About the Author

Dr Lindsay Gething is Director of the Nursing Research Centre for Adaptation in Disability and Illness. She also is Team Leader of the Community Disability and Ageing Program (CDAP). Both are centred in the Faculty of Nursing at the University of Sydney. The CDAP is actively involved in research and education into issues associated with disability and with ageing. Dr Gething obtained her PhD from the University of Melbourne and her Bachelor of Arts from the University of New South Wales. She is registered to practise as a psychologist in NSW and is a member of the Australian Psychological Society. She is also an associate member of Persons with Disabilities (PWD) Inc. (NSW), President of the Carers' Association of NSW, and Member of the Policy Advisory Committee for the NSW Council on Ageing. Dr Gething has published widely in professional journals and her other books include *Working with Older People*, *Lifespan Development* and *Managing Research Effectively*. She was leader of the team which developed the Disability Awareness Package which is used in several countries by government, nongovernment, community and educational organisations to provide pre- and in-service disability awareness training to professionals and service providers.

D1572218

PERSON to PERSON

A guide for professionals working
with people with disabilities

THIRD EDITION

Lindsay Gething

PhD, BA (Hons), MAPsS, NSWPsych Reg
Associate Professor

*Director of the Nursing Research Centre for
Adaptation in Health and Illness and
Team Leader of the Community Disability and Ageing Program*

·P·A·U·L·H·
BROOKES
PUBLISHING Co

Baltimore • London • Toronto • Sydney

Paul H. Brookes Publishing Co.
PO Box 10624
Baltimore, Maryland 21285-0624

Printed and bound in Australia.

Library of Congress Cataloging-in-Publication data
Gething, Lindsay.
    Person to person : a guide for professionals working with people
with disabilities / Lindsay Gething. — 3rd ed.
       p. cm.
    Includes bibliographical references and index.
    ISBN 1-55766-320-3
    1. Handicapped. 2. Handicapped—Public opinion. 3. Handicapped—Care.
4. Handicapped—Australia—Case studies. I. Title.
RA644.5.G47 1997
362.4'045—dc21
                                                     97-20354
                                                     CIP

to
TIM AND DAVID

CONTENTS

PREFACE

Each of the editions of *Person to Person* has involved major changes and additions. The book's evolution reflects developments in the disability field, in philosophies regarding service provision, in what are regarded as appropriate attitudes and beliefs about people with disabilities and in accepted beliefs about the rights and obligations of people with disabilities within society. These developments reflect the contributions and lobbying of people with disabilities and their colleagues who have worked tirelessly to demand equity and equality, and to be accepted as valued individuals.

The philosophy of this book is that people with disabilities are *people first* and disabled second. They have the same rights and responsibilities as others. Like all people, they have strengths, limitations and special needs. Unfortunately, common myths in our community focus on limitations and often result in people with disabilities being stereotyped as being alike. This means that individuality is overlooked and particular strengths, wishes and needs are not taken into account.

During the last decade government philosophy in Australia has changed from a welfare-based philosophy to a rights-based model of service provision and community living for people with disabilities. These changes, which are reflected in legislation, demand major alterations in attitudes and beliefs on the part of professionals in regard to their own roles, the nature of their interactions with clients with disabilities, the roles of their clients in decision making, and acknowledgment of clients as complex individuals.

A wide range of professionals work closely and regularly with people with disabilities. These professionals include psychologists, lawyers, librarians, architects, engineers, opticians, occupational therapists, speech pathologists, physiotherapists (physical therapists), dentists, nurses, teachers, educators, medical practitioners, social workers and welfare workers. These people are working in the community and many of them provide services for all people, whether or not they have a disability.

The knowledge and approach of these professionals have profound implications for the quality of life for people with disabilities. Each professional has been trained in a specific area and sometimes there is the danger of focusing on this expertise to the neglect of other areas. For example, there may be a temptation for a physiotherapist (physical therapist) to focus on muscle function in the person with spinal injury and to overlook the client's psychological and personal reactions to acquiring a disability. Such a focus may inhibit effective decision making and result in less than optimal services and rehabilitation. It is important for a professional to have a perspective which extends beyond his or her particular area of expertise to incorporate an overall and holistic view of life with a disability.

The book is designed to provide increased understanding about life with a disability. It takes an *holistic* view of life with a disability by emphasising that each person is a unique individual who has many characteristics and is the product of a unique set of life experiences. In line with this philosophy, the book provides only essential coverage of medical descriptions associated with disability and focuses on personal, family, social and cultural issues associated with living with disability. It presents disability from the perspective of ten major domains in life: health, work, marriage, forming relationships, housing and community living, social relationships, creative expression, education, growth and development, and future prospects.

The recurrent theme of this book is that *people* have disabilities. People without disabilities often have difficulty in looking beyond a disability to recognise and be aware of the actual person – a person who has feelings, opinions, financial worries, family commitments, sporting interests, sexual partners and all the other concerns and features that go with everyday life. These factors must all be taken into account by a professional if effective and appropriate services are to be provided.

People report changes in community attitudes and beliefs about disability and life with a disability. Many myths are gradually being broken down and people with disabilities are being accepted as members of an integrated society. However, there is still a long way to go. Evidence suggests that negative attitudes are still prevalent in the community. It also suggests that many service providers, health, welfare and education professionals hold attitudes and inaccurate beliefs and can help perpetuate myths prevalent in society. Important results of the formation and perpetuation of negative attitudes include ongoing features of practice which persist despite changes in legislation and philosophy. These features include unequal relationships between professional and client and the tendency to focus on problems associated with disability rather than viewing the client or consumer as a whole person.

It has been argued that it is often in the interests of professionals and their organisations to retain old stereotypes and myths because these actually have short-term benefits. They provide short-cuts which are attractive in times of funding cuts and limited financial resources. It is quicker and easier to apply a stereotype or label than to find out about a person by getting to know him or her as an individual. However, short-term benefits are outweighed by the long-term disadvantages of inappropriate and less than optimal service provision.

The aim of this book is to convey an holistic approach and to promote the view of people with disabilities as active and able individuals who have much to contribute and who are entitled to have a say in decisions which affect their lives.

The first two chapters of the book cover general issues associated with having a disability. Each of the remaining 14 chapters focuses on a specific disability area. Each chapter follows a similar format. It first covers issues for the particular disability associated with personal adjustment, sexuality, being a parent, family/community living, appropriate behaviours, and strategies for interaction. The later pages of each chapter cover medical descriptions (where appropriate), definitions, incidence/prevalence, diagnosis, treatment, services, supports, equipment and additional costs. Each chapter closes with a list of further readings and a list of resource organisations, both of which are designed to provide direction for the reader who wishes to obtain further information.

The last section of the book contains a series of personal accounts given by people with disabilities. These accounts are not intended to give extensive coverage of all disability types included in the book or to cover all important life events. It would be impossible to do this, as people with disabilities are individuals and no two people conduct their lives in the same way. Rather, these accounts demonstrate the impact of disability on life experiences and show some of the ways that people adjust to their disability to deal effectively and successfully with important life events. These accounts clearly demonstrate the profound influence of factors external to the individual in creating handicaps and limitations which affect quality of life and the range of opportunities available to someone with a disability.

ACKNOWLEDGMENTS

Gratitude and appreciation are expressed to the many individuals and organisations who have contributed to this book. These contributions have been made over three editions. Some people have been involved in preparation of more than one edition, while others have played a part for one edition only. Each of these people has made his or her mark on the philosophy and content of the book.

Special thanks go to all those people who willingly shared personal insights into living with a disability. Their honesty and openness enables issues covered in the book to come to life for the reader.

Acknowledgment is made to Rosemary Leonard and Kate O'Loughlin who worked with the author and were included as co-authors on the first edition. Acknowledgment is made also to Tracey Poynter, Felicity Reynolds, Glenn Redmayne, Louise Cahill and Melanie James who were part of the research team who worked with the author to develop the Disability Awareness Package (first and second editions). This package formed the basis for the second and third editions of *Person to Person* and, when used in conjunction with this book, forms a useful tool for anyone wishing to provide disability awareness training.

Other people who contributed to at least one edition of the book are: Dr C. E. Miller, Virginia Adams, Gary Banks, Zanna Baron, Dr Roy Beran, Jock Blair, Jaleen Caples, Denise Chapman, Gillian Church, Alisa Coleman, Narelle Coleman, Maria Dalgleish, John Ferris, Dr Simon Hammond, Joan Hansen, Freda Hillson, Libby Harricks, David and Jenny Heckendorf, Jim Henderson, Margaret Hope, Christine Johnston, Lindy Kerr, Greg Killeen, Joanne Lawrence, Sandra and Des Lean-Fore, Claire Lisle, Pietro Lo Surdo, Bernadette Lowther, Susan McAviney, Peter Mahoney, Professor Graeme Morgan, John Moxon, Bronwyn Moye, Margaret Olah, Susan Molloy, Jo Sabolcec, Lea Sorensen, Evelyn Rushton, Professor David Sillence, Syd Sinclair, Judy Stenmark, David Stern, Wendy Turner and Darren Watzinger.

Organisations that reviewed chapters for the third edition are: the Arthritis Foundation of NSW, Australian Quadriplegic Association, Brain Injury Association of NSW, Deaf Society of NSW, Diabetes Australia – NSW, Epilepsy Association of NSW, Mental Health Coordinating Council Inc., Muscular Dystrophy Association of NSW, NSW Council for Intellectual Disability, Paraplegic and Quadriplegic Association of NSW, the Royal Blind Society of NSW, the Self Help for Hard of Hearing People (SHHH), Short Statured People of Australia, Inc., and the Spastic Centre of NSW. The chapter on amputation was reviewed and revised by Anne Hillman from the School of Occupational Therapy, Faculty of Health Sciences, University of Sydney and Jean Halcrow. The chapter on intellectual disability was reviewed by Gwynnyth Llewellyn, also from the School of Occupational Therapy in the Faculty of Health Sciences at the University of Sydney.

Several of the diagrams and photographs in this book were provided by the Faculty of Health Sciences at the University of Sydney.

CHAPTER 1

LIVING WITH A DISABILITY

What does the term 'disability' mean?

It is important to remember that each person is an individual whose personal characteristics are moulded by life experiences which may include those associated with having a disability. The following quotes show that the meaning of disability varies greatly from one individual to another.

> In my own words, a disability is any physical, sensory, psychiatric or learning barrier that makes a person different from the norm. It's important to realise that people with disabilities are people first and their disability is secondary: although it is an integral part of their life, disability must not be the dominant force in it.
>
> Angus, who is vision impaired

> A person with a disability is one who has an impediment in everyday life. This does not mean we are unable to contribute to society in a positive and meaningful way.
>
> Marcus, who has schizophrenia

> Disability is something that is with you all the time. That doesn't mean I think about it all the time, but to cope with it you have to know it's there and make the best of it. It can be your friend or enemy.
>
> Nathan, who has cerebral palsy

These quotes raise questions about the definition of 'normality'. What is 'normal'? The meaning of this term varies greatly from one individual to another, from one culture to another and from one situation to the next. Table 1.1 lists some definitions given by people with disabilities. After this, the term is not used again to refer to people without disabilities as it contradicts the philosophy of this book, which is that people should be accepted on their own terms and not judged against a criterion which does not exist in reality.

Thus, normality is a perception which reflects the eye of the beholder and the values of the society in which a person lives. Abnormality and the extent to which presence of disability is linked with abnormality reflect features which lie outside the person: they reflect society, the perception of others and how society deals with differences between individuals. Disability and abnormality are social constructs.

Definition of disability

Disability is the functional consequence of an impairment or change in body or human functioning. The extent to which disability affects a person's life (handicap) depends very much upon the environments in which a person lives – social,

1

Table 1.1: What is 'normality'?

'Normality' is having full function and being able to do what you want to do when you want. It is having choices and being like the majority of people.

John, who has a spinal cord injury

Normality to me is living a lifestyle that I am happy with and have some control over; but what is normal?

Meg, who has paraplegia

Being normal is to fit into the norm of a community's life. People without disabilities perceive normality as not using any aids such as white canes, wheelchairs or hearing aids. It would be great to think of a future society where these aids are part and parcel of a normal way of life.

Angus, who is vision impaired

I have a diversity of friends – some with disabilities, some without. Some of my friends are quite successful. It is my experience that people who reckon they don't have a disability can put up a positive appearance, yet they too have all sorts of usual hidden disabilities (emotional, relationships, inadequacies and so on).

Maria, who has mental illness

Being 'normal' is only one person's perception and not always reality. So, it doesn't hold any importance for me. For example, if being 'normal' means being average, then I'm glad I'm not 'normal'.

Nathan, who has cerebral palsy

---

cultural, psychological and physical. Some broad factors which influence life experiences and how the person adjusts include: length of time the person has had his or her disability(ies), family history and supports, schooling and education, own acceptance of disability, whether the disability was acquired or congenital, how early interventions and services were introduced to the person, and the nature of the environment in which the person receives services (for example, whether they foster independence or dependence within the individual).

International classification

The above definition focuses on functional and lifestyle consequences for the individual, rather than on medical causation. The definition published by the World Health Organization in 1980 (International Classification of Impairments, Disabilities and Handicaps, or ICIDH) is currently the most widely-accepted definition. It has received some criticism and several teams are working to revise it (see below). However, it is used in this book because it incorporates three levels in its sequence: *impairment*, *disability* and *handicap*. These terms are in wide current usage and it is important that they are used in a consistent way and according to the following definitions in order to avoid misunderstandings. The WHO definition specifies that:

- *Impairment* is concerned with loss or abnormality of psychological, physiological or anatomical structure or function or appearance.
- *Disability* is any restriction or lack (resulting from an impairment) of ability to perform an activity in the manner or within the range generally expected for a human being. Some disabilities are hidden or invisible while others are visible. These disabilities have different implications.
- *Handicap* is a disadvantage for a given individual resulting from an impairment or a disability. Handicap reflects interaction with and adaptation to surroundings (including the cultural, social and physical environments) in which the person lives. Handicaps prevent the fulfilment of roles that are appropriate according to the age, gender, social and cultural features of an individual.

The distinction between *disability* and *handicap* is important. Wright (1983) argues that the term disability should be used to refer to the functional condition of the person, while the term handicap should refer to psychological, social and behavioural consequences of that condition. From this point of view, attitudes held in the community influence the extent to which disability becomes a handicap. Stigma, stereotyping, prejudice and discriminatory practices occurring in society are major sources of handicap, as are factors such as impoverishment due to high health care costs, barriers which block access and mobility, and lack of appropriate service provision. Earlier government policy in many countries contributed to handicap in that it resulted in over-emphasis on institutional service solutions.

One criticism of the WHO definition is that it implies a causal relationship between impairment, disability and handicap. Authors have criticised this sequence, saying that the reverse also can be true. That is, handicaps such as social disadvantage and deprivation can result in impairments and/or disabilities. The definition also has been criticised in terms of the potential negative effects associated with labelling. This criticism is largely directed at work in progress to specify in detail characteristics and conditions at each of the three levels. Rioux (1995) points out that such specificity confuses the person with characteristics being classified, does not allow for individual differences and is potentially dangerous if it is used in applications such as in determining the amount of compensation or social benefits a person is entitled to. She argues that a detailed system of definition could serve to further disenfranchise people with disabilities and to deny their rights if the system is used to distinguish a person from others in a way that makes him or her socially inferior or if care and treatment (which include law, policy and political rights) are developed by society on the basis of such a label of social inferiority. Pfeiffer (1994) also is critical of the current WHO approach. He argues that disability is a natural part of life and that most people will be disabled at some time during their lives. He argues that disability is not a health or medical issue. Disability is not a sickness, but the WHO promotes a view of illness, difference and deficiency by using terminology such as 'abnormality' and by its support of moves to develop a detailed specification of features and conditions at each level of the classification. He believes that disability is a political issue and that the feature of disability should not be used to separate people.

Despite these criticisms, authors such as Rioux and Pfeiffer do not experience difficulty with the concepts underlying the WHO definition in its broadest terms (the three levels). These levels are used in the following chapters as they illustrate the basic philosophy of the book: that disability and handicaps are social phenomena or constructs which do not necessarily have to occur, but reflect the physical, social and attitudinal barriers that society imposes on people with disabilities. Barriers result from attitudes and social policy which use disability as a characteristic to set a person apart from others and which do not place a high value on providing an environment which is accessible for all people. More work is required by the involved research teams such as those in Quebec (Fougeyrollas, 1995) to convince critics that a detailed specification of characteristics within each of the three levels does not, in itself, form a further source of handicap in terms of labelling of individuals with disabilities.

One benefit of this work to date has been its success in emphasising the wide range of factors outside the individual which promote disadvantage and handicap. This specification has potentially positive benefits when used to identify possible areas of need and to guide service provision as suggested in the framework developed by Madden, Black and Wen (1995). These authors report the results of a workshop which used the classification as a basis for making recommendations regarding the nature and structure of services provided to people with disabilities by the Australian government.

Definitions currently used as the basis for government policy and service provision emphasise functional limitations rather than causation. Functional limitations are seen as more important considerations when designing strategies to minimise the handicap experienced by an individual. For example, current Australian Commonwealth and state legislation specifies that:

> *a person is in the target group if the person has a disability (however arising and whether or not of a chronic episodic nature):*
>
> *(a) that is attributable to an intellectual, psychiatric, sensory, physical or like impairment or to a combination of such impairments; and*
> *(b) that is likely to be permanent; and*
> *(c) that results in:*
> > *(i) a significantly reduced capacity in one or more major life activities, such as communication, learning, mobility, decision-making or self-care; and*
> > *(ii) the need for support, whether or not of an ongoing nature.*
>
> Disability Services Act 1993 (NSW)

A similar approach is taken in the *Americans with Disabilities Act 1990* (ADA), which defines disability to mean, 'with respect to an individual, a physical or mental impairment that substantially limits one or more of the major life activities of such an individual, a record of such impairment, or being regarded as having such an impairment'. According to Patrick et al. (1994) this definition takes into account both the context of the person's disability and the societal response. A person may not be as disabled or disadvantaged by an impairment as by the way society treats him or her.

Prevalence of disability

In 1993 it was estimated that 18 per cent of the Australian population had a disability and 14.2 per cent of the population was classified as having a handicap (thus, not all people who regard themselves as having a disability, regard themselves as handicapped). Of the these people, 51 per cent were males and 49 per cent were females.

The 1991 Health and Activity Limitations Survey (Statistics Canada, 1992) indicated that 15.5 per cent of the Canadian population (or 4.2 million people) reported some level of disability. This proportion represented an increase from the previous data collection in 1986 where 13.2 per cent of the population emerged as having a disability. Statistics Canada attributed this increase to the ageing of the Canadian population, greater willingness of people to acknowledge disability and more accurate data-capturing methods. In Canada, older age groups are over-represented among people with disabilities. Thus, 7 per cent of people with disabilities were aged under 15 years as compared with 14 per cent being aged between 35 and 54 years, and 43.3 per cent being aged over 65 years.

Kemp (1995) states that people with disabilities make up 20 per cent of the population in the United States. Of these people, 50 per cent have some form of physical disability. He summarises the following statistics about Americans with disabilities: there is an unemployment rate of 70 per cent among those who wish to work, a third of people aged over 65 years have some form of disability and a quarter of adults with disabilities live in poverty.

Variables affecting reaction to disability

Type, causation and age of onset may influence a person's particular set of life experiences and how he or she lives with disability. People are unique, but there are some factors which affect how people adapt to disability.

Type of disability

Disabling conditions are usually divided into four groupings:

- *sensory* – for example, deafness, hearing impairment, blindness, visual impairment;
- *physical* – for example, spinal cord injury, diabetes, acquired brain injury, multiple sclerosis, cerebral palsy, muscular dystrophy, arthritis, amputation and short stature;
- *mental illness/psychiatric disability* – for example, schizophrenia, manic depression (bipolar mood disorder), depression, dementia;
- *intellectual*.

It is important to note that many people have multiple disabilities. For example, it is not uncommon for people with cerebral palsy to experience both physical disability resulting in the use of a wheelchair and sensory disability associated with hearing impairment. It is also possible that intellectual disability will accompany a physical or sensory disability.

Causes of disability

Disabling conditions can be broadly classified into four groups according to whether they are inherited, congenital, acquired or of unknown origin.

Inherited disabilities. These are passed down from the parents through genetic transmission or result from a genetic defect or mutation. Examples of inherited conditions are muscular dystrophy, retinitis pigmentosa (a form of visual impair-ment), Down syndrome and spina bifida.

Congenital disabilities. These result from infections in the mother during preg-nancy, a typical development during pregnancy, or injury during or soon after birth.

Table 1.2: What are the greatest implications of your disability for you?

Changes to all physical capabilities and the way you do things. I deal with them by focusing on what I can do and developing a new lifestyle and enjoyments (for example, work, sports).

Con, who has a spinal cord injury

The limitations of physical access to services, buildings and so on which limits your involvement in society, education, employment and recreation. The extra costs that a severe disability attracts. The health problems that may arise due to a spinal cord injury (for example, pressure sores, urinary tract infections, chest infections).

Matt, who has a spinal cord injury

Mobility, safety and information access.

Yola, who is blind

My greatest problem is lack of money due to an inability to cope with work. I rationalise this by seeing there are many people worse off than me. Despite this, I would like to be financially independent. I am not a greedy person, but I find the financial struggle difficult.

Marcus, who has schizophrenia

This is a very difficult question to answer because the implications of my disability change from day to day. This is why I must continue to deal with the implications on a day-to-day basis. It means that I have more to deal with than the average person.

Nathan, who has cerebral palsy

Cerebral palsy is an example of a congenital impairment. Other examples are intellectual disability associated with metabolic disturbance such as PKU and hearing impairment resulting from the mother contracting German measles during pregnancy. The impact of congenital disability often is not so much to do with dealing with rapid change (as in acquired disability), but gradual adaptation to a life where disability influences how others react to us. It can affect opportunities to determine self-worth, perceived attractiveness to others (both sexually and in general) and development of body image. Such issues can be particularly important during the teenage years, when the person is adjusting to growing up, just like everyone else. This is an important time for formation of self-identity and for deciding whether we like ourselves. How others react to us influences such processes.

Acquired disabilities. These result from accident, injury, disease, substance abuse or illness during life. Examples include amputation, multiple sclerosis, traumatic spinal cord injury, arthritis, diabetes and acquired brain injury. How people react to a loss is influenced by the strategies they have already developed for dealing with losses and changes in life in general. It also is influenced by their values and previous lifestyle. A person who places great value on body strength and attractiveness may react differently to disability than someone whose priorities lie elsewhere. Body image is an important part of our self-identity, self-image, or sense of who we are. A major change to one's body requires adjustment to body image and may result in mourning for loss of the previous body image or functioning and feeling 'half a person'. Sexuality is an important part of a person's identity, both physically and emotionally. Disability may require changes to ways of expressing sexuality and to a person's ideal of a sexually attractive person. Changes demanded by acquisition of a disability form further issues that the person must work through in coming to terms with having a disability. Previous beliefs and attitudes, whether conscious or not, must be challenged and resolved by the person with a disability.

Origin unknown. The precise origin of an impairment cannot be determined in some cases. This is often the case for intellectual disabilities and for many forms of mental illness.

Age of onset

Overall, the occurrence of disability increases with age. Many disabilities reflect lifestyle habits extending over many decades. Thus, incidences of heart disease, diabetes, arthritis and cancer are higher in older age groups. Other disabilities such as vision and hearing impairment also tend to be more prevalent in older age groups. However, there are also forms of impairment which occur early in life. Disabilities such as cerebral palsy only originate early in life. Other disabilities can first emerge at any age, but tend to have a higher incidence in certain age groups. Thus, acquired spinal cord injury and acquired brain injury have their highest incidence in young adult males.

In some inherited and all congenital conditions, the person has never experienced life without disability. This can mean that the person has had many years to adapt to the condition. On the other hand, the person may not have reached many developmental milestones in the same way or at the same time as a nondisabled person.

In contrast, acquired disability after the earliest years of life demands major changes to lifestyle, often under sudden and traumatic circumstances. This can entail major crises in adjustment; however, the person has lived previously without the disability and has had opportunities often denied to people with an inherited or congenital disability.

Severity of disability

Severity of disability affects a person's reactions and the limitations experienced.

Visibility-invisibility

People with 'hidden' disabilities such as diabetes and epilepsy can experience different reactions from those with highly visible disabilities such as spinal cord injury, muscular dystrophy and amputation. Having a hidden disability means that it is possible to mix with others without them being aware of the disability. This can create conflicts for the person with the disability about self-disclosure, identity confusion and fear of being found out. Robinson (1988) outlines three strategies often used by people with invisible disabilities, with acquired disabilities or with disabilities which are not visible to others in their early stages. Some people use all three strategies, others use perhaps only one.

- A person may choose not to publicly acknowledge the disability and may try to conceal it. Changes in lifestyle may be required to achieve this and people report feeling dishonest and as leading a false life. For example, a person with MS may explain a stay in hospital to others by reference to a brief holiday. This strategy requires quick thinking and can be associated with anxiety and the fear of being found out. It is particularly likely to be adopted when employment is jeopardised.
- Other people acknowledge their disability but try to maintain a 'normal' identity and to carry on life with disability treated as an important but accepted part of life. They choose to continue to mix with people without disabilities, but may find this difficult if the disability becomes more obvious and negative attitudes make others less willing to treat them as they did before. This reluctance by others can be devastating.
- Other people may take a different approach by separating themselves from previous friends (who do not have a disability) and by choosing only to mix with other people who have a disability. Life is redesigned around the disability. The person may feel safe as contacts are restricted to those who know about and understand disability, but the person is denied access to a wide range of social contacts and experiences.

The experience of disability is not the same for everyone. Its impact is modified by the individual and the strategies he or she uses to adjust to life. Each individual is a highly complex being with personality, behaviour and adjustment styles being the end product of years of experience in a number of realms: cultural, social, personal and physical. While being formed by this diversity of experience, the individual reciprocates to shape his or her environments in return. The experience of disability is an important feature which affects both the individual and members of his or her immediate family and the wider social and cultural environment.

It is important to take an *holistic* view of the range of factors operating at any one time within an individual, and his or her family and social/cultural environments. Focusing on one aspect (for example, the physical) while neglecting other factors is likely to produce a misleading picture which does not acknowledge diversity of need or ability.

Stages of coming to terms with disability

Many people find it useful to apply Kübler-Ross's (1969) five stages of bereavement to the experiences of people who have acquired disability and to their family and friends. These outline a series of stages that people tend to pass through following a major loss. The theory has been applied to a range of major losses, including divorce, death of a child, death of a loved person, retrenchment from a job, impending death, and failure to achieve an important goal such as passing an important examination or getting into a certain university course.

Kübler-Ross argues that movement through these stages is essential in adjusting to a major loss. However, people differ in the length of time they take to pass through stages and to reach the final stage of acceptance of the loss. Some people never reach this stage.

Stage 1: Shock. The person's life has been overturned. She or he feels disoriented, frightened, worried about the future.

Stage 2: Denial/bargaining. After the initial shock, the person may retreat into a state of refusing to admit that permanent disability has occurred. The person may dream of a miracle cure or insist that, with sufficient effort, life will be as it was before. Families, in their efforts to be comforting, may unwittingly reinforce denial. In its initial stages, denial is regarded as healthy as it gives the person and family time to overcome initial anguish. However, if it continues too long, it can become counterproductive and interfere with successful adjustment.

Stage 3: Anger. This comes with the realisation that disablement is permanent. People feel unfairly treated by life. Often anger is directed towards others in the person's life and it is important that family members and professionals do not take this anger personally. It is part of the healing process, but should not be encouraged or sanctioned.

Stage 4: Depression. This stage occurs with awareness of the extent of disability or loss. Feelings of lack of control over the environment and helplessness are crucial factors (Seligman, 1975, 1992). Depression may occur at any time during the healing process and may recur over many months. Some people contemplate suicide. Any sign of depression is a cue for counselling.

Stage 5: Adaptation or acceptance. The impairment and accompanying disability are accepted. In most people, acceptance occurs between one and two years after they first learned about the disability. However, acceptance is not always constructive. Some people reach the stage of acceptance of disability and wanting to make the best out of life, but others harbour bitterness and resentment, others accept their fate passively, and yet others aggressively attack life trying to prove that they can do all they could do before, and more.

Bereavement is a natural and typical response to a major loss. Disability is one example of such a loss and is likely to be associated with grieving on the part of the individual, family and close friends. It is important to remember that most people do manage to come to terms with this loss and discover that there is a worthwhile life afterwards.

Double disadvantage

The term 'double disadvantage' refers to people who experience disadvantages in addition to those associated with their disability. This term is often applied to people from non-majority cultures in a particular country or region, to people who live in remote or isolated areas and to women.

Before embarking on a discussion of these groups, it is important to emphasise key points made by authors such as Bostock (1991), Lim (1993a and b), Moss (1993) and Scott (1993):

> *People are unique and just as people with disabilities are individuals, so are members of gender, ethnic and racial groups. It is important not to stereotype members of such groups or to assume that they have similar interests, values and needs. Unless diversity is acknowledged and taken into account, the needs of the individual will not be met.*

Although people are unique, there are many broad issues which generalise across groups of people with disabilities. Such issues are marginalisation, difficulties in obtaining access to appropriate services and failure of service delivery personnel to acknowledge individual differences in needs, requirements and the impact of disability on life.

Membership of a non-majority cultural group. Lee (1988) defines culture as the way we do things: our routine of sleeping, bathing, dressing, eating and so on. It is also the way we greet friends, make a telephone call, what we consider to be good and bad manners. Culture is not only the way we do things and the language we speak, it is also our attitudes, thoughts, expectations, goals and values. It includes perspectives on male/female roles, child rearing practices, sexuality, concepts of independence, family obligations, recreation, work, health, welfare, sickness and rehabilitation. A culture is not static but is constantly changing. People within a cultural group vary in many ways.

Disadvantages associated with having a disability are likely to be compounded for a person who comes from a non-majority culture. This person may experience additional difficulties associated with prejudice, stereotyping, devaluation, and gaining access to culturally sensitive services (Livanos & Karraz, 1992).

Living in a remote or rural area. Disadvantage is compounded for people with disabilities who live outside major urban centres, especially when large distances from services and resources are not considered in the design and delivery of services (Brentnall & Dunlop, 1985). Lack of adequate transport infrastructure to take people to and from services and to enable them to participate in community life are further sources of handicap. Such features also can result in segregation, hampered social development and in continued entrenchment in the rural community of the belief that people with and without disabilities are different. The nature of service provision also contributes to disadvantage. For example, organisations which tend to implement service delivery models which are effective in the city, but do not necessarily work elsewhere are unlikely to meet the needs of their rurally-based clients. Additionally, most professionals receive their training in the city where course content is focused on advice, techniques and appliances which are suitable for an urban environment and may not be appropriate in the country. Until recently, urban-based courses have contained little material about rural practice. Other difficulties experienced by rural residents with disabilities surround the availability of up-to-date information about technological advances and therapy, diagnosis and treatment. Outdated attitudes among the general community and professionals also create difficulties as these do not reflect current philosophies regarding service provision (Gething et al., 1994).

Being a woman. Writers such as Quinn (1994) and Traustadottir (1990) have criticised policy and decision makers in their neglect of issues for women with disabilities. Traustadottir argues that women with disabilities have historically been neglected by leaders and scholars of both of the disadvantaged groups to which they belong. Her review of the literature revealed women with disabilities have been neglected in disability studies and in feminist scholarship.

Evidence suggests that the experience of disability is different for women, however most research and policy focuses on the needs of men or assumes that issues are the same for both sexes.

Gender differences on the experience of disability begin from birth. Parents tend to be more protective of daughters than of sons with disabilities. They also often have subtly lower expectations and are more likely to discourage community living and self-sufficiency for their daughters (National Information Center for Children and Youth with Handicaps, 1990).

Cooper (1993) summarises figures published by the Australian Bureau of Statistics (1988) which indicate that gender affects experiences associated with having a disability. She concludes that Australian women with disabilities are more likely to live in an institution, are less likely to work for money, less likely to own a house, and less likely to receive requested personal care and household assistance. Bowe (1983) reports similar patterns in the United States where women with disabilities are likely to be poorer than their male counterparts, and are less likely to receive adequate disability benefits. Altman (1985) and Ficke (1991) argue that American women with disabilities are less likely than men to obtain vocational rehabilitation. Also, Ficke argues that vocational rehabilitation for women tends to be centred around stereotyped roles such as homemaker and office work. Wagle (1994, p. 44) reports that women with disabilities 'face crushing underemployment and unemployment rates'. She argues that barriers which exclude women with disabilities from the workforce include discrimination, negative employer attitudes, and lack of access to training and to educational opportunities. Many women with disabilities have never held paid jobs. This heightens their vulnerability to being marginalised, isolated and outside the mainstream of society. The barriers for women with disabilities to participate in the areas of employment and training are quite formidable – the double disadvantage of the separation of people with disabilities in the community and the discriminatory forces which have acted in the past to prevent women's entry into further education and employment combine to marginalise them (Hiscock, 1991).

Thus, presence of disability in a woman is likely to influence her options in regard to the range of vocational roles she may fulfil in society. Gender differences also emerge in regard to caregiving. A man with a disability is likely to have a female caregiver at home to perform chores and to provide assistance. This is not the case for a woman with a disability who receives little caregiving support and may, herself, be required to care for others (Quinn, 1994). Many women with disabilities have children. However, most women with disabilities fall into older age groups and many are responsible for providing care to a frail partner or spouse. Women tend to adopt caregiving as an expected part of their role (in our culture women are still expected to be the major caregivers). However, it is more difficult for a woman who does not wish to adopt this role to refuse it than it is for a man. Walmsley (1993) points out that women often do not have socially accepted reasons (such as being in paid employment) for not being a carer. Thus, the experience of having a disability and caregiving is different for men and women.

The irony of the situation is that women with disabilities are often regarded as being asexual (Oliver, 1991), more likely to never marry or to marry later (Asch & Fine, 1988; Hannaford, 1989) and are discouraged from having children because it is believed that they are not capable of caring for them (Walmsley, 1993). However, they are expected to be capable carers of other people with disabilities and are less likely to receive care themselves than are men with disabilities.

Issues of personal safety and vulnerability are important for most people in modern society. These fears may be more pronounced for people with disabilities and for women. They may inhibit a person's freedom in moving around the community and may result in parents and the family of a woman or girl with a disability adopting overprotective behaviours over and above those they would regard as necessary for a male or for siblings who do not have a disability. Evidence suggests that people with disabilities, especially women, are vulnerable to sexual abuse (Doucette, 1986; Fine & Asch, 1988; Sobsey, 1994, Wright-Felske & Hughson, 1991). This is a phenomenon which occurs for people with disabilities of both genders, but is particularly an issue for women and which impacts on their life experiences.

The above factors result in major differences in the experiences of men and women with disabilities, indicating that gender must be taken into account in design of policy and of services. The disadvantages are compounded by isolation and a society which is often ignorant and even hostile to the needs of women with disabilities. All of these factors have contributed to feelings of inadequacy and lack of clear role definition for many women with disabilities. Furthermore, women with disabilities have few female role models who demonstrate socially-acceptable models of achievement and success (Fine & Asch, 1988). These features interfere with quality of life and affect self-esteem, resulting in a self-reinforcing cycle of failure and feelings of inadequacy (Schaefer, 1985). Women with disabilities have access to fewer socially-sanctioned roles than either non-disabled women or men with disabilities. Expectations of gender roles and a woman's perceived failure to fulfil them can result in anxiety, guilt and feelings of inadequacy. Problems are compounded by conventional images of beauty and attractiveness which apply particularly to women in our society and make it difficult for some women with disabilities to come to terms with their body image (Quinn, 1994). Some women feel compelled to live up to the ideal of femininity to prove that they are 'normal' (Orr, 1984) while some feel they are treated as asexual by others.

Differences also occur between women with and without disabilities. For example, a study of reproductive health and access to care (Nosek, Rintala & Young, 1995) reported that, compared with their counterparts without disability, younger women with physical disabilities are significantly more likely to have had a hysterectomy, less likely to receive regular pelvic examinations, more likely to lack basic knowledge about their reproductive health, and to be regarded by physicians and professionals as asexual and not in need of reproductive health care. The project also revealed that many women with physical disabilities are married and have children, but at a lower rate than women without disabilities. They also were less sexually active.

Sexuality and disability

As Vargo (1985, p. 15) stated: 'Each [person with a disability] is a person first, a sexual person second and a disabled person third'. However, many members of society respond to the person with a disability on the third level only. Often disability brings special issues associated with developing a sense of sexuality and sexual identity. For someone with an acquired disability, major changes to self-image and sexual identity may be demanded. Miller (1993) describes the experience as learning to accept a 'new skin' in which we must live. Learning to accept physical changes to one's body is complicated by the emotional impact of these changes. A person may feel frustrated, betrayed by his or her body, grief over perceived losses and self-hatred. Self-acceptance is also complicated by changes in the behaviour of others toward the person. How we perceive the way others see us greatly affects how we see ourselves (the 'looking-glass phenomenon'). The person must learn that self-esteem does not have to depend on traditional measures of acceptability, beauty and perfection (Miller, 1993).

For someone with a congenital or longstanding condition, the feature of disability is likely to have influenced from childhood the development of sexuality and how the person perceives him or herself as a sexual being. Toleno (1994) states that as a person born with blindness, she underwent a three-part journey to attaining her sexuality and feeling a 'whole' woman. These stages were: knowing and accepting, respecting and liking, and celebrating and appropriately caring for her body. Part of this process involved learning strategies that were useful for someone who was blind, including using verbal and body language in place of visual attraction when establishing a relationship.

Violence, abuse and disability

People with disabilities, like other marginalised groups, are vulnerable to violence and abuse. The evidence in support of this statement is alarming. For example, Stimson & Best (1991) report that 40 per cent of women with disabilities have been sexually assaulted or abused and 83 per cent will be abused sometime in their lifetime; Sullivan, Vernon & Scanlan (1987) report that 59 per cent of girls and 54 per cent of boys who were deaf had been sexually abused; Jacobson (1989) and Jacobson & Richardson (1987) report that 68 per cent of psychiatric outpatients and 81 per cent of psychiatric inpatients have been victims of major sexual assault; Pillemar & Moore (1990) report that 10 per cent of nurses and aides in nursing and immediate care facilities admitted to having physically abused their clients; and Ulicny et al. (1990) report that 10 per cent of consumers of attendant home care services had been abused by their service providers.

> *I was manipulated, battered, and physically and emotionally pushed around in two hospitals. Within two months, they had physically pushed me into an acute arthritic flare-up. I went from using a cane to using a wheelchair.*
>
> DisAbled Womens Network, 1995, p. 32

Ticoll (1994) conducted a review of the growing literature on this topic. She defines violence against people with disabilities as:

- occurring in the context of systemic discrimination in which there is often an imbalance of power; and
- including both overt and subtle forms of abuse which may or may not be considered to be criminal acts.

The Roeher Institute (1995) and Ticoll (1994) argue that people with disabilities are more likely than others to experience:

- *physical abuse* including hitting, shaking, burning; the administration of poisonous substances or inappropriate drugs; inappropriate handling, personal or medical care; overuse of restraint or inappropriate behaviour modification; experimental treatment;
- *sexual abuse* including unwanted or forced sexual contact, touching or displays of sexual parts, threats of harm or coercion with sexual activity, denial of sexuality, denial of sexual education and information, forced abortion or sterilisation.

He raped me over and over again from the time I was four until I was eleven. Unlike my other sisters, I couldn't run away from him. I was sexually abused because I had a mobility impairment.

DisAbled Womens Network, 1995, p. 32

- *psychological and emotional abuse* including lack of love and affection, verbal attacks, taunting, threats (for example, of withdrawal of services and/or of institutionalisation), insults and harassment.
- *neglect and acts of omission* including ignoring nutritional, medical or other physical needs; withholding of the necessities of life, failure to provide required medical care or appropriate educational services.
- *financial exploitation* including denial of access to, and control over, individuals' own funds and the misuse of their financial resources.

Factors reported by the Roeher Institute (1993) and Ticoll (1994) to precipitate exposure of people with disabilities to violence are negative public attitudes toward disability, social isolation of people with disabilities and their families, reliance of people with disabilities on others for care, unequal power relationships between people with disabilities and carers/service providers, lack of support for caregivers, lack of opportunities for people with disabilities to develop social skills, the nature of the disability itself, gender (females are more likely to be abused), poverty, lack of control or choice of people with disabilities over their personal affairs, lack of perceived credibility of people with disabilities when they report abuse, socialisation of people with disabilities to be compliant, drug and alcohol abuse by perpetrators, and ineffective safeguards.

Family reactions

Families are all different and the ways they incorporate disability into life differ. As with the individual, the impact of disability is likely to be influenced by age of onset, severity and type of disability of the family member. It also is influenced by factors such as the roles and position of the individuals before acquiring disability: whether they were wage earners, what responsibilities they had within the family, and so on.

When a child with a disability is born into a family, adjustment will be required on the part of each member, with some individuals and some families adjusting more successfully than others (Speigle & Van den Pol, 1993). Much of the literature about families paints a somewhat bleak picture about the stress and hardship they encounter. This does not have to be so. Certainly, some families do experience major difficulties which are never adequately resolved. Others, however, adjust successfully and the member with a disability is loved and valued.

There is a range of reactions that families might display.

Overprotectiveness. Parents may become overwatchful and overprotective, wanting to reduce the hurt they believe their child may experience from other people and from failing to do what other children can do. However, learning one's limitations is part of growing up, as is learning one's strengths. Overprotection can increase dependence and can deny the child experiences associated with growing up, testing the world and establishing skills and competence. The child may feel constantly watched and that he or she has no time alone. Overprotectiveness can contribute to the fears that many parents experience about what will happen in the future when they are no longer able to care for their child with a disability.

Family unity. Some people argue that the likelihood of family breakdown increases in families where a member has a disability. This is controversial and there are many factors which can contribute to family breakdown. Whether the family remains a functional unit depends on family characteristics and its strategies before disability became a reality. Many families with a person with a disability become more close-knit and stronger.

Financial costs. Most disabilities impose an added financial burden on families. Direct costs may be associated with a loss of income from either a breadwinner becoming disabled or from a parent choosing to stay at home to care for a family member with a disability. Indirect costs are associated with home modifications, travel to and from appointments, laundry bills and other day-to-day costs which are likely to be higher for a person with a disability. These costs are in addition to the considerable costs which are often associated with purchase of special equipment and aids.

Family patterns and relationships. For many people with a child with a disability there are rigorous demands associated with everyday care and therapy. In some cases, family life seems to become centred around treatment patterns and hospital visits, leaving little time for family relationships and outings. These demands may create conflict and resentment among siblings who may feel jealous, left out, and that they are not receiving enough attention from their parents who always seem to be involved with the child with a disability. These siblings may also become unwilling to bring friends home because they feel ashamed. In contrast, siblings in other families may assist the parents with therapy and caring for the child with a disability. They accept the child as part of the family unit, including him or her in games and activities.

> *My brother and I are completely different people, so I don't think we would be close even if I was not disabled. I think that when we were younger he may have been envious of the 'special treatment' that I received. Also, he had a more difficult time at school because both he and I went to the same primary and high schools and he was always seen as 'the brother of the boy in the wheelchair'.*
>
> Nathan, who has cerebral palsy

Friends and the extended family. Adult friends may feel uncomfortable and find it difficult to socialise with the family. Well-meaning people may compound problems by relating stories of difficulties encountered by other people or by urging the family to institutionalise the family member with a disability. Others may perceive the disability as a tragedy and may convey this through their behaviour towards members of the family who may not welcome expressions of sorrow or pity. Statements that the family is 'wonderful' and 'has performed miracles' also often do not help.

Other reactions. Some parents experience feelings of inferiority and worthlessness because they believe that they have an imperfect baby. They may see themselves as damaged. From time to time they may wish that their child had died or would die, a wish they feel cannot be shared and which makes them feel guilty. Some parents blame themselves for their child's disability. This blame is usually unfounded and unrealistic. They may blame themselves for something that happened during the pregnancy, childbirth or soon afterwards. It may be that they are carriers of a genetic condition that they were not aware of beforehand. There may be anxiety that other children (already living or still to be born) may inherit the disability. If the disability develops after birth (for example, Duchenne muscular dystrophy), parents may spend anxious years looking for any telling signs in other children. These feelings are common and natural reactions, which must not be dismissed as maladaptive. Rather they must be recognised and the family must be given time and assistance in working through their reactions.

Use of services. The roles and experiences of family members have changed considerably over the last 20 years. The advent of policies of integration, de-institutionalisation and community living mean that most people with disabilities remain with their families. These policies are generally regarded as improving quality of life for people with disabilities, but it is only recently that policy makers have begun to turn their attention to impacts on the family. This is a highly controversial issue. Often it is argued that caring creates a largely unacknowledged burden on the family, particularly on the principal carers of people who are disabled and dependent. The family requires access to a variety of community-based services, including home care, transport options, occupational therapy, employment services, family doctor, hospital medical team, special equipment, aids, home adaptation, home nursing, assistance with legal and financial matters, supportive counselling and respite care (Stopford, 1988).

Families differ in the extent to which they use services and supports within the community. Families who make extensive use of services and support groups often find that it helps them accept the presence of disability. Those that make little attempt to find out about services and refuse them when offered may do so because they have yet to come to terms with the disability, do not want to be singled out as different or feel reluctant to acknowledge that they are incapable of dealing with needs on their own. An element of guilt may prevent acceptance of help. It should be recognised that there are families who may choose not to seek out services, or refuse them when offered, as they are meeting needs on their own.

Positive aspects. How families adjust to disability is greatly influenced by the strategies they have developed for dealing with life in general. Despite all that has been said above, it must be repeated that many families have reaped benefits from having a member with a disability. They talk of the unconditional love provided by their child with a disability, and feelings of pride at achievements and progress.

Caregivers

With the shift from institutional care to caring for a person with a disability at home, issues for carers become increasingly important (Bozic, Hermann & Schofield, 1993). Researchers have suggested that caregiving has the potential to have many negative aspects. Words like 'burden', 'stress' and 'strain' crop up frequently in the literature where common experiences are reported to include depression, loneliness and isolation. Many of these negative consequences reflect the level of support available for carers in the community. Carers report receiving little support (either formal or informal) in their role. Community or family supports often are not adequate or carers do not choose to use them. Despite these negative consequences, many carers report positive experiences associated with their role. They feel a sense of commitment and love for the person they are caring for and gain satisfaction from seeing benefits from their work. People vary in their reactions to the caregiving role. These differences reflect personal and environmental characteristics. Thus, for example, Tetreault (1994) reports that the perception of load associated with caring for a child with a physical disability was influenced by the stability and closeness of the relationship between the parents, the extent to which they shared responsibilities and the extent to which the parents (particularly the mother) made use of available supports and resources.

Women. Traditionally, providing care has been considered a female role. Although both men and women play important roles in childrearing in modern society, the bulk of responsibility still tends to fall on the shoulders of women. Many of these people are younger women with a disabled child or family member. Some are middle-aged women caring for a parent with a disability. Others are older women who are caregivers for a spouse who is frail or has a disability. Women are carers who are largely hidden within society and their contribution is rarely acknowledged. Many people regard this phenomenon as a feminist concern as it suggests inequality related to gender, which is likely to grow as governments increasingly rely on informal and unpaid caregivers to maintain people with disabilities in the community. It has been argued that, unless acknowledgment is made of this contribution, women's unpaid work will continue to be taken for granted and women will continue to be caught between conflicting values pertaining to motherhood, marriage, family bonds, self-fulfilment and work. Findings reported by Traustadottir (1991) confirm this argument. She found that families of children with a disability are more likely to follow traditional patterns of the father working outside the home and mother working within home than are other families in the community. She argued that an increased demand for traditional women's activities within the home, such as caring for a child with a disability, create tremendous pressures which deny a woman opportunities to enter the public work arena or to maintain outside paid employment.

As said above, the issue of caring is important for women with disabilities. A woman with a disability is less likely than a male counterpart to have someone available to assist with everyday chores and tasks. Many woman with disabilities are responsible for providing care for others. Such care may be provided for children or by older women with disabilities for a frail partner or spouse.

Older carers. The issue of caring is becoming increasingly important as there is a growing number of people who are now old (or are reaching old age) and providing care for adult offspring, or a spouse or partner who has a disability(ies). Longer life expectancies (both for people with and without disabilities), along with the dismantling of institutions mean that there is an increasing number of older parents who act as carers for adult dependent children (Greenberg et al., 1993). Currently, little is known about this group of ageing carers. However, it is likely that, as well as experiencing concerns about maintaining the day-to-day carer's role, older parents worry about the future (how long they will be able to maintain their role and what will happen to their child when they themselves are either too frail to continue or have died). Lewin (1990) supported this view in an article in the *New York Times* which noted that in the United States there are now at least 200 000 people with intellectual disabilities who are over the age of 60 years. The article focused on the anxiety of parents who are providing care and support for their ageing adult offspring with intellectual disability. Many of these parents were facing issues they had not expected to encounter, as they had been told when their child was young that his or her life expectancy was short and it was unlikely that the child would outlive his or her parents.

As with other issues associated with disability, individuals differ in how they adjust to life experiences, with some coping strategies generally more effective than others. Greenberg et al. (1993) found that older mothers of adult offspring with either intellectual disability or mental illness were likely to report less stress if they had a wide social network, a cohesive family structure, and if their children were involved in out-of-home programs and activities.

Respite care

Respite care is an important service which gives both dependent people with disabilities and their carers a break. Respite care involves other people taking responsibility for the care of a person and it can be provided in the home, in institutions and in community centres. Fink (1994) notes that ideal respite care respects personal dignity, relieves carer responsibilities and provides services in a flexible, non-judgmental way which meets the needs of all members of the household. It is important that such care is age- and culturally-appropriate and that it is attractive to both the person with the disability and carers. It should help the carer to get back into regular life. Respite care may occur for short periods on a regular basis or may occur for a longer period to allow the family to have a holiday or break. It also provides the person with the disability with recreation, education and experiences outside the home.

Disability and ageing

The ageing patterns in most Western countries means that many people with life-long disabilities or those acquired earlier in life are living longer and also that there are more older people who acquire disability later in life. These two factors mean that ageing with disability is becoming an important issue. However, it is only recently that researchers have begun to direct their attention to issues associated with ageing and disability and there still tends to be a focus on research and policy development in regard to members of younger age groups.

Ageing in people with long-term disabilities

Evidence suggests that the presence of disability affects the ageing process. For example, a report published by the Ontario Federation for Cerebral Palsy (1993) indicates that people with disabilities tend to experience the changes associated with the ageing process earlier than others. However, it is controversial as to whether these premature changes are a consequence of cerebral palsy or are the result of life-long receipt of treatments and therapies. The impact of disability on health has been demonstrated by a national survey of women with physical disabilities which was conducted in the United States. The research team reported that 'disability is a risk factor for acquiring secondary chronic diseases at a younger age than women without primary disabling conditions' (Foley, 1995, p. 1).

Five chronic conditions which were uniformly reported significantly more often by women with physical disabilities were osteoporosis, chronic urinary tract infections, kidney disease, restrictive lung disease and heart disease. Women with disabilities also reported higher rates of depression. Overall, 78 per cent of women with disabilities who were aged 40 years and older reported at least one chronic health problem as compared with 52 per cent of the women without disabilities. The conclusion reached by the researchers was that conditions common in older women occurred earlier in women with disabilities.

Changes in function associated with the ageing process

Durrance (1992) notes that many bodily changes occur as the years go by. Changes include loss of elasticity in connective tissue, decreases in cell renewal and decreases in the sensitivity of some cells. However, she points out that a large reserve capacity compensates for much of this loss and that we can work to maximise efficiency through exercise. Nevertheless, the incidence of many impairments increases with age. Some impairments are the result of a lifetime of use of parts of the body (for example, arthritis), while others reflect changes to body organs (for example, vision and hearing impairment).

The combination of disability and ageing can have many psychological impacts on the individual. Minnes (1992) argues that depression, anxiety and fear are common reactions. There may be fear about the future, about continuing independence, about institutionalisation and reinstitutionalisation (for some people with a life-long disability).

It has been suggested that myths and misunderstandings on the part of health service providers may serve to prolong and exacerbate disability. For example, evidence suggests that a large percentage of health providers wrongly believe that senility and decline in the senses are inevitable aspects of ageing (Gething & Fethney, 1995). If a provider holds such myths, he or she is less likely to take action to reduce an impairment and so the older person is forced to live with an unnecessary level of disability. Such a conclusion was reached in the report published by the Ontario Federation for Cerebral Palsy (1993) which found that health care providers lacked knowledge about the effects of ageing on long-standing disability and were unable to provide advice about strategies to minimise the effects of ageing.

RESOURCE LIST

All care has been taken to ensure that all information is correct at the time of publishing. However, responsibility for the accuracy of this information is not accepted by the writer. The list of resource organisations contained in this chapter is not intended to be exhaustive. It notes national organisations only. The reader is referred to local community directories for further information and for local branches of national organisations. Inclusion of services and organisations should not be taken as a recommendation.

DISABILITY UMBRELLA ORGANISATIONS

Australia

ACROD Limited
PO Box 60
Curtin ACT 2605
Ph 06 282 4333
Fax 06 281 3488

Disabled Peoples' International (Australia)
PO Box 169,
Curtin ACT 2605

Ph/TTY 06 282 3025
Fax 06 282 3800

Canada

Council of Canadians with Disabilities
Suite 926, 294 Portage Avenue
Winnipeg, MB R3C 0B9
Ph 204 947 0303
Fax 204 942 4625

New Zealand

DPA New Zealand
PO Box 27-524
Wellington 6035
Ph 04 801 9100
Fax 04 801 9565

Assembly of People with Disabilities
PO Box 10138
Wellington
Ph 04 472 2626
Fax 04 472 2624

United Kingdom

RADAR (Royal Association for Disability
& Rehabilitation)

12 City Forum, 250 City Road
London EC1V 8AF
Ph 0171 250 3222
Fax 0171 250 0212

United States

Disability International USA
C/- University of San Francisco
    Rehabilitation Administration
2130 Fulton Street
San Francisco, CA 94117
Ph 415 422 2534
Fax 415 422 2551

INFORMATION NETWORKS

Australia

DINA – Disability Information Network Australia. DINA is a national group of disability information providers with interest in resource and information sharing and networking. The aim of DINA is to facilitate cooperation and communication between information services for people with a disability in all states and territories.
Fax: 06 273 5483
NICAN – a national information service on recreation, tourism, sport and the arts for people with disabilities. NICAN provides information on organisations around Australia offering the above activities. Enquiries from anyone in Australia are welcome. Information is provided free of charge.

Reply paid 028, PO Box 407
Curtin ACT 2605
Ph 008 806769
TTY 06 2824333
Fax 06 2853714

Canada

Disability Information Services of Canada
Suite 304, 501-18th Avenue S.W.
Calgary, AB T2S 0C7
Ph 403 244 2836
TTY/TDD 403 229 2177
Fax 403 229 1878

United States

National Organization on Disability
910 16th Street NW
Suite 600
Washington, DC 20006
Ph 202 293 5960
Fax 202 293 7999

FURTHER READING

Australian Bureau of Statistics (1993). *Disability, ageing and carers: summary of findings.* Canberra: Commonwealth Government Printer. Cat. No. 4430.0

Bostock, L. (1991). Access and equity for people with a double disadvantage. *Australian Disability Review*, 2, 3–8.

Bozic, S., Hermann, H. & Schofield, H. (1993). *A profile of carers in Victoria: analysis of the ABS survey of disabled and aged persons 1988.* Melbourne: Victorian Health Foundation.

Cooper, M. (1993). Discrimination against women with disabilities. *Australian Disability Review*, 4, 69–72.

Ellis, J., & Whaite, A. (1987). *From me . . . to you: advice to parents of children with special needs*. Sydney: Williams & Wilkins and Associates.

Fine, M. & Asch, A. (1988). *Women and disabiities*. Philadelphia, PA: Temple University Press.

Gething, L. (1994a). Aboriginality and disability. *Aboriginal and Islander Health Worker Journal*, 18, 29–34.

Gething, L. (1995). A case study of Aboriginal people with disabilities. *Australian Disability Review*, 94–4, 77–87.

Gething, L., Poynter, T., Redmayne, G. & Reynolds, F. (1994). *Across the divide: distance, diversity and disability. Volumes I and II*. Sydney: The University of Sydney.

Moss, I. (1993). Double disadvantage. *Australian Disability Review*, 23–7.

Munford, R. & Martin, S. (1994). *Disability studies: thinking critically about disability*. Palmerston, New Zealand: Massey University.

Orr, K. (1984). Consulting women with disabilities. *Australian Disability Review*, 3, 14–18.

Quinn, P. (1994). America's disability policy: another double standard? *Affilia*, Spring, 45–57.

Rix, P. (undated) *Living with a disability and dying for a break: a study of respite care*. Sydney: Disability Council of NSW.

Robinson, I. (1988). *Multiple sclerosis*. London: Routledge.

Seligman, M. (1992). *Helplessness: on development, depression and death*. New York: W. H. Freeman & Co.

Sobsey, D. (1994). *Violence and abuse in the lives of people with disabilities: the end of silent acceptance*. Baltimore, MD: Paul H. Brookes.

Stopford, V. (1988). *Understanding disability: causes, characteristics and coping*. Caulfield, Vic: Edward Arnold.

World Health Organization (1980). *International classification of impairments, disabilities and handicaps*. Geneva.

Wright, B. A. (1983). *Physical disability: a social-psychological approach*. New York: Harper.

CHAPTER 2

PHILOSOPHY, LEGISLATION, ATTITUDES AND SERVICE PROVISION

Major changes have occurred over the last ten or fifteen years in philosophies, legislation, and models of service provision. Until just over a decade ago most people with severe disabilities lived in institutions and obtained services from specialist organisations. Now, most live in the community and use generic services available to all people.

Many of the recent changes in policies and in government philosophy and legislation can be attributed to the determination and hard work of people with disabilities. International Year of Disabled Persons occurred in 1981 and marked a time of upsurge in feelings of common identity among people with disabilities, and an acknowledgment of their rights. This International Year was a milestone as it brought into prominence many issues associated with equality of opportunity, access and quality of life. Although its benefits are disputed by some, few would deny that it provided a marker for the participation of people with disabilities in decision making and in the promotion of change. The Year saw an increase in the activity of advocacy groups and political lobby groups. It also brought to fruition the previous years of lobbying and work in which people with disabilities had been involved. One of the most important outcomes of the Year was the World Program of Action Concerning Disabled Persons. Both the World Program and the International Year emphasised the right of people with disabilities to the same opportunities as other citizens and to an equal share in improvements in living conditions resulting from economic and social development.

These developments occurred in the context of two philosophical approaches: the principles of *normalisation* and *empowerment*.

Principle of normalisation. Wolfensberger's (1972) basic philosophy is that socially-valued roles should be supported and defended for people who are at risk of social devaluation and that all people have the right to 'normal' life experiences. Normalisation is not concerned with trying to make all people 'normal', but with providing services which are the same or as close as possible to those provided for others. This position follows Nirije (1967) who stated that all people should be able to participate in the normal rhythms and routines of the human life cycle: they should be able to participate in daily events such as cooking, going to work, shopping; in annual rhythms such as wearing different clothes in winter and summer; and in the life cycle by doing things which are appropriate to their chronological age. Normalisation (now more commonly known as social role valorisation) is also concerned with freedom of choice: the right to make decisions about what you eat, where you live, what type of job you do, and so on. It is argued

22

that service provision should take into account the principle that all people have the right to develop and achieve to the best of their abilities.

Empowerment philosophy. Empowerment means enabling. In the context of service provision, it means that the aim is to assist people to acquire skills and abilities so that they are able to take control of their own lives. This is in direct contrast with earlier philosophies and models of service provision which were based on concepts of helping and unequal relationships between service providers and clients. The following two quotes provide insight into the meaning of this concept to people with disabilities. Empowerment is:

> . . . *a process by which individuals gain mastery over their lives and a critical understanding of their environment.*
>
> Zimmerman et al., 1992, p. 708 cited by Dempsey, 1994

> *Empowerment implies that many competencies are already present or at least possible. Empowerment implies that what you see as inadequate functioning is a result of social structure and lack of resources which make it impossible for the existing competencies to operate. [Empowerment] implies that in those cases where new competencies need to be learned, they are best learned in a context of living life rather than in artificial programs where everyone, including the person learning, knows that it is really the expert who is in charge.*
>
> Rappaport, 1981, p. 16

Concepts of normalisation and empowerment have been reflected in the world-wide move towards rights-based models of service provision and community living. The United Nations Standard Rules on Equalization of Opportunities for Persons with Disabilities underpins legislation and changing approaches in many countries. Three concepts are defined in the UN Rules as being at the heart of disability policy: prevention, rehabilitation and equalisation of opportunities. The *Americans with Disabilities Act 1990* (ADA) incorporates these concepts. The Act established 'a clear and comprehensive prohibition of discrimination on the basis of disability . . . [it] provid[ed] a sound legal framework for the practical implementation of the inalienable right of people with disabilities to participate equally in the mainstream of society'. It outlaws discrimination in wide areas of life including employment, public services (including public transportation), public accommodation, services operated by the private sector, and telecommunications. The focus of the ADA is on routine activities, services and facilities that people use in the course of everyday life. The Act incorporates a staged introduction process. This staged introduction meant that many American service providers were less antagonistic than they would have been if immediate compliance had been required. It also offset irrational fears that implementation of the Act would damage the American economy. In Australia, the commonwealth *Disability Services Act 1986* and the *Disability Discrimination Act 1992* are consistent with the philosophy underlying the United Nations Standard Rules. These Acts are designed to promote equity and equality of access to a wide range of services within the community. The *Disability Services Act* is accompanied by a set of standards which government and government funded organisations must use to ensure that models of service provision are appropriate and meet specified requirements. Each state has its equivalent to the

Figure 2.1: This cartoon displays the effects that barriers can have on community participation. Legislation is designed to ensure access for all to community facilities and activities

Figure 2.2: The fact that having a disability does not prevent you from having fun and enjoying sport is captured in this cartoon

Cartoons reproduced with permission of People with Disabilities Participation Division, Australian Sports Commission.

Disability Services Act. People with disabilities and their organisations have had an integral and essential role in the development and implementation of this legislation.

Five important themes which run through government philosophies and legislation are:

- Services and policy should be consumer-focused – consumers have a right to be, and should be, consulted.
- People with disabilities have the same rights and obligations as others in the community.
- Whenever possible, services should be provided by generic organisations used by all members of a community.
- Services should be individualised and enable people to reach their potential in terms of quality of life, integration within everyday community life and its activities, and achievement of aspirations.
- People with disabilities should actively participate in decisions, both on an individual basis and in terms of policy-making and implementation.

Many Australian state governments have developed strategies for implementing the above changes in policy and practice. The Australian Disability Strategy seeks to implement practices which reflect contemporary thinking in terms of the rights-based model of service provision. It aims to establish mechanisms for meeting the objectives of the *Disability Services Act 1986*, the *Disability Discrimination Act 1992* and the UN Standard Rules on the Equalization of Opportunities for Persons with Disabilities. It aims to establish appropriate mechanisms at all levels of government and the community for achieving equal opportunity objectives. To date, a draft for the strategy has been developed and consultations are still under way (Bidmeade, 1994).

Canada has approached legislation differently. Rather than having specific legislation relating to people with disabilities, Canada has included these people in human rights legislation applying to all Canadians. Specific mention is made of disability in Section 15 of the Canadian Charter on Rights and Freedoms (1982). This Charter is the supreme law of Canada and states that 'every individual is equal before and under the law and has the right to equal protection and equal benefit of the law without discrimination and, in particular, without discrimination based on race, national or ethnic origin, colour, religion, sex, age, marital status or mental or physical disability'. Some provincial (state) governments have adopted legislation specifically to protect the rights of people with disabilities. For example, the *Ontarians with Disabilities Act 1994* (ODA) is concerned with ensuring equal access to areas such as post-secondary education, transportation, government publications, training programs and communication. The *Ontario Long Term Care Act 1995*, supports care for people in the comfort and dignity of their own home; creates a bill of rights, and safeguards and appeals for users of community services; establishes a framework for multiservice agencies; and helps remove bureaucratic obstacles to care by creating uniform eligibility criteria across the province. One strategy it has initiated is amalgamation of a range of services previously provided by separate organisations, so that they are now administered by an umbrella organisation. Multiservice agencies (MSAs) mean that access to services such as housework and cleaning, nursing, personal support, occupational therapy, physiotherapy and Meals on Wheels will be possible through one phone call and one assessment. This change is designed to promote integrated health and social in-home community home services, to reduce fragmentation, to provide easier access and easier coordination (Tiessen, 1995). This system has similar intentions to the HACC (Home and Community Care) program established by the Australian government in 1985.

Disability discrimination legislation has been passed in the United Kingdom. The United Kingdom *Disability Discrimination Act* was passed into law on 8 November, 1995. This Act has six parts. The first defines disability. The second makes it unlawful for employers of more than 20 people to discriminate. The third relates to discrimination in the provision of goods or services, excluding education and transport. The fourth requires schools and colleges to set annual disability statements and goals. The fifth gives the government power to make recommendations regarding accessibility of taxis and buses as from 1999, and the sixth part establishes the National Disability Council to advise government.

Despite these major changes and admirable intentions, evidence suggests that in many countries, issues are yet to be satisfactorily tackled in regard to equity and equality for people with disabilities. For example, the Australian National Inquiry into Human Rights of People with Mental Illness (Burdekin, 1993) concluded that people affected by mental illness are among the most vulnerable and disadvantaged in the community. The report argues that these people experience widespread discrimination and are denied the rights and services to which they are entitled. Clearly there is a long way to go before philosophies are fully reflected in the policy and practice of service agencies and in the life opportunities for people with disabilities.

One of the major factors hindering the implementation of new legislation is associated with the widespread negative attitudes and beliefs about disability within the community. These set apart people with disabilities as being less than equal and different from others. Such attitudes exist not just within the general population, but also within professional groups. They are demonstrated in behaviours and practice.

Attitudes and beliefs

Most people are well intentioned and wish to treat others equitably; that is, to behave in a way consistent with positive attitudes. However, there is evidence to suggest that definitions of what constitutes positive attitudes and behaviour differ between people with and without a disability. This discrepancy hinders effective interaction and can create conflict. Makas (1988) found that people without disabilities defined positive attitudes and behaviour as reflecting a desire to be well meaning, helpful and considerate. For people with disabilities, a positive orientation meant dispensing with the special category of disability altogether and promoting civil and social rights. They did not want to be treated as different or as in need of help, but wanted an environment in which they could do things for themselves. In this context of differing perceptions and aspirations, the offer of help from a nondisabled person, although well meaning, may be interpreted by the person with a disability as being patronising and taking away any possibility of being independent, ordinary and competent.

This difference in orientation is consistent with the 'insider-outsider' concept developed by Wright (1975a and b, 1980, 1983). Wright argues that people without disabilities, who have had little personal and mutually-rewarding contact with people with disabilities, tend to hold negative and stereotyped or 'succumbing' views which focus on the handicap and tragedy associated with disability. 'Outsiders' are likely to display 'spread' in their perceptions by extending perceived limitations beyond the disability to include personality and other characteristics having no necessary relationship with the disability. They also tend to hold a view which concentrates on the difficulties and heartbreak of being disabled. People who hold such views attribute disability and handicap to the individual and focus on interventions which aim to decrease the handicap associated with disability by *changing the person*.

In contrast, 'insiders' who have had close contact tend to develop a 'coping' framework which views disability as only one feature of a multifaceted person who has abilities as well as disabilities. Insiders attribute handicaps to features of the environment, rather than to the individual with a disability and focus on interventions which aim to *change the environment* (for example, architectural barriers, affirmative action legislation).

The phenomenon of spread was demonstrated in a study conducted by the author (Gething, 1988, 1992b). Here, trainee health professionals viewed a videotape of a young adult applying for job and then made assessments of the applicant and whether he or she should get the job. Twelve versions of the video were made in which sex, personality (shy versus brash) and presence of disability were varied. Parallel pairs of videos for the applicant with and without a disability (the applicant used a wheelchair) were identical except for brief shots at the beginning and end of the interview where the applicant walked or wheeled into and out of the session. Otherwise, the applicant was viewed from the waist up. Results indicated that presence/absence of disability was the overriding factor influencing judgments. It was more influential than sex or personality. The feature of disability led to a general devaluing of the applicant in a wide range of characteristics as perceived by the students. Among other things, the applicant was seen as less well adjusted, less capable, less happy, and more anxious.

Goffman's landmark work, which was published in 1965, regarded people with disabilities as members of a minority group which is set apart, treated as different and stigmatised by other members of society. Wright (1983) expands this view to argue that anything which deviates from cultural norms stands out and is perceived negatively. These attitudes have become part of the fabric of society and are deeply entrenched in service provision. Society has encouraged the view of difference and separateness by creating 'special schools', using special buses in which children travel to and from school, and by establishing specialist institutions which are often in locations which are remote from the rest of the population.

Recent legislation is designed to force change. Models of service provision which segregate people with and without disabilities are now outlawed. For example, 'cradle to grave' institutions which provide life-long services and living quarters for people with disabilities are now being closed in favour of community living.

However, attitude change has not necessarily kept abreast of changes in legislation. An anecdotal example emerged for the author in a recent study of rurally-based general practitioners in NSW, Australia. This study was designed to assess disability awareness of these medical professionals in order to make recommendations for in-service education. One phase of the study involved distributing questionnaires. The author and her team spent considerable time debating what terminology to use when referring to people with disabilities in the questionnaire. In the end it was decided to use the term 'client' as it conveys a message of equality in the service provision situation. The term was not well received by a section of respondents. Angry phone calls and letters indicated that 'doctors have patients, solicitors and prostitutes have clients'. It would seem that those people who chose to correct the researcher were still operating under a 'medical model' which fosters an unequal power relationship rather than the 'community' or 'holistic' model advocated by government and in which consumer/client equality and rights are strongly promoted. (It should be noted, that most respondents were enthusiastic about the project and cooperated fully with data collections.)

Factors underlying attitudes

Considerable discussion has centred around why negative attitudes exist. However, one conclusion that does seem to be agreed upon is that these reactions are reflected in behaviour in terms of discomfort in social interaction (Evans, 1976) and in less than optimal service provision (for example, Chubon, 1982; Roush, 1976).

Factors underlying negative attitudes are summarised below and are based on Gething (1984) and Livneh (1988):

- *Fear of the unknown* or anxiety associated with being unsure of how to behave and what to expect from the person with a disability.
- *Threat to security* or to the view of the world as a fair place after viewing a person who appears to be 'suffering' from an undeserved fate.
- *Fear of becoming disabled* or feelings of vulnerability.
- *Guilt* or 'why did this misfortune happen to this person and not to me, she/he is no more deserving of it'.
- *Aversion to difficulties*, weakness and a less than perfect body.

Such beliefs are widespread in the community. For example, Covington (1995) reports results of a Harris Poll conducted in 1992. In this poll, 58 per cent of Americans agreed that they felt anxious, uncertain and uncomfortable when meeting someone with a disability. A large proportion of the sample also reported that they feared people with disabilities.

Prejudices can arise from cultural values which prefer beauty, youth, intelligence and strength, and socialisation or passing of stereotypes from one generation to the next.

Goodwill (1994) summarises the following images of disability in popular culture:

- *Humanitarian,* where disability is viewed as a misfortune. This form of portrayal is commonly used in telethons and to encourage people to give to charities. In the past, organisations of people with disabilities contributed to perpetuating myths and enhancing the sense of difference. Fortunately, beauty contests which reinforced the high value placed on physical attractiveness and campaigns which encouraged people to give money out of pity are now largely a thing of the past. Most organisations now feature constructive issues in their campaigns and aim to convey people with disabilities as valued individuals with special needs.
- *Medical*, where disability is viewed as a sickness. This form of portrayal is particularly found in hospitals and medical settings.
- *Outsider*, where the person with a disability is viewed as other and seen as separate and different from other people, as demonstrated in their portrayal in stories and cartoons as monsters and evil characters.
- *Religious*, where disability is seen as part of a divine plan.
- *Retribution*, where disability is seen as a punishment for sins.
- *Social control*, where disability is seen as a threat to society, as conveyed in horror shows and by monsters.

- *Zoological*, where the person with a disability is seen as a pet or an object of entertainment, as seen in circuses, wrestling, freak shows and dwarf tossing.

Attitudes and behaviours of service providers

The behaviours and attitudes of service providers have a major impact on their effectiveness and on the satisfaction experienced by clients. All of us are able to recall examples of where effective behaviour resulted in an excellent service, leaving us feeling that our needs had been attended to and that we were satisfied with the outcomes (see Table 2.1).

Unfortunately, we also can all cite examples of less-than-adequate service provision which left us feeling angry, frustrated, disillusioned and determined never to use the service again. Sometimes, there is little choice: there may not be other professionals or services located in the area where we live. This means either putting up with an unsatisfactory service or not going again (see Table 2.2).

As discussed above, 'insiders' tend to attribute handicaps associated with disability to the environment while 'outsiders' attribute them to qualities of people with the disability. Such a difference has major implications for education, health services, policy and planning. Professionals who are 'outsiders' are likely to reach different decisions from those who are 'insiders'.

Evidence suggests that health and community workers hold attitudes which are typical of those in the general population, and that prevalent myths are institution-alised within health professions. Holmes & Karst (1990) argue that myths are shortcuts that enable a professional to form stereotypical views in lieu of interaction aimed at understanding a client. Such myths result in a person with a disability being looked upon as a *type* of client rather than as an individual.

De Loach & Greer 1981 list professional behaviours which imply low opinions of clients and rob them of their humanness. These include:

- interpreting as 'abnormal', behaviours by people with disabilities which are generally considered 'normal' in others (for example, displays of emotion);

Table 2.1: Good experiences with service providers

Good acute health care team (doctors, nurses and other professionals). They especially acknowledged the importance of my family and friends.

College, in particular the disability officer, has been very supportive and willing to help in any way.

John, who has a spinal cord injury

Friendly, helpful nurses and doctors. Despite the horror and intense suffering I went though, the system was able to help me back to reality.

Marcus, who has schizophrenia

When 'health professionals' care about their work and realise that they don't know everything and that you know something.

Nathan, who has cerebral palsy

Table 2.2: Bad experiences with service providers

Poor long-term support and being pushed in a direction I didn't want to go. I feel I've had to achieve most things myself through trial and error and talking to other people. I was not offered any counselling or answers to important questions (such as sexuality). Everyone was generalised into a mould.

Barbara, who has cerebral palsy

Taxi drivers, especially those in my country town, have a very poor attitude — they tend to talk down to you and throw your wheelchair around.

John, who has a spinal cord injury

I remember attending my first interview with a service provider. I was accompanied by my guide dog, but the counsellor kept offering me printed material to read. This has left me with a poor impression of their service.

Angus, who is vision impaired

High turnover of staff meant that in one service over five years I was managed by 11 different people. This made it very difficult to form a relationship which was not only comfortable, but also efficient.

Ruth, who has MS

Sometimes professionals are rude and insensitive. Psychiatrists often think they know what is best for you and don't listen to what the client thinks. The doctors are often wrong and prescribing medication seems to be hit-and-miss.

Ashish, who has schizophrenia

- overemphasising the effects of disability on adjustment;
- underestimating the potential of a client with a disability;
- treating clients in terms of their disabilities rather than in terms of other personal characteristics.

Thinking along the lines of the medical model also affects professional attitudes and behaviours. This model focuses on changing the individual, to the neglect of social and other environmental factors which affect the lives of people with disabilities. It also affects the goals of service provision and influences recommendations made by professionals. Stuifbergen (1995) argues that professionals who have experienced educational situations and practice settings that depend heavily on the medical model find it difficult to view individuals with disabilities as fully capable of health. In the medical model, health means an absence of illness. Many professionals have difficulty in separating illness from disability. Stuifbergen cites Pender (1987) who argues that health and impairment are not on the same continuum. Absence of impairment is not a prerequisite for health. Health and disability can coexist. Stuifbergen argues that difficulty in separating these concepts is one reason for the neglect of, and lack of information about, health promotion issues for people with disabilities. This provides one illustration of how attitudes, beliefs and lack of accurate information can have major impacts on service provision for people with disabilities. Maynard (1995) argues that an important aspect of community education and health professional roles should be to facilitate and develop health promotion programs in order to assist an individual in maintaining an optimal level of functioning. If a professional believes that health is inconsistent with having a disability, she or he is unlikely to encourage health-promoting behaviours.

Most people with disabilities are healthy and able to make decisions about their own lives. However, many service providers do not seem aware of this. They expect the client to be a passive recipient of information and to behave in ways indicative of helplessness and dependence (Crisp, 1987). People with disabilities who fight against such stereotyping or who try to maintain control over their own lives are often viewed as aggressive and difficult, while those who are dependent are regarded as 'good' and cooperative. Either way, the person loses in terms of dignity, quality of life and individuality (Lindemann, 1981).

Professionals provide powerful models. Their conscious and unconscious behaviour conveys messages and expectations to the client with a disability. Crisp (1987) argues that professionals should work to encourage clients to be active and independent. One means is to work with the client as a co-manager in planning, operation and evaluation of service provision. Other ways are to interact with clients in terms of their asset value, not limitations; to deal with social and physical environmental factors which face clients; and to encourage clients to take an active role in working for change in themselves and in the environment. Such strategies encourage people with disabilities to adopt a constructive view of life and to regard themselves as powerful individuals who can have control over the world and the things that happen.

Wright (1980) makes a series of points which are still highly relevant for service providers:

- Most people with disabilities are not passive, they do and must take charge of their lives.
- People with disabilities are individuals, each has his or her own past experiences, personality, strategies for dealing with life, and needs.
- Severity of disability is as much a function of physical and social environmental barriers, as of personal impairment (if not more so). An important part of service provision is to act on the environment to minimise barriers.
- People with disabilities, like everyone else, have strengths and limitations. It is important to emphasise assets.
- Service provision should not focus on problems so that assets and abilities are overlooked.
- As with any relationship between two people, it is important that both the person with a disability and service provider make adjustments to promote successful interaction.

RIGHTS AND RESPONSIBILITIES

Philosophies of empowerment and normalisation have major implications for the quality of client–professional relationships and for the rights and responsibilities of each person when working together in such a relationship.

Rights for the client/consumer with a disability include:

- to live in and be part of the community;
- to make decisions that affect his or her life;
- to realise his or her individual capacities for physical, social, emotional and intellectual development;
- to receive protection from exploitation and discrimination;
- to receive services which are appropriate and timely, regardless of age, sexual preference, ethnicity, race, religion or marital status;
- to have personal information kept confidential and not released to others without permission.

Responsibilities for the client/consumer with a disability:

- to be clear, specific and precise when instructing a carer/enabler;
- to respect the rights of others;
- to ask questions when unsure about aspects of service provision or programs;
- to participate fully in decision making;
- to inform service providers if aspects of a program or treatment are or are not working effectively;
- to keep to agreements made with service providers about aspects of a program, therapy or support.

Rights for a service provider, carer or enabler:

- to work without being harassed;
- to refuse to give services he or she regards as inappropriate;
- to have privacy and confidentiality.

Responsibilities for a service provider, carer or enabler:

- to respect the privacy and confidentiality of consumers/clients;
- to allow clients/consumers to be informed of, and have input into the services they receive;
- to inform clients/consumers of their rights and responsibilities;
- to provide information about types of services offered, and to make informed decisions about their usage, outcomes and benefits;
- to seek information as needed;
- to provide services which are flexible and appropriate to the client/consumer's needs;
- to provide services agreed upon with the client/consumer.

Principles of service provision

The following principles are useful to remember:

People first, disability second. People with disabilities are like anyone else. They experience the same range of emotions, needs, interests; and issues associated with growing up, self-esteem, sexuality and so on.

People with disabilities are individuals. People with disabilities, like all of us, are individuals, but are often handicapped by diagnosis and associated labels. It is important to resist the temptation to assume that everyone with a particular disabling condition has the same needs and interests. Remember to take gender, racial, ethnic, age and other differences into account. Respect for the individual is vital, as is listening and accepting as useful the information people with disabilities convey about their experiences and needs.

Disability is an inconvenience and affects the way a person achieves his or her desired lifestyle. However, most people with disabilities do not sit around and contemplate their disabilities. They carry on with their lives. Most have lives similar to others: they go to work, pay taxes, go shopping, go out for dinner, marry, have children and so on.

A universal expectation. This is to have a healthy life and healthy children. Acquisition of disability or discovery that one's child is less-than-perfect changes life and hopes for the future. In both cases, the person with disability and/or close family members are likely to experience stages of reaction similar to those Kübler-Ross (1969) associates with bereavement.

Respect the rights of someone with a disability. All of us are entitled to be treated with dignity and to have allowances made for our special needs. Be prepared to offer help or to give assistance when asked, but do not be offended if your offer is refused. Accept a person's right to privacy, do not ask personal questions about the disability until you feel you know him or her well enough (see Table 2.3).

Table 2.3: Suggestions for client-professional relationships

Client	Professional
Be clear about what you want (or do not want). Be organised, think ahead about what you need and will say.	Remember that this person is like anyone else, except for special needs associated with disability.
Make sure you are talking to the right person.	Remember that many difficulties reflect society's attitudes, rather than the impairment itself.
You are entitled to information; knowledge is a right, not a privilege.	Focus on abilities rather than disabilities.
Stop apologising for what you cannot do.	Encourage the person to do everything she or he wants to, and set goals.
Do not be put off with vague explanations or jargon.	Be patient, let the person set his or her own pace.
Resist the temptation to exploit the role of a 'sick person'.	Give responsibility as soon as the person is ready.
Ensure your opinion is heard and taken into account, but retain a calm attitude and keep your temper.	Speak directly to the person, do not use a companion as a go-between.

Important principles which acknowledge the individuality of people with disabilities and their rights to belong to the community are:

- *'Customer focus'*. People with disabilities are individuals and consumers of services which must have an individual focus rather than stereotyping people and assuming that, because they have a disability, they have the same needs, interests and abilities.
- Services (both generic and disability-specific) should assist people with disabilities in achieving *empowerment, independence, quality of life* and *access* to facilities.
- People with disabilities must play an *active and equal role* in the planning and implementation of services.
- Most people with disabilities are not ill or sick, therefore models of service provision and organisations which are responsible for providing services must focus on *wellness and well people*.
- Regions and areas are different, and service provision must be *flexible* to take into account geographic, social and economic variation.

Language and behaviour

Also important is the language we use to refer to people with disabilities (McCrindle, 1995). Language affects the way we think and conveys our attitudes to others. Appropriate language puts *people first* and the disability second. Language should also convey capability rather than depict a person as helpless and tragic. Thus, the appropriate term is *people with disabilities*. This terminology extends to references to people with particular types of disability. Thus, the following terms are the ones to use: person with intellectual disability, person with cerebral palsy, person who uses a wheelchair, person with schizophrenia, person living with AIDS, and so on.

However, there is a balance. Euphemisms for disability or sugar-coated terms such as 'handi-capable' and 'physically challenged' are viewed by many people with disabilities as being patronising and confusing (Weitz, 1992).

It is not appropriate to use terms such as 'lad' or 'kid' when referring to adults who have a disability. A useful guide is whether you would like to be called by a particular term. If not, then it is not suitable to use with someone with a disability.

Professional language contains many stereotypes of people with disabilities which are conveyed by using labels based on medical diagnoses. Such labels tend to focus on deficits rather than on strengths and overlook differences between people. They provide a shortcut in professional discussions and an easy way to deal with and think about people with disabilities (Weitz, 1992). The importance of the effects of language was recognised by the Illinois Department of Rehabilitation Services (1994) which published a set of guidelines for journalists when writing about people with disabilities. These guidelines included inappropriate and appropriate terminology for people with disabilities.

Our behaviours convey important messages about what we think of other people. All people have the right to be treated with dignity and respect, and for their wishes to be taken into account. Interaction is a two-way process, both parties have responsibilities and rights. Any relationship or interaction involves modifications or 'accommodations' in which *both* people adjust their behaviours to suit the needs and characteristics of the other. Modifications made during interaction with

Table 2.4: Strategies for interaction

Person with a disability	Other person
Tell the other person if any form of assistance is required.	Ask the person if help is required, but do not insist and do not assist without asking first.
Let people know what you wish to do yourself.	If you are unsure of how to behave, ask the person. Accept the fact that disability exists, do not try to pretend it is not there.
Do not let people treat you like an invalid.	Regard and treat the person as healthy.
Do not assume that everyone knows and understands your disability.	Be aware of the environment and how it may present difficulties.
Become aware of your rights and be firm about your rights to access, independence and privacy.	Do not talk about the person as if he or she is not present or cannot understand or speak for himself or herself.
Be aware and tolerant if another person seems uncomfortable in social situations.	As in any conversation, maintain eye contact as far as possible.
If your speech is affected be prepared to repeat what has not been understood.	Be willing to communicate in different ways (for example, using an alphabet board).
Be polite when offered assistance. Such offers, although sometimes misguided, are usually well meant.	Remember, people differ in their needs, interests, personalities and approach to life.

a person with a disability represent just one form of the many accommodations that we make in our everyday lives.

Table 2.4 provides suggestions for interaction in any context, whether it involves a professional–client interaction, meeting of friends, community interaction or whatever.

FURTHER READING

Bidmeade, I. (1994). *Legislation and integration: an audit of legislation which impacts upon the integration of people with a disability in Australia.* Intellectual Disability Services Council.

Chubon, R. A. (1982). An analysis of research dealing with the attitudes of professionals toward disability. *Journal of Rehabilitation,* 48, 25–9.

Crisp, R. A. (1987). Helping relationships: key issues. *Australian Disability Review,* 1, 56–9.

De Loach, C. & Greer, B. G. (1981). *Adjustment to severe physical disability.* New York: McGraw-Hill.

Geskie, M. A. & Salasek, J. L. (1988). Attitudes of health care personnel toward persons with disabilities. In H. E. Yuker (ed). *Attitudes toward people with disabilities.* New York: Springer.

Gething, L. (1992). Judgements by health professionals of personality characteristics of people with visible disabilities. *Social Science and Medicine,* 34, 809–15.

Gething, L. (1994). The interaction with disabled persons scale. *Journal of Personality and Social Behavior,* 9, 23–42.

Goffman. E. (1965). *Notes on the management of a spoiled identity.* Harmondsworth: Penguin.

Holmes, G. E. & Karst, R. H. (1990). The institutionalisation of disability myths: impact on vocational rehabilitation services. *Journal of Rehabilitation,* 56, 20–7.

Illinois Department of Rehabilitation Services (1994). Handicapping language: a guide for journalists and the public. *Remedial and Special Education,* 15, 60–2.

Livneh, H. (1988). A dimensional perspective on the origin of negative attitudes toward persons with disabilities. In H. E. Yuker (ed). *Attitudes toward people with disabilities.* New York: Springer.

Makas, E. (1988). Positive attitudes toward disabled people: disabled and nondisabled persons' perspectives. *Journal of Social Issues,* 44, 49–61.

McCrindle, K. (1995). War on words: label versus euphemism. *Disability Today,* 4, 18–22.

Roush, S. E. (1976). Health professionals as contributors to attitudes toward persons with disabilities. A special communication. *Physical Therapy,* 66, 1551–4.

Wright, B. A. (1983). *Physical disability: a social-psychological approach.* New York: Harper.

Yuker, H. E. (1988). The effects of contact on attitudes toward disabled persons: some empirical generalizations. In H. E. Yuker (ed). *Attitudes toward people with disabilities.* New York: Springer.

CHAPTER 3

ACQUIRED BRAIN INJURY

Brain injury may be acquired as a result of trauma through accidents and violence, or through non-traumatic causes such as strokes, substance abuse, medical misadventure and disease. For many people, acquired brain injury occurs suddenly and without warning. For others, it can reflect gradual deterioration. Either way, major changes to lifestyle are usually required. Implications for the individual depend on the extent and location of injury.

LIVING WITH ACQUIRED BRAIN INJURY

There are a range of possible outcomes for people sustaining a brain injury and it is difficult to predict what these will be in the early months. Sometimes the damage will be minimal and will cause little or no difficulty in returning to everyday life. After other injuries, people may be left with very serious difficulties which will require a long period of rehabilitation and adjustment. Rehabilitation is an ongoing process and gains can be made for some years following the injury.

In general, people who sustain brain injury may experience permanent disabilities in each of three functional areas:

1. physical (or motor-sensory);
2. cognitive (or intellectual);
3. behavioural (or personality).

Consequences for the individual vary, depending on which areas of the brain were injured and how much brain tissue was destroyed. Commonly, motor control and coordination are affected. Other common disabilities include paralysis or weakness on one side of the body (hemiplegia), loss, decrease or even increase in one or more sensations, slow or slurred speech or aphasia, and altered social and emotional behaviour. Some people experience confusion (Duckworth, 1987).

These disabilities are likely to result in major changes to life opportunities and aspirations. They also increase the possibility of occurrence of secondary disabilities. Marge (1995) stated that substance abuse was an issue for 50 per cent of people with acquired brain injury in the United States. Other common occurrences for these people cited by Marge include reinjury because of poor risk-taking judgment, subsequent vehicle accidents, falls, violent outbursts, being a victim of violence by others, mobility limitations which can influence the adequacy of self-care, difficulties in maintaining employment, and obesity.

Personal adjustment

Reactions for the individual greatly depend on the extent and location of injury within the brain and may also vary depending on the person's age. However, the sudden and unexpected nature of many forms of brain injury mean that the person experiences sudden disruption to his or her life and will need to make unplanned adjustments to everyday living. This involves a process of coming to terms with the disability and incorporating it into one's lifestyle. Not surprisingly many people experience the stages of loss and bereavement outlined by Kübler-Ross (1969) and summarised in Chapter 1. These are healthy grieving processes associated with sudden and/or major loss.

> *I thought at first that it would be the way people reacted to me that would bother me the most but in fact it's often the small things like struggling to check the change someone's given me, things that I know I used to do easily before the accident.*
>
> Sophia, who acquired a brain injury 13 years ago

Acquired brain injury can mean major adjustments to lifestyle, abilities aspirations and self-identity. One of the most distressing outcomes for people who have had a brain injury and their families is the sense that they are 'not the same person'. Damage to certain parts of the brain can exaggerate or modify a person's personality and the way they behave, so that although they are the same person, they seem different. Some of these changes may be temporary or may reduce over time.

Cognitive and behavioural disabilities can be 'hidden disabilities' that are not readily apparent and that are often most disabling for the person with a brain injury because of their effects on people around them. The 'hidden' nature of the impairment may produce conflicts and ambivalence in relating to others. For example, some people may prefer not to 'disclose' their disability because of the stigma they perceive is attached to it. However, clues to the presence of impairment may be contained in the person's behaviour and thought processes. Not knowing that the person has brain injury may lead others to misinterpret these.

The disability(ies) experienced by some people with a brain injury may prevent them from being independent in activities of daily living, and/or in finding employment. In the longer term, some people may experience difficulty establishing, developing and maintaining relationships because of cognitive and behavioural changes. A person who has had a brain injury can at times be difficult to live with because of the cognitive, emotional and social effects of his or her injury.

People with severe cognitive and behavioural problems who are not engaged in work, educational or social activities, may find it difficult to fill their time. Loneliness and inability to obtain paid employment can have detrimental effects on self-esteem and confidence and people sometimes experience periods of boredom, depression and/or anxiety. Or it can result in the person becoming demanding, intolerant and sometimes aggressive. However, as noted with other disabling conditions, people who have had a brain injury are individuals and display a range of personality characteristics like others in the community. Contrary to popular myth, they are not necessarily aggressive, not are they likely to display inappropriate sexual behaviour.

> *I noticed my personality had changed from quiet, introverted to noisy, extroverted and outspoken.*
>
> Russell, who acquired a brain injury as a result of a car accident

Not everyone who has had a brain injury will experience these changes and many people can overcome problems with support and assistance.

Sexuality

Studies on sexuality following brain injury commonly indicate changes in sex drive and sexual behaviour. Lezak (1978) cited in Ponsford, Sloan & Snow (1995) has reported that people who have had a brain injury may experience either a loss of sex drive or an increase in sexual desire. In a more recent study cited in Ponsford, Sloan & Snow and conducted by Kreutzer & Zasler (1989), over half of the people reported a decline in sex drive with only 14 per cent reporting an increase. A large number of people in the sample reported significant changes in sexual behaviour and over half reported decreases in self-confidence, decline in sexual appeal and an increase in feelings of depression.

According to Ponsford, Sloan & Snow (1995), in spite of the fact that research findings indicate major changes in sexual behaviour, sexual issues are not routinely discussed as part of a rehabilitation program. Orchison and Simpson (1995) state that workers in the area of brain injury need access to clear information about sexuality and need to feel comfortable about discussing these issues if they are to provide appropriate support for people who have had a brain injury. Such issues may have a great impact on a person's life.

Moreover, there is some evidence that the partners of people who have had a brain injury also experience a reduction in sex drive (Rosenbaum & Najenson, 1976; cited in Ponsford, Sloan & Snow, 1995). Some reasons for this include stress, loss of attraction, a perception of personality change in the person who has sustained the injury and a decline in the quality of the relationship.

It is important to recognise that people who have had a brain injury have the same relationship and sexual needs as other people and that these should be met. However, even when people's sexual needs are met, they may in some instances behave in sexually disinhibited ways, as people with a brain injury are more likely to have difficulties with disinhibition than they are with increased sexual drive. According to Orchison & Simpson (1995), people can exhibit disinhibited sexual behaviour even when their sexual drive has remained the same or decreased after an injury. Sexually disinhibited behaviour is frequently part of a broader pattern of disinhibited behaviour and is best managed through the consistent use of simple behavioural techniques (Orchison & Simpson). Most people with cognitive disabilities can learn appropriate sexual behaviour. The content and method of teaching information must be modified to suit the needs of the individual.

People who have had a brain injury are as varied in their sexual knowledge and experience as the rest of the community. Some will be assisted in dealing with post-injury experiences by their pre-injury knowledge and experience. Some may have lost some social sensitivity or have developed sexual disinhibition or have lost self-esteem which undermines their confidence and ability to have a sexual relationship. It is important to provide support to assist people to deal with these issues (Orchison & Simpson, 1995).

In a relationship where one partner has had a brain injury with consequent severe disabilities, the uninjured partner may carry most of the responsibility for keeping the relationship together. There may be many role changes within the relationship because of the needs of the person who has had a brain injury. A person may find that his or her partner is no longer the 'same person' and has become a frustrated, difficult, dependent adult needing supervision, support and/or care. There may be problems in resuming and maintaining a satisfying sexual relationship because of physical and/or personality changes. Some partnerships may falter and possibly break down under the impact of all these stresses. Griffith

& Lemberg (1993) discuss issues associated with sexuality for a person with acquired brain injury. Their book is a guide for both the person who is brain injured and the family.

Being a parent

Two mothers who have had a brain injury have written a composite story about their lives as parents following brain injury (Brain Injury Women's Network, 1995). They state that the major readjustments that occurred in their relationships with their children resulted from changes in emotional control, personality or behaviour following their injury. These changes resulted in memory loss, lack of initiative, impulsiveness, low libido, and low tolerance levels. These changes create a great deal of stress and tension for all family members. Often people make a good physical recovery, but behave in ways that may upset or embarrass their children. Younger children may be too embarrassed to bring friends home from school or may fall into the habit of avoiding the parent who has had a brain injury because they have difficulty in dealing with the changed behaviour. Parents talk about the need for children to have some counselling and to talk through their feelings concerning the changes in their family.

Family

The majority of people who have sustained a brain injury return home to live with their families. This may have a significant impact on family life. For people with severe disability(ies) who require considerable care and support, the impact of the brain injury can be as great for the family as for the person with the brain injury. A young adult who has left the parents' home and has been working and/or studying or living with someone may have to return to live with parents. Perhaps an older brother was once greatly admired by his younger siblings for his sporting prowess and now seems to be dependent. A father may find his son to be a different person and not the person he once was so proud of. These changes require major adjustments to values, perceptions and lifestyle for all concerned.

Families may be required to provide personal care for someone with physical disabilities and/or ongoing supervision and support for someone with cognitive disabilities.

> *Owing to the fact that my family had their sights set firmly on the regaining of independence for me, I was given a free rein to make mistakes and fall down, which invariably taught me in the end to fend for myself.*
>
> Russell

The person's cognitive and behavioural problems may alienate their family/carers from friends and support people, resulting in the family and carers becoming socially isolated as their friends withdraw their social contact.

The situation facing children and adolescents with a brain injury is different from that for adults. Brain injury in adults may result in a significant loss of acquired skills and independence, as well as changes in personality and altered relationships. Children and adolescents with a brain injury may lose not only existing skills, but potential skills as the brain injury alters the course of their development. In very young children, the effects of the brain injury may not become apparent until later in life.

As children usually remain at home with their families until they are adults, there is an acute need for families with a child who has had a brain injury to have access to long-term support, respite care services and counselling. Adolescence may be more difficult and stressful than it would be otherwise, and the family may need extensive help and support as the child becomes older and progresses through puberty.

Many of the above reactions are summarised in a study reported by Bogod (1995). Interviews were held with men with acquired brain injury, their partners or spouses and children. For the men, their greatest fear was losing independence. Many felt that their wives had taken on responsibilities that once were the husband's and felt 'baby sat'. Tasks which were once simple now required much more energy to complete. Many of the men had had to change to a less well-paid and less prestigious job. The men believed that one of the most successful factors in recovery was being able to communicate freely and openly with their partner. The men were adamant about being allowed to experience 'the dignity of risk'. They wanted to be allowed to do things for themselves. They wanted to experience the self-esteem that comes from attempting to manage one's own life. They believed that falling self-esteem was not a result of the brain injury in itself. Rather, it resulted from the consequences of losing a job or from changes in their roles within the family.

Wives frequently made the comment: 'He isn't the same person I married'. They reported feeling burdened and stressed. Sometimes, they felt obligated to care for someone who was now a stranger. They felt their personal energies and resources were stretched to the limit and that they had little time to themselves. Many reported that they felt isolated, lonely and misunderstood. They commented that the most important aspect of the brain injury for them was loss of companionship and emotional support. They commented that the injury had taken away their best friend. Women commented that an important step in adjustment and coming to terms with the disability was realisation that their husband would never be the same again and acknowledgment that recovery would take a long time.

Changing roles had to be accepted by both partners. Women had to learn to be willing to get men to do household duties and men had to become willing to take on such responsibilities. Many women reported that they had to take on increased responsibilities outside the home and had to learn to be assertive in dealing with professionals and other family members and in making family decisions. They found support groups to be very helpful. They also reported that it was important to schedule time for oneself.

Children felt confused and frightened by the changes they saw in their father. Sometimes a child needed extra attention to help deal with changes, but perceived that the mother was too busy caring for her husband and did not have sufficient time to give the children.

This research highlights the major life changes for men after acquiring brain injury. Similarly marked changes can be expected for women.

Community living

Acquired brain injury is often called a 'hidden disability' because its long-term problems are usually in the areas of thinking and behaviour, which are not as easy to see and to recognise as many physical disabilities. As a consequence, the difficulties faced by people who have had brain injury may be ignored or misunderstood. People with acquired brain injury may be seen, even by their friends and family, as lazy or hard to get along with. In general, there is very little understanding and knowledge in the community about brain injury. Negative community attitudes and destructive family relationships can provoke inappropriate behaviour so it is important to ensure that people do not feel:

- devalued;
- threatened or attacked;
- frustrated or confined.

Some people who have had a brain injury may have difficulty accepting their disability and adjusting to the new self and changed roles. This may result in loss of self-esteem and social isolation. Some strategies that have been adopted to deal with these issues include:

- Formation of self-help and self-advocacy groups where people can provide support for each other.
- Personal counselling.
- Supporting people to re-establish community networks and reintegrate into the community.
- Support for the whole family to assess the family system and to change the system to suit the changed circumstances.

One of the most serious consequences of brain injury is social isolation. The person who has had a brain injury may exhibit changes in personality and behaviour as a result of the injury which can isolate him or her from a range of previously supportive social relationships. One strategy which is providing positive outcomes is the 'Circles of Support' network which comprises people who have been nominated by a person who has sustained brain injury. This group of people meet on a regular basis to assist the person to achieve his or her nominated goals. Although initially the support may be provided in a formal and organised manner, often these networks provide a source of informal friendships and facilitate community integration.

Access

People who have had a brain injury have the same right to the use of goods and services in society as do other people. One area in which people may experience difficulties is that of public transport. As a consequence of the injury, some people have mobility problems requiring specialised provisions to enable them to use public transport which should be safe, affordable, easy to use and accessible to people with all forms of disability. Some people who have had a brain injury may find it difficult to ask for information at places such as railway stations and may require clearly identified information booths, as well as ticketing information in visual as well as written formats. It is essential that all transport staff have training in the specialised needs and supports that may be required by people who have had a brain injury.

Driving is an important source of independence and self-esteem for many people. It also influences a person's ability to work and to participate in community life. The issue of determining whether a person with acquired brain injury is able to drive again is complex. Handler & Patterson (1995) discuss issues associated with tests to ensure that a person is able to drive safely. They point out that no single test is appropriate, rather a range of tests should be available to ensure that the individual abilities and impairments of each individual can be determined.

Education

Acquired brain injury occurs most often in the 15–24 year age group. The next most common age group is in children under 15 years of age. Education is a particularly important issue for people in these age groups and forms a central part of the rehabilitation process. To make it a success, transition from rehabilitation to school requires careful planning to ensure that the child, family and teachers are equipped to deal with issues.

Mira & Tyler (1991) argue that return to school is not the end point of rehabilitation and that children often return to education while recovery is still taking place. What happens at school will influence recovery. Some features of education programs can assist recovery. These include regular schedules and timetables and the commitment of the education system to building on previous skills in all children, not just those with acquired brain injury. The school system also has specialists available who provide training in language and motor skills. School also is important for families in helping them to adapt to changes in functioning.

School may help the child face the limits imposed by brain injury. It may help the child develop a more realistic view of his or her new self. Thus, school teachers are likely to have a crucial influence on the child's development and rehabilitation. Their attitudes and knowledge about brain injury are important. Mira & Tyler (1991) argue that it is vital that teachers are sensitive to the challenges that brain injury presents to a child.

In some cases, behaviour problems may interfere with school progress. Mira & Tyler contend that these are more likely to occur in children who had problems before their brain injury.

Employment

Gaining employment after sustaining a brain injury is a major issue. Roessler, Schriner & Price (1992) report that 70 per cent of people with acquired brain injury remain unemployed seven years after the accident. As acquired brain injury occurs mostly in people who are in their teens and early adulthood, the high unemployment rate represents one of the serious implications of this form of disability on everyday life.

Roessler et al. (1992) and Wehman et al. (1991) discuss strategies for assisting someone with acquired brain injury to return to the workplace. As with education, careful planning is required to ease the person back into employment and to ensure that modifications are made which make work possible. Roessler et al. argue that currently there is a poor knowledge base from which to develop and implement rehabilitation strategies. However, important aspects to consider are improving the individual's self-awareness of capabilities and limitations, developing realistic employment expectations and dealing with changed emotions and information processing abilities. These authors argue that these steps must be taken before job placement. Wehman et al. focus on issues surrounding training at the work site. The individual may need to learn new ways of doing things, so job modification and job retention counselling are important facets of rehabilitation. Additionally, ongoing assessment should be conducted of how the person is managing at work both in terms of the vocational and social aspects of employment.

PERSON TO PERSON

Appropriate behaviours

It is important to treat the person with respect, dignity and as an individual. People who have had a brain injury are all different, with unique needs and potentials.

Service provider attitudes and awareness are important factors in terms of access for people who have had a brain injury. This is an area which has been identified as a priority if people who have had a brain injury are to receive adequate levels of long-term community support which are essential for community reintegration.

People who have had a brain injury do not usually have intellectual disabilities. When interacting with them, it is important to enhance their sense of self-worth and self-esteem. This can be done by talking directly to the person who has sustained the brain injury rather than their carer, involving the person in activities and assisting him or her in other appropriate ways if this is required.

It is important to remember that some people may have difficulty in social situations by sometimes saying and doing things that may embarrass themselves or others. Consequently, they may avoid social contact and lose self-confidence and self-esteem. One way of facilitating community reintegration is to foster existing social networks. Some of the following principles may be useful to keep in mind when encouraging interaction:

* Be aware of the impact of the brain injury on the person.
* Be prepared to listen and understand the person's point of view.
* Reinforce and reward appropriate behaviour in social situations.
* Avoid negative attitudes and stereotyping.
* Treat the person with respect.
* Communicate clearly in a straightforward manner.
* Remember that every person is an individual with individual capacities and capabilities.

Strategies for interaction

Table 3.1: Strategies for successful interaction

Person who has had a brain injury	Other person
If assistance is required, ask for it and make your needs clear to the person who is assisting.	Do not assume assistance is needed.
Be aware of your rights and be firm but polite about your rights to access, independence, privacy, and so on.	Talk directly to the person.
Ask the person to repeat or re-explain things if they are not clear.	Communicate in a clear, straightforward way.
Remember that you have a right to participate in decision making in areas that affect your life.	Involve people in making decisions and assist and support them in this process if required.

MORE INFORMATION ABOUT ACQUIRED BRAIN INJURY

Definition

In terms of the World Health Organization (1980) definition:

- *Impairment* refers to damage to the brain.
- *Disability* refers to lack of, loss of or reduction in movement, cognitive and behavioural changes.
- *Handicap* refers to reduction in ability to perform everyday tasks, limitations in job opportunities and social isolation.

The outcome of brain injury will be different for each person depending on how much damage has occurred and on what part of the brain has been damaged. The following description of the parts and functions of the brain demonstrates that implications of acquired brain injury are closely linked to the extent and location of the injury.

Parts of the brain

The hind brain. As the spinal cord enters the skull it swells to form what is called the hind brain. The spinal cord runs the length of the back up into the brain and carries messages between the limbs and the brain. The hind brain consist of the medulla, pons and cerebellum. The *medulla* plays an important role in the control of vital functions such as breathing, heart rate and blood pressure. This is the part of the brain that keeps us alive, and therefore damage to this area can be fatal.

The human central nervous system consists of the spinal cord and the brain.

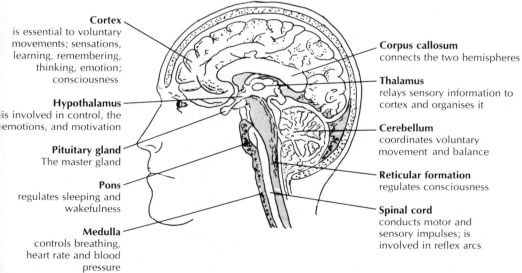

Cortex
is essential to voluntary movements; sensations, learning, remembering, thinking, emotion; consciousness

Hypothalamus
is involved in control, the emotions, and motivation

Pituitary gland
The master gland

Pons
regulates sleeping and wakefulness

Medulla
controls breathing, heart rate and blood pressure

Corpus callosum
connects the two hemispheres

Thalamus
relays sensory information to cortex and organises it

Cerebellum
coordinates voluntary movement and balance

Reticular formation
regulates consciousness

Spinal cord
conducts motor and sensory impulses; is involved in reflex arcs

Figure 3.1: The brain and its functions

Reproduced with permission from Brain Injury Society of NSW

The *pons*, which is a bulb at the top of the medulla, is largely responsible for the regulation of sleep and wakefulness. If certain areas of the pons are damaged, we are likely to experience difficulty in either going to sleep or waking up again.

At the back of the hind brain is the *cerebellum*, which enables us to coordinate large movements and to maintain our balance. Injury to the cerebellum is likely to result in jerky, uncoordinated movements and trouble with keeping balance.

The midbrain. The section of the brain slightly above the hind brain is called the midbrain. The most important part of the midbrain is called the *reticular formation*. The role of the reticular formation is to regulate consciousness by sending messages throughout the brain and by enabling the brain to process information.

The forebrain. This section of the brain is divided into two halves called hemispheres. The hemispheres are very similar in structure although they tend to have different functions. In general, the left hemisphere specialises in tasks which require an analysis of information (for example, reading, writing, speaking and doing mathematics). The right hemisphere is more proficient at tasks that involve the integration of information (for example, recognising faces, constructing designs). The two hemispheres are joined by a band of fibres known as the *corpus callosum*. If this area is damaged, the two hemispheres will be unable to communicate. This communication between hemispheres is extremely important because each hemisphere is responsible for the opposite side of the body. For example, the left hemisphere sends messages to, and receives message from, the right side of the body but not the left. To get information about the left side of the body, the left hemisphere must rely on the right hemisphere. This crossing over of control (contra lateral control) explains why damage to one hemisphere (for example, the left) might result in motor difficulties on the other side of the body (for example, right). In each of these hemispheres, there are a number of parts, including the thalamus, the hypothaiamus, the limbic system and the cortex.

The *thalamus* acts as a relay station which allows incoming information to be sent to the brain. If this area is injured it is likely that information will not pass efficiently through the central nervous system.

The *hypothalamus* is in the centre of the forebrain and is involved in many different processes. Its primary function is to control basic human drives and motivations such as hunger, thirst and sexuality. The hypothalamus is also involved in the production and control of emotions and the regulation of body temperature. Damage to the hypothalamus is likely to cause dramatic changes to behaviour, such as excessive eating and drinking, uncontrolled emotions, altered sex drive and fluctuating body temperature.

Slightly below the hypothalamus is the *pituitary gland*. This gland is part of the endocrine system and is not considered to be part of the brain. However, the hypothalamus and pituitary gland together regulate the flow of hormones through the body. These hormones are responsible for many body functions, such as the maintenance of fluid levels, weight, blood sugar level, production of sperm and the sex hormones (testosterone, progesterone, oestrogen, etc), salt level and immune reactions.

The *limbic system* is connected with the hypothalamus and incorporates a number of structures that are involved in our ability to remember information and to feel and express emotions. Injury in this area can result in memory problems and excessive emotional expression (for example, unexplained laughing or crying).

The outer layer of the forebrain is called the *cortex*, and it can be divided in four major sections or lobes. The front part of the cortex (above our eyes) is called the *frontal lobe*, the middle portion at the top of the cortex is called the *parietal lobe*, and the middle portion and the side of the cortex (near our ears) is called the *temporal lobe*. The final part of the cortex is the portion at the very back which is called the *occipital lobe*.

Causes

> *When I was 16 years old and doing Year 11 at the local high school, during my half yearly exam period, whilst riding my bicycle down the dirt road, I swerved to avoid a car and fell off my bicycle. When I reached home I began to be sick, looked pale and was drifting in and out of consciousness, I also had a huge lump appearing out of my forehead.*
>
> Trinh, who acquired a brain injury when he was a schoolboy

Brain injury may be acquired directly through trauma to the head (for example, as incurred in road accidents, falls, sporting accidents, violent assault, near drowning and gunshot wounds) or indirectly through non-traumatic causes such as strokes, infections, tumours, substance abuse, degeneration, disease, medical misadventure and haemorrhage.

Other terms such as 'head injury' may be used to refer to 'brain injury' but this is misleading because it confuses the true location, potential cause and nature of the injury. In the case of direct injury, the amount of damage to the brain will largely depend on the type of injury received.

Local trauma injury. With this type of injury, there may be damage both to the skull and the brain. This type of injury may result from an assault to the head.

Crush injury. The head remains stationary while compressed between two opposing forces. Gross skull fractures may occur, yet consciousness is not lost and brain injury may not occur.

Acceleration–deceleration injury. This is the usual traffic accident injury, but similar damage may also occur from local trauma or blows to the head. The significant feature is that the head is accelerated or decelerated. It is rather like the effect when the brakes are jammed on in a car. People are thrown forward to the dashboard (if not seat-belted). In this type of accident, the brain inside the head is thrown forward onto the spheroidal ridges – bony prominences inside the skull. This type of injury usually causes significant damage to the frontal and temporal lobes. As a result of laceration, haemorrhage may occur. Blood clots are removed through burr holes drilled in the skull.

Incidence and prevalence

Each year an estimated 10 000 people will incur traumatic brain injury in New South Wales, Australia. For each 1000 people who survive a severe brain injury, 125 will have a severe disability, ten will be in a persistent coma for months, 225 will have a moderate disability, and 640 will experience a good recovery but possibly with some ongoing cognitive and/or behavioural problems. Incidence and outcomes in percentage terms for other states in Australia are similar to those experienced in NSW.

In Canada, which has a population of 30 million people, approximately 40 000 people acquire brain injury each year. Of these people, 70 per cent have acquired brain injury from motor accidents with other common causes being sporting accidents and falls (Dawson, 1994).

In the United States, two million people receive a head injury each year. Of these, 500 000 to 750 000 require hospitalisation and 75 000 to 100 000 result in death. It has been reported that 80 per cent of these injuries result from motor vehicle accidents, 21 per cent from falls, 12 per cent from assault and violence and 10 per cent from sport and recreation.

Age. Brain injury is disproportionately concentrated in the young, particularly young males. While people aged 17 to 25 years constitute 15 per cent of the population in Western countries, they account for 40 per cent of brain injuries. Brain injury is the main cause of disability incurred by young people aged 16–30 years. In the United States the most common causes of acquired brain injury in children, adolescents and young adults are motor vehicle accidents (pedestrian, driver or passenger), falls, bicycle accidents and recreational and sporting accidents (Mira & Tyler, 1991). In the United States, 75 per cent of acquired brain injury due to motor vehicle accidents occurs in males aged 18–30 years.

Gender. The ratio of males to females incurring brain injuries is three to one.

People of Aboriginal backgrounds. Australian Aboriginal populations experience a range of acute and chronic diseases and conditions generally not seen in other Australian populations. These can result in physical, sensory, intellectual and mental impairment. Bostock (1991) reports that alcohol and drug addiction, petrol and glue sniffing are common in some communities and can cause brain damage. Levels of domestic violence also are high and can result in temporary and permanent brain injury. Aboriginal communities are very concerned about these problems and are doing a great deal to combat them.

Other sources of acquired brain injury include working in manual jobs in isolated locations. The manual nature of the work increases the likelihood of accidents and distance means that there is considerable delay before the person can receive treatment that might reduce or avoid permanent damage.

Residents of remote and rural areas. The nature of work in remote and rural areas enhances the risk of acquired brain injury. Humphreys, Rolley & Weinand (1992) suggest a relationship between lifestyle, working environment and health. Smith, Forbes & Cooke (1993) discuss issues associated with caring for someone with an acquired brain injury in a remote location. They argue that distance and isolation often place the carer in the position of having to carry out principal aspects of a rehabilitation program. This can create high levels of stress and can compound stresses and adjustments required by a family. Lack of information is also a problem in remote areas at all stages of rehabilitation. The survey conducted by Smith, Forbes & Cooke revealed that carers of people with newly-acquired brain injury felt that they did not have the required skills to be a full-time carer in an isolated location.

I have an adult daughter who has severe brain injury and is extremely disabled. She is partially mobile and I have to care for all her needs. There are no services for her. What will happen to her when I die?

Marie, who lives in a remote area of NSW

Diagnosis

According to Ponsford, Sloan & Snow (1995), after recovering consciousness, most people who have had a traumatic brain injury demonstrate a range of ongoing cognitive and behavioural problems. These vary widely in their nature and severity, depending on a range of factors including location and severity of the injury and the characteristics of the person prior to injury.

In many instances, the duration of loss of consciousness may be an important determinant of the severity of the injury. In the case of more severe injury, the person may lose consciousness and be in a state of coma for days, weeks, or even months. The measure which is used most often to rate the depth of coma is the Glascow Coma Scale (Jennett et al., 1976). A small percentage of people pass from coma into a state in which they may have a range of primitive reflex movements but do not appear to be responsive to their environment. After emerging from coma, the person may be disoriented for a period of time. This is referred to as post-traumatic amnesia.

People who lose consciousness for a short period of time, less than 20 minutes, are diagnosed as having mild brain injury. These people may still experience a range of symptoms which include headache, dizziness, sensitivity to noise or bright lights, ringing in the ears (tinnitus), blurred or double vision, restlessness, insomnia, reduced speed of thinking, reduced concentration and memory problems, fatigue, irritability, anxiety and depression (Ponsford, Sloan & Snow 1995). Some people do not have these symptoms on a long-term basis, but symptoms may persist for some time.

Treatment and rehabilitation

When a person has acquired a brain injury, he or she will probably be admitted to a casualty/emergency department of a major hospital. If the person is simply concussed, he or she may be held for neurological observation and then dis-charged. If the injury is serious, surgery may be required and the person will be transferred to a medical ward.

I was taken to hospital and when I arrived was operated on immediately to relieve the intercranial pressure in my head. This was done by placing a bore hole in my head after shaving my hair off.

Trinh

Some people recover quickly and may be discharged home from the ward while others will require rehabilitation and will be transferred from the hospital to a rehabilitation unit.

I was flown to a top Sydney hospital where a craniotomy was performed to remove the blood clot. An hour after the operation the doctors pronounced me brain dead. The next morning they said I was going to be in a 'vegetative state' for the rest of my life and needed to go into an institution. However, two days later I came out of coma and lapsed into unconsciousness for two weeks.

Trinh

By the time people leave hospital, most will no longer have medical problems but a small percentage (about 5 per cent) of people who have incurred a traumatic brain injury will develop epilepsy. The period of rehabilitation may vary in both intensity and duration and may be provided on an in-patient and/or an out-patient basis. Most people who have had a brain injury make a good recovery; 10 per cent will have severe ongoing disabilities.

Services and supports

The person who has had a brain injury and the family/carers may require a range of services to maximise the injured person's ability to participate in community life. Services that might be required include:

- living skills training;
- behaviour management programs to deal with behaviour that might be aggressive, difficult, annoying and/or inappropriate;
- counselling to help the person with the brain injury and his or her family/carers deal with the emotional and psychosocial impact of the injury and resulting disability(ies);
- sexual counselling;
- education and support for friends;
- personal care for people with physical disabilities;
- respite care;
- further education;
- vocational training and placement;
- supported employment;
- appropriate and meaningful leisure, recreational and cultural activities;
- opportunities to develop recreational interests;
- domiciliary support, such as Meals on Wheels, cleaning and home maintenance;
- home modification and special equipment;
- accommodation and support;
- opportunities to engage in social activities that are appropriate to the nature and level of disability(ies) and the lifestyle of the person and his or her family.

Because of the relatively young age of the majority of people who have had a brain injury, it must be anticipated that support services may be required for a long time, perhaps 40–50 years or more. For people who have a brain injury and who are living with their parents, there will come a time when others must assume the primary care-giving roles that may have been fulfilled by ageing parents.

There is a small number of services which specifically target people who have had a brain injury. Some traditional community services are currently used by people who have had a brain injury, but staff in these services often lack specialised knowledge, training and expertise.

There were no appropriate services available [and I had] to integrate myself into what services were on offer. These were often incomplete

and frequently left me feeling like a round peg attempting to enter a
square hole; but I felt right about what I was doing.

Trinh

Equipment

Common experiences with acquired brain injury are reduced concentration, difficulty in remembering things, and fatigue. These can affect day-to-day activities. A
range of equipment can assist. Memory aids include wall calendars, noticeboards,
post-it notes and planning diaries. Accidents can be avoided by using electrical
appliances which turn off automatically and so avoid a kettle boiling dry or toast
burning, for example.

Additional costs

Additional financial costs are associated with changes in employment opportunities, the need to purchase specialised equipment that is appropriate to the nature
of the injury, and the need to pay for the services of personal care attendants for
many daily living activities. Contrary to popular myth, only about 20–30 per cent
of people who have had a brain injury receive compensation.

Hidden costs include low self-esteem, limited social contacts, poor support
networks and limited specialised services.

RESOURCE ORGANISATIONS

All care has been taken to ensure that all information is correct at the time of publishing;
however, responsibility for the accuracy of this information is not accepted by the writer. The
list of resource organisations contained in this chapter is not intended to be exhaustive – it
provides national organisations only. The reader is referred to local community directories for
further information and for local branches of national organisations. Inclusion of services and
organisations should not be taken as a recommendation.

Australia

Head Injury Council of Australia (HICOA)
PO Box 82
Mawson ACT 2607
Ph 06 290 2253
Fax 06 290 2252

National Brain Injury Foundation
16 Burwood Street (PO Box 33)
Hughes ACT 2605
Ph 06 282 2880
Fax 06 282 2684

New Zealand

Head Injury Society of New Zealand
12 Hawthorne Road
Opawa, Christchurch

Canada

The Association for the Neurologically
    Disabled of Canada
59 Clement Road
Etobicoke ON M9R 1Y5
Ph 416 244 1992

United Kingdom

National Head Injury Association
7 King Edward Court
King Edward Street
Nottingham NG 1EW

United States

Brain Injury Association
Suite 100, 1776 Massachusets Avenue
   NW
Washington DC 20036 1904
Ph 1 800 4444 6443 or 202 296 6443
Fax 202 296 8550

FURTHER READING

Bogod, N. (1995). A family affair. *Disability Today,* 4 (1), 26–40.

Brooks, N., Campsie, L., Symington, C., Beattie, A., & McKinlay, W. (1986). The five year outcome of severe blunt head injury: a relative's view. *Journal of Neurology, Neurosurgery and Psychiatry,* 49, 764–70.

Crisp, R. A. (1992). Return to work after traumatic brain injury. *Journal of Rehabilitation,* Oct/Nov/Dec, 27–33.

Dawson, D. (1994). Tricks for better recall: overcoming memory problems after a brain injury. *Abilities,* Summer, 23.

Elsass, L. & Kinsella, G. (1987). Social interaction following severe closed head injury. *Psychological Medicine,* 17, 57–78.

Gronwall, D., Wrightson, P., & Wadell, P. (1990). *Head injury, the facts: a guide for families and care-givers.* Oxford: Oxford University Press.

Kreutzer, J. S. & Wehman, P. (1990). *Community integration following traumatic brain injury.* Baltimore: Paul H. Brookes.

Mira, M. P. & Tyler, J. S. (1991). Students with traumatic brain injury: making the transition from hospital to school. *Focus on Exceptional Children,* 23, 1–12.

Perlez, A., Furlong, M., & McLachlan, D. (1989). Family-centred rehabilitation: Family therapy for the head injured and their relatives, in R. Harris, R. Burns & R. Rees (eds). *Recovery from brain injury: expectations, needs and processes.* Adelaide: Institute for the Study of Learning Difficulties.

Ponsford, J. (1987). Practical issues in working with the head injured. Paper presented at the Headway Victoria Kaleidoscope Conference, Melbourne.

Ponsford, J., Sloan, S. & Snow, P. (1995). *Traumatic brain injury: rehabilitation of everyday adaptive living.* Hillsdale: Lawrence Erlbaum & Associates.

Williams, J. M. & Kay, T. (1991). *Head injury: a family matter.* Baltimore: Paul H. Brookes.

CHAPTER 4

AMPUTATION

Amputation may occur as a result of a birth defect (congenital), following trauma (such as a motor vehicle accident), or may be conducted surgically in order to halt a potentially fatal disease process.

Amputation of a limb or part of a limb has major physical and psychological implications. Children born without a body part are able accommodate for that loss in their development, but must deal with the attitudes of others to their loss. Amputation later in life results in an alteration of the person's functional capacity and body image. It may lead to important changes in the person's way of life. Psychological and emotional adjustments are required, as well as physical adaptation.

Amputations can be of a minor or major nature, from the loss of the tip of a finger right through to the loss of an entire limb or limbs. When a limb is surgically removed the surgeon attempts to retain the longest possible length compatible with viable tissue and to shape the stump for the wearing of an artificial limb (prosthesis).

LIVING WITH AMPUTATION

Loss of function is the most obvious implication of amputation. A lower limb amputation causes mobility problems. Upper limb amputation affects manual dexterity. It also can mean a change in dominance. For example, if part of the right upper limb is removed, a right-handed person will probably prefer to use the left hand to perform tasks requiring fine coordination, even though they are able to use a prosthesis for their right arm well.

A lower limb prosthesis helps replace bodily function in a way that is far more satisfactory than the use of crutches or a wheelchair, because it allows for an unobtrusive walking pattern and frees the upper limbs for carrying out everyday tasks. In addition, prostheses are useful when people want to resume their usual work, sporting or leisure activities. There are specialised protheses to give people the freedom to resume almost any sport or leisure activity. Elite athletes with an amputation can run, jump and throw and are able to compete in the full range of events at a high level of international competition.

Using a prosthesis can also be important in restoring body image. The wearing of a lower limb prosthesis will make it much less obvious to others that a limb is missing and the person is likely to feel less self-conscious. People who have upper limb loss may choose to use an upper limb prosthesis that has a hook type terminal device, affording a high level of function; or they may choose to have a passive hand that has little or no function, but is cosmetically more acceptable to the person (both types are illustrated in Figure 4.1). Some people use an upper limb prosthesis which is electrically powered and controlled by the action of remaining muscles.

However, a prosthesis will never be as good as the missing limb as it will not entirely fill the function of the limb. The absence of sensation in the prosthetic body part limits the degree of function that can be obtained because no feedback is

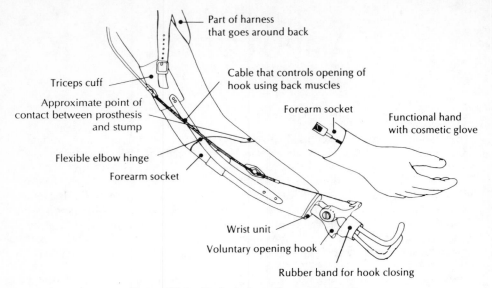

Part of harness
that goes around back

Cable that controls opening of
hook using back muscles

Triceps cuff

Approximate point of
contact between prosthesis
and stump

Forearm socket

Functional hand
with cosmetic glove

Flexible elbow hinge

Forearm socket

Wrist unit

Voluntary opening hook

Rubber band for hook closing

Figure 4.1: Right below-elbow prosthesis

available from the prosthesis. This loss of sensation is of less importance in the lower limb prosthesis, although it has implications for stability and balance. In the upper limb, on the other hand, the lack of feedback results in a marked loss of dexterity.

The level of amputation also affects the degree to which a prosthesis provides a satisfactory substitute. As a general rule, the greater number of functioning joints the person retains, the more successful the prosthetic fitting is. There may also be physical difficulties in wearing a prosthesis such as discomfort, excessive perspiration, fatigue, mechanical failure, noise, and problems with use and control of the prosthesis.

In the industrialised world, the overwhelming majority of people with amputations – whether congenital, traumatic or surgical – are fitted with a prosthesis. Most of these achieve a satisfactory result. Lower limb amputations are more common than those of the upper limbs, and lower limb prostheses have a particularly high success rate, providing functional mobility to people of all age groups. The most significant exceptions to this are the few people who have had bilateral high-level lower limb amputations. Often the energy expenditure required and the level of function achieved mean that a wheelchair is chosen as a more realistic and comfortable option for mobility.

People with a high-level amputation of a single limb can learn adapted methods and lead a satisfying life without a prosthesis. However, those with bilateral upper limb loss usually find prostheses can give them a satisfactory level of independence.

PHANTOM LIMB SENSATION

After traumatic or surgical amputation, most people experience the sensation that their limb is still present. This is part of the adjustment process and occurs until the brain accepts that the limb is not there. It is not uncommon for people to think that they are becoming mentally affected until they are reassured otherwise. These sensations usually fade with time, although they may continue to recur occasionally. This type of sensation is often referred to as 'phantom limb'. People describe it in various ways. One person may experience general tingling while another may describe a very specific itch in the ankle that is no longer there. It is common with high-level limb loss that the foot or the hand are felt to be in their expected anatomical position initially, but as time goes by, they are perceived as gradually moving up towards the amputation site. Often wearing the prosthesis dispels the sensation.

Phantom limb is generally painless. There is another condition, which is pathological, known as phantom pain. It can become intolerable and in some cases results in severe pain which may be described as cramping, shooting, burning, or crushing; however, this is rare. These days, phantom limb pain can be dealt with effectively with appropriate management in the early stages. It is not common for it to persist beyond a few months.

Personal adjustment

The amount of time it takes to adjust to having an amputation varies between individuals. Adjustment is influenced by such factors as age, gender, family support, cultural background, education, occupation and extent of disability. Besides the loss of function, a change in body image occurs. Some people need to change their occupation.

The loss of an upper limb has much greater significance psychologically than the loss of a lower limb. People use their hands as an expressional adjunct to communication, to manage their own personal hygiene, to carry out sporting and leisure activities and to do their job. As Wynn Parry (1981, p. 1) says:

> *The hand is capable of the strongest grasp and the most delicate touch; its rich and complex sensory innervation allows the finest judgement of texture, volume and temperature. The value of a strong and well co-ordinated hand in such activities as writing, painting and manipulating tools is obvious. Less obvious perhaps is the extent to which the hand is a reflection of personality and a vital organ of expression. One has only to consider the manual signs and attitudes of an oriental dancer, the benediction of a priest, the gestures of a conductor or a Gallic raconteur, to realize how much more is the hand than a prehensile and sensory tool.*

People who have an amputation must come to terms with their loss. Many go through the stages outlined by Elizabeth Kübler-Ross (1969) and summarised in Chapter 1 of this book. These stages are denial ('It can't be happening to me'), anger ('Why me?'), bargaining (looking for a way out), depression and acceptance. These stages represent healthy reactions to a loss and an important part of a professional's role is to recognise and work with the person through the grieving process. Having an awareness of the stages can also help the service provider and the person's family to understand the behaviours being displayed. However, it is important not to stereotype people. Grieving is a complex process and each person approaches it in a unique way. People vary in the time spent in each stage, some may jump a stage, others may go through a particular stage more than once. Some never reach final acceptance.

> *Learning to adjust came slowly. I was impatient, and for almost a year I had to cope with crutches, bandages, hating everyone and thinking that I'd never walk again and questioning 'Why me?'.*
>
> Penny

Life experiences both before and after the amputation contribute strongly to the way in which a person is able to deal with the loss of a body part. A teenager who has not yet established a clear self-identity is likely to have more difficulty coming to terms with the effects of a limb loss than an adult who is in a strong, stable relationship.

Most people who have an amputation are over 55 years of age. The majority of these are lower limb amputations and the most common cause is vascular disease. Developing the ability to use a prosthesis may take longer for someone in this age group than for a younger person. However, a good functional result is usual. One restriction to prosthetic use is congestive cardiac failure because of the energy demands of using a lower limb prosthesis. A wheelchair may be a more practical option than a prosthesis for such people. Sometimes older people have other conditions (such as arthritis) that also affect their mobility. In this case a mobility aid such as a stick or crutches may be needed in addition to the prosthesis.

> *Whatever image Peter has got of himself, his body is his body, and the limb is an extension which he puts on and off.*
>
> Noella, whose son was born with a deformed arm

Sexuality

Changes to a person's body image may make him or her feel less masculine or feminine. A person growing up with amputation may feel different from other people of the same age. When starting a relationship, the person may feel anxious and embarrassed about a girlfriend or boyfriend finding out about the limb loss because of a fear of rejection. For this reason, teenage girls may discard an upper limb prosthesis at or after puberty even though they have been wearing it effectively for years, because it is a visible sign of being different.

In general, there is no loss of sexual function for either men or women, but outside a stable relationship there are added psychological pressures. Fear of rejection may inhibit the development of relationships. The person may experience some awkwardness during sexual intimacy because of the practical difficulties of balance and stability and also because of the element of exposure and risk. Someone who is in a stable relationship and loses a limb in an accident may fear rejection by their partner. The partner may indeed have difficulty coming to terms with the limb loss. Touch is an important part of relating to other people. Someone with amputated arms may be restricted in the enjoyment of touching and caressing.

Being a parent

Those with lower limb amputations who are using a prosthesis successfully will notice few problems. Lifting a child may pose problems that will be overcome as the child learns to climb up rather than expecting to be lifted. For those with an upper limb amputation, the loss of manual dexterity may mean that tasks such as dressing, bathing and picking up a small baby are difficult. Appropriate advice about equipment and adaptive techniques will assist these people in fulfilling their parenting role to their satisfaction.

Family

Family support and acceptance is important. The person who has strong supports is in a better position to deal effectively with the loss of a limb.

A partner or spouse may be overprotective when an adult acquires a disability. The partner also may be concerned about the effects of the disability on his or her own life. For example, whether it makes their partner more dependent and thus restricts the person's own and shared life options.

There are likely to be differences in the parents' reaction between congenital and acquired limb loss in a child. As Biggs (1994) states: 'The immediate parental reaction to the birth of an infant with a deficiency is one of shock, disappointment and sadness instead of the happiness they expected. They may feel that they are responsible for causing the deformity, they may feel guilty because they feel angry or repulsed, or may deny these human feelings, which are too threatening to acknowledge at the time. As well as coping with their own feelings, parents must also cope with those of family, friends and hospital personnel, and, later on, society.'

> *My husband had the job of phoning the relatives. We didn't have any plan in mind as a way of telling them. A close friend burst into tears when she was told. She wasn't able to speak to me for two days. People don't know what to say.'*
>
> Noella

Acquired disability in a child is a shock to parents and they also have to make adjustments to the new situation. Some parents may over-protect the child, even into adulthood.

> *The child who is accepted in the family as an equal member in his/her own right will be able to overcome most of the difficulties he/she encounters. The overall objective . . . is to assist the family in making it possible for the child to reach full physical potential and emotional stability.*
>
> Biggs, 1994, p. 5

Community living

> *One kid used to call me 'peg'. That hurt, but I knew that if I didn't accept it I would be in trouble. I had to live with it, although it did frustrate me.*
>
> Brian, who was born with part of his lower leg missing

Friends and others may have difficulty in accepting that the person is different. People who have acquired a disability often mention that they have lost friends. Social contacts are important. Research has shown that people with amputation

Figure 4.2: Making music with one hand

who have strong social contacts, especially outside the home, are more likely to be successful in rehabilitation.

The level of acceptance that the person experiences may differ from culture to culture. Some cultures value physical wholeness and beauty very highly. Any physical impairment may have a negative effect on the way the community interacts with the person. In some countries hands may be amputated as a punishment, so the loss of a hand, say, in an industrial accident, in such countries may have serious consequences in terms of social acceptance. For many people, however, an amputation does not mean that talents, skills and tasks are no longer possible, or that others will not accept them as they are − as illustrated in Figure 4.2.

Access

For those with a lower limb amputation and successful prosthetic fitting it is possible to live an active life and to achieve satisfactory access to all aspects of community life. Often, if no mobility aid is used, other people may be unaware that the person is in any way different.

Driving a car is possible for all those with an amputation once appropriate adaptations of the controls have been made and the person has been trained in their use. Review and, if necessary, reclassification of the person's driving licence legalises these changes and allows regular driving.

For those who use a wheelchair, there are the usual issues attached to community access for wheelchairs. Many public buildings are not wheelchair accessible. Uneven pavements, sharp changes in ground level and the absence of kerb ramps make moving about in the community difficult for this group of people, despite various initiatives to improve community accessibility.

For those with an upper limb amputation, the loss is more obvious to others. Other people's attitudes may therefore impinge further. In the past, this may have led to discrimination against people in employment and in social situations. The Australian *Disability Discrimination Act 1992* provides remedies for the consequences of such discrimination.

Education

> *The reaction of my classmates was mixed. Those who were close friends accepted me, others acted like I had a disease.*
>
> Penny

Biggs (1994, p. 5) describes how the situation described by Penny can be ameliorated:

> *It is important that parents communicate effectively with school personnel about the child's abilities and the devices the child uses, before school starts. Sometimes it is appropriate for the occupational therapist to be there too, particularly when teachers are anxious, and understandably so, about having a limb-deficient child in the class. After a clear, honest explanation to the other children at the beginning of term, the child can settle in to be an active, participating member of the class without having to contend with curious looks and remarks.*

Children and adults who have had an amputation may require assistance in adapting to the educational environment. Generally, amputation does not cause major difficulties unless, for example, the dominant limb or both arms have been amputated. In such a case, the child may need an amanuensis for examinations, a tape recorder, a computer, a software package for one-handed typing, adjustments to seating and to desk heights, as well as modification to the method of carrying schoolbooks while managing public transport.

As a result of mainstreaming, schools and tertiary institutions frequently have experienced counsellors who liaise with health workers to ensure the person settles satisfactorily into the class environment with the appropriate modifications.

Employment

Restrictions in employment depend on the site of the amputation. Some occupations which involve a high degree of manual dexterity, mobility or long periods of standing may not be suitable. However, there are very few jobs which are unsuitable for those with amputations, particularly if modifications are made to available equipment or techniques for doing a job. As in the case with other disabilities, it is important not to assume that, because a person has an arm or a leg missing, a job is not suitable.

Exceptions are jobs with a heavy manual labouring component. Occupations which may be manageable in the short term for a young person who has had a traumatic amputation may be detrimental to their health as they grow older. For example an outdoor job requiring a high level of manual labour may be possible for a vigorous young person but may not be sustainable over the long term as the person moves into middle age. 'Today's young amputee is tomorrow's middle aged amputee with decreased physical capacity' (Halcrow, 1994, pp. 5–36). Long-term manual labour can cause musculo-skeletal problems. Those with an amputation have to work in an less ergonomically satisfactory way, leading to stress to their joints over the long term. There is a greater need for those who have had an amputation to plan their employment future carefully.

PERSON TO PERSON

Other people's attitudes are important in influencing how a person approaches life as an amputee. The opinion of one's peers is as important to someone with limb loss as it is to anyone else in the community. Limb loss is a badge. It is overt and it is never going to change. Like many disabilities, an amputation can single out a person as different.

Prosthetic componentry is improving all the time, however, and these advances are providing people with opportunities to achieve higher skill levels in many activities. An increase in skill usually leads to an increase in confidence.

Appropriate language and behaviour

Some people feel uncomfortable and unsure of how to behave when meeting a person with an amputation. A person who has had an amputation for a long time will have developed strategies for coping with the discomfort of others. He or she will probably be used to putting others at ease and the interaction will flow

Table 4.1: Strategies for successful interaction

Person who has had an amputation	Other person
Let the other person know if any form of assistance is required.	Ask the person before attempting to provide any form of assistance.
If the other person seems to be uncomfortable, perhaps you can facilitate interaction by using humour to make him or her feel more at ease. However, do not use humour which puts yourself or the other person down.	If are unsure of how to behave appropriately, ask the person.
	If the person's right arm is missing, offer your left arm to shake his or her left hand. Often the person will anticipate your discomfort and will initiate the greeting.
If you do not want to answer questions about your amputation, indicate this to the other person if he or she asks questions.	If you feel embarrassed, humour and goodwill will often overcome the problem.
	Do not ask questions about the amputation until you are well acquainted with the person.

smoothly, because he or she accepts the responsibility for the comfort of others. For example, if a handshake is a customary greeting, it is likely that an experienced person with right upper limb loss will offer a reversed left hand. On the other hand, someone who is still adjusting to limb loss may have difficulty managing another person's discomfort. In this case, a relaxed and friendly attitude will ease the situation for both people.

Strategies for successful interaction

It is important to remember that people who have had an amputation are like other people in other respects. They experience the same needs, desires and aspirations. They have the same range of abilities, intelligence and personality types as other people. They generally will have accepted their disability and learned how to deal with it.

MORE INFORMATION ABOUT AMPUTATION

Definition

According to the World Health Organization (1980) definition as applied to limb loss:

- *Impairment* refers to the loss of a limb or part of a limb.
- *Disability* refers to restrictions in manual dexterity and mobility.
- *Handicap* refers to limitations placed on the person by the physical and social environment, because that environment demands a type of performance in relation to upper-limb function and mobility that will disadvantage those with limb loss in carrying out of their life roles.

Causes

Congenital. Usually the cause of limb deficiency is unknown. In a few cases there is a hereditary basis for the deformities. There are some syndromes that result in congenital limb deficiency along with other problems. Amputation in utero due to vascular conditions occurs in about 10 per cent of cases seen. The aetiology is unknown.

Trauma. Amputations may result from accidents which have caused severe damage or have severed a limb. Industrial and road accidents, wars and land mines have been major contributions to traumatic amputation. Unlike other forms of amputations, most traumatic amputation happens to young people. Their injuries may result in amputation at the time of the accident (traumatic amputation) or subsequently because the part is so badly damaged that it cannot be repaired.

Poor circulation. This is one of the most common causes of amputation in older age groups. Peripheral vascular disease causes a narrowing or hardening of the arteries of the limbs which may reduce the supply of blood to the lower limbs so much that it damages the tissues and causes gangrene. Gangrene in this instance is not associated with infection and is called dry gangrene. Most amputations in older people are performed on lower limbs as a result of this process.

Chronic infection. Gangrene which is associated with infection is often accompanied by substantial drainage problems and is called wet gangrene. It is common in people with diabetes because of low resistance to infection. Chronic osteomyelitis and infections which occur after injuries to a limb may necessitate amputation because of the extensive nature of infection.

Tumours. Malignant (cancerous) tumours, such as cancer of the bone, may necessitate an amputation. However, the need for amputation in this situation is becoming less frequent with improvements in treatments such as chemotherapy and radiation therapy.

Paralysis. Sometimes a limb is paralysed as a result of a severe brachial plexus lesion. It may hang loosely and be seen as useless and unattractive. In these cases, the person may choose to have the paralysed limb amputated after sufficient time has elapsed to ensure that no further nerve recovery is possible. A prosthesis can be fitted which at least provides some function.

Deformity. Parents may choose to have the deformed limb of a child amputated and replaced by a prosthesis for functional or cosmetic reasons.

Incidence and prevalence

The overwhelming majority of amputations (outside war zones) are lower limb amputations, and the primary causes of lower limb amputation are vascular deficiencies (smoking and diabetes are common causes of such deficiencies). In 1982, in Australia, the incidence of amputation per annum was 22.5 per 100 000 people. In the same year in the United Kingdom it was 31 per 100 000 people. Improvements in vascular surgery designed to save the leg from the effects of vascular disease are credited with the lower rate of amputation in Australia compared with the United Kingdom, where the same techniques were not practised to the same extent (Jones, 1990). People aged 50 years and over make up 80 per cent of those having amputation for these causes. The majority of people wearing prostheses around the world are aged 55 years and over.

> When I tried on my first limb (prosthesis), wow! The feeling of standing on my own two feet was hard to explain. I felt like running, jumping — all at once, but these came later, after walking one step at a time.
>
> Penny

Services and supports

The prosthetic team. A specialist medical physician is the team leader. He or she manages the process of rehabilitation, including prosthetic prescription. The physician is responsible for the ongoing welfare of the person with the limb loss, including pain management, prescription and checking the prosthesis and coordination of the program. A prosthetist designs, makes, fits and repairs artificial limbs (prostheses). An orthotist designs, makes, fits and repairs orthopaedic braces (orthoses) and other devices. The physiotherapist carries out post-operative care, pre-prosthetic management and gait re-education. In addition, physiotherapists have a primary responsibility for lower limb rehabilitation. The occupational therapist is responsible for promoting positive functional outcomes including environmental modifications to the person's home and car, attention to transport and their job, and achieving competence in the home and community. In addition, occupational therapists have a primary responsibility for upper limb rehabilitation.

Support groups. Support organisations specifically for people with major limb loss exist in every state in Australia and in most other industrialised countries. In some countries there are separate sporting associations. In Australia there is a national organisation called 'Amputees United of Australia'.

Equipment

Active research and development is ongoing into prosthetic components, materials and manufacturing techniques. With each improvement, a greater range of options is available which diminishes the disability and enables the person to participate in an ever-increasing range of sporting and employment options. The improvements in technology, however, do come at a great financial cost to either the individual user or to the community who fund it in various ways.

RESOURCE ORGANISATIONS

All care has been taken to ensure that all information is correct at the time of publishing; however, responsibility for the accuracy of this information is not accepted by the writer. The list of resource organisations contained in this chapter is not intended to be exhaustive; it lists national organisations only. The reader is referred to local community directories for further information and for local branches of national organisations. Inclusion of services and organisations should not be taken as a recommendation.

Australia

Amputees United of Australia Inc.
67 Sunbeam Creseent
East Devonport Tas 7318
Ph 02 9742 5243

Canada

The War Amps
2827 Riverside Drive
Ottawa ON K1V 0C4
Ph 613 731 3821

New Zealand

Amputee Society
(Federation of New Zealand Inc)
213a Bay View Road
St Clair
Dunedin
Ph 03 455 6347

United Kingdom

The Limbless Association
Roehampton Rehabilitation Centre
Roehampton Lane
London SW1S 5PR
Ph 1817 881 777
Fax 1817 883 444

United States

ACA (Amputee Coalition of America)
PO Box 2528
Knoxville TN 37901
Ph 423 524 8772 or 1 888 AMP KNOW
Fax 423 525 7917

The International Society of Prosthetics and Orthotics (ISPO) is an international society for health professionals with branches in each state of Australia, and in Canada, America, the United Kingdom and many other countries.

FURTHER READING

American Academy of Orthopaedic Surgeons (1981). *Atlas of limb prosthetics. Surgical and prosthetic principles.* St. Louis: C. V. Mosby.

Burgess, E. M. & Rappoport, A. (1992). *Physical fitness: a guide for individuals with lower limb loss.* Washington, DC: Department of Veterans Affairs.

Drake, H. (1981). *It's only a leg!* Sydney: Sydney Better Communication.

Dumpleton, H. (1989). *Addups and takeaways.* Kogarah, NSW: Kezza Enterprises.

Goodman, S. & Nunn, C. (eds). (1992). *Coaching amputee athletes.* Canberra: Australian Sports Commission.

Olivett, B. L. (1995). Conventional fitting of the adult amputee. In J. M. Hunter, E. J. Mackin & A. D. Callahan (eds), *Rehabilitation of the hand: surgery and therapy* (4th edn), pp. 1223–40. St. Louis: C. V. Mosby.

Pillet, J. & Mackin, E. J. (1995). Aesthetic hand prosthesis: its psychologic and functional potential. In J. M. Hunter, E. J. Mackin & A. D. Callahan (eds), *Rehabilitation of the hand: surgery and therapy* (4th edn), pp. 1253–66. St. Louis: Mosby.

Ravot, K. (ed). *Amputee News.* (Newsletter available to members of The Amputee Association of NSW.)

Setochi, Y. & Rosenfelder, R. (eds). (1982). *The limb deficient child.* Springfield, Ill: Charles C. Thomas.

CHAPTER 5

ARTHRITIS

Arthritis is a very common condition and primarily a disease of middle and late life, although it can occur at any age. Approximately 70 per cent of people will seek treatment for musculo-skeletal symptoms at some time in their lives. A significant proportion of these people will be diagnosed as having arthritis. It is a disease of the joints, especially in the ligaments, cartilage and synovium.

The term 'arthritis' is often linked with rheumatism. Rheumatism is, however, a term which is often used to denote any type of ache or pain in the muscles and joints for which there is no other explanation.

Over 200 types of arthritis have been identified. This chapter looks at the two most common types: rheumatoid arthritis and osteoarthritis.

Rheumatoid arthritis (RA) is an inflammatory disease which affects the joints and can also affect organs in the body. Inflammation begins in the joint lining or synovium which becomes inflamed, making it thick and swollen. The reason for this is unknown. Large quantities of synovial fluid are produced and the combination of swelling of the joint lining and production of increased fluid makes the joint itself swollen. The joints are affected in a symmetrical fashion; that is, both hands and/or feet are involved.

RA can lead to pain, stiffness and deformity. It often appears suddenly and usually affects several joints (polyarthritis). The early symptoms are usually swollen, stiff, sore knuckles or base of the toes. Hands, feet, wrists, elbows and knees are the parts of the body most often involved. They can become stiff and painful, especially in the morning after overnight rest. RA can influence general health: it can bring on fevers, tiredness, weight loss and lack of energy. One of the most common symptoms is fatigue. Stiffness and pain are affected by changes in the weather: a sudden drop in the barometric pressure or a sudden rise in the humidity produces increased stiffness and pain in many people with rheumatoid arthritis (Brewer & Angel, 1993). Extremely cold temperatures cause increased pain because they increase a person's perception of his or her pain. Another prominent feature is the rheumatoid nodule, a painless lump under the skin. Nodules occur on the bony part of forearms, around ankles and in fingers.

Inflammation is a feature of RA that can lead to damage of the joints and organs. Figure 5.1 displays the joints most commonly affected.

Rheumatoid arthritis usually begins in people aged between 20 and 50 years and is three times more prevalent in women than in men (Vierck, 1991). However, it can occur at any age and one of the forms in children is called Still's disease (Stopford, 1988). RA sometimes is active for six to eight years and then levels off, but in other cases it can occur for prolonged periods.

> *It all started so suddenly. One minute I was rescuing my two-year-old daughter who was trying to leave home, the next I had collapsed on the step. My ankle was sore and stiff and then it started to swell up.*
>
> Jacqueline

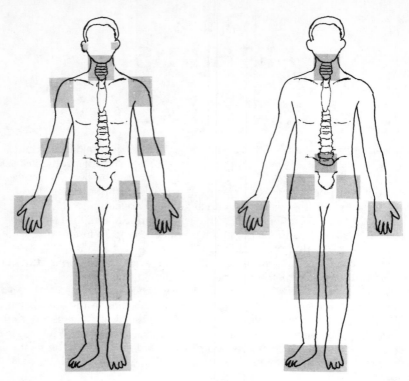

Figure 5.1: Joints commonly affected by rheumatoid arthritis

Figure 5.2: Joints commonly affected by osteoarthritis

Juvenile rheumatoid arthritis (JRA) is the form of arthritis which affects children. JRA is a chronic disease of childhood with swelling, pain and tenderness of at least one joint and lasting longer than six weeks. It affects three girls for every boy and usually involves the same joints on both sides of the body – knees, wrists, joints in the fingers (that is, it is symmetrical). There are three types of JRA. Pauciarticular JRA (pauci means few; that is, few joints are involved) is the mildest form and is associated with very few swollen joints and pain. In polyarticular JRA more joints are involved and the child may be more severely affected. This form of JRA is potentially very destructive to the joints and requires active treatment. Systemic JRA (also known as Still's disease) can affect several organs in the body including the heart, liver, spleen, lymph nodes and kidneys, as well as many joints. It is associated with anaemia, fatigue, fever and a rash.

Osteoarthritis (OA) is the most common form of arthritis. It is a disease in which the cartilage breaks down and it has many causes, only some of which are known. Heredity factors, obesity, repetitive stress to joints, extreme trauma (such as from a fracture through the joint) all may be involved. It is rarely evident before 50 years of age and more women are affected than men. It is not necessarily a part of the ageing process (Vierck, 1991). Unlike rheumatoid arthritis, osteoarthritis is inflammatory and is not a general illness, but is restricted to isolated joints (monoarthritis). It does not cause redness or swelling. It is characterised by a degeneration of the cartilage that protects the bone and results in gradual deterioration of the joints. Osteoarthritis is most common in the hips, base of the spine and knees because these joints are subject to the most pressure and strain. Joints that have been injured, infected or strained by bad posture are also more prone to damage. Similarly, heavy manual work and repetitive work can wear out joints. Figure 5.2 displays the joints most commonly affected.

> *I was almost fifty when I acquired osteoarthritis. My mother had osteoarthritis and so I knew how it could affect me. The lower lumbar section of my spine was the first to be affected, then my hands began to ache. Now my feet and knees are also affected.*
>
> Mary

LIVING WITH ARTHRITIS

> *Arthritis is a disability I had to face and accept. I am restricted in what I can do, but it doesn't mean I can't get out and live.*
>
> Mary

Personal adjustment

Osteoarthritis and rheumatoid arthritis tend to have different effects on lifestyles. OA for the most part affects older people and may affect only one or two joints. It does not cause fatigue or extreme debilitation and generally is not labelled as being a serious illness, rather it is seen as a problem that is chronic and that may, at times, cause medium to severe pain and stiffness. The common scenario for OA would be of a woman in her mid 60s who has moderate OA in one knee or hip which causes moderate disability. In such a case, OA would create difficulties in using public transport and shopping, and would also cause some pain. For the most part, people learn to live with OA by doing something to help themselves. Exercise is one of the most important aspects of the management of OA, and when this is done correctly it helps to decrease pain, to make muscles and bones stronger and to help the person feel better about himself or herself.

In the case of RA, some people may be shocked to find that discomfort is a sign of serious illness. Other people become gradually aware over time of the extent of their condition. There can be a long period of uncertainty about whether it will be possible to continue in the present lifestyle. Sometimes people are relieved to find that their pain and difficulties are taken seriously by others and to find out that treatments are available which can bring some relief. Considering that there are more than 200 different types of arthritis, it is sometimes difficult to reach a definitive diagnosis early on.

> *What I found hard was to accept that something was wrong. Once I did, there was a life I had to live. I take one day at a time.*
>
> Ron

An important part of the personal adjustments associated with arthritis is learning how to participate actively in treatment and to become a *self-manager* of the disease of arthritis. People with arthritis learn how to protect affected joints and how to help themselves with a well-balanced diet, physiotherapy (physical therapy) and exercise programs. They also learn to move and rest in ways which will not cause deformity. An exercise program designed for the person with arthritis is one of the most important factors in overall management. Some people find that these changes require a considerable amount of self-discipline which can be frustrating, especially when there are no immediate improvements in the condition.

I have to be careful not to overdo it. Too much knitting, piano playing or working at the computer keyboard will make my wrists sore. It's a matter of management. Swimming is the only form of exercise I enjoy.

Jacqueline

At first the person may try to hide symptoms. However, as disabilities become more pronounced, it becomes necessary to negotiate recognition of the disability with others and to make adjustments to everyday living. Negotiations include family relationships, adjustments of roles and management of anxiety. They are part of legitimising and accepting the disability. Many people with disabilities (such as arthritis) 'walk a tightrope' during the negotiation process. They experience conflict between the need to gain as much help as possible and the desire to retain self-esteem and independence. Resolution of this conflict is important to the person and to those around him or her.

Sexuality

Sexuality is an important part of a person's identity. Arthritis does not generally affect areas of the body (including the brain) that allow a person to enjoy sensual and sexual stimulation. However, when a person's body is affected by arthritis, movements (particularly in the hips and lower spine) become awkward, strength may decline and appearance may change. Bodily changes associated with RA can often affect self-esteem and sexuality. These changes can result in a person feeling less feminine or masculine. It may take a lot of time and possibly counselling for a person to work through negative feelings. Some people are embarrassed to talk to their partners about sex and assume that their partners find them unattractive. In turn, the partner may then assume that sexual intimacy is unwanted or may fear that sex will create more pain. Some of the drugs used to treat RA can cause unpleasant bodily changes (for example, cortico-steroids can cause an increased risk of osteoporosis, thinning of the skin, an increase in facial hair and increased weight) and can affect the libido.

Planning can help to reduce the pain and stiffness which may prevent the enjoyment of sexual relations. It can be helpful to choose the most comfortable time of day, have a warm bath beforehand, to do relaxation exercises for stiff joints and to take medicines for pain relief. Both partners may discover that good sexual relations do not have to be spontaneous. In addition to planning, a couple may find intercourse enjoyable if they adopt a new, more comfortable position that imposes less strain on the joints. Couples may have to experiment to find the best position; for example, lying on the side.

I could forego the brace if I put two huge plaster casts on my legs at night. The casts were extremely uncomfortable for my husband, as well as for me, but we couldn't help seeing the funny side.

Jacqueline

There are several booklets available that give information on new and innovative positions that may be easier to adopt during sex (for example, Arthritis Foundation of Australia, undated, a and b).

Girls who develop rheumatoid arthritis as teenagers may be particularly conscious of their disability if they have friends who spend a lot of time beautifying themselves and discussing the latest fashions, many of which may be unsuitable for someone with arthritis. For instance, high-heeled shoes could be tiring and painful while flimsy clothes may not be warm enough to protect sore joints.

Being a parent

The discussion here will focus on rheumatoid arthritis as this is more likely to occur in someone of child-bearing age than is osteoarthritis. RA does not cause loss of fertility; however, not feeling well or being in poor physical shape because of illness does reduce the ability to become pregnant. Many women with RA have a complete or almost complete remission of symptoms from the early months of pregnancy and this lasts until six weeks or so after delivery (Brewer & Angel, 1993). Babies are no more likely to have birth problems or to be premature than babies of other mothers. Remission after the third month means that the mother can stop taking her medications to reduce the symptoms of rheumatoid arthritis. However, the use of aspirin and anti-inflammatory drugs in the first three months is generally treated with caution. The effects of some of these drugs in pregnancy have not been studied sufficiently and so they should not be considered safe. Aspirin is not recommended for nursing mothers as it shows up in breast milk. Use of medications should be discussed with a medical practitioner before becoming pregnant and also during pregnancy.

Children of women with rheumatoid arthritis have a greater likelihood than others of developing the condition at some time in their lives.

If the mother has serious impairments from her rheumatoid arthritis she may need help with the physical side of caring for a baby. Fine motor movements such as using safety pins can be painful and difficult. Now many aids are available to make life easier for mother and baby.

Family

It is important to note that someone with RA may not have any visible signs of illness or deformity, but may experience extreme pain, fatigue and discomfort. Lack of visible signs and fluctuations in symptoms may result in misunderstanding and underestimation by others of the pain and limitations associated with arthritis. Fluctuation also may create anxiety and uncertainty in family members who are not sure whether the person is able to manage independently or safely.

If the person with arthritis is a woman, it may be difficult for the rest of the family to accept that she now needs care or that she needs to rest during the day. Some women find it hard to ask for the help they need, especially if their husband or partner has very definite views on gender roles.

My children are supportive but it hasn't affected my husband at all. He expects that I should be able to do all the things I used to.

Mary

When people have to give up work because of arthritis, their families may resent economic hardship and changes in roles. On the other hand, a supportive family can help the person come to terms with such changes and can directly help with day-to-day household tasks. It is very important that the partner or spouse has a good understanding of arthritis and how it affects the person both internally and externally, as well as psychologically.

Community living

Acceptance means the person accepting that he or she has arthritis and then doing something about it. Acceptance also involves family, friends and workmates accepting the changes in the person, both physically and emotionally. The unpredictability of arthritis (especially RA) is one of the things that people with this disability most often complain about. Because arthritis runs a course (generally of exacerbations and remissions) sometimes it can be difficult to plan for the future. Personal adjustments are an essential part of living with arthritis and sometimes it is possible only to take each day as it comes.

The diagnosis of arthritis in children and teenagers can be devastating for both the person and the family. Diagnosis of RA in young adults can be equally devastating with the worry, not only of pain and deformity, but of its effects on relationships and on the future.

'What have I done to deserve this?' is a common reaction. Uncertainty about the future also is another common reaction. Acceptance is often reached through a series of emotional upheavals and adjustments. Realising that there will be good and bad days, weeks and months is another important part of acceptance.

Communicating feelings with family, friends, teachers and fellow workers is vital. Others do not always know how the person with arthritis feels or that he or she is in pain. It is important for the person to educate others about arthritis and what it means to live with it. It also is important for the person with arthritis to keep up everyday activities as far as possible, to encourage integration and acceptance by others. It also is important that the person feels good about himself or herself and wants to feel included.

Access

Government bodies now recognise the needs of people with physical disabilities. This recognition has given rise to a wide range of new services and modifications being made to existing ones. For example, all public buildings must now provide ramps, access and toilets for people with disabilities. Public transport is also becoming more accessible; for example, new buses have lifts and provision for wheelchairs.

The Australian *Disability Discrimination Act 1992* states that no person should be hampered from travelling on public transport by the nature of their physical disability. Thus, having stiff knees and hips due to arthritis should not stop a person travelling on a train. Easy access is still not possible at many railway stations and for other forms of transport. However, gradually public transport is being converted. The *Disability Discrimination Act* says that people should report discrimination such as in the above example. Letters can be sent to the Australian Disability Commissioner or to the local municipal councils. The more people who make written complains, the more things are likely to change.

An occupational therapist can give advice about providing access in the home. A home visit can be made to see what modifications are required to bathrooms, kitchens, stairs and so on. Other organisations such as ACROD (Australian Council for the Rehabilitation of the Disabled), TAD (Technical Aid for the Disabled) and ILC (Independent Living Centres) can give assistance where access at home is a problem.

Education

Osteoarthritis rarely occurs in school-age children, but rheumatoid arthritis occurs in a considerable number of young teenage girls and children. Schoolwork may be interrupted by stiff, sore hands and wrists which make it painful to write. Computers may help here but may require special adaptations to enable the person to use them with comfort.

Young girls with rheumatoid arthritis also may lack energy and be prone to fevers, both of which can affect school participation and performance. Appearance is often all-important in teenage years and when young men and women experience deformities and changes to their appearance, it can have a devastating effect on self-esteem.

Sometimes children and teenagers may have to miss school for prolonged periods or, when at school, are not able to join in all the sporting or social activities. It is important that children or teenagers with arthritis are not excluded from any activity which is within reason or made to feel that they are 'second best' if they are too sick to participate.

Education can also be important for older people who may need to change their lifestyle as a result of acquiring arthritis. Retraining may be required for a less physically-demanding occupation or to learn new ways of accomplishing domestic duties. Retraining may be particularly important when a person's occupation or daily activities aggravate the arthritis. However, the demands of a retraining program must also be considered. For example, courses which require considerable written work can be difficult when hands or wrists are affected.

> *I had to do a three-hour exam, but I knew I couldn't write for three hours. I decided to break up the time with frequent rests and aspirin, so my answers had to be very concise. I found out later that I just missed out on getting the top grade.*
>
> Jacqueline

New technology, such as lap-top computers, can do a great deal to assist a person with arthritis in both education and employment.

Employment

If a person becomes overtired or generally run-down from rheumatoid arthritis, it may be necessary to take extensive sick leave or to give up work. However, there are treatments which can stabilise the condition and ease symptoms so that the person can go back to work. If a person's previous job involved high levels of manual dexterity or strain on involved joints, he or she will have to learn new ways to work, probably using special equipment. The advice of a physiotherapist (physical therapist) and occupational therapist is invaluable in adjusting the workplace to accommodate a person with RA. Nevertheless, some occupations are incompatible with the treatment of RA and a change in employment becomes essential.

In a suitable work environment, the majority of people with rheumatoid arthritis (85 per cent) can expect to continue to work until retirement age. The main problem is convincing the employer that the person can still work efficiently and can make a worthwhile contribution.

The situation is different for people with osteoarthritis. If the wearing out of a joint results from engaging in a particular occupation, then it is unlikely that work conditions can be changed sufficiently to protect the joint completely. Without protection, the condition of the joint will rapidly worsen. Splinting of the hand or elbow may be a solution and the worker must then learn to use other joints to perform the job.

PERSON TO PERSON

Appropriate language and behaviours

Reactions of other people are mixed. People only notice when I'm eating. Some stare at me but I try to take no notice. I'd like to tell them that I hope they never get it because arthritis is painful.

Mary

Treatment for arthritis is not a cure, but aims at control of the symptoms. People with arthritis need to feel that they are mastering their situation and that they can make decisions about their work and social activities without interference from others. They need to feel they have some control over their arthritis and their lives.

A person may strive to maintain previous activities and lifestyle, particularly if those around underestimate the effects of pain and the restrictions created by arthritis, and seem unwilling to make allowances for these. In striving to meet the high expectations of others, people with arthritis can further damage affected joints. Thus, it is important for those around the person with arthritis to acknowledge the disability and the effects it has on lifestyle and personal well-being. It is important to understand what the person can and cannot do and to be aware of the importance of the adjustments the person has to make. It also is important to remember that effects of arthritis vary greatly between individuals and also within an individual from one time to another. This means that the person may be able to do more on some days than on others.

I don't want people to help me all the time. I just want them to react to me as me. They are capable of doing things I can't do, but I can do things they can't do. It balances out.

Ron

It is important to be responsive to the individual at all times. However, this does not mean that the person should be over-protected or denied opportunities to try new things or take risks.

Strategies for successful interaction

Table 5.1: Strategies for successful interaction

Person with arthritis	Other person
Let people know if you are unable to carry out tasks.	Don't make assumptions about the person's physical abilities.
On the other hand, don't let them treat you like an invalid when you are confident of your ability.	Don't make assumptions about the degree of pain associated with arthritis. It can range from a mild twinge to extremely painful.
Remember your own experience may not be the same as that of others.	Remember your own experience may not be the same as another's.
It is common for people to feel depressed or anxious. Be prepared to seek help if you feel you need it.	Offer assistance if a person appears to need help, but do not insist.

MORE INFORMATION ABOUT ARTHRITIS

Definition

According to the World Health Organization (1980) definition:

- *Impairment* refers to damage in the joints, bones and other relevant parts of the body.
- *Disability* refers to associated pain, deformity and functional limitations.
- *Handicap* is reflected in reduction in ability to participate in everyday activities and to live an independent life.

Rheumatoid arthritis. This is a disease of the synovium. The joint on the right-hand side of Figure 5.3 is unaffected by arthritis and the joint on the left is arthritic. In the musculo-skeletal system there are two types of joints, movable (for example, the knee and wrist) and non-movable (for example, in the skull). Movable joints are called synovial joints. The bones in a movable joint are held in place by tendons and ligaments. Within the joint, the ends of the bones are protected by cartilage, a tough, resilient substance which can be slightly compressed to absorb shock as the limb moves. The joint is enclosed in a capsule lined with the synovial membrane or synovium. This produces synovial fluid which lubricates the joint and nourishes the cartilage. In rheumatoid arthritis, the body's immune system appears to turn on itself, causing an inflammatory reaction. In an arthritic joint, the synovium is inflamed and an excess of synovial fluid is produced, causing the swelling around the joint. The swelling can pull the ligament that keeps the joint in place, causing pain and deformity (see Figure 5.4). The course of events is unpredictable. Rheumatoid arthritis can be mild or severe, it can deteriorate rapidly or suddenly

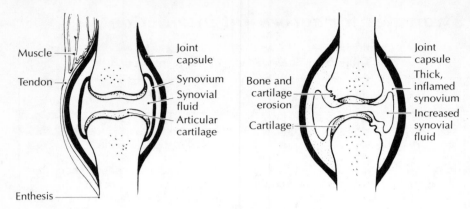

Figure 5.3: Rheumatoid arthritis

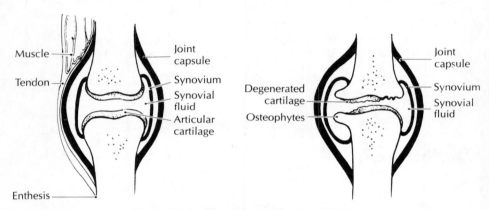

Figure 5.4: The effects of osteoarthritis

improve. Of all people with rheumatoid arthritis, 70 per cent will gradually get better of their own accord, 8 per cent will have a fluctuating condition, 10 per cent will have major long-term effects and 12 per cent will become severely disabled.

> *I wasn't very impressed when the doctor diagnosed arthritis. That was something that made people a bit stiff in old age!*
>
> Jacqueline

Osteoarthritis. X-rays of people aged over 60 years show that most have varying degrees of joint damage from this condition. All cartilage wears out to some extent, but in some people this process is more rapid and more marked. As it wears out, cartilage loses its elasticity, cracks and flakes off. The cartilage cannot repair itself and, as it deteriorates, the bone underneath becomes harder and thicker. The bone may grow out over the joint and cysts may develop. The ligaments and synovium also become stiff and sore. Pain and stiffness are the most common symptoms of OA.

Causes

The causes of rheumatoid arthritis are unknown, but it has been linked with the tissue type or genetic marker called HLA-DR3. Contrary to popular belief, rheumatoid arthritis is not caused by dampness, draughts or vitamin deficiencies. However, damp and cold can exacerbate the condition.

It seems likely that genetic characteristics predispose some people to certain forms of juvenile rheumatoid arthritis. Stress does not cause RA, but may exacerbate it.

Scientists have long regarded osteoarthritis as a necessary part of ageing and its cause has not been determined. However, the view of inevitability has been disputed by researchers who argue that it results from years of wear and tear rather than the ageing process. Recent evidence suggests that more severe cases may be associated with a genetic defect or mutation. This evidence is very recent and is subject to verification.

Incidence and prevalence

Figures for the prevalence of arthritis are not readily available for many countries and those that are available vary widely between authors. For example, the Arthritis Foundation of USA (1993) cites the prevalence of rheumatoid arthritis in the United States as three to ten cases per 1000 with overall figures for that country being about seven million people. In contrast, Pitzele (1985) cites the prevalence of osteoarthritis and rheumatoid arthritis within the American population as being 16 million each. The most recent figures for the United States indicate that 673 000 people have arthritis and related disorders, while 5 048 000 have osteoarthritis and allied conditions (La Plante & Carlson, 1996)

In Australia it is estimated that around 11 per cent of the population (or 1 935 500 people) have arthritis (Australian Bureau of Statistics, 1990). Watts (1995) states that almost four million Canadians have some form of arthritis. Of these people, around 273 000 have rheumatoid arthritis and 2.7 million have osteoarthritis. Around 6000 Canadian children have a form of arthritis.

Rheumatoid arthritis affects three women for every man. It mainly affects women in their 30s and 40s but can also occur in children and in people over 65 years of age.

Osteoarthritis (OA) is largely a disease of middle and old age with 90 per cent of people showing some visible changes in their cartilage by the fifth decade of life, although 20 per cent of older people have a moderate or severe case. Men and women differ in frequency and type. Women tend to have OA in their fingers more often, while men tend to have it in their knees and hips. Area of residence also seems important. The warmer the climate, the worse OA is (Brewer & Angel, 1993). Weight also is important, OA of the knees and hips is worse in obese people. Overuse by ballet dancers, gymnasts and athletes can cause injury to the joints and bring on OA, which also can occur as a result of a life of repeated-motion injury, such as from years of using a keyboard under poor ergonomic conditions and from operating machines in factories.

Contrary to popular belief, arthritis is not a disease confined to older groups in the population. Some types are more likely to occur in older people, but there are types of arthritis, such as juvenile rheumatoid arthritis which begin in childhood.

Figure 5.5: A woman showing the effects of arthritis on her hand and knee joints

Diagnosis

Rheumatoid arthritis is diagnosed through medical history, physical examination and laboratory tests, specifically blood tests. The latter confirm the presence of inflammation in the system. Later on, X-rays show what joint damage may have occurred. They also can show how well the person is responding to treatment. X-rays early on in RA are not particularly useful as radiographic evidence in the first year is not usually visible.

Osteoarthritis is often diagnosed on the basis of a physical examination, medical history and X-rays. X-rays will show whether the changes in the joints that usually accompany the disease are present.

Treatment

It is not known why RA often improves by itself. There is no medical cure for it, but these days treatment can control symptoms such as pain and swelling and can prevent long-term damage to the joint. Early diagnosis and treatment of RA can be critical to obtaining a good outcome. Because RA varies greatly from person to person, treatment must be geared to the individual. Some common treatments are noted below.

Medication. Fairly high, constant doses of aspirin or paracetamol, and anti-inflammatory drugs are used to decrease pain and inflammation. Some drugs can have side effects but fewer than 1 in 20 people has to stop a medicine because of bad side effects. The corticosteroid group of drugs ('steroids') are among the most effective anti-inflammatory drugs known; however, they have major side effects. Early effects include water retention, increased appetite, high blood pressure, insomnia and impaired vision. Continued use can lead to mood changes, increased fatty tissue in the cheeks, neck and shoulders, weakened arm and leg muscles, osteoporosis and increased facial hair. In children, these drugs can slow growth. The greatest dangers with long-term usage are loss of the body's protein and a masking of infection which can lead to serious complications if untreated (Arthritis Society of Canada, 1994). To minimise side effects, dosages are kept as low as possible and the course of therapy is kept as short as possible. It also is important to take the medication as prescribed and not to make adjustments without the knowledge of the prescribing doctor. Currently, slow-acting anti-rheumatic drugs are the mainstay of treatment of RA.

Gold treatment is a method which has variable results and has been found to assist some people with rheumatoid arthritis. It involves injections of gold salts.

Exercise. This is important to keep joints flexible and to build up and preserve muscle strength. It helps to decrease pain and to keep muscles, ligaments and bones strong, but most importantly exercise makes people feel better mentally, and more able to cope with everyday life.

Splinting. Splinting may be necessary to maintain inflamed joints in a good, safe position and thus to prevent deformities and pain. Wrists, hands and knees are commonly splinted in RA. While a joint is inflamed it needs to be rested, but at other times exercise is crucial to help prevent stiffness and deformity.

Heat. Heat from hot packs, hot wax, baths, hot baths, electric mitts and infra-red lamps can also bring relief. Heat is often particularly useful in the morning when a person feels stiff and in pain. Heat helps muscles to relax, thereby helping to decrease pain. *Ice* can also help to relieve pain.

TENS. TENS (or transcutaneous electronic nerve stimulation) is designed to block pain messages to the brain. Electrode pads are placed on the painful area and a mild electric current is pulsed into the muscle tissue for about 15 minutes.

Rest. This helps relieve pain and inflammation, but must be balanced with exercise and activity in order to avoid increased stiffness.

Nutrition. Good nutrition and healthy weight are both important. It is important to know how food may affect the absorption of drugs and medication. Being overweight places extra stress on weight-bearing joints, hips, knees and feet, and can worsen the pain and inflammation associated with arthritis.

Hydrotherapy. Exercise in a warm bath assists many people with arthritis.

Treatment for osteoarthritis centres around movement and exercise. Medications such as paracetamol are also used A walking stick can help prevent further wear on an arthritic hip or knee. Heat and cold applications ease discomfort, while acupuncture, massage and weight control have been found to be effective for some people. In severe cases, hip and knee joint replacement are now common. Joint replacement surgery replaces bone with metal and plastic parts and can restore mobility and relieve severe pain. The joints most commonly replaced are the hips and knees (Powers, 1992).

Brewer and Angel (1993) recommend moderate and regular exercise and activity (especially swimming) as helpful. People with OA also report that walking and using an exercise bike are useful forms of exercise. Hydrotherapy is also of benefit for OA.

SERVICES AND SUPPORTS

Management of arthritis involves teamwork. The person with arthritis is the central member of this team, which involves many people. It is important that the person feels that he or she is an active part of this team and knows that the other members are there to help. This approach is essential if the person is to achieve self-management of the arthritis.

Many professionals are involved in treating and supporting people with arthritis. The family medical practitioner is the coordinator of care and can assist with many health care issues. In cases of RA and other severe arthritis, the expertise of a rheumatologist may be called upon. A podiatrist may be involved in treating problems related to the feet. He or she examines the feet and recommends specific types of footwear and devices designed to ease pain and to make life more comfortable. Major foot surgery is usually handled by an orthopaedic surgeon.

A nurse may be involved in ongoing education of the person and family. Physiotherapy is one of the most important aspects of treatment of arthritis. While the medical practitioner attempts to control inflammation and damage of joints through medication, the physical therapist helps maintain the mobility needed for daily activities. He or she evaluates individual needs, shows new ways of doing everyday tasks and teaches exercises. A personal exercise program also will be involved. Hydrotherapy may be used to bring pain relief. An occupational therapist helps the person to be independent and to go about daily routines while conserving energy and minimising damage to joints. He or she may design and fit splints or other devices needed to support and protect weakened joints and to help prevent deformities. The occupational therapist also can advise on adaptations to the bathroom, kitchen and other rooms in the house. The aim is to improve the person's functioning around the home.

A social worker can help with emotional and social concerns. He or she is knowledgeable about community resources and supports. A nutritionist may be consulted about which foods to eat and the ways medications affect the body. A psychologist or psychiatrist may provide counselling to help the person put into perspective the problems associated with arthritis.

As said above, acupuncture also has been found to be effective for acute pain relief as have chiropractic, massage therapy and heat treatment. Biofeedback is being taught today as a way of learning relaxation techniques and of controlling involuntary reflexes. For example, with people with Raynaud's phenomenon, it may be possible to increase blood flow to the hands or feet. By reducing stress and relaxing tight muscles it may be possible to reduce the level of pain and need for medication. Deep breathing and self-hypnosis can also be used to facilitate relaxation and control of pain. Thus, Tai Chi, Feldenkrais and meditation are also useful in managing arthritis.

The services of an opthalmologist may be required in certain types of inflammatory arthritis, such as juvenile arthritis and rheumatoid arthritis, which can be associated with inflammation of the blood vessels and ducts of the eyes. Also, some medications can affect vision.

An orthopaedic surgeon is an integral part of the management team as joint repair is common. Surgery can range from cleaning up bone and cartilage debris in a joint capsule to complete replacement of a joint.

The contribution of a pharmacist is important as he or she knows a great deal about medications and their possible interactions or side-effects and can educate the person with arthritis.

It is important to remember that the person with arthritis is the central member of the team working to manage the effects of this impairment. An active partnership with professionals is an important part of maintaining a feeling of control over one's life and disability. The person should keep informed, ask questions and not be overwhelmed by the condition. The Arthritis Society of Canada (1991) states that it is important for the client to speak up when something goes wrong, to be prepared (be well informed and have questions ready), be honest (for example, admit if he or she has stopped taking a medication), be precise (in the description of symptoms and events) and be willing to discuss aspects of social and private life (in order to reveal what events influence the condition). It also is important for the person with arthritis to take medications as prescribed (for example, if a scheduled dose is missed, a double dose should not be taken next time without first consulting a doctor or pharmacist). It also is important for the person to report any persistent side-effects and not to substitute drugs without the doctor's knowledge. The person with arthritis should also take an active role in treatment and therapies such as exercise, dietary change, self-education and remaining active.

Equipment

There are many aids and pieces of equipment which can help the person with arthritis in carrying out daily tasks. Labour-saving devices are essential around the home as routine tasks can take much longer and can cause considerable frustration without them. Velcro fasteners and zippers are easier to use than buttons. Adapted eating utensils enable a person with limited manual dexterity to continue feeding himself or herself. Access to such equipment enhances feelings of independence and capability.

Equipment such as crutches and walking sticks must be fitted by a health professional as harm can be caused by an inappropriate or ill-fitting device. Some people use rubber-tipped canes while quad canes are also useful.

Devices are available to assist in holding pens and pencils. Wrist and hand rest attachments are available for a computer keyboard. Book folders are available which hold up a book for the person. Dozens of special devices are available to enable a person with arthritis to open car doors, turn on the ignition, drive and to turn lights on and off at home. There are phone holders, cordless phones and catapult seats which push the person up out of the chair. Grippers and non-slip pads assist people in doing everyday tasks. Occupational therapists are the best people to give advice about equipment and where to obtain it.

RESOURCE ORGANISATIONS

All care has been taken to ensure that all information is correct at the time of publishing; however, responsibility for the accuracy of this information is not accepted by the writer. The list of resource organisations contained in this chapter is not intended to be exhaustive; it provides national organisations only. The reader is referred to local community directories for further information and for local branches of national organisations. Inclusion of services and organisations should not be taken as a recommendation.

Australia

Arthritis Foundation of Australia
Suite 902A, 33 Bligh Street
Sydney NSW 2000
GPO Box 121
Sydney NSW 2001
Ph 02 9221 2456
Fax 02 9232 2538

Canada

Arthritis Society
Suite 410, 250 Bloor Street East
Toronto ON M4W 3P2
Ph 416 967 1414
Fax 416 967 7171

United States

Arthritis Foundation
PO Box 19000
Atlanta GA 30326
Ph 404 872 7100 or 1 800 283 7800
Fax 404 872 0457

New Zealand

Arthritis Foundation of New Zealand
150 Featherstone Street
PO Box 10-020
Wellington
Ph 4 721 427
Fax 4 723 967

United Kingdom

Arthritis Care
18 Stephenson Way
London NW1 2HD
Ph 0171 916 1500
Fax 0171 916 1505

Arthritis and Rheumatism Council
    for Research (ARC)
Copeman House St Mary's Court
St Mary's Gate
Chesterfield
Derbyshire S41 7TD
Ph 01246 558 033
Fax 01246 558 007

FURTHER READING

Arthritis Foundation of Australia (undated, a.). *Osteoarthritis*. Sydney: AFA.
Arthritis Foundation of Australia (undated, b.). *Rheumatoid arthritis*. Sydney: AFA.
Brewer, E. J. & Angel, K. C. (1993). *The arthritis sourcebook*. Los Angeles: Lowell House.
Fries, J. F. (1990). *Arthritis: a comprehensive guide*. Reading, MA: Addison Wesley.
Littlejohn, G. (1989). *Rheumatism: a consumer's guide*. Ivanhoe, Vic: Fraser Publications.
Lorig, K. & Fries, J. F. (1990). *The arthritis help book*. Reading, MA: Addison Wesley.
Powers, M. C. (1992). *Arthritis*. New York: Chelsea House Publishers.
Vierck, E. (1991). *Keys to understanding arthritis*. New York: Barron's Educational Series.
Watts, R. (1995). Arthritis. *Disability Today*, 4 (4), 10–17.

CHAPTER 6
CEREBRAL PALSY

Actually being 'spastic' is not a popular disability. There was a time when I wouldn't admit to being 'spastic'. I would say that I had polio. To say I was 'spastic' meant that I wasn't quite right in the head. As you get older, the more people you tell that you have cerebral palsy, the better because it educates them. It destroys the stereotype.

Monica

Cerebral means 'of the brain' and palsy means 'lack of muscle control'. Cerebral palsy is a non-progressive disorder of movement and posture that results from damage to parts of the developing brain before, during or shortly after birth. Thus, it is a disability that is present from very early in life and has always been part of the person's life. As it occurs early in the lifespan, it can interfere with a person's progression through developmental milestones (Lindemann, 1981). As such, it is often classified as a developmental disability.

Cerebral palsy is a complex set of conditions which vary from individual to individual. It affects nerve, motor or movement function within the person, which can result in one or more of the following characteristics: tight muscles, poor coordination of limbs, uncontrollable or jerky movements, poor balance and difficulty with speech and eating. Multiple disability is not uncommon in cerebral palsy. Impairments can range from mild to severe. About 40 per cent of people with cerebral palsy are affected in terms of at least one of the following: speech, vision, epilepsy, gait, balance, coordination, hearing and sensation (Stanley, Watson & Mauger, 1987). Contrary to popular belief, intellectual disability does not necessarily accompany cerebral palsy (although it can occur).

The type and extent of disability reflects the areas of the brain that are damaged. Much also depends on the general environment in which individuals grow up as to how they develop their potential and learn to manage their lives as independently as possible. There are wide individual differences between all people, but in those with cerebral palsy these differences are even more complex and variable. No two people will have the same set of challenges. Handicap can result from being treated differently from others or from being protected from everyday life experiences. Thus, the extent and type of handicap varies between individuals and precludes the use of stereotypes and labels to describe people with cerebral palsy. All people are individuals and are unique.

Cerebral palsy affects my body, but not my soul. My mind and my soul are free.

David

LIVING WITH CEREBRAL PALSY

I think my disability has made me a stronger, tougher and perhaps wiser person than I might have been. I also tend to have greater respect for people who are not disabled but have shown the same strength and toughness to come through what I see as difficult situations.

Nathan

Individual differences are wide. For some people, the effects of cerebral palsy are mild. However, for others it may mean severe or profound disability. In its more severe forms, a person may be unable to walk, may use a wheelchair and be dependent on others for mobility and for assistance with everyday tasks. For other people, mobility aids such as callipers, braces, crutches and walking sticks will help them to be independent. While for others, disability has a limited impact. Effects on speech may arise from the effects of cerebral palsy on control of the muscles involved in tongue and lip movements. There is sometimes difficulty in organising and selecting speech as a result of damage to the speech centre in the brain. This can result in slurring, stuttering, delayed responses, unclear speech and unclear pronunciation. Communication can become frustrating for both the speaker and listener; patience is required on both sides.

Slowness of speech may be incorrectly seen by some members of the community as a sign of intellectual disability. Clumsy gait is also often used to make this inference. However, this is not necessarily so. Around 50 per cent of people with cerebral palsy fall into the average or superior ranges of intellectual functioning. This percentage corresponds with that for the general population. People with cerebral palsy generally do better in intelligence tests based on verbal ability than in those involving motor tasks. This difference reflects the nature of their disability, rather than their intellectual capabilities and provides a good example of how standard intelligence tests can be inappropriate tools for assessment.

Some people with cerebral palsy have hearing disabilities which are associated with high frequency loss, difficulty in attaching meaning to sounds, and in localising sounds as a result of the inability or difficulty in stabilising head movements and keeping the head upright. The most common form of visual disability associated with cerebral palsy is internal strabismus (where the eyes turn inwards). Also common is reduced visual acuity which may reflect damage to the visual cortex. Vision may be affected by involuntary eye movements. Visual problems can cause difficulties with spatial orientation, recognition of words and acquiring living skills.

Personal adjustment

An individual's reactions to having a disability vary depending on his or her own personality, abilities, needs and environment. Other important factors include the strategies a person has chosen for living his or her life, available support systems, and social networks. This is the same for everyone, not just someone with a disability.

Communication is an essential part of the formation of friendships and personal relationships. Communication difficulties can hinder development and growth of social relationships and deny the person full expression of thoughts and feelings. Many methods of communication, such as electronic communicators, alphabet boards, computers, signs and symbols are used (these are described later in the chapter).

Sometimes a person's view of his or her disability is more handicapping than the disability itself. Some people do not feel 'whole', others feel they must 'make up' for their disability and drive themselves further than their capacities permit. They may feel self-conscious about their speech or gait. These feelings are often a reaction to how people have been treated by others.

> *For the first couple of years at high school I did not fit in very well. I originally thought it was only because I was disabled, but I found out that it was mainly because I was being an idiot and it had very little to do with being in a wheelchair. I changed my behaviour and the hassling stopped.*
>
> Nathan

Many people lack the confidence to try something new or to take the initiative. This may result from beliefs which persuade them that they are not capable or experienced enough to be independent, from the overprotectiveness of family and society and from messages people receive from others. Dependency on other people to assist with everyday activities, along with isolation through being kept at home or in a residential facility, can hinder a person's development and the person may become very passive in his or her approach to life. Activities that others take for granted may present a challenge to a person who has had few opportunities to make his or her own decisions. Thus, the decision to leave a sheltered workshop (activity centre) to find open employment may create fear and uncertainty. Likewise, lifestyle changes required in moving to one's own residence from an institution or from one's parents' home may seem to present insurmountable problems. It also can be difficult to form and maintain relationships with peers. This can result in social deprivation. For example, many people with cerebral palsy experience deprivation in the form of touching by other people. This important aspect of life which most of us take for granted can be denied people with cerebral palsy by others who are afraid of making physical contact. Hugging, kissing, touching, caressing are important parts of healthy development and in shaping a person's attitudes toward himself/herself and toward others. If others show repugnance, it is likely that the person with cerebral palsy will internalise this disgust towards himself or herself. Empowerment, support and encouragement are very important ingredients that people with and without disabilities can provide each other to build up self-confidence and self-esteem.

Some people find it is easier to stay at home rather than to mix with strangers. This solution may be safe but denies opportunities to make friends and enjoy social and recreational activities.

In the teenage years, special issues may arise in coming to terms with the presence of disability, body image and a sense of personal worth. In a society preoccupied with health, fitness and body image, impairments can influence self-esteem and make the person feel self-conscious and different.

Some people with disabilities choose to avoid others with similar disabilities. They do not wish to be identified as 'one of them'. In contrast, others may prefer only to mix with other people with disabilities, feeling that by doing so, they obtain mutual support and understanding and avoid negative behaviours from other people.

Slowness in completing tasks and clumsiness in walking can lead others to falsely assume that a person has an intellectual impairment. This compounds the stigma associated with cerebral palsy.

Sometimes other people think we are intellectually impaired because of our slowness and clumsiness. People working with us need to be patient and unhurried. Above all, they should listen to and value what we say. It is a big effort to say it sometimes, so please take the trouble to listen. Our self-esteem often is very low in this society which is so preoccupied with health, fitness and body image. We don't want to feel any more different, more devalued or more disempowered. Sometimes it's easier to stay at home than to try to mix with the community out there.

Sandra and Bill

Sexuality

I remember writing something about my first sexual encounter, questioning my lover. Is this person doing it because they want to do it, or are they taking pity on me?

Jacob

Sexuality is an important part of a person's identity, both physically and emotionally. People growing up with a severe physical disability such as cerebral palsy may feel that they are not sexually attractive and may be reluctant to become sexually involved. Body image can be affected by the physically disabling aspects of cerebral palsy. Clinical use of the body in medical assessment, treatment, and intensive physiotherapy (physical therapy) can sometimes result in a feeling of detachment from it. This is something that many professionals seem unaware of.

Limited mobility or spasms may result in awkwardness during sexual intimacy. This can often be overcome by obtaining professional advice and with discussion and experimentation with one's partner in order to find expressions of intimacy and a range of positions which are satisfying. Many people with cerebral palsy will need the assistance of another person in positioning them or in undressing them for sexual activity. This may cause embarrassment for the attendant, feelings of invasion of privacy, or concern about the mode of sexual expression that the person uses. Carers and assistants may need to examine their own attitudes carefully in order to respect the wishes, rights and privacy of the individual with a disability. The service provider has the right to refuse to assist if he or she wishes. This is a sensitive area which is still being tackled by many human service agencies, yet the person with a disability has a right to have sexual needs met just as he or she has the right to have other everyday needs, such as bathing and toileting, met.

Cerebral palsy does not in itself have any bearing on a person's fertility or ability to conceive a child. Contraception methods depend on the ability of the user and also upon education the user has received. Paralysis, spasms, stiffness, deformity or limited manual coordination can make the use of condoms, foams or diaphragms impossible or impractical. Insertion of an IUD could be painful or difficult for a person whose pelvic structure is deformed. The diaphragm may slip out of position if pelvic muscles are weak. Contraceptive tablets are more frequently prescribed, but these may not be the desired choice of the individual.

Pregnancy may be difficult for a woman with cerebral palsy. It can complicate existing balance problems and low back pain may occur as the pregnancy advances. Childbirth can be more difficult because of spasms inhibiting the woman's ability to 'bear down' or push. It has become more usual for women with cerebral palsy to have caesarean rather than vaginal births.

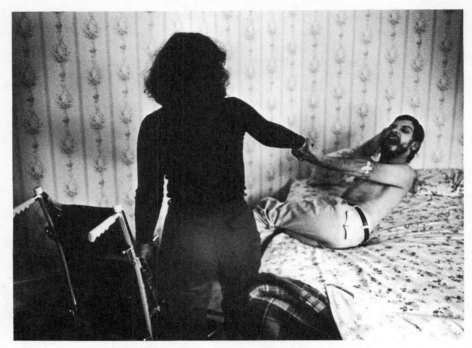

Figure 6.1: The everyday task of dressing and getting up

Being a parent

Sexual functioning and reproduction are not affected by cerebral palsy. People with cerebral palsy can and do have children. As cerebral palsy is not known to be hereditary, it is unlikely to occur in the next generation. If it does occur, its causes are the same for the children of other members of the population (see later in the chapter). But being a parent comes with its own responsibilities and demands, and so the decision whether or not to have children must take these into account.

Each parent develops his or her own strategies for child rearing and for enforcing discipline within the household. A parent with cerebral palsy may require special strategies in parenting:

> *It was fine when they were little, but now I find having a disability has its problems, especially in controlling my two girls. Talking at them is not the answer because they learn that I can't follow it through. Tactics are important. It never seemed to bother them that I am different, they've always accepted things. I have to watch that I don't place too much responsibility on my elder daughter.*
>
> Sue

Ageing and having cerebral palsy

In most cases, the life expectancy of people with cerebral palsy is similar to that of people in the general population (Overereynder et al., 1992). However, until recently most research and interest has focused on children with cerebral palsy, to the neglect of adults and issues associated with ageing. A report published by the Ontario Federation for Cerebral Palsy in 1993 indicates that physical challenges associated with cerebral palsy seem to intensify with age. Increased pain, increased spasticity, loss of endurance, loss of strength, fatigue and declining mobility were noted by all respondents included in the survey. Evidence, both from people with cerebral palsy and from physiatrists (medical doctors specialising in physical medicine and rehabilitation) who participated in the survey, suggested changes associated with ageing begin earlier for people with cerebral palsy than they do for other members of the population. However, it is controversial as to whether such changes are due to premature ageing or reflect secondary disabilities resulting from years of therapy and treatment, or reflect insufficient treatment.

Respondents also reported that health care providers lacked knowledge about disability and ageing and were unable to provide advice about strategies which could delay physical deterioration.

Marge (1994) and Dorval (1994) also discuss changes occurring with ageing for people with cerebral palsy. Marge makes the point that many service providers wrongly view conditions such as cerebral palsy as static. Rather, he argues that disability should be perceived as a condition undergoing changes at all times and, if not controlled, these changes can result in further disability and handicap. Marge and Dorval specify the following as potential concerns for people with cerebral palsy who are ageing: depression, adjustments in social relationships, mobility limitations, joint and muscle pain, difficulties with balance, progressive contractions, bladder and bowel incontinence, gastrointestinal problems, dental problems, pneumonia and respiratory complications, pressure sores, cardiovascular disorders and spasticity changes.

Marge (1994) presents a set of health promotion strategies for people with cerebral palsy which parallel those recommended for all people (whether they do or do not have a disability). These strategies include: improved diet and nutrition; reduction or elimination of tobacco, alcohol and drug use; weight control; physical exercise and activity; access to primary health care; strong social supports; control of environmental hazards (such as noise pollution and water contamination); achievement of an adequate income; sound stress management; and adequate rest and sleep.

Family

Denial, anger and rejection are grief reactions many family members feel when their long-awaited baby is finally diagnosed as having cerebral palsy. Often this diagnosis is not given until the parents or other family members have become aware that their baby is not reaching developmental milestones such as sitting up, walking and reaching out.

> *Poor Mum and Dad went through a terrible time. They didn't realise anything was wrong. Bear in mind I was their first child and the fact that my legs crossed when my nappy was changed didn't mean much. At nine months when I was propped up with cushions, they thought I was a bit backward. I went to many specialists who said I had rickets and all sorts of weird and wonderful things. At four years of age I was finally diagnosed at the Spastic Centre.*
>
> Monica

As with other disabilities, life with a family member who has a disability need not necessarily be tragic. Although the incidence of family breakdown is higher in such families than in the general population, disability can strengthen family relationships and promote pride in helping and in observing progress.

Having a disability puts me and my relationship with my parents on a different level than my brother's relationship with them. Sometimes I feel closer to them and sometimes I feel that my disability is a barrier between us. For example, my Dad and I are good mates and it is a hassle when I'd like to help him with physical work and I just can't do it.

Nathan

Regular planned respite care is important so that people can have a 'break' from caring and being cared for. The importance of respite care cannot be overemphasised. Care in the community must be shared, it should not just be the responsibility of one family member. Planned respite care is a needed component to preventing handicap, isolation and social disadvantage. For many people with cerebral palsy, respite services are difficult to access because of the person's high care needs.

Parents are not immune from attitudes which are prevalent in the community. For example, they may have difficulty in accepting that their son or daughter is growing up, has sexual needs and wants to take part in adult activities such as having a boyfriend or girlfriend or moving out of the family home.

Community living

Most people with cerebral palsy live in the community in their own homes or in the family home. Some live in nursing homes as they grow older, but this living arrangement should be a person's own choice which should be respected. All people (whether they have a disability or not) have the right to live as full a life as possible and to be able to make choices. However, these choices are to a degree limited for many people with cerebral palsy. Government support is no longer assured, nor is accommodation automatically provided in special-purpose nursing homes. Nevertheless, there are still choices that people can make.

Changes in government funding mean that greater emphasis is now placed on care in the community and 'ageing in place', rather than institutional care. The danger is that old supports are taken away before new supports are in place and are shown to be working effectively. Successful community living requires a whole range of organised and coordinated community support services, including adapted housing and living equipment, home help, home nursing, assistance with shopping, transport, employment and recreation, personal care, supportive counselling, living skills training and respite care.

Over the last ten years, many changes have occurred in legislation and community living for people with disabilities such as cerebral palsy. Disability services, anti-discrimination and equal opportunity legislation specify requirements and set standards for service provision and equality of access. These advances reflect the hard work and lobbying on the part of people with disabilities, their supporters and their representative organisations.

It's the segregation when you're disabled. I remember at ten years of age, in Sunday school, feeling different. I had to work harder at being friends with them.

Milton

Community attitudes have been changing and are becoming less negative towards people with cerebral palsy. Such change is particularly evident in children who have belonged to classes containing both children with and without disabilities. However, cerebral palsy still is not widely understood within the community. People with this disability may look different, walk strangely or talk unclearly and other people often do not know how to deal with such unfamiliarities. Strangeness and uncertainty arouse fear and pity, leading to efforts to avoid interacting with people with cerebral palsy. Fears are compounded by myths that cerebral palsy is 'catching' or that people can be dangerous and unpredictable. Other common beliefs are that people with cerebral palsy are helpless and overwhelmed by their disability. Community education plays a vital role in breaking down such myths and fostering acceptance. When presented with something strange or novel, some people may stare or act self-consciously, and sometimes are rude. These reactions are frustrating and devaluing for the person with cerebral palsy.

I think attitudes have greatly improved on a community level. On a more personal level, the average non-disabled person is not aware of the differences between disabilities. It is important that they realise that we are not the same. Our disabilities are not the same and we, as individuals, are not the same.

Nathan

It is important for community acceptance that people are seen as 'part of' their community, living, working and interacting with other community members. Many organisations undergoing 'deinstitutionalisation' (that is, changing their focus of service provision from institution-based to community-based) have special transitional programs of social education, living skills, and other community access programs to enable their members to integrate into their new settings. Peer support is invaluable at this time, as others who have succeeded in 'moving out' into new environments can give confidence and support. A helpful strategy is for organisations to assist their members with disabilities in developing their own individual plans for the future or to assist families with disabled members living at home to develop family future plans that link them with community service providers.

Access

Access means many things, not just building ramps into houses and buildings. It means not having barriers that prevent movement into and around one's house and garden, going to the movies or the shops or to a sports club, seeing a football match, enrolling and successfully completing a university or technical course, going to a party, driving a car, using public transport, going sailing or fishing, opening a bank account or raising a loan, travelling to a holiday destination, boarding a plane or a train, going to the toilet, having a shower, turning on the TV and choosing a

Figure 6.2: A young woman with cerebral palsy has difficulty with a long set of steps, but she is not the only one

program, and so on. Access to all of these activities is affected by many things including attitudes of others, architectural design, suitable transport facilities, community services, and the ways in which service provision is designed.

Education

Early intervention and pre school programs are staffed by specialist teachers and therapists. Most allow for individual assessment and therapy for infant and pre-school children. Programs include stimulation and sensory experiences, physiotherapy (physical therapy) and occupational and speech therapy to enhance the child's strengths and capabilities. They also provide useful peer support for parents.

> *Certain teachers at my school thought that a person in a wheelchair should not be worried about friendships or any social life with other people. Some teachers actively discouraged my friends from being seen with me.*
>
> Nathan

Government education policy now mainstreams and integrates all students with disabilities. With early intervention programs more and more children with mild to moderate motor impairment are entering regular classes. Some special classes and support units are available for students with special needs within regular schools. In special and mainstream schools, children have access to physiotherapy, occupational therapy and speech therapy, in addition to a school program which is often specially devised for the individual. The special school has the advantage of offering treatment and specialised education, as well as a sense of identification with other children with a similar disability. However, it also has the disadvantage of isolating children from their local community and from wider peer group involvement. This carries over into social and recreational activities. Often friendships in special schools may also be confined to friends who live in other localities and who are not available outside school.

Mobility aids may be needed to improve access to some places such as specialised work areas. Slowness in handwriting, typing or speech may require the use of special techniques which enable the person to record lecture notes and to prepare and sit for examinations. Most tertiary institutions have disability advisers to assist students with disabilities and to adapt the educational environment to their needs.

Developments in computer technology have had a major impact on educational opportunities and teaching strategies used with children and adults with disabilities. Training in such technology is now an essential part of all special education and also is vital in the training of special education teachers.

Employment

> *At this time I am unemployed. Employment is the best example of disability having a negative impact on my life. It does limit my career choices and even casual work options. I mean, how many people with disabilities work on a check-out as their first job?*
>
> Nathan

With a greater emphasis on integration, community acceptance, and legislation for equal employment opportunities, the range of employment options has increased for people with cerebral palsy. However, people are still disadvantaged. People who are obviously physically disabled are less likely to be employed, regardless of their intellectual abilities (Chamberlain, 1984).

The attitudes of counsellors, educators, family and employers are important in influencing job selection, vocational training and rehabilitation strategies. However, employment choices are limited to some extent by the severity of the disability. Some people achieve high levels of education and develop the social, communication and professional skills to succeed in the labour market. Some people's employment is centred around unskilled and semi-skilled jobs, while for others intellectual disability and limited mobility mean that 'sheltered employment' is the best option.

Additional costs

Health care needs may be partially met by government or private insurance and are no different from those of other people. Equipment costs may sometimes be subsidised by government programs such as the PADP (Program of Aids for Disabled People) which is funded by the Australian Home and Community Care (HACC) Program. However, this assistance is means tested. There are some interest-free loan schemes which assist with the purchase of wheelchairs, environmental control systems and communication systems for people with disabilities who are employed.

PERSON TO PERSON

Appropriate language and behaviour

Service provider attitudes and awareness are key factors in the ability of people with disabilities to successfully gain access to generic services used by all members of the community. People with cerebral palsy argue that, although important changes have occurred, there is still considerable room for enhanced awareness and sensitivity to their needs as consumers.

Language and labels convey a great deal about one's attitudes. Use of inappropriate terms such as 'spazo' and 'cripple' perpetuates negative beliefs. It is unfortunate that the term 'spastic' is used in this negative way in the community when historically it has been in the title of many organisations representing people with cerebral palsy.

> I get angry with how people are presented. Headlines such as 'crippled girl wins . . .' are disgusting. 'Crippled' and 'spastic' are such terrible words.
>
> Monica

Language has a powerful effect on behaviours and attitudes. Words and behaviours of others about disability convey messages to the person with a disability which, in turn, influence their aspirations, expectations and self-esteem.

Each person is an individual. The label 'cerebral palsy' should not be used as a shortcut for evaluating and 'understanding' the person. Full understanding comes through getting to know the person and his or her strengths and limitations. Remember: 'people first' and that the disability is secondary to being a person.

Interaction is a two-way process. A good philosophy is: 'Look, listen, understand and treat me as you would like me to treat you'. Communication for a person with cerebral palsy can be difficult if speech is affected. However, conversations can be successful if both people with and without disability are prepared to participate and use all the possible communication skills and cues that are available. People who have speech limitations usually do not mind repeating what they have said if the listener has not understood. Interactive, two-way conversation may simply require greater concentration and more patient listening. Where responses are delayed or 'written' communication is necessary, there is still potential for effective communication.

Barriers to successful communication with a person who has cerebral palsy may include difficulties in initiating and maintaining conversation, reluctance of the listener to adapt interaction patterns, difficulties with communication devices and slowness of speech. Hugo & Lloyd (1990) list the following as key factors cited by people with cerebral palsy as interfering with effective communication:

- frustration at not being able to respond;
- being ignored, particularly by professionals;
- lack of awareness and understanding on the part of others;
- lack of ability or the opportunities to convey needs and desires;
- lack of knowledge about up-to-date technology.

Table 6.1 conveys that responsibility for successful interaction is the responsibility of all parties involved. Both people with and without disabilities are responsible for behaving appropriately and taking positive steps to make interactions successful with other community members.

> *Socially, having a disability can be an asset or a great liability depending on two main things. The most important thing is to be comfortable with your disability so that the people you are with can be comfortable with it, too. The second thing I have learned is that you are easily remembered by people. So, if you go out and you are comfortable in yourself, then people will respect you and remember you for it.*
>
> Nathan

MORE INFORMATION ABOUT CEREBRAL PALSY

Cerebral palsy is a group of conditions caused by damage to the central nervous system before, during or following birth. It impairs motor functioning and muscle growth. The person may have one or more of the following characteristics: tight muscles, impaired speech and muscle coordination, jerking, uncontrollable movements or poor balance. Cerebral palsy can range from mild to severe, and may be accompanied by other disabilities such as poor visual perception, hearing impairment, limited verbal communication, and intellectual disability or epilepsy.

'Cerebral' refers to the cerebrum or cerebral cortex of the brain where motor and sensory activities are controlled. 'Palsy' is defined as a loss of motor or sensory function in some part of the body.

Definition

In terms of the World Health Organization (1980) definitions:

- *Impairment* refers to damage in the cerebrum, with area and extent of damage determining disability.
- *Disability* refers to loss of functions such as ability to move limbs, balance, hearing and vision.

Table 6.1: Strategies for successful interaction

Person with cerebral palsy	Other person
Retain your sense of humour and dignity.	Treat the person with dignity. Use age-appropriate language.
Be patient, but persistent.	When talking to someone with a communication disability, be patient. Resist the temptation to interrupt or to answer on behalf of the person.
Be a good listener.	
It is all right to remind the person gently that you are not deaf or a child and that you have something to say.	Never walk away, turn away, drum a rhythm on the table: this is rude and suggests you are feeling impatient.
Do not assume that all people know or understand what cerebral palsy is; many do not.	Be aware of the environment and the difficulties that it can present for people with severe physical disabilities.
If assistance is needed, ask for it and make your needs known to the person who is assisting.	Be willing to communicate in different ways if necessary, such as using an alphabet board, verbal and non-verbal cues.
Be prepared to communicate in the way best suited to you.	
If your speech is affected, be prepared to repeat if you have not been understood.	Talk directly to the person. Do not talk about the person as if she or he is not physically present or cannot understand and speak for himself or herself. As in any conversation, maintain eye contact as far as possible; for example, sit down if appropriate.
Become aware of your rights and be firm and protective about your rights to access, independence and privacy.	
Be assertive and stand up for your rights.	Never do anything which may disempower or devalue the person. Assistance in certain circumstances might be required – ask the person if it is needed.
Be aware and tolerant of the other person's discomfort in social situations.	

Table 6.1: *Continued*

Person with cerebral palsy	Other person
Remember you are a member of society with the same rights and responsibilities as others. Remember that you are an equal partner in any relationship. You are entitled to have input in decision making which concerns your life and well-being.	At first the person's speech may seem difficult to understand. After a while you will find that it begins to make sense and that you are able to understand it. Try to imagine how you would feel if you were that person. Do not pretend that you have understood the person, ask him or her to repeat comments until you do understand. Be aware of mobility difficulties. Obtain information from the person about particular mobility requirements. Find out the places in your area that are accessible to people using mobility aids. Respond with understanding if the person knocks over a cup, needs help to go to the toilet, can't speak, or accidentally hits you.

- *Handicap* refers to the consequences of disability such as difficulty in performing everyday tasks, in speaking clearly, in obtaining a mainstream education, in gaining access to public buildings which do not permit wheelchair access, housing and transport systems which do not account for the needs of people with disabilities, and prejudice in others.

The brain

The nervous system is made up of nerve cells and nerve fibres and is divided into the central nervous system (CNS) and peripheral nervous system (PNS). These parts work in close relationship; each receives and transmits messages to and from the other. Effective functioning depends upon harmony in this relationship.

The *central nervous system* consists of the brain and spinal cord. Cerebral palsy arises from damage to the brain which is briefly described below and illustrated in Figure 6.3. The brain is contained within the cavity of the skull. It is made up of the forebrain, midbrain and hind brain.

The *forebrain* comprises the cerebrum, and its enclosed structures. The *cerebrum* is the largest part of the brain and is divided into right and left hemispheres. In right-handed people, the left hemisphere predominates and vice versa with left-handed people. Each hemisphere is made up of four ill-defined lobes – frontal,

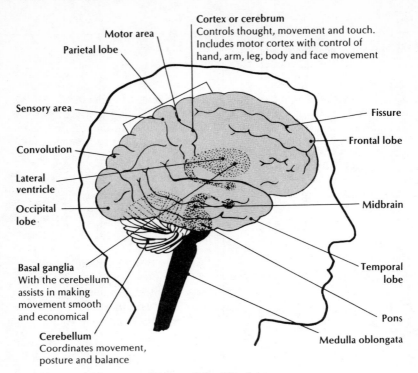

Figure 6.3: The brain

parietal, occipital and temporal – according to the part of the skull they occupy. The functions of these lobes differ. The surface of the lobes is called the cerebral cortex and has many convolutions, separated by clefts and fissures. This arrangement increases the surface area of the brain and separates areas with different functions.

A section through the hemispheres shows that the outer layer (cortex) is darker in colour ('grey matter') and is made up of nerve cells. The deeper layers are paler ('white matter') and are made up of nerve fibres. Deep inside each hemisphere lie the lateral ventricles, thalamus, basal ganglia and internal capsule. The *lateral ventricles* are two cavities in the lower and medial part of the hemisphere. They produce a pale fluid – cerebrospinal fluid (CSF) – which passes out to surrounding surfaces of the brain and spinal cord. This facilitates movement and maintains intercranial pressure. It probably also has a part to play in reducing the effect of injury.

The *thalamus* and *basal ganglia* lie close to and behind the ventricles. They are made up of nerve cells and act as relaying stations for messages passing from one part of the brain to another and also for afferent (incoming) nerves carrying messages from the spinal cord. They are, therefore, very closely involved in injury affecting any part of the brain. The *internal capsule* is a pathway through which all nerves to and from the cortex pass. It lies close to and just to the side of the thalamus which it separates from the basal ganglia.

The *mid brain* is the smallest part of the brain and is about two centimetres in length. It lies below the forebrain and connects the thalamic region to the hind brain. It contains collections of nerve cells (ganglia or nuclei) but is mainly made up of nerve fibres passing to and from the cerebrum.

The *hind brain* comprises the pons, cerebellum and the medulla oblongata. The *pons* is the front part of the hind brain and is situated in front of the cerebellum with which it connects. Below, it is directly continuous with the medulla oblongata. Cross-section shows a preponderance of grey matter, indicating cell structures which act as relaying stations to the cerebrum, cerebellum, thalamus and the basal ganglia. Many nerves originate in the pons, and in addition to this, it accommodates the nerves passing to and from the brain, the medulla oblongata and the spinal cord.

The *cerebellum* is situated below the cerebrum and behind the pons. It consists of two cerebellar hemispheres and a narrow median strip. The surface is marked by curved fissures, some deeper than others, which divide the organ into lobules. It is made up of grey and white matter arranged in the same way as that of the cerebrum. In addition to the cortex there are four masses of grey matter in each hemisphere. There are cell stations on the efferent (outgoing) nerves from the cerebellar cortex. The *medulla oblongata* extends from the lower part of the pons to the exit from the skull where it is directly continuous with the spinal cord. It has a structure similar to the pons and contains nerve cell masses relaying nerves originating in the pons as well as nerves passing to and from the brain.

Physiology

The basic structure of the nervous system is the nerve unit which consists of a single nerve cell and a nerve fibre with its nerve endings. These units vary in length and are grouped in bundles to form a nerve which may carry impulses or messages either to or from the brain. Those going to the brain are 'afferent' nerves and carry impulses of sensation (pain, touch and temperature). These messages are relayed in the thalamus to the appropriate area of the cortex. If the cortex is damaged, as in cerebral palsy, some of these impulses can be interpreted in the thalamus so sensation may not be completely lost.

Nerves going from the brain are 'efferent' nerves. These may originate in the cerebral cortex (motor area), in the cerebellum or in the nuclei of the pons and medulla. By means of these nerves, the cerebrum is connected with all parts of the brain as well as with all parts of the body.

The cerebellum is the ultimate refinement and coordination centre of the brain. Normal functioning of the brain results in smooth, controlled and coordinated movement and normal sensation. Damage to any part will produce either failure of function or abnormal function, both of which are reflected in cerebral palsy. As stated above, the type and degree of impairment depends upon the site of the damage and its extent. Because all parts of the brain are interconnected, injury to one area may cause interference with function of other areas such as speech, vision, hearing, balance and walking. As a result, cerebral palsy may have a variety of symptoms. However, for convenience, it can be divided into four major forms, listed below in descending order of frequency.

Types of cerebral palsy

Clinicians generally classify cerebral palsy on the basis of neurological syndromes which are highly complex and difficult to characterise. Examination of a person with cerebral palsy will show a variety of signs. The following classification is often used, but has two serious drawbacks: the changing nature of clinical signs in an individual over time and clinician's differing interpretations of the terms used in the description of signs. These drawbacks make comparisons of different statistical datasets difficult.

- *Spastic hemiplegia*. This is mostly associated with weakness which is unilateral (on one side of the body). Twenty-five per cent of people with this form have epilepsy. Athetoid movement in the affected side is often prominent.
- *Spastic diplegia and ataxic diplegia*. Here involvement is on both sides of the body and is relatively minor in both forms. Major signs occur in the lower limbs and hips.
- *Spastic quadriplegia*. The person is affected in four limbs. The trunk, hands and face are also likely to be affected. Learning difficulties and epilepsy also may be present.
- *Ataxic/hypotonia*. In this form, muscle tone is diminished and ataxia is present.
- *Athetosis/dyskinesia*. The major features include uncoordinated movements. Muscle tone may fluctuate.
- *Mixed types*. In some people, the motor disorder is hard to classify into the above groupings. Tone may be variable, various degrees of ataxia may be seen, athetosis may not be a major feature.

A variety of terms is used to describe the clinical features of people with cerebral palsy:

- *Hypertonia* refers to increased resistance to passive movement of the limb. The reflexes also may be affected. *Hypotonia* refers to decreased muscle tone, resulting in soft and floppy muscles. Some reflexes also may be affected.
- *Spasticity* refers to increased muscle tone with abnormal resistance to passive movement. Reflexes also may be affected.
- *Rigidity* refers to uncoordinated voluntary movement, generally occurring in the arms and hands. Control of the head and trunk may be affected as may gait.
- *Athetosis* refers to movement extraneous to the desired task. It results in slow, perhaps writhing movement.
- *Dystonia* refers to fluctuating tone in which a person's muscle tone is increased or decreased.
- *Ataxia* is a poor sense of balance, making walking and coordination difficult. Typically the lower limbs are affected more than the upper limbs. The person is likely to show an unsteady and lurching gait, creating an appearance which is often misunderstood as suggesting the person is 'drunk'. Speech may be slowed and even slurred.

People with cerebral palsy usually have some limb control. Cerebral palsy is not progressive. The brain damage does not get worse. Some degeneration of muscles may occur as the person gets older. Regular therapy can prevent this.

Causes

Cerebral palsy is not hereditary and it is rare for more than one case to occur in the same family. It originates before birth, during birth or within seven days after birth. Most diagnoses are made by five years of age. The following are accepted causes.

Before birth. Reports (for example, Blair & Stanley, 1988) suggest that problems during intrauterine development account for the largest proportion of known cases of cerebral palsy. These may result from:

- infections in the mother during pregnancy (for example, German measles or rubella);
- abnormal brain development during pregnancy;
- malnutrition;
- toxic effects, such as foetal alcohol syndrome (FAS);
- disorders in the mother such as diabetes;
- restriction of fetal circulation, a knot in the umbilical cord or the cord wound around the neck or a limb;
- unknown causes, possibly genetic;
- placental insufficiency, usually resulting from maternal disease or injury.

During birth. Possible causes include:

- insufficient oxygen (asphyxia) to the baby's brain during birth, either because of a prolonged and difficult birth or because of inadequate resuscitation immediately after birth;
- birth injury occurring as a result of a difficult forceps delivery;
- cerebral haemorrhage;
- premature birth (the risk of cerebral palsy increases as birth weight declines).

After birth. Possible causes include:

- infection;
- head injury;
- cerebral haemorrhage;
- child abuse.

It was assumed for many years that most causes of cerebral palsy were asphyxia and other problems at the time of birth (Paneth & Stark, 1983). This has been questioned (Blair & Stanley, 1988) and most researchers now agree that factors during pregnancy are more influential.

It is believed that postnatal causes of cerebral palsy account for approximately 10 per cent of all cases, with most of these occurring in infancy. In older children, traumatic brain injury is the main risk. Such injury may occur because of meningitis or other infections affecting the brain, child abuse or from toxic effects such as lead poisoning.

Incidence and prevalence

This is not easy to determine with any great deal of precision, but studies show a remarkable consistency of prevalence rates. It is estimated that two people per 1000 in the population have cerebral palsy (Stanley & Watson, 1988: Stopford, 1988), with 10 per cent of these people having a disability of a postnatal origin. In Australia there is no national system of notification of cerebral palsy, however there is a state register in Western Australia. Similarly, no Canadian statistics are available, but estimates indicate that cerebral palsy occurs in between 1.5 to three cases per 1000 births. Statistics from the United States vary: between one and three in 1000 babies are born with cerebral palsy. This means that, conservatively, there are between 3500 and 4000 babies born with cerebral palsy each year in the United States (Overeyender et al., 1992). In the United States 211 000 people have cerebral palsy (LaPlante & Carlson, 1996)

Evidence is lacking about demographic influences on the incidence rates of cerebral palsy.

Diagnosis

Computerised axial tomography (CAT) scans and magnetic resonance imaging (MRI) can help identify lesions in the brain. This technology may enable some children who are considered as at risk of having cerebral palsy to be diagnosed early. However, for most people, it is months or years before a firm diagnosis is made (Ontario Federation for Cerebral Palsy, 1994). A child with cerebral palsy may be late in reaching developmental milestones and may feel unusually stiff or floppy. However, observations are made over time in order to rule out other explanations before a diagnosis of cerebral palsy is made. This period of uncertainty and waiting can cause considerable stress for the parents and supportive counselling can assist.

Treatment

There is no known cure for cerebral palsy. However, its effects may be modified by therapy and medication, and secondary disabilities can be alleviated.

Treatment involves the coordinated action of a wide range of health, education and service professionals as well as a wide range of services and activities. Treatment will not overcome the damage to the brain, but prevents effects becoming more serious and helps the person become more independent. In most Western countries treatment is carried out by a multidisciplinary team of occupational therapists, physiotherapists (physical therapists), social workers, psychologists, medical doctors and physiatrists. Few disabilities involve such a wide range of health professionals in their treatment. Regular physiotherapy is the most likely ongoing need for people with cerebral palsy. Orthopaedic surgery to correct postural, limb or spine problems can be useful. Occupational therapists advise on posture aids and ergonomic design for independent living and the workplace. Speech pathologists assist with communication aids and techniques and adaptive device design such as voice synthesisers and special communicators. Other therapy approaches include hydrotherapy, counselling, acupuncture, aromatherapy and nutritional advice. Hydrotherapy and aquatic activities provide opportunities for relaxation and body control. There are also many alternative and complementary treatments that use, for example, acupuncture, reflexology, aromatherapy and massage.

A wide range of professionals may assist with problems which arise as a result of cerebral palsy. Diagnosis and assessment of these and associated disabilities should be made early in life to ensure appropriate treatment. Early intervention programs are important to maximise the child's abilities and to minimise developmental delays.

Services and supports

Most services are provided free of charge at specialist organisations for people with cerebral palsy. They aim to enable and facilitate each individual with cerebral palsy to reach goals and to live as independently as possible. Specialised services are provided throughout a person's life, but gradually more and more services are being provided within the general community. Counselling services tend to be limited for people with cerebral palsy and, even when available, may be inaccessible or difficult for someone who cannot use the usual forms of communication. A sign language interpreter or someone familiar with the particular communication device being used may be required. This situation also may arise for personal care attendants for whom it may be necessary to learn the symbols and signs used by the person with cerebral palsy to communicate.

Equipment

To be effective, an aid should assist function, save energy and help (not worsen) the disabling condition. A wide range of aids are available which enable people with cerebral palsy to live independent lives. Aids can simplify eating, grooming, dressing and help with the tasks of daily living and the workplace. Computers, telephones, reading and writing appliances, voice synthesisers and symbols are used to augment communication and interaction with others. Car adaptations such as adapted controls and transfer aids make driving possible for some. Wheelchairs, walkers, hoists, lifts and ramps increase mobility. Many useful products are available that cover almost every area and activity of daily life, ranging from expensive equipment to simple gadgets. These include large-handled eating utensils, grab sticks and electronic door openers.

Equipment advice can be gained from specialist disability organisations such as Independent Living Centres (ILCs), specialist organisations, Technical Aid for the Disabled (TAD) and hospital and government rehabilitation centres. It also is contained in advice and material published by and for people with disabilities.

Specialised adaptations that are not commercially available are designed by TAD, which is a voluntary organisation that assists people with disabilities to be as independent as possible. Many people find novel, unorthodox and often simple solutions to outwit their limitations, and TAD volunteers and engineers often assist them to do this.

Computers not only help people to communicate with others but also help them interact with and control their environments more effectively. Computer programs have been developed specifically to perform this task. There is a comprehensive range of software that provides state-of-the art augmentative communication, computer access and education programs. Modified computers are available with specialised keyboards and other features which suit the needs of someone with limited manual dexterity. Other devices employ synthesised speech and require the user to type the message in letter by letter to produce spoken output.

> *I use an electric and a manual wheelchair as well as a computer. I regularly use a disabled taxi for transport. These things have greatly improved my mobility and my written communication.*
>
> Nathan, who is 19 years of age

Ways to communicate

There are many other forms of communication besides verbal speech. These include eye contact, nods of the head, communication boards, 'touch talkers', 'liberators', 'light talkers' and handsigning. Augmentive communication is widely used by people with speech limitations associated with cerebral palsy. Chedd (1995) describes augmentive communication as involving pictures, sign language, computers, voice output devices and letter boards. These are designed to supplement or replace speech. The challenge for therapists is to find the combination which best suits the individual and enables him or her to maximise communication skills.

Facilitated communication (FC) is another system which is used to assist communication in people with limited speech. This method – publicised by Australian, Rosemary Crossley – involves the technique of hand-over-hand spelling out of words. A piece of cardboard with letters of the alphabet on it is held in front of the person with a disability. With the assistance of a facilitator he or she points to letters to spell out words. This method is used with adults and children. In countries such as the United States, use of FC is controversial and its benefits are debated. Often it is used with people with a range of disabilities. Orelove and Sobsey, 1966 discuss some of the controversy, which centres on the role of the facilitator in moving the person's hands to spell out letters. Some have raised the possibility that the facilitator may influence the communication. They assert that messages produced in FC come from the facilitator, not the person with disabilities. Others regard FC as a means of opening new worlds for people otherwise unable to communicate and that it enables people to gain expression and greater control of their lives.

RESOURCE ORGANISATIONS

All care has been taken to ensure that all information is correct at the time of publishing. However, responsibility for the accuracy of this information is not accepted by the writer. The list of resource organisations contained in this chapter is not intended to be exhaustive. It lists national organisations. The reader is referred to local community directories for further information and for local branches of national organisations. Inclusion of services and organisations should not be taken as a recommendation.

Australia

Australian Cerebral Palsy Association
C/- The Cerebral Palsy Association
  of WA Ltd
106 Bradford Street
Coollbinia WA 6050
PO Box 61
Mt Lawley WA 6050
Ph 09 443 0211
Fax 09 444 7299

Refer to your local telephone directory for state addresses of the local Spastic Centre of the Cerebral Palsy Association. For NSW, the address is as follows:
Spastic Centre of NSW
189 Allambie Road
Allambie Heights NSW 2100
PO Box 184

Brookvale NSW 2100
Ph 02 9451 9022
Fax 02 9451 4877

Canada

The Ontario
Federation for Cerebral Palsy
Suite 104, 1630 Lawrence
Avenue West
Toronto

New Zealand

Cerebral Palsy Society
PO Box 24042
Royal Oak
Auckland
Ph 09 358 1854
Fax 09 358 0732

United Kingdom

Scope (formerly the Spastics Society)
Church Drive, Rhos on Sea
Colwyn Bay
Clwyd LL28 4LL
Ph (01492) 547 777

United States

United Cerebral Palsy Associations Inc.
Suite 706, 1660 L Street, NW
Washington, DC 20036
Ph 800 USA-5-UCP or 202 776 0406
Fax 202 776 0414

FURTHER READING

Baumgart, D. (1990). *Augmentative and alternative communication systems for persons with moderate and severe disabilities.* Baltimore: Paul H. Brookes.

Bergman, T. (1991). *Going places: children living with cerebral palsy.* Milwaukee: G. S. Childrens' Books.

Cathels, B. A. & Reddihough, D. S. (1993). The health care of young adults with cerebral palsy. *Medical Journal of Australia,* 159, 444–6.

Chedd, N. A. (1995). Getting started with augmentive communication. *Exceptional Parent,* May, 34–9.

Cogher, L., Savage, E. & Smith, M. (eds) (1992). *Cerebral palsy: management of disability series.* London: Chapman Hall.

Dormans, J. P. & Pellegrino, L. (in press). *Caring for children with cerebral palsy*: A team approach. Baltimore: Paul H. Brookes.

Dorval, J. (1994). Achieving and maintaining body systems integrity and function: clinical issues. *Preventing secondary conditions associated with spina bifida or cerebral palsy: proceedings and recommendations of a symposium.* Washington: Spina Bifida Association of America.

Eicher, P. S. & Batshaw, M. L. (1993). Cerebral palsy. *Paediatrics Clinics of North America,* 40, 537–51.

Garner, A., Lipsky, D. & Turnbull, A. (1991). *Supporting families with a child with a disability.* Baltimore: Paul H. Brookes.

Geralis, E. (1991). *Children with cerebral palsy: a parents' guide.* Rockville, MD: Woodbine House.

Goldfarb, L. A., Brotherson, M. J., Summers, J. A. & Turnbull, A. P. (1986). *Meeting the challenge of disability or chronic illness: a family guide.* Baltimore: Paul H. Brookes.

Johnston, C. (ed.) (1993). *Does this child need help: identification and early intervention.* Sydney: NSW Education and Training Foundation and the Australian Early Intervention Association (NSW Chapter) Inc.

Kerr, L. (1994). Care for the carers: bridging the gaps. Paper presented to the International Cerebral Palsy Society, Cambridge, United Kingdom.

Levine, K. & Wharton, R. (1995). Facilitated communication: what parents should know. *Exceptional Parent,* May, 40–53.

Marge, S. (1994). Toward a state of well-being: promoting healthy behaviors to prevent secondary conditions. *Preventing secondary conditions associated with spina bifida or cerebral palsy: proceedings and recommendations of a symposium.* Washington: Spina Bifida Association of America.

Orelove, F. P. & Sobsey, R. N. (1996) *Educating children with multiple disabilities: a transdisciplinary approach* (3rd edn). Baltimore: Paul H. Brookes.

Overeyender, J., Turk, M., Dalton, A. & Janicki, M. P. (1992). *I'm worried about the future: the aging of adults with cerebral palsy.* New York: New York Developmental Disabilities Planning Council.

Pimm, P. (1992). Physiological burnout and functional skill loss in cerebrl palsy. *Interlink,* 4, 18–21.

Stanton, M. (1992). *Cerebral palsy: a practical guide.* London: Optima Publishers.

Stopford, V. (1988). *Understanding disability: causes, characteristics and coping.* Caulfield, Vic: Edward Arnold.

Twigg, J. & Atkin, K. (1994). *Carers: perceived policy and practice in informal care.* Oxford: Oxford University Press.

CHAPTER 7
DIABETES MELLITUS

Diabetes touches every part of your life. Everything that affects it has to be carefully managed.

Brackenridge & Dolinar (1993, p. 7)

Diabetes mellitus is a disease of uncertain causes and which is characterised by high blood glucose levels. It is a chronic disorder of the pancreas in which very little or insufficient insulin is produced to meet demands or in which it is not used effectively by the body. Insulin is a substance produced by the pancreas to break down glucose (sugar) in the blood. Without insulin, sugar in food cannot be converted into the energy required to sustain life. Instead, the unused sugar accumulates in the blood and spills out into the urine. Diabetes can affect many of the chemical processes and tissues in the body. It is a multi-system disorder (Hillson, 1992).

The majority of people with diabetes develop it in adulthood. There are two major types of diabetes mellitus – insulin-dependent and non–insulin-dependent diabetes mellitus.

Type I or insulin-dependent diabetes mellitus (IDDM) generally has an early onset and is also known as juvenile onset diabetes. It is the type of diabetes that children, adolescents and young adults get. The pancreas ceases to produce insulin, making the administration of insulin by injection necessary for the rest of a person's life. The symptoms of Type I are more rapid in onset and generally more severe than in Type II. No one knows why children develop diabetes. It is known, however, that the disorder is not the result of poor eating habits, nor is it infectious (Canadian Diabetes Association, 1994). Symptoms include abnormal thirst, frequent urination, rapid and unexplained loss of weight, unusual hunger, irritability, weakness, fatigue, nausea and vomiting.

I was constantly tired and depressed. Because I had only just recently got married and had a busy job, I put it down to stress. I felt tired and sick a lot of the time. I would get headaches, was extremely thirsty and I was losing weight.

Sarah

Type II or non-insulin-dependent diabetes mellitus (NIDDM) is the more common form of diabetes – 85 per cent of people with diabetes have this form. It usually affects people over the age of 40 and is also called mature-onset diabetes. It is associated, not with a lack of insulin, but with an inability of the body tissues to use glucose in response to insulin. It usually has a gradual onset and may be controlled by diet and exercise or by diet and tablets. Insulin injections are sometimes required.

LIVING WITH DIABETES MELLITUS

If diabetes goes unrecognised or is inadequately treated, the person is susceptible to a wide range of illnesses and disabilities. These are outlined later in the chapter. However, it is important to note at this point that early detection, regular checkups, health monitoring and a healthy lifestyle are vital to avoid or minimise disabilities which can result from diabetes. This is why diabetes organisations and governments conduct regular campaigns to enhance diabetes awareness. Complications associated with diabetes are the fifth major cause of death from disease in Australia.

Personal adjustment

As with other disabilities, many people experience grief reactions following the diagnosis of diabetes, going through the stages of shock, denial, anger, depression and acceptance. Older people may find changes particularly distressing and as they also may have to come to terms with the fact of age-related complications such as failing sight (Stopford, 1988). People should be encouraged to work through their sense of loss and bereavement. However, the denial stage should be treated with caution as it may result in nonadherence to treatment and failure to perform routine urine and blood testing (Cohen, 1982).

As diabetes cannot be cured, the person has to come to terms with a new self and a new lifestyle. People with diabetes are able to do most of the things they could do prior to diagnosis, however spontaneity may be impaired. Food intake and injections must be planned. Changes may be required to daily routine, eating and exercise habits, consumption of alcohol and smoking behaviours. It is important to realise, however, that many of the changes required are similar to those other people make in order to have a more healthy lifestyle: more exercise, a balanced diet, stopping smoking and so on.

It may take time for the person to accept that he or she will be taking medication for the rest of his or her life. At first the limitations imposed by the need for regular meals, regular monitoring of blood levels and regular doses of insulin may seem intrusive and overwhelming but most people adjust to this and incorporate requirements into their regular routine so that injecting a dose of insulin becomes a habit like brushing the teeth.

> *I have discovered that diabetes doesn't have to my restrict life. I know the types of food I should eat and I don't find it difficult to accommodate them within my everyday diet. I guess I'm getting used to having diabetes.*
>
> Sarah

People taking medication to control blood glucose levels (that is, insulin or certain types of tablets) are at risk of hypoglycaemic episodes. This is a serious situation which, if not recognised and treated, may lead to insulin coma. If it occurs in a public place, it may, at the very least, cause embarrassment for the person with diabetes as well as shock for others who are not aware of what is happening or of how to help. This is why it is important for a person to ensure that friends, relatives, workmates and teachers are aware of the presence of diabetes and what to do to help. Table 7.1 later in the chapter outlines steps to take to assist the person.

Most people know very little about diabetes until it happens to them. They hear stories of the dramatic aspects and this can result in unrealistic and exaggerated fears. One of the first tasks for a person diagnosed with diabetes is to overcome these fears and to obtain a realistic picture of the impact diabetes will have on his or her life.

Many people with Type I diabetes are diagnosed during their adolescent years. This can be a time of turmoil for many teenagers anyway and the advent of diabetes can compound difficulties in forming a self-identity. A common problem in teenagers with Type I diabetes is the effects that changes in hormone production associated with puberty have on their condition. Most people manage these changes well, but some teenagers use their diabetes as a way of venting anger against others. Brackenridge and Dolinar (1993) say that it is not unusual for a teenager to miss meals and insulin injections in order to 'get back' at parents. Some may do it as a way of establishing a sense of who they are and how they are different from others. It is important for parents to recognise the motivation behind these behaviours. It also is important for both parents and teenagers to be aware that the body cannot grow and develop to its full potential unless blood glucose levels are kept in control.

> *Dye your hair blue if you want, but, for goodness sake, don't skip your insulin.*
>
> Brackenridge & Dolinar (1993, p. 186)

Frank (1995) reports that 20–25 per cent of adolescents drop out of medical care after graduating from paediatric to adult clinics. This means they do not receive regular checkups at a time when important changes are occurring: going off to university, leaving home, starting a career, and so on. Frank suggests that transition strategies are necessary to assist the teenager in meeting the demands of adult care.

Sexuality

There is no reason why people with diabetes cannot look forward to marriage and parenthood. Contrary to popular myth, men with diabetes are not usually impotent (Hillson, 1987), however young men who have had a long duration of diabetes with poor control often have erectile dysfunction associated with nerve damage and restricted blood flow to the penis. This situation characterises 50 per cent of men with diabetes who are aged over 50 years and 60 per cent over 60 years.

Sexual intercourse uses up energy which might lead to a hypoglycaemic reaction (hypo). People at risk of hypos may need to take precautions to prevent these from occurring. Because of hormonal changes, some women with diabetes find that they need to adjust their insulin with every period.

Being a parent

Studies suggest that one in 200 pregnant women have diabetes. In one-third of these women, diabetes was pre-existing. In the other two-thirds, the women developed *gestational diabetes* (GDM) which remits soon after delivery, however the woman is at increased risk of diabetes developing during subsequent pregnancies or later in life. Between 10 per cent and 25 per cent of women with GDM have been found to have diabetes by one year following the birth of their baby. About 60 per cent of these women have diabetes or impaired glucose tolerance within 10–15 years. GDM occurs in 5–10 per cent of pregnancies. It develops during pregnancy because the pregnancy hormones cause resistance to the action of insulin. The baby may gain excess weight, leading to a difficult labour and delivery. The baby also may have low blood glucose levels or breathing difficulties in the first few days of life and has a higher chance of becoming jaundiced. Babies of women with gestational diabetes are monitored for the first 24–48 hours in case of hypoglycaemia or respiratory distress. Blood glucose levels are also checked regularly.

Gestational diabetes is a biochemical manifestation and is usually controlled by diet, although some women require insulin injections (Gething, Papalia & Olds, 1995). The woman will be required to check her blood glucose level regularly by using the finger prick test. Control of blood sugar is necessary to control the amount of glucose which passes to the baby. Extra glucose in the baby's blood causes the baby's pancreas to take more insulin, which in turn acts as an extra growth hormone. Thus, the mother's high glucose levels interfere with the baby's maturation and growth

A woman with Type I or Type II diabetes has the same chance of having a healthy child as do other women if blood glucose levels are well controlled prior to and following conception. However, birth defects are twice as common in babies of mothers with diabetes if the diabetes has not been well controlled. If diabetes is not well managed prior to conception and during pregnancy, there is a higher risk of perinatal mortality. However, for mothers with well-managed diabetes, the risks are the same as for the general population. Dangers are associated with repeated high blood glucose levels and persistent ketones (see later in the chapter). If maternal blood glucose levels are not controlled, there is a greatly increased risk of still birth and congenital abnormality in the newborn.

The woman with diabetes who wishes to become pregnant should consult her health-care team and have a thorough diabetes check-up beforehand. She should also regularly monitor her blood glucose levels during pregnancy as insulin requirements to achieve good diabetes control are likely to change as the pregnancy progresses. For example, insulin needs tend to drop in the first three months because the baby is using the mother's glucose, whereas in the third month insulin requirements increase because hormones secreted by the placenta interfere with its action (Canadian Diabetes Association, 1995a).

There is no reason why a mother with diabetes should not breastfeed her baby, as long as her diet and insulin are adjusted to meet her nutritional needs.

If the mother or father has Type II diabetes, the baby has around a 50 per cent chance of inheriting a tendency to develop diabetes. In Type I diabetes, heredity is less of a factor. A gene is required from both parents to develop Type I diabetes. About 5–6 per cent of children with a parent with Type I diabetes develop the tendency to become diabetic. If both parents have diabetes, the risk of their children developing diabetes at some time in their lives is 25–30 per cent.

Healthy lifestyle

A healthy lifestyle is important for everyone and many of the following recommendations which are made for people with diabetes should be heeded by all of us. Careful adherence to all aspects of routine and lifestyle can do a great deal to maintain good health and to minimise side effects. Particularly important are:

- following a healthy, balanced meal plan and eating a varied and healthy diet, with low fat, low added sugar and high fibre content;

- eating regular meals which are evenly spaced throughout the day;
- not skipping or delaying meals;
- having regular exercise;
- achieving and maintaining a weight which is in normal limits for one's height;
- taking insulin and/or oral antidiabetic tablets as prescribed;
- a regular review of diabetes control to ensure strategies are effective;
- regular monitoring and maintenance of good blood glucose levels;
- not smoking;
- drinking alcohol in moderation and only when diabetes is well controlled;
- having blood pressure checked regularly and treating hypertension if necessary;
- having eyes checked every year by a specialist;
- having urine checked every year for protein;
- examining feet regularly for signs of broken skin or infection;
- minimising the effects of stress.

Family

Diagnosis of diabetes can result in major changes in routine for the child and family. Diagnosis may be met with feelings of relief when parents learn that their child's health will improve and that diabetes can be controlled. Sometimes the parents may blame themselves for their child's diabetes and its effect on family and everyday living. They also may feel guilt over high or low blood sugar levels which are not always predictable or preventable (Anderson, Henderson & Whittaker, 1995).

Parents will have the added responsibility for diabetes control and for monitoring if a young child is affected. Anderson, Henderson and Whittaker (1995) give useful advice for parents of a young child with diabetes. These include dealing with a finicky eater, testing and injecting, and dealing with low blood sugar levels. Initially, changes may seem to be overwhelming but, with the assistance of a competent health care team, limitations can be minimised and it will be unnecessary to prepare 'special' foods. However, this may mean that changes in eating habits occur for everyone in the family.

Initially, some parents dread giving injections and may overcompensate by showering the child with presents. These reactions can increase dependency in the child and can lead to high levels of stress within the family as a whole.

Siblings may resent the changes and the extra attention that their brother or sister is receiving. Parents may become overwatchful and overprotective, ever mindful of their constant fear of hypogylcaemia. The issues of diet and injections can sometimes be used as a source of conflict between parents and child. Some of this conflict can be avoided if the child sees the parent as someone who is helping him or her stay healthy rather than as someone who is always 'checking up' on how well the condition is being managed.

In time most parents and children adapt to changes in routine and get used to them. In most cases, a child with well-managed diabetes can maintain good health, do well at school and participate in sports.

Community living

> *Everyone else took it lightly, everybody said: 'Get on with it, you have to go back to work'. . . . At work they wouldn't let me have time off to go to the clinic.*
>
> Trocher (1995, p. 24)

Diabetes in most people is an invisible disability. Therefore, other people tend to underestimate its effects on lifestyle and the importance of the person adhering to routines and eating plans. Others may think the person is being unreasonable by refusing food which has been offered. It is the responsibility of the person with diabetes to inform others of his or her needs. It also is the responsibility of others to respect these needs. Diabetes organisations such as Diabetes Australia have published pamphlets to assist in preparing meals for guests who have diabetes. Such publications assist the person with diabetes in explaining his or her requirements to friends and also help the host to ensure that guests have an enjoyable meal.

Education

People with well-managed diabetes participate in mainstream education. However, it is important that teachers are aware when they have a pupil with diabetes and know what to do in a case of hypoglycaemia (low blood sugar) or hyperglycaemia (high blood sugar). It is also important for teachers to know what to do in case of illness and when to contact the parents. Children with diabetes should be encouraged to participate in as many school activities as they choose. They should not be excluded from school excursions. For those who wish to participate in vigorous physical activity, good planning is important to ensure that the blood sugar balance is maintained.

Diabetes education forms an important part of treating and controlling the disease and of avoiding complications for both adults and children. Diabetes associations and diabetic education centres play important roles in conveying knowledge and in teaching strategies for effective management.

Employment

A wide range of employment is possible; however, it is important to select a job which will not unduly affect diabetes management. For this reason, jobs involving shift work, high levels of stress, or heavy work need to be carefully considered. Advice on additional precautions and strategies is essential so that a successful career may be combined with good diabetes management.

People with diabetes should avoid activities where sudden unconsciousness could result in injury or death (for example, climbing high ladders or sports such as hang-gliding or abseiling). Airline pilots, drivers of passenger vehicles, firefighters and divers who require insulin will probably not be able to continue in their current occupation.

PERSON TO PERSON

Appropriate language and behaviour

As diabetes is an invisible disability, other people may not be aware of the effects it has on the person's lifestyle. Even though they may be aware of dietary requirements and the need for regular meals, others may underestimate the importance of these and may believe that there is no harm in occasionally breaking rules. This can make it very difficult for the person with diabetes who does not want to offend a friend by refusing to eat inappropriate food or who is unable to delay his or her meal until other people feel ready to eat.

Table 7.1: Strategies for successful interaction

Person with diabetes	Other person
Explain to others about your diabetes, including its symptoms, and what steps to take in case of hypoglycaemia. Also explain dietary requirements. Wear a disc that notifies others that you have diabetes and which gives instructions on what to do in case of an emergency.	Learn what to do in case of hypoglycaemia. Remember and respect any special needs. Even though the disability is invisible, do not forget that the person with diabetes may need special consideration. On the other hand, do not treat the person like an invalid. He or she is likely to be well and healthy.

It is important for people who know someone with diabetes to learn about the symptoms of hypoglycaemia and about steps which can be taken to assist the person if necessary. It is also important to know that some people with diabetes are unaware during an episode that they need attention and may have difficulty in stating their needs.

Special note should be taken of dietary requirements, however it should be remembered that in most ways the person with diabetes is no different from anyone else. 'Kid glove' treatment should be avoided as should attempts to restrict the person's independence. Such behaviour is demeaning and irritating for the person with diabetes. It is essential for self-esteem and feelings of capability that the person be able to strive and to achieve in ways open to others.

My husband has had to learn about diabetes. He knows what to do if I have a hypo. He has been very supportive.

Sarah

MORE INFORMATION ABOUT DIABETES MELLITUS

Definition

Type I diabetes results from the failure of the pancreas to produce insulin – the reasons for this are not fully understood. The pancreas is a gland situated on the posterior wall of the upper part of the abdomen. It is in close relation to the upper part of the abdomen (duodenum) and lies behind the stomach. The pancreas also is responsible for producing secretions which aid digestion. These are known as pancreatic enzymes and enter the duodenum via the pancreatic duct. Insulin is a hormone produced by the beta cells in the islets of Langerhans in the pancreas and is required to allow glucose to move into cells where it is turned into energy. It is secreted directly into the blood.

According to the World Health Organization (1980) definition:

- *Impairment* in Type I diabetes mellitus is associated with the failure of the pancreas to produce insulin and in Type II is associated with the inability of body tissues to use glucose effectively.
- *Disability* reflects damage which can occur to body organs if the diabetes is not kept under control, including blindness, neuropathy (nerve damage) and kidney failure.
- *Handicap* reflects the limitations on lifestyle that result from disabilities associated with poor control of blood glucose levels.

Poor control of blood glucose levels can result in hyperglycaemia and hypoglycaemia.

Hyperglycaemia results when the blood glucose level is high. Symptoms include tiredness, thirst, passage of large quantities of urine, dehydration, general feelings of being unwell and blurred vision. Hyperglycaemia can result from too low doses of insulin or tablets, insufficient exercise, too much sugary food or carbohydrates, being overweight, stress, acute infections, trauma, and taking some medications (for example, cortisone).

Hypoglycaemia develops if blood glucose levels become too low. Symptoms may include trembling, sweating, weakness, headaches, fatigue, palpitations, pallor, tingling in the body and blurred vision. If not treated immediately, the person becomes confused with slurred speech, drowsiness and behaviour changes such as irritability, crying and staggering as if drunk. In more severe cases, unconsciousness (insulin coma) develops. Hypogylcaemia can result from missed meals, extra activity without additional carbohydrates, excessive alcohol intake and errors in insulin dosage (Cohen, 1986). Glucagon is regarded as the best treatment for severe low blood sugar levels if the person is conscious and able to swallow. It is a hormone that works in opposition to insulin. It is recommended that people with diabetes carry a glucagon emergency kit and make sure that friends and family know how to use it. Most people also carry jelly beans or a high sugar sweet for less severe cases of low blood sugar. 'Hypos' are rapid in onset and, once treatment is given, symptoms generally disappear in about five minutes.

Table 7.2 summarises behaviours which can be taken to avoid hyperglycaemia and hypoglycaemia. It also outlines action to be taken by others in the case of either condition arising.

Causes

It is believed that Type I is associated with an inherited susceptibility which is triggered by external factors such as viral infections. Diabetes Australia (1988) explains that the disease process involves immunological damage to the insulin-secreting cells which may continue for years before diabetes becomes evident. Stopford (1988) states that if one child already has Type I diabetes, the risk to siblings is about one in 13. If one parent has Type I diabetes, the risk to the child is one in 50. If both parents are affected, the risk to the child is one in eight.

In Type II (NIDDM), onset is influenced by a number of risk factors. These are grouped into modifiable and non-modifiable factors. Age and family history are non-modifiable factors, while lifestyle factors such as diet, obesity, lack of physical activity and stress are modifiable. Diabetes also may be associated with a drop in the efficiency of insulin caused by certain drugs and disorders. It is not caused by eating too much sugar, but poor eating habits and excess weight are common causes.

Table 7.2: Steps to avoid hyperglycaemia and hypoglycaemia

Prevention	
Hyperglycaemia	**Hypoglycaemia**
Work with your health care team to establish a reasonable balance between food, exercise and medication. Maintain a normal body weight. Monitor blood sugar levels regularly. Maintain a regular exercise regimen. Be aware of the effects that medications such as cortisone can have on blood glucose levels. Learn how to adjust the dose of insulin or tablets on sick days if necessary. Avoid too much sugar and carbohydrates in food.	Take the correct dose of insulin or tablets every day. Never miss meals or snacks, eat on time and consume all the recommended food. Drink only minimal alcohol. If it is being consumed, eat some extra carbohydrate food to reduce the risk of a 'hypo'. Be aware of symptoms. Carry some quickly-absorbed sugar and eat it at the first sign of a 'hypo'. If you have a stomach upset, take your insulin, sip sugary fluids and consult your doctor. Monitor blood glucose levels regularly.

Treatment

For both hyperglycaemia and hypoglycaemia
Explain to relatives, friends, workmates and teachers so that they will know how to help.

Hypoglycaemia
What to do if someone is in a diabetic coma.

- Never give fluids to an unconscious person.
- Lie the person on his or her side.
- Call a doctor or ambulance.
- Give an injection of one unit (1 mg) of glucagon. Every person with diabetes who uses insulin should discuss this with his or her doctor and family members should be prepared.
- When the person wakes, give sugar followed by carbohydrate food.

As mentioned in the section titled 'Being a parent', some women develop gestational diabetes during pregnancy.

Incidence and prevalence

It is estimated that round 3 per cent of the population in Australia are affected by diabetes at any one time (Diabetes Australia, 1988). Estimates for the United Kingdom and United States are around 2 per cent of the population (Stopford, 1988; Garner, 1981). In the United States, 2 569 000 people have diabetes. The vast majority of these people were reported as not experiencing complications (LaPlante & Carlson, 1996). In Canada, around one million people (3 per cent of the population) are living with diabetes (Pettit-Crossman, 1994). Many of these people are undiagnosed.

The prevalence of Type I (IDDM) in children under five years of age is estimated at one per 10 000. This figure rises to six per 10 000 for children aged between five and nine years, ten per 10 000 for those aged between ten and 14 years and 15 per 10 000 for those aged between 15 and 19 years (Diabetes Australia, 1988). Type I accounts for around 15 per cent of all people with diabetes.

Type II (NIDDM) is far more common than IDDM and tends to occur in people aged over 40 years. In the United Kingdom, about one in 130 people have NIDDM and know about it, another one in 100 have it without realising (Hillson, 1992).

Age. Mature onset diabetes (Type II or NIDDM) is the form most likely to go unnoticed and is sometimes called the 'silent killer'. It is regarded as a disease associated with the ageing process and old age, and the risk of developing Type II increases with age. About 13 per cent of people over 65 years of age are affected.

Race. Diabetes is more common in some racial groups. For example, in some Australian Aboriginal communities, the rate of Type II is six times higher than that in the general population. It also is more common among people who are Chinese, South-East Asian, Pacific Islander, New Zealand Maori, Middle Eastern, African or who are of Caribbean origin.

Diagnosis

Typical symptoms are excessive thirst, frequent passing of urine, weight loss, tiredness, skin and genital infections. Dehydration and diabetic coma may be features of acute cases. In older people, there may be no symptoms and diagnosis is made in the course of a routine health check. The symptoms of diabetes mellitus are summarised in Table 7.3. Urgent medical attention should be sought if symptoms are recognised. Untreated diabetes can result in disability, and, in severe cases, death.

The following tests are used to diagnose diabetes (details of techniques for monitoring the ongoing effectiveness of control are outlined later in the chapter in the section titled 'Ongoing monitoring').

- Testing blood for elevated sugar glucose levels.
- Testing urine. Urinalysis is used as an inexpensive screening test, but is not sufficiently precise to be used alone. It tests the level of glucose in the urine as an indicator of high blood glucose levels. Some (usually older) people with

Table 7.3: Signs and symptoms of diabetes

Type I **Insulin-dependent diabetes**	**Type II** **Non-insulin-dependent diabetes**

Abnormal thirst.
Excessive urination.
Rapid loss of weight, despite
   unusual hunger.
Irritability.
Weakness and fatigue.
   Skin infections and slow healing.
Nausea and vomiting.
	May include Type I symptoms plus:
	   Family history of diabetes.
	   Easy fatigue.
	   Excessive weight.
	   Blurred vision.
	   Tingling, numbness in feet.

diabetes show no sign of glucose in the urine, even though levels in the blood may be elevated. For this reason, urine testing is not recommended.
- The islet-cell antibody test – a new technique that involves testing for immune system antibodies. It is believed that these antibodies react against the insulin-secreting beta cells of the pancreas as if they were foreign. The test can be used to identify people likely to develop Type I diabetes before symptoms occur. Evidence emerging from the use of this test indicates that Type I develops over a period of several years, even though symptoms tend to come on suddenly. Thus, the test provides an early warning system before blood glucose levels start to rise (Brackenridge & Dolinar, 1993, Colman, 1989).

Associated impairment and disability

Cardiovascular problems are most likely to occur in long-standing and inadequately-controlled diabetes. Persistently raised blood glucose levels result in damage to and narrowing of the blood vessels. This damage is exaggerated by smoking. Hypertension results from reduced blood flow, predisposing the person to coronary artery disease and insufficient blood supply to the lower limbs. Pain may be experienced in the legs on exertion. Burns, cuts and minor injuries may be slow to heal and readily become infected. This can lead to gangrene and amputation. Complications associated with diabetes are the cause of half of all amputations.

Retinopathy (damage to the blood vessels in the eyes, making them weak and resulting in fluid leakage into the back of the eye – see Chapter 16) can also result from diabetes. This can be treated with laser beam treatment (photocoagulation) if detected early. Another form of treatment is vitrectomy, where the damaged part of the eye is removed and replaced with artificial material. One-third of people with diabetes have retinopathy and in one-third of cases it is vision-threatening (Royal Australian College of General Practitioners, 1989). Refractive errors can result from alteration in the lens shape owing to changes in blood glucose concentrations, and leading to blurred vision. Premature cataracts can occur in people with diabetes and result in blurred vision and intolerance of glare. Regular eye checkups are important for early detection and treatment. Diabetes is the cause of 15 per cent of all blindness. It is the leading cause of blindness in the United States. However, most people with diabetes do not become blind. It is believed that good control of blood glucose and blood pressure can prevent diabetic retinopathy.

Neuropathy or nerve damage is one of the most debilitating complications of diabetes. It results partly from damage to nerves by high blood glucose levels and partly from damage to the small blood vessels nourishing the nerves. There are two main types of neuropathy. Peripheral neuropathy is more common and affects peripheral nerves which control the sense of feeling and muscle movement. It can affect sensation, temperature discrimination, and feelings of pain, especially in the feet and limbs. Thus, people with diabetes must take special care with their feet and should consult a podiatrist (or chiropodist) for treatment of corns, calluses, ingrown toenails and other conditions. Nerve pain, tingling, numbness and burning sensations in the feet and hands may be the first warning of diabetes. The other type of neuropathy affects autonomic nerves which control the autonomic function of the heart, other organs and glands. If undetected, neuropathy can result in sexual impotence, difficulties with bladder and bowel control and loss of muscle power.

Nephropathy or kidney disease may occur because of damage to the small blood vessels of the kidneys. Such damage results from long-term high blood glucose levels and is more common in Type I diabetes. Damage prevents the kidney from working properly. Waste products are not removed and remain in the blood to act as poisons. Also, important blood nutrients (such as protein) can be lost in the urine. High blood pressure may exacerbate the condition.

Regular checks and control of hypertension (high blood pressure) form an important part of treatment of diabetes to lower risk factors for retinopathy, kidney disease and cardiovascular disease (Royal Australian College of General Practitioners, 1989).

Treatment

Diabetes is a disease which has been known for thousands of years; however, effective treatment has only been possible since 1921. Previously, people wasted away and died. Before insulin was available, diagnosis of Type I diabetes mellitus meant death in six months to two years. With the discovery and availability of insulin, diabetes is no longer necessarily fatal. The aim of treatment is to enable the person to live an active life, to be free of episodes of high and low blood glucose levels which can lead to hospitalisation, to avoid long-term complications and to enable children to achieve healthy growth and development.

Type I diabetes is treated with a combination of diet, exercise and insulin injections which are administered at regular times during the day. The traditional method of giving insulin is by using a syringe. A newer method is to use a pen injector. There are different regimens to suit the needs of the individual.

I cope quite well now and the regimen I have chosen means that I give myself four injections every day. Some people choose to inject their insulin once or twice a day, but this usually means that they must eat at set times. I chose my regimen because it gives me more flexibility in my daily routine. I give myself one injection of long-acting insulin every night and then I inject short-acting insulin half an hour before each meal during the day.

Sarah

Type II is treated either with diet and exercise alone, or with a combination of diet, exercise and medication taken in the form of tablets. Diet is important to control both weight and blood glucose levels. Insulin does not work as effectively when the person is overweight. Many people who are diagnosed with diabetes in middle or late life can reduce blood glucose levels by diet and exercise alone. A healthy diet should be high in fibre and low in fat, with adequate amounts of complex carbohydrates and protein. Tablets do not contain insulin and only work when the body is producing some insulin. They do not replace the benefit of healthy eating and exercise.

Ongoing monitoring

An important part of treatment and control is regular medical monitoring in which the doctor checks the eyes, blood pressure, feet, weight, height and injection sites. In addition, the person must conduct regular checks of blood glucose levels. Blood testing has taken over from urinalysis as the most popular method.

Urine testing is still used to monitor levels of ketones in people treated with insulin. Ketones are formed from fat when the body cannot use sugar to produce energy. Testing for ketones is particularly important during pregnancy and for people with insulin-treated diabetes who are ill or who have high blood glucose levels. Checking for ketones takes only a few seconds. A dipstick is passed through the urine stream and compared to a ketone colour chart. This shows how many ketones are present. Presence of ketones indicates a need for extra insulin.

Blood glucose testing is carried out by pricking the finger (using an automatic finger pricker) and placing a drop of blood onto a test strip. The change in colour of the test strip indicates the level of sugar in the blood. Pocket-sized machines called glucometers are available to test the strip electronically. These give a digital readout of the blood sugar level.

Urine testing provides an indirect, approximate measure of blood sugar. It is not as accurate as blood glucose tests. A dipstick is passed through the urine stream and is then compared to a colour chart to estimate the amount of sugar present.

Monitoring is important to check that blood glucose levels are within normal limits. Deviation from this range can have severe consequences. For this reason, national diabetes associations implement major education programs which are designed to provide the person with more information about how to properly manage diabetes. Figure 7.1 summarises the effects of insulin on glucose and fat metabolism.

It is generally recommended that a blood glucose monitor be used to test blood glucose levels before meals and at bed time. Such regular checks show the pattern of blood glucose control. Patterns tell more than a single test value which gives a snapshot picture of the blood glucose level at a particular point in a day.

The glycosylated haemoglobin test can be used to look at blood glucose levels over several weeks. This test looks at the amount of glucose coating on red blood cells and helps reveal the overall effectiveness of diabetes control. It tells the average blood glucose level for the past two or three months. This test cannot be self-administered and a sample of blood must be analysed in a laboratory.

Services and supports

People with diabetes are now actively involved in their own care. A team of professionals works to assist them. The local general medical practitioner arranges

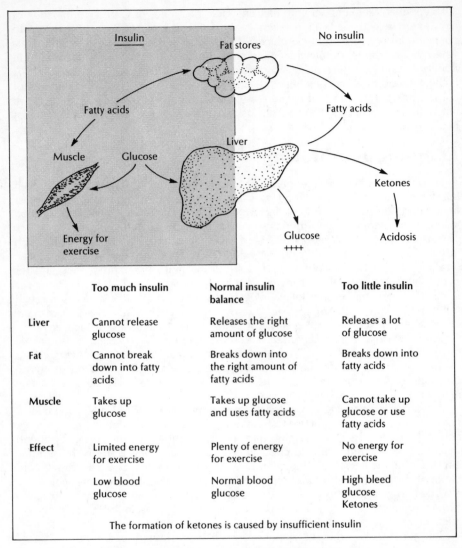

The following labels appear in the diagram:

Insulin — Fat stores — No insulin
Fatty acids — Fatty acids
Muscle — Glucose — Liver — Ketones
Energy for exercise — Glucose ++++ — Acidosis

	Too much insulin	Normal insulin balance	Too little insulin
Liver	Cannot release glucose	Releases the right amount of glucose	Releases a lot of glucose
Fat	Cannot break down into fatty acids	Breaks down into the right amount of fatty acids	Breaks down into fatty acids
Muscle	Takes up glucose	Takes up glucose and uses fatty acids	Cannot take up glucose or use fatty acids
Effect	Limited energy for exercise	Plenty of energy for exercise	No energy for exercise
	Low blood glucose	Normal blood glucose	High bleed glucose Ketones

The formation of ketones is caused by insufficient insulin

Figure 7.1: Insulin in glucose and fat metabolism

Reproduced with permission from Hillson R. (1987). Diabetes: A beyond basics guide. *London: McDonald & Co.*

for initial diagnosis and supervises ongoing care and treatment. A dietitian should advise on healthy eating patterns. A diabetes educator has the job of helping the person to learn how to control his or her diabetes. Educators usually are nurses or dietitians who are specially trained in both diabetes and teaching. They teach about insulin, what to eat, care for the feet, and other day-to-day strategies for healthy living. A podiatrist may be consulted to assist with foot problems.

Equipment

People with diabetes use a range of equipment to assist with management. Their needs include blood glucose meters, test strips, syringes, and appropriate footwear.

Additional costs

As said above, a range of equipment and prescription drugs are required on a daily basis. Not all of these are covered by medical insurance or by government subsidies. It is important to be aware of subsidies available locally.

RESOURCE ORGANISATIONS

All care has been taken to ensure that all information is correct at the time of publishing. However, responsibility for the accuracy of this information is not accepted by the writer. The list of resource organisations contained in this chapter is not intended to be exhaustive, and provides national organisations only. The reader is referred to local community directories for further information and for local branches of national organisations. Inclusion of services and organisations should not be taken as a recommendation.

Australia

Diabetes Australia
5/9 Phipps Place
Deakin ACT 2600
Ph 06 285 3277
Fax 06 285 2881

Juvenile Diabetes Foundation of Australia
PO Box 1500
Chatswood NSW 2067

Canada

Juvenile Diabetes Foundation Canada
89 Granton Drive
Richmond Hill, ON L4B 2N5
Ph 1 800 668 0274 or 905 889 4171
Fax 905 889 4209

The Canadian Diabetes Association
Suite 1001, 15 Toronto Street
Toronto, ON M5C 2E3
Ph 416 363 3373
Fax 416 363 3393

New Zealand

Diabetes New Zealand
PO Box 54
Oamaru NZ
Tel (03) 434 8110
Fax (03) 434 5281

United Kingdom

British Diabetic Association
10 Queen Anne Street
London W1M 0BD

United States

The American Diabetes Association
National Centre
PO Box 25757
1660 Duke Street
Alexandria, VA 22314
Ph 703 549 1500
Fax 703 549 6995

FURTHER READING

Anderson, K., Henderson, G. & Whittaker, C. (1995). No small task. *Diabetes Dialogue*, 42 (3), 6–13.

Brackenridge, B. P. & Dolinar, R. O. (1993). *Diabetes 101: a pure and simple guide for people who use insulin*. Minneapolis: Chronimed Publishing, PO Box 47945, Minneapolis, MN 55447–9727.

Canadian Diabetes Association. (1994–95). (A series of booklets about living with diabetes.) 15 Toronto Street, Toronto, ON M5C 2E3.

Hillson, R. (1992). *Diabetes: a new guide.* London: Optima.

Little, M. (1991). *Diabetes.* New York: Chelsea House Publishers.

Pettit-Crossman, S. (1994). Diabetes and nutrition. *Abilities,* Fall issue, 28–31.

Royal Australian College of General Practitioners (1989). *A guide to the management of diabetes in general practice.* Canberra.

Trocher, M. (1995). The road to wellness. *Diabetes Dialogue,* 43 (2), 23–6.

CHAPTER 8
EPILEPSY

Epilepsy is a hidden disability which is associated with stigma and fear in our society. There are several types of epilepsy, each having different implications for the individual. Additional factors which influence the impact of epilepsy include age of onset, severity, type of seizures and the forms of treatment which are being used. For most people, epilepsy is an episodic disorder and it is those recurring 'odd moments' that influence their lifestyle. For some people, seizures occur only during sleep and so have little effect on daily life, but for others epilepsy requires major modifications to lifestyle. Each person is unique and one cannot apply a strict set of characteristics to individuals with epilepsy.

There are many misconceptions about epilepsy. It is not a disease or an illness. People with epilepsy do not necessarily have brain damage nor an intellectual disability. They are not violent or crazy (Devinsky, 1994).

Epilepsy is a condition associated with recurrent and sudden discharges of impulses from nerve cells in the brain (seizures) that cause a change in how a person feels, senses things or behaves. These discharges can be detected by recording the electrical activity within the brain (electroencephalography or EEG) which shows that different types of seizure reflect the different sites of cells in which discharges begin, and the way in which they spread. Seizures may be the result of an inherited tendency, a brain injury, or the cause may be unknown (Devinsky, 1994).

Epilepsy is often referred to as 'a storm in the brain' . . . Storms blow up frequently, often without warning . . . There's a pattern to the storms, with similar things happening each time, yet even this may change with time . . . frequent storms present difficulties and tensions but they're only one aspect of the way you live, once you're used to it and understand what's happening, you're NOT FRIGHTENED.

Yanko (1992)

Seizures can be associated with many effects, including physical sensations like tingling in the fingers which may gradually extend up the arm, or a strange taste or smell, ringing in the ears, temporary loss of awareness, and convulsions. For some, an aura is recognised as the first stage of a seizure and these people may be able to take action to prevent a seizure. Sometimes, resting or relaxation techniques may be effective.

There are two major types of seizure:

- A *generalised* seizure involves widespread excessive electrical activity which involves both cerebral hemispheres from the outset and is associated with loss of consciousness. These convulsive seizures involve the body's entire network of muscles and motor activities. For example, in a generalised tonic–clonic seizure, the person may fall to the ground, go stiff and then jerk his or her limbs.

121

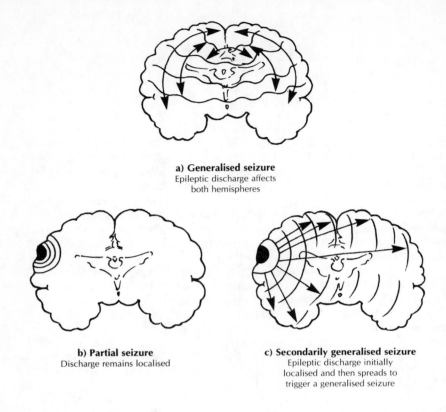

a) Generalised seizure
Epileptic discharge affects
both hemispheres

b) Partial seizure
Discharge remains localised

c) Secondarily generalised seizure
Epileptic discharge initially
localised and then spreads to
trigger a generalised seizure

Figure 8.1: Diagrammatic representation of electrical discharges

Sometimes the person may cry out before going stiff (this results from muscle tightening which pushes air out of the body). Loss of bladder or bowel control may occur. Some people vomit, others may go blue in the face. Other types of generalised seizures are mentioned in Table 8.3 (see later in the chapter).

- A *partial* seizure starts in one cerebral hemisphere and remains there. In some cases, partial seizures may spread to the other side and become what is termed *secondarily generalised*.

These two forms of epilepsy differ in their diagnostic tests and in appropriate medications used to treat them.

LIVING WITH EPILEPSY

While epilepsy is a disorder of brain functioning, it does not mean that the person is intellectually impaired. The range of intelligence for people with epilepsy reflects that for the general population. Intellectual impairment may result from epilepsy associated with extensive damage to the brain or from birth trauma which causes intellectual impairment and disability.

In most cases, seizures can be reduced with medication, adequate rest and a healthy lifestyle. For some people, seizures may be triggered by certain stimuli and they can take steps to reduce the likelihood of a seizure. It is important for these people to become aware of triggers and to take steps to reduce the possibility of encountering them. This may mean avoiding flashing lights or noisy environments. Adequate rest and moderate alcohol intake are also important. A woman for whom seizures are linked with menstruation can take precautions at the appropriate time.

Personal adjustment

Most people with epilepsy deal very well with their disability: They do not regard it as a disability and it does not restrict them from leading very full and satisfying lives. However, having an 'invisible' or 'hidden' disability can create dilemmas associated with self-disclosure versus concealment. Historical myths about epilepsy have resulted in stigma and misunderstanding, making many people with epilepsy reluctant to disclose it. Most people with epilepsy can move around in the community without having their disability detected. By not disclosing his or her epilepsy, a person is able to avoid community attitudes associated with having a disability. However, if others unexpectedly discover that the person has epilepsy, they may feel resentment, anger and mistrust.

West (1986, cited in Buchanan, 1994) identifies three patterns of behaviour in regard to concealment. These stages have similarities with those outlined by Robinson (1988) and discussed in Chapter 1.

- *Successful concealment* where the person and family make sure that epilepsy remains unknown to most other people.
- *Failed concealment* where the person and family remain committed to concealment, even though others have become aware of the epilepsy (perhaps because the person has had a seizure).
- *Disclosure* where the person and the family are open about epilepsy from the start.

Stigma and misinformation in the general population affect the way the person with epilepsy feels about his or her disability. Brown (1993) argues that young people with epilepsy report feeling embarrassed and reluctant to disclose their epilepsy to others, resulting in them leading a double life.

> *They run the other way and they also think you're contagious. It makes me want to cry because I've lost so many good friends.*
>
> 18-year-old woman quoted by Brown (1993)

Disclosure may be argued to be the most adaptive strategy in that it avoids feelings of living a double life, removes the need to spend time and effort in maintaining the deception and reduces the likelihood of failing to come to terms with the presence of disability.

Mittan (1988) summarises fears reported by many people with epilepsy in regard to their seizures. Common fears are the fear of injury, fear of what happens during and after a seizure (what I do and how others react), fear of losing something during a seizure (for example, that a temporary paralysis may become permanent) and fear of death. For those few people unable to predict when a seizure will occur, feelings of helplessness and vulnerability may arise because they are never sure when the next seizure will occur. These reactions, together with rejection resulting from being left out of school, social and sporting activities, can damage self-image and feelings of worth.

The problem is you never know when the next one will strike and there's this feeling that it will happen at the wrong time in the wrong place.

19-year-old man quoted by Brown (1993)

Lack of confidence, together with conflict about whether to disclose the presence of disability can create uncertainty and ambivalence about social relationships. Changes in behaviour on the part of other people who have unexpectedly experienced a seizure or 'found out' about the undisclosed disability can cause guilt, cynicism and resentment in the person with epilepsy.

Onset of epilepsy during adolescence can have many implications for the teenager who is seeking greater independence and establishing a sense of self-identity. Overprotection is a common reaction on the part of parents, and teachers may be too lenient, encouraging a belief in the teenager that he or she deserves special attention. Adolescence is often a time of questioning and rebellion. This may be a factor in the regularity in which medications are taken. The teenager may feel angry and resentful about having epilepsy. Not taking the medications may be a way of pretending that epilepsy does not exist. For an adolescent, the social and psychological milestones of maturity and independence represented by a driver's licence and owning a car may be denied.

A person may have to rely on public transport or family and friends to get around. It can be frustrating and limiting for an adult to forfeit a driver's licence because of the onset of seizures. Depending on local regulations, a person may need to be seizure-free during the daytime for a period of up to two years before being eligible for a licence.

Occurrences which are commonplace in other people's lives can have major consequences for someone with epilepsy. One drink too many, a busy day at work, or a late-night party may be enough to trigger a seizure. However, people with epilepsy are able to do (and do) most of the things that others can. The guide for all of us is: everything in moderation and avoid excess.

Sexuality

Epilepsy does not directly affect sexual functioning or reproduction. However, a person with epilepsy may have experienced rejection when he or she has mentioned the disability to a potential partner. If the person is not open about having epilepsy, this may create the fear of letting another person come close enough to, perhaps, discover the secret. Even when a person is not trying to hide the disability, it is hard to know when and how to mention it.

A relationship may not develop smoothly if the partner does not understand about epilepsy. The partner may be embarrassed or frightened by a major seizure. On the other hand, simple absence seizures might look as though the person has lost interest or is not paying attention.

My partners get rather offended if I 'forget' an important piece of information or if I'm not paying attention at an intimate moment.

Jeff

Being a parent

Many issues arise in regard to having children. Many are concerned about the possibility of handing epilepsy on to the child. If one or both parents have epilepsy, the risk of handing it on to their children is five times higher than in the general population; however, if the parents' epilepsy is acquired, there is no risk of handing it on. The following summary comes from Buchanan (1994).

Approximately one-third of women with epilepsy will show no change in seizure control during pregnancy, one-third will show an improvement and one-third will show some deterioration (usually in the first three months of pregnancy).

There is evidence that antiepileptic medication can affect the fetus. Most abnormalities are minor (for example, broad bridge of the nose and tapered fingers), however some are severe (for example, heart defects, cleft palate, spina bifida and mild intellectual disability). It is generally regarded that the risks of stopping treatment are greater than the risk of defects to the infant.

Antiepileptic medications taken by the mother during pregnancy may have some effect on the baby immediately after birth as they are transmitted across the placenta. Possible effects include drowsiness and a mild tendency towards bleeding which responds to Vitamin K (Buchanan, 1994). Some infants may show a withdrawal reaction to the medication, including irritability, jitteriness and poor sucking. These features are not common, nor are they generally regarded as serious.

Antiepileptic medications appear in breast milk, but do not have major effects on the baby. There is no reason why a mother with epilepsy should not breastfeed, if she wishes to.

Family

Seizures can be very frightening to observe, especially if they occur in early childhood. Parents may become overprotective, fearing that the child may have a seizure while away from home. Parents are likely to have many questions: Will the child grow out of the seizures? Is the child likely to get hurt or to be in danger? Many parents worry that epilepsy is associated with intellectual impairment. This does not necessarily follow.

> *My early memories are of double vision, seeing the world from a cot. My mother was afraid of me having fits when out of sight, of falling down back steps. I was forever being pulled back from edges of cliffs, long before it was necessary.*
>
> Eleanor, who has had epilepsy since early childhood

Onset of epilepsy in adulthood is likely to result in changes in lifestyle and family relationships.

> *It has made a difference to my life. I was married with two boys, but I think that it probably would have been a pretty hard thing for my wife to take and we finished up getting divorced. She took the two boys with her. I still see them, but the hardest thing was the splitting up of the home and how it affected the boys.*
>
> Richard

Community living

> *Prejudice is like a social Exocet missile, a long range destroyer of self-esteem.*
>
> Taylor (1987)

Many people with epilepsy feel discriminated against; however the extent of stigma and prejudice is somewhat controversial. Buchanan (1994) argues that levels of public intolerance and ignorance are not as high as many people claim. Rather, he argues, indifference seems more common in modern society. He also states somewhat controversially that the stigma perceived by people with epilepsy and their families is actually more severe than real stigma. Certainly, real stigma does occur, but he argues that the common strategy of hiding the disability disrupts peoples' lives and that the fear of being stigmatised is actually greater in its effects than is real stigma. Many people, however, do not regard their epilepsy as a disability and do not let any associated stigma interfere with their lives.

Nevertheless, unexpectedly witnessing a seizure can be frightening and can reinforce community views that people with epilepsy are dangerous and violent. Many members of the general public are not aware that there are many forms of epilepsy. Most are only aware of the tonic–clonic form.

Access

Issues concerning access often relate to other people's attitudes. Fears and mis-understandings about epilepsy often make it difficult to obtain satisfying employment or to join in community life.

Education

Most children with epilepsy attend mainstream schools. Epilepsy is related to deficits in intellectual functioning in only a few cases; however, learning ability may be affected by the condition and by the medication taken to control seizures. Learning difficulties may be associated with specific types of epilepsy. Concentration may be a problem for people with absence seizures, whereas memory and recall difficulties may occur with some forms of partial seizures. A child who has absence seizures several times a day may have difficulty with schoolwork. Important details in both formal teaching and class interaction are missed. The teacher may interpret the 'absences' as deliberate inattention or disobedience.

> *She had a lot of ridicule at school. Her absences were not visible to anybody else, but she would miss part of a conversation and come back to make an irrelevant remark. People would laugh at her and call her stupid.*
>
> Anne's mother

Seizure control through medication should enable the child to participate fully in school life. However, parents should discuss their child's epilepsy with the school and with teachers. An explanation to classmates about epilepsy is important in developing an accepting attitude among the child's peers.

> *If I've any objections to my schooling it is that teachers and pupils weren't educated to know how to treat epilepsy – some panicked or felt threatened. When my academic work suffered, I was treated as if I wasn't trying, rather than that I had problems.*
>
> Joe

Employment

Negative attitudes of employers raise major difficulties. For example, it is widely believed that people with epilepsy are unreliable, unpredictable, volatile and are dangerous in jobs such as those involving the operation of machinery. This is not so: people with epilepsy show the same range of personality characteristics as others. Organisations representing people with epilepsy are doing much to address these myths. Nevertheless, some high-risk occupations may be inadvisable. Many companies include questions on job application forms about whether a person has any impairments. Disclosure of epilepsy can mean that the person is denied the chance of attending an interview. Failure to disclose such information can make the person feel dishonest and opens up the possibility of dismissal if the disability is discovered. Thus, when applying for a job, a person with epilepsy is encouraged to be honest and positive about disability. It should be noted that many countries have legislation such as Australia's *Disability Discrimination Act 1992* which makes illegal the failure to interview a person on the grounds of their disability. If a person with epilepsy believes that he or she has been discriminated against in this way, there are formal mechanisms to lay a complaint through the Human Rights Commission.

> *She is finding it difficult to get a job, even though she is qualified, because at least 90 per cent of the advertised welfare worker jobs require applicants to hold a driver's licence. The other 10 per cent have shift work or travelling which are problems for her because she needs ten hours sleep each night because of her medication.*
>
> Anne's mother

An important feature of government strategies is to encourage employers to modify the workplace and job requirements to enable a person with a disability to do a job successfully. The above quote displays two job characteristics which denied Anne getting a job, but which could have been addressed by flexibility within the workplace. The quote illustrates the argument raised in Chapter 1 that handicap associated with disability is a reflection of the environment rather than of the person him or herself. Quite often only minor modifications are required to permit access to employment for someone with a disability. In many cases, these modifications benefit all employees, both with and without disability. Organisations representing people with disabilities can assist in devising modifications to the workplace.

PERSON TO PERSON

Appropriate language and behaviour

For most people with epilepsy, their disability is under control and they lead lives similar to those of other people. It is important for members of the community to recognise this and not to use epilepsy as a way of discriminating against a person in terms of employment, education or other aspects of community life.

Such discrimination has resulted in a reluctance on the part of many people with epilepsy to disclose their disability. However, honesty and openness with friends, acquaintances and workmates can be used constructively to assist members of the community in coming to understand about this disability and about the individual who has epilepsy. It also helps the person to come to grips with having epilepsy.

Strategies for successful interaction

Table 8.1: Strategies for successful interaction

Person with epilepsy	Other person
Tell friends and fellow workers about your epilepsy and what to do should a seizure occur.	Remember that epilepsy is not a disease. It is a sporadic disorder which, on occasions, can interrupt an otherwise healthy life.
After witnessing a seizure, friends might need reassurance that you are not physically hurt.	If you know someone with epilepsy, ask about the seizures and whether he or she is likely to require help.
	If you are present when a person has a seizure, do not leave. Offer support, but do not make a fuss as this could cause embarrassment.

People who have regular contact with someone who has epilepsy should learn procedures in the event that a seizure takes place. Table 8.2 outlines first aid treatment for the three most common types of epilepsy: tonic–clonic seizures, complex partial seizures and absence seizures.

MORE INFORMATION ABOUT EPILEPSY

Definition

Epilepsy is associated with a sudden discharge of electrical activity from the brain. A number of words are used to describe seizures and these include: turns, black-outs, fits and convulsions. In terms of the World Health Organization (1980) definitions:

- *Impairment* refers to a chemical abnormality or damage to the brain.
- *Disability* refers to interferences in functioning such as those associated with loss of consciousness and lapses in concentration.
- *Handicap* refers to experiences such as limitations in job opportunities and being able to drive a car, difficulties encountered in school as a result of frequent losses in consciousness (especially in simple absence seizures), and isolation resulting from other people's fears.

Seizures usually are brief, recurrent and sporadic. There are many types of seizures and they vary in their location in the brain and in the extent of involvement within the cerebral cortex (or cerebrum) of the brain. Figure 8.2 displays the areas of the brain relevant in epilepsy.

Your jaw tightens and it's like you can't feel your tongue. Your whole teeth feel like cement. All your muscles in your neck go still and all of a sudden you can't talk properly. No one knows what you're thinking

Table 8.2: First aid

Seizure type	What it looks like	What to do
Generalised tonic-clonic	The body may go stiff; the person becomes unconscious and may fall. The body begins jerking. Saliva may drain from the mouth and the person may lose control of the bladder. The face may turn grey or blue because the person is not breathing properly.	1. Stay calm, even through the seizure may look frightening. 2. Remain with the person. 3. Protect them from injury: • Remove hard objects from on or around the person. • Put something soft under the head. 4. Help the person to breath: • Turn onto the side when jerking stops, or sooner if possible, so that saliva can drain. This also allows the tongue to fall forward. 5. Tell the person he or she has had a seizure and that everything is OK. 6. *Do not* try to stop the jerking. 7. *Do not* put anything in the mouth. (*See below)
Absence	The person will suddenly lose awareness. They may stare, their eyes might roll back or their eyelids flutter. This type of seizure may happen many times each day. It starts suddenly, lasts a few seconds and stops suddenly. The person doesn't remember anything that has happened.	1. Recognise that the seizure has occurred. 2. Repeat any information the person may have missed.

Table 8.2: *Continued*

Seizure type	What it looks like	What to do
Complex partial	The person may behave very strangely; they may appear to make sounds with their lips, may fiddle with clothes.	1. Remain with the person. 2. Protect the person from injury; he or she is unaware of the surroundings. 3. Guide the person gently and keep him or her safe. 4. Tell the person he or she has had a seizure and that everything is OK.

* NB. Call for emergency medical assistance if a convulsive seizure lasts more than five minutes or if one seizure immediately follows another without the person regaining consciousness (status epilepticus). *Table reproduced with the permission of the Epilepsy Foundation of Victoria.*

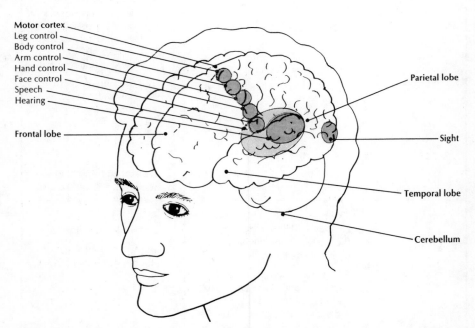

Figure 8.2: Diagrammatic view of the brain showing some of the areas of body control

and it gets the better of you. Then you go bang against something and you're unconscious.

A 19-year-old woman quoted by Brown (1993)

Factors which can trigger seizure

People with epilepsy sometimes find there are events which will trigger off seizures. These include:

- *Lack of sleep.* This is particularly important during adolescence, where a good night's sleep is not always a priority.
- *Menstruation.* Some women with epilepsy find that their seizure frequency increases just prior to or during their periods. This type of epilepsy is called catamenial epilepsy. It is thought that this type of epilepsy may be related to hormonal changes that occur during this phase of the menstrual cycle. It has been suggested that fluid retention may be partly to blame for this increase in seizures.
- *Stress.* This can be either physical or emotional. Also, when a person is feeling stressed, sleep may not be easy.
- *Alcohol.* This tends to reduce inhibitions and has the potential to increase seizure frequency. Alcohol also does not mix well with antiepileptic medications and may make the person more drowsy. Seizures also can occur during the alcohol withdrawal phase.
- *Infections.* Many children with epilepsy have increased seizure frequency during periods of infection. Even children who have good control of their seizures may experience an increase in seizure frequency during infections such as tonsillitis.
- *Drugs.* Some types of medication are known to induce seizures, including tricyclic antidepressant drugs, phenothiazines, very high doses of penicillin, some aminophylline preparations and a drug called methylphenidate (Ritalin). Withdrawal of drugs can also be a trigger. Such drugs include barbiturates, diazepam (Valium, Ducene), clonazepam (Rivotril), as well as the sudden withdrawal of antiepileptic drugs.

Major forms of epilepsy

Primary epilepsy. This results from a chemical abnormality in the brain which sometimes allows seizures to occur. If someone has primary epilepsy it means that the exact cause of the epilepsy cannot be found.

Secondary epilepsy. This is easier to understand because it means that the seizures are secondary to something else. An abnormality in the brain can be found which may have been present at birth or may be the result of a head injury or brain infection, resulting in a scar. These brain abnormalities can be detected on the neuro-imaging tests such as magnetic resonance imaging (MRI), single photon emission computerised tomography (SPECT) and positron emission tomography (PET).

As stated earlier, there are two major types of seizure: *generalised* and *partial*. The International classification of seizure types is given in Table 8.3 and Figure 8.3. Table 8.3 is designed to demonstrate the wide variety of seizures that can occur.

The following summary of major primary and secondary generalised and partial seizure types is based on Devinsky (1994).

Primary generalised seizures. *Absence seizures* (petit mal) are brief episodes of staring with impaired awareness and responsiveness. Episodes usually last less than ten seconds, but may last as long as 20 seconds. They begin and end suddenly with

Table 8.3: International classification of epileptic seizures

I. **Generalised seizures** (convulsive or non-convulsive)
   A. *Absence seizures*
      1. Absence seizures
      2. Atypical absence seizures
   B. *Myoclonic seizures*
   C. *Clonic seizures*
   D. *Tonic seizures*
   E. *Tonic-clonic seizures*
   F. *Atonic seizures (astatic seizures)*

II. **Partial seizures**

   A. *Simple partial seizures* (consciousness not impaired)
      1. With motor symptoms
      2. With somatosensory or special sensory symptoms
      3. With autonomic symptoms
      4. With psychic symptoms

   B. *Complex partial seizures* (with impairment of consciousness)
      1. Beginning as simple partial seizures and progressing to impairment of consciousness.
         a. With no other features
         b. With features as in partial seizures
         c. With automatisms
      2. With impairment of consciousness at onset
         a. With no other features
         b. With features as in partial seizures
         c. With automatisms

   C. *Partial seizures evolving to secondarily generalised seizures*
      1. Simple partial seizures evolving to generalised seizures
      2. Complex partial seizures evolving to generalised seizures
      3. Simple partial seizures evolving to complex partial seizures to generalised seizure

III. **Unclassified epileptic seizures**
   Includes all seizures that cannot be classified because of inadequate or incomplete data and some that defy classification in other described categories. This includes some neonatal seizures, such as rhythmic eye movements, chewing and swimming movements.

Source: International League Against Epilepsy (1981).

A. Partial seizures (Epilepsy originates from one location.)

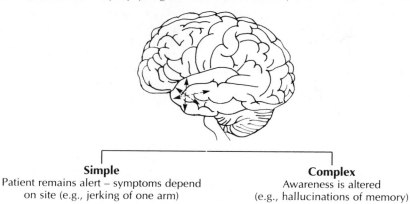

Simple
Patient remains alert – symptoms depend on site (e.g., jerking of one arm)

Complex
Awareness is altered (e.g., hallucinations of memory)

Both forms of partial epilepsy may, on occasion, develop into tonic-clonic seizures if the abnormal electrical activity spreads beyond its normal confines.

B. Generalised seizures (Seizure activity involves the whole brain – no single region can be identified as the source.)

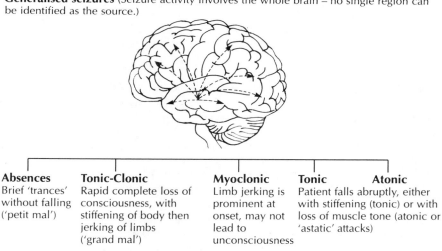

Absences
Brief 'trances' without falling ('petit mal')

Tonic-Clonic
Rapid complete loss of consciousness, with stiffening of body then jerking of limbs ('grand mal')

Myoclonic
Limb jerking is prominent at onset, may not lead to unconsciousness

Tonic

Atonic
Patient falls abruptly, either with stiffening (tonic) or with loss of muscle tone (atonic or 'astatic' attacks)

Figure 8.3: Epileptic seizures: classification

Reproduced with permission from The Neurological Centre, Westmead Hospital, Sydney (1993).
Epilepsy: a booklet for the information of patients.

no warning. Afterwards the person is alert and attentive. They generally begin between four and 14 years of age and, in 75 per cent of people, do not continue after 18 years of age. *Myotonic seizures* are brief, shock-like jerks of a muscle or group of muscles, usually in the neck, shoulders, upper arms, body and upper legs. *Clonic seizures* may involve jerking (clonic) movements on both sides of the body, but without stiffening while *tonic seizures* are associated with sudden stiffening. *Tonic–clonic seizures* (grand mal) are convulsive seizures where the person briefly stiffens and loses consciousness, falls and often utters a cry resulting from air being forced through the contracting vocal cords. Stiffening is followed by jerking of the arms and legs. Seizures last from one to three minutes. There may be excessive saliva production, sometimes incorrectly described as 'foaming at the mouth'. Biting of the tongue or cheek may cause bleeding. Loss of urine, or occasionally, a bowel movement may occur. After the convulsion, the person may be tired and confused, and may fall asleep. Some people become agitated or depressed. Table 8.2 summarises first aid steps to assist with someone who has had a tonic–clonic seizure. *Atonic seizures* are brief spells associated with sudden loss in muscle strength, causing eyelids to droop, the head to nod, an object to be dropped, or the person may fall to the ground.

Partial seizures. These are restricted to one hemisphere of the brain and mostly arise from the temporal or frontal lobes. *Simple partial seizures* cause a diverse group of symptoms, some of which (for example, abdominal discomfort) may not be recognised as epilepsy. Motor seizures involve a change in muscle activity while sensory seizures involve a change in sensation such as a feeling of 'pins and needles' or of seeing a red ball. *Autonomic seizures* cause changes in part of the nervous system (limbic system) which control bodily functions, resulting in strange or unpleasant sensations in the abdomen, chest or head. Changes may occur in heart rate and breathing, and goose bumps may come on for no apparent reason. *Psychic seizures* cause changes to the brain that affect thinking, feeling and experiencing. They can result in experiences such as garbled speech, inability to find the right word, and alteration to perception of time. They also can cause sudden changes in emotion, such as fear, anxiety, depression and happiness.

Complex partial seizures. Here consciousness may be impaired, but is not lost. Typically, the person stares and is unable to respond to questions or instructions. Automatisms (automatic movements) usually occur and can include lip smacking, chewing, tapping or clasping the hands, grunts or more complex acts such as stirring movements. More rare forms include disrobing, screaming and bizarre movements. These seizures last from 30 seconds to three minutes and are commonly accompanied by auras or warnings which are actually simple partial seizures. Afterwards, the person may feel lethargy or confusion for a few minutes.

Secondary generalised seizures. These result when a restricted burst of excessive electrical activity spreads to involve both sides of the brain. As a result, a partial seizure may become a secondarily generalised tonic–clonic seizure.

The period immediately following a seizure is called the *postictal period*. Its length and symptoms vary, depending on the type of seizure. Absence seizures may not be followed by any symptoms while after a complex partial seizure the person may feel confused and tired for between five and 15 minutes. After a tonic–clonic seizure, there may be muscle soreness, headaches and pain in the tongue and cheek (if they were bitten). The person also may be confused and tired, and may fall asleep for a period. (Devinsky, 1994).

Causes

- *Lack of oxygen to the brain (hypoxia).* This causes damage to brain cells and may subsequently lead to epilepsy. Hypoxia may occur during birth or as a result of a stroke where the blood supply to a particular area of the brain is cut off.

- *Brain damage*. This can result from a head injury. This injury may cause scar tissue and later the person may experience seizures.
- *Tumours*. A frequent fear when seizures first start is that they are the result of a brain tumour. This is a very uncommon cause of epilepsy, especially in children, and can be detected on neuro-imaging tests.
- *Infections*. These can cause damage to brain tissue and include meningitis (bacterial infection) and encephalitis (viral infection) which are the most common types of infection resulting in epilepsy. However, infections transmitted from mother to baby during pregnancy and by some parasites (for example, sheep tapeworm and dog tapeworm) have been known to cause damage to brain tissues, resulting in seizures.
- *Inheritance*. If one parent has epilepsy the chances of a child developing epilepsy are about the same as in the general population (1–2 per cent). If both parents have epilepsy, chances increase to around 10 per cent. Epilepsy in itself is not inherited but the cause may be. In some inherited conditions, epilepsy is a symptom of the condition.

Incidence and prevalence

It is estimated that there are 36 000 Australians who have epilepsy. Around five to ten thousand new cases of epilepsy appear each year in Australia (Brown, 1993). Around 1–2 per cent of the population has some form of epilepsy. In the United States there are 583 000 people diagnosed as having a form of epilepsy (LaPlante & Carlson, 1996). The world-wide prevalence is generally accepted to be 1–2 per cent, but tends to be higher in third world countries (Gerrits, 1994).

Age. For most people (64 per cent of the population), their first seizure has occurred by the end of primary school, while nearly all people who have epilepsy have experienced their first seizure by the end of young adulthood (93 per cent). Many young children have convulsions associated with high temperatures. Others may have absence seizures which cease during adolescence. For some people, their first seizure may not occur until well into adult life.

> *My first seizure happened when I was 43 years old. The only thing I could put it down to was a serious knock on my head which happened several years previously.*
>
> Richard

In older age groups, over 50 per cent of seizures are partial in nature. This is because strokes and other vascular events which occur in older people produce local areas of brain damage. For an older person, diagnosis of epilepsy can mean loss of independence and a tendency towards social isolation. It takes longer for an older person to recover from a seizure (Buchanan, 1994).

Gender. Figures are slightly higher for men, who are more likely to experience head injuries in work and sport. However, as mentioned above, there is a cause of epilepsy specific to women. Buchanan (1994) notes that a relationship between the menstrual cycle and seizures has long been recognised. This is referred to as catamenial epilepsy. Little is understood about why this occurs and why treatments work for some women, but not for others.

Diagnosis

Diagnosis takes into account medical history, physical examination, laboratory tests and neurological examination. A history of recurrent seizures is an important consideration (Barnes & Krasnoff, 1973) as are family and personal history, including pregnancy, birth, development and accidents. Physical examination is made to determine any nutritional or metabolic disturbances. Neurological examination is conducted through skull X-rays, tests of the senses and EEG which helps detect abnormal electrical activity in the brain. The type of brainwave varies with the type of seizure. Seizures vary with the different forms of epilepsy, but for any one person the pattern is fairly consistent.

Treatment

Medication. Approximately 70–75 per cent of people with epilepsy gain good seizure control using antiepileptic medications. Around one-quarter of people do not respond well to medications. The aim of medical treatment is monotherapy (use of one drug only). Antiepileptic medications may need to be taken twice a day, and some only once a day. There are many types of antiepileptic medications. Some of the more commonly-used medications are phenytoin (Dilantin), sodium valproate (Epilim), carbamazepine (Tegretol), lamotrigine (Lamictal) and vigabatrin (Sabril).

Antiepileptic medications are not without side effects and choice of a drug depends on the degree of seizure control and possibility of side effects outweighing the benefits of control. The following quotations come from Brown (1993):

> *I see everybody with so much energy and I get so jealous because I'm always like a zombie.*
>
> 18-year-old woman

> *My sister gave me a brand new $400 Italian leather suit and I can't fit into it because of what these tablets are doing.*
>
> 17-year-old woman

> *I get rashes like these and then I get scars all over my legs and body.*
>
> 12-year-old girl

> *I just get a headache or something, I just feel like chopping my head off and grabbing someone else's head.*
>
> 14-year-old girl

Surgery. A small number of people benefit from surgery. These people have epilepsy which is focused in the temporal lobe and thus have complex partial seizures. Surgery involves the removal of part of the temporal lobe and currently 60 to 70 per cent of people become seizure-free after the operation.

Services and supports

Services are available nationally and locally for people with epilepsy, their families, carers and other members of the community. These agencies provide information, counselling and group activities. Although epilepsy organisations vary in the services they offer, most will provide literature and videos suitable for a range of people; counsellors to assist with social issues such as leisure, education and employment; group activities such as self-help groups, social outings and social clubs. Comprehensive epilepsy centres exist in many capital cities of the world. These centres provide expert medical care for people with epilepsy.

RESOURCE ORGANISATIONS

All care has been taken to ensure that all information is correct at the time of publishing. However, responsibility for the accuracy of this information is not accepted by the writer. The list of resource organisations contained in this chapter is not intended to be exhaustive – it provides national organisations only. The reader is referred to local community directories for further information and for local branches of national organisations. Inclusion of services and organisations should not be taken as a recommendation.

Australia

National Epilepsy Association of Australia
1st Floor, 74 Macquarie Street
PO Box 224
Parramatta NSW 2150
Ph 02 9891 6118
Fax 02 9891 6137

New Zealand

Epilepsy Association of New Zealand
610 Victoria Street
Hamilton
Ph 07 834 3556
Fax 07 834 3553

United Kingdom

British Epilepsy Association
Anstey House
40 Hanover Square
Leeds LS3 1BE
Ph 0532 439 393
Fax 0532 428804

The National Society for Epilepsy
Chafont St Peter
Gerrards Cross
Bucks SL9 0RT
Ph 0494 873 991
Fax 0494 871 927

United States

Epilepsy Foundation of America
4351 Garden City Drive
Landover, MD 20785 2267
Ph 1 800 332 1000 or 301 459 3700
Fax 301 577 2684

Canada

Epilepsy Canada
Suite 745, 1470 Peel Street
Montreal, Quebec H3A 1T1
Ph 514 845 7855
Fax 514 845 7866

FURTHER READING

Beaumont, M. (1987). *Epilepsy in education, a manual for teachers.* Melbourne: National Epilepsy Association of Australia Inc.
Brown, R. (1993). *Young people and epilepsy.* Melbourne: National Epilepsy Association of Australia Inc.
Buchanan, N. (1990). *Epilepsy questions and answers.* Sydney: MacLennan & Petty.
Buchanan, N. (1994). *Understanding epilepsy.* Sydney: Simon and Schuster.
Dahl, J. (1992). *Epilepsy.* Seattle: Hogrefe & Huber, Publishers.
Devinsky, O. (1994). *A guide to understanding and living with epilepsy.* Philadelphia: F.A. Davis Co.
Freeman, J., Vining, E. & Pillas, D. (1993). *Seizures and epilepsy in childhood.* Baltimore: The Johns Hopkins University Press.

Goss, S. (1989). *Ragged owlet*. Sydney: Houghton Mifflin.

Goss, S. (1995). *I can live with that*. Melbourne: Epilepsy Foundation of Victoria.

Gram, L. & Dam, M. (1995). *Epilepsy explained*. Copenhagen: Munksgaard.

Gumnit, R. (1995). *The epilepsy handbook*. New York: Raven Press.

Human Rights Commission (1984). *Epilepsy and human rights*. Occasional Paper No. 7. Canberra: Australian Government Publishing Service.

Landau, E. (1994). *Epilepsy*. New York: Twenty First Century Books.

La Plante, E. (1993). *Seized*. New York: Harper Collins.

Mittan, R. (1988). *Living well with epilepsy*. Wellington, NZ: New Zealand Epilepsy Association.

Richard, A. & Reiter, J. (1990). *Epilepsy: a new approach*. New York: Prentice Hall.

Yanko, S. (1992). *Coming to terms with epilepsy*. Sydney: Allen & Unwin.

CHAPTER 9

HEARING IMPAIRMENT AND DEAFNESS

Hearing loss is a generic term used to describe impairment which may range from mild to profound. It can occur in high and/or low frequencies, and can affect one or both ears, to the same or different extents. There are many types of hearing loss, each having different implications for the individual and for everyday life. As with vision loss, it is important to distinguish between types. Of particular importance are the distinctions between *deafness*, *hearing impairment* and being *hard of hearing*. These are the most commonly used definitions associated with this disability.

Deafness. A person who is deaf has a severe or profound hearing loss from, at or near birth and mainly relies upon vision to communicate, whether through lip-reading, gestures, cued speech, finger-spelling and/or sign language. In this book a capital letter is used for the word Deaf when reference is being made to members of the Deaf community or culture and to the Deaf sign language.

Hearing impairment. Although definitions vary, the term 'hearing impaired' is used here to refer to a person who has acquired a hearing loss after learning to speak, has a mild, moderate or even a severe or profound loss, communicates orally and makes maximum use of his or her residual hearing with the assistance of amplification. This classification may be used interchangeably with the terms 'hard of hearing' or 'partially deaf'.

Hard of hearing. This term increasingly is being used in place of 'hearing impaired' to refer to a hearing loss of a moderate to profound level. The World Federation of the Deaf agreed in 1991 that the term 'hearing impaired' was not acceptable and that the terms 'deaf' and 'hard of hearing' should be used (Moore & Levitan, 1993).

The extent of hearing loss and the time at which it occurred have major implications for the individual and how he or she processes information and communicates with others. It is important to be aware that many issues are different for people who are deaf and people who are hearing impaired.

LIVING WITH DEAFNESS AND HEARING IMPAIRMENT

Extent of hearing loss

The impact of a hearing loss depends on its extent and other factors including age of onset and the prior opportunity the person has had to acquire spoken language. Boyd & Young (1981) summarise major factors as being:

139

- Severity of loss in decibel level (see later in the chapter).
- The age at time of loss and age at time of diagnosis. The earlier the loss, the greater the barriers to learning and to developing communication skills.
- The audiometric frequency loss pattern. Hearing losses involving high-frequency loss of 1000–4000 hertz result in low speech discrimination. Losses which are approximately equal at all frequencies can be relieved by amplification through use of a hearing aid.
- Accompanying vision impairment. Reception of speech through lip-reading and signing requires adequate vision.
- Whether the loss is stable, progressive or fluctuating. A stable loss is more amenable to treatment and adaptation.
- Other organic impairments, such as those associated with brain injury involving the speech centre.

Pre-lingual and post-lingual hearing loss

'Lingual' refers to language. Those people who have an acquired hearing loss (that is, they acquire their hearing loss after the age of three years) have a communication base rooted in knowledge of spoken language (post-lingual), unlike people who were either born deaf or lost their hearing before the age of three years (pre-lingual). Absence of spoken speech does not indicate less intelligence or that a person is physically unable to communicate through speech. Deaf people usually have operational voice boxes. The ability to speak is usually determined by the age of onset of hearing loss. If hearing loss occurs before the acquisition of speech, then speech may never be heard and therefore cannot be learned through the usual process of imitation. If a person learned to speak before hearing loss occurred, he or she may already have established good speech patterns. It is the memory of these speech patterns, *not* an ability to hear, that enables these deaf people to speak well. In some cases, people who have lost their hearing prior to learning speech can be rigorously trained to use their residual hearing to understand speech and develop speech skills.

Table 9.2 outlines the effects of hearing loss for people in whom loss occurred before learning to speak. It is important to note that Table 9.2 refers to spoken language. A person can be fluent in a signed language but have no knowledge of, or skills in, speech.

To illustrate the implications for everyday functioning, Table 9.3 highlights differences in the daily routines of a hearing person and someone who is deaf. It should be noted that people with a hearing impairment may also use some or all of these strategies and there will always be exceptions and variations to these strategies.

Associated consequences

The variety of types and degree of hearing loss mean that impairment involves more than just a general loss of sound. Hearing loss can take several forms, each of which has particular consequences for the individual.

Specific frequency loss. Relatively few hearing losses are uniform across several frequencies. Because the frequency of sound waves determine their pitch (see the section titled 'The mechanism of hearing' later in the chapter), an impairment can be associated with a low-frequency or high-frequency loss. For example, some

Table 9.1: Hearing loss and associated disability

Average hearing levels (0.5,1,2,4 KHZ)	Level of impairment	Handicap	Probable needs
10–14 dB	Normal	Hears all speech sounds	
15–24 dB	Slight	May have problems hearing clearly in difficult listening situations (for example, meetings, classrooms). Vowel sounds heard, but may miss unvoiced consonant sounds.	Awareness of hearing loss and need to adopt good listening strategies to optimise communication. A child will probably adjust adequately at school but may have mild dysfunction in learning language.
25–40 dB	Mild	Difficulty with faint speech. May have problems in background noise. Could have an effect on language development. Able to understand spoken conversation at a distance of 1 metre, will miss much of class discussions.	Could use hearing aids and/or assistive listening devices. Need to adopt good listening strategies to optimise communication. A child would have speech problems, with mild spoken language retardation and inattention at school.
41–55 dB	Moderate	Group discussion very difficult to follow. Frequent difficulty with understanding normal speech. Delayed language development in children.	Would benefit from hearing aids. Need speech reading instruction and auditory training. A child is likely to have limited speech and vocabulary and may misumderstand directions and be inattentive.
56–70 dB	Moderate/severe	Greater difficulty with understanding speech and following conversations in general listening situations.	Would definitely benefit from hearing aids. Need speech reading instruction and auditory training.
71–90 dB	Severe	Great difficulty with understanding speech. Can only understand loud conversation. Sounds are distorted, poor discrimination of consonant. May hear loud environmental sounds, for example, sirens. Relies heavily on visual cues for communication.	Requires substantial amplification and extensive auditory training and speech reading instruction. Spoken language unlikely to be learned without early amplification.
91 dB	Profound	Hears no speech. May hear some loud sounds, poor discrimination, sound is very distorted, marked effect on language and speech development.	Requires powerful hearing aids. Could be a candidate for a cochlear implant or vibrotactile device. May require interpreter or special assistance.

Source: *SSSH News*, Summer, 1993; Lindeman, J.E. (ed) Psychological and behavioral aspects of disability. New York: Plenum Press, p. 379.

Table 9.2: Some effects of pre-lingual hearing loss

Degree of hearing loss

Profound hearing loss
  Poor spoken language
  Little benefit from hearing-aids
  Limited potential for speech

Severe hearing loss
  Spoken language affected
  Hearing aids may assist

Moderate hearing loss
  Amplification and additional speech training where necessary will result in increased capacity to acquire spoken language and speech development

Mild hearing loss
  Good spoken language and speech acquisition
  Hearing aids prescribed in only some cases

Table 9.3: Everyday routines of a hearing person as compared with a person who is deaf or hearing impaired

Hearing person	Person with a hearing loss
• Alarm rings	• Alarm flashes and/or vibrates
• Puts radio on	• Puts hearing aids on
• Converses using hearing as the primary sense (eg, speech)	• Converses using vision as the primary sense (eg, sign language)
• Uses telephone	• Uses TTY (telephone typewriter)
• Attends meetings	• Attends meetings with an interpreter
• Workmates call to get attention	• Workmates use visual or tactile means to get attention (eg, wave, stamp, tap on the shoulder)
• Communicates at work using speech	• Communicates at work using writing
• Meaningful conversation with workmates	• Superficial conversation with workmates
• Aware of why something out-of-the-ordinary is happening	• Unsure of why an unusual event is occurring and must wait till later to find out (often to be given only a brief explanation or to be told it was not important!)
• Arrival of friend signalled by a ringing doorbell	• Arrival of friend signalled by a flashing light instead of a doorbell

people with a hearing impairment cannot detect low-pitched sounds such as vowel sounds. In their case, it is rather like trying to read a sentence with the vowels omitted:

Th- w- -th-r w-s w-nd-rf-l y-st-rd-y.

However, for high-frequency loss, it is like trying to understand a sentence with the consonants omitted:

I- i- -oi- - -o -ai- -o-a-.[1]

High-frequency losses are more common.

Difficulty in locating sound. This occurs particularly with unilateral hearing loss (in one ear only) and makes it difficult to locate the direction from which ambulance, police sirens or other sounds are coming.

Difficulty in speech discrimination. In situations where there is background noise, particularly in large gatherings of people, such as at parties or conferences, a person with a hearing impairment can experience difficulties in communication. It is almost impossible to differentiate speech in these situations. This experience can be one of the first signs of hearing loss.

Sound distortion. A particular effect of sound distortion is that it makes a taken-for-granted experience, such as the enjoyment of music, almost impossible for a person with hearing impairment. Thus, many forms of entertainment, such as concerts, opera and theatre, cannot be enjoyed.

Abnormal volume perception. A slight increase in volume of sound may be experienced as uncomfortably loud and sometimes even painful. For example, sudden changes in film sound effects or intensity of background music may cause discomfort.

Tinnitus. This refers to 'noises' (such as ringing, buzzing or hissing) in the ears or head that other people cannot hear. Tinnitus may be intermittent or continuous. It is frequently related to hearing loss and can be a very annoying aspect of the impairment.

Dizziness and loss of balance. This may occur because fluid levels in the inner ear which regulate balance are altered.

PRESENCE OF OTHER DISABILITIES

People with a hearing loss are more likely to have multiple disabilities than other people with disabilities. These disabilities are also likely to affect everyday living and further contribute to the diversity between individuals.

---

[1] The weather was wonderful yesterday.
  It is going to rain today.

Communication

The main issue associated with hearing loss is not so much the inability to hear as the barriers to communication that result.

> *The high frequencies are necessary to learn speech and I had enough high frequency hearing to do this, except that I was slow to speak and confused sounds like 'horse' and 'house'. People thought I had a learning problem.*
>
> Anne

Many people who are deaf or have a hearing impairment have vocal ability and are able to learn to use their voices. However, because they cannot hear themselves, some people cannot readily control the tone and loudness of their voices. Even with years of training, a person who acquired a severe impairment early in life may have speech which is difficult to understand. Often other people find that they are able to understand once they have become familiar with the person's speech. Nevertheless, this form of communication can be frustrating, tiring and open to misinterpretation for both people with and without hearing impairment.

> *Sometimes I got things wrong and in a group I made a fool of myself by making inappropriate comments. I could never have a relaxed conversation; it was always a strain . . . Hearing was a guessing game. I'd hear a bit and guess the rest. It's extremely frustrating.*
>
> Emily

Other alternatives exist to reliance on the spoken word. There are three categories of communication methods: oral, manual and written.

Oral communication. This relies on hearing and speech to communicate. Many people with a severe or profound hearing loss also communicate orally. Mildly and moderately hearing-impaired people usually communicate using the oral method. This means of communication is assisted by the use of hearing aids to maximise any hearing present. In oral/aural communication, speech is used for expressive communication and lip-reading is used for receptive communication.

- *Lip-reading (receptive).* Lip-reading is very difficult because only 30–40 per cent of what we say is visible on the lips. This is because some sounds look exactly the same on the lips; for example, m, b and p. Further, some sounds are extremely difficult to see on the lips (such as s and t). There is a lot of guesswork in lip-reading. The more predictable something is, the easier it is to lip-read. Familiarity with the context and the speaker helps too. It is usually much easier for hearing people to lip-read than deaf people because they often know the language better. This is also why it is easier for someone with an acquired hearing-loss (hearing was lost after they learnt to speak) to lip-read. Lip-reading is a skill which must be learned and practised regularly.
- *Speech (expressive).* Often the speech of a deaf person or a person with hearing impairment is not very clear. This is because they have not had the opportunity to clearly hear speech and can only imitate what they do hear.
- *Cued speech.* This is a phonetically-based code of English. It involves the use of hand movements near the face to represent the *sound* of the word (not its

Figure 9.1: A combination of lip-reading and a hearing aid enable this man to communicate about technical matters with his co-worker

spelling). There are four hand positions (throat, chin, side of mouth and next to face) and eight hand shapes which represent the consonants and vowels. The aim of cueing is to take the ambiguity out of lip-reading. Cueing improves lip-reading from 30–40 per cent up to 96–99 per cent accuracy. Cueing is no longer widely used and is not taught in Australia.

Manual communication. Schembri (1995) states that manual communication is a cover term that refers to any communication which is achieved using the hands rather than the voice. The term is often used to refer to any of the following forms of communication: gesture, mime, Auslan, finger spelling, Pidgin Sign English and Signed English. The following description of these forms of communication are taken from Schembri:

- *Gesture.* Both hearing and deaf people use and understand gestures (for example, waving your hand for goodbye), but these gestures cannot be used to communicate a great deal of information. Deaf people may use gesture to communicate basic concepts with hearing people who do not sign, but they do not provide an effective means of communication and cannot be used in place of sign or spoken language.
- *Mime.* This involves acting out of real-life activities. Deaf people may use elements of mime to communicate with hearing people who do not sign, and aspects of mime are incorporated into sign languages like Auslan. However, in

itself mimed communication is not sufficient as an efficient communication system.

- *Sign language (Auslan).* Auslan, or Australian Sign Language, is the language of the Australian Deaf community. It is a highly structured and highly complex linguistic system that is comparable to spoken languages in that it can be used to express the same range of meanings and can be used in a wide range of situations. Sign languages have evolved naturally wherever deaf people have gathered to form communities. Versions differ within English-speaking countries. This means that a person who is Australian and Deaf will not use the same version of sign language as someone in the United States (ASL or American Sign Language) or the United Kingdom. There are even some regional differences in signs within Australia. However, it is likely that people from these countries will be able to understand each other. Sign languages make use of individual signs which are organised into grammatical systems. Signs have specific meanings just like the words of spoken languages, and can be combined with other signs. Just as the words of English are built from a limited set of sounds, so the signs of Auslan are put together from a limited set of hand shapes, locations on the body and movements. More than one sign may be required to convey a particular word. These signs are then organised into larger units such as phrases and sentences. Auslan has its own grammar which is not based on the grammar of any spoken language, such as English. Auslan differs from English in many ways. Auslan is the natural, living, every-day language of Australian Deaf people, with its own vocabulary and grammar and the same expressive capacity as any spoken language. It is a complete language in its own right and has no written form. It is recognised by Australia's National Language Policy. The people who use Auslan constitute a distinct social and cultural group, more like an ethnic community. Signing interpreters are available through the Ethnic Affairs Commission in NSW and similar organisations elsewhere. They are necessary for the deaf person who uses sign language if he or she is to have full access to information when interacting with people who communicate through spoken English, particularly in important situations.
- *Finger spelling.* This is comprised of 26 hand shapes representing the 26 letters of the English alphabet. Finger spelling is regularly mixed in with signing by Auslan users, but should not be confused with signing. Words are finger-spelt when there is no sign for them (for example, words like 'pizza', 'kindergarten' or 'karaoke'). It is used to spell out English words, letter by letter. There are two finger spelling alphabets in use in Australia. The British two-handed alphabet is the most widely used, but some Catholic signers also use the one-handed alphabet which has its origins in Ireland. Although finger spelling is an important part of Auslan, few deaf people rely exclusively on this method of communication.
- *Pidgin Sign English.* Most often when people using Signed English and people using Auslan talk to each other, they meet somewhere in the middle between Signed English and Auslan. When this happens Pidgin Signed English (PSE) results. PSE is not a language. It does not have a grammatical structure. It is not taught, it just spontaneously happens. PSE appears to be highly variable in structure, depending on the language background and attitudes of the signers involved.
- *Signed English.* This is the representation of English in the signed form. It was developed for use in educating deaf children and its aim is to represent English,

Figure 9.2: Finger spelling in action

Reproduced with the permission of the Deaf Society of NSW.

word for word, on the hands. Signs are produced in English word order with many additional signs to represent English grammatical items. Signed English is really 'English on your hands', word-for-word. This is really a sign 'code' not a sign language. Because Signed English is actually English, it is quite easy for hearing people to learn by simply learning a sign for each word and so was expected to be useful for hearing teachers in Deaf education. However, it has not been as successful as anticipated. In practice it takes twice as long to produce a sentence as in English or Auslan. As a result, exact versions are rarely reproduced and a form of Pidgin Sign English results. Many deaf people strongly reject the use of Signed English and advocate the use of Auslan in the classroom, with English taught as a second language. Signed English is an artificially contrived code (as compared with Auslan which is a naturally-occurring language) and is not widely used by deaf people.

Written communication

Writing. Sometimes deaf people's written English is not clear. This may be the case when a deaf person's first language is Auslan and English is their second language. Other signing deaf adults may come from non-signing hearing families where communication in the home was difficult and they may not have fully acquired either English or Auslan in their childhood. Variations in literacy skills

Figure 9.3: Sign language used in an everyday situation

within the overall Australian population make it difficult to make generalisations about the skills of deaf people in written English, however research indicates that many deaf people's written skills frequently do not match those of their hearing peers. Thus it is important for a hearing person to look for the basic message a deaf person is trying to convey through writing rather than to focus on the grammatical correctness of their written English.

Reading. Evidence suggests that the average reading age of deaf school-leavers is eight years and nine months, although many deaf people achieve scores no different from their hearing peers. It is important to keep in mind that giving a deaf person a sheet packed with information is not the easy way out if you want to communicate. If you must write, try to keep things simple – without being patronising. Some things that can make it easier for deaf people to understand what you have written are:

- Do not use double negatives (for example, 'He is not unhappy with your work').
- Try not to use 'when' unless you are referring to time. Take the sentence: 'Please give me that book when you are finished'. With this sentence a deaf person is likely to think you are asking when he or she will be finished. It would be better to ask: 'Please give me that book after you have finished reading'.
- Try not to use 'it'. Rather, keep on referring to what you are talking about by its name.
- Avoid idioms such as 'It's raining cats and dogs'.
- Avoid complex sentences.

A memo, e-mail, handout or overhead which is packed with details may not be the most appropriate way to communicate information to someone who is deaf (Schembri, 1995).

The Deaf community

Deaf people who use sign language and are members of the Deaf community do not see deafness as a 'disability'. They see themselves as members of a linguistic group with their own culture and language, not as a 'disabled' group. Deaf culture is a set of learned behaviours of a group of deaf people who have their own language, values and beliefs, rules for behaviour and traditions (Lewis, 1987). For example, behaviour in this culture involves greater use of facial expressions, a more direct approach to personal interaction (for example, comments about physical appearance), visual or tactile ways of getting attention (such as waving, flashing lights or stamping feet) and long goodbyes. Auslan is the accepted language. Within the Deaf community many have chosen not to use spoken speech which has traditionally been forced upon them. Even with years of speech and auditory training, many people who are deaf have endured humiliation and pain from the reactions of others to their 'strange' voices. Some people therefore choose not to use their voices (Moore & Levitan, 1993).

For several years, members of the Deaf community have been lobbying to have themselves recognised as an ethnic group having their own culture. In Australia, Auslan is now recognised by the Australian government as a language in its National Languages Policy. This recognition has come in NSW with the decision to include this group within the realm of activities of the NSW Ethnic Affairs Commission.

Sometimes hearing people see deafness as a problem to be 'cured' whereas the Deaf community accepts deafness as one aspect of a person's identity. Sign language is recognised as a valid form of communication. Acceptance by the hearing community of English as a deaf person's second language acknowledges the existence of the Deaf community as a different, but equally valid, culture.

Personal adjustment

Two variables which are important in determining the implications of hearing loss are:

* the age of onset;
* the degree of hearing loss.

Table 9.4: Important beliefs within the Deaf culture

* Deafness is accepted and seen as a positive part of a person's identity.
* The focus is on what Deaf people can do (unlimited abilities).
* Sign language (Auslan) is encouraged and seen as an everyday way of communication.
* English is accepted as a Deaf person's second language.
* Deaf people are regarded as just as intelligent as hearing people.
* Full recognition is given to the existence of a Deaf community.

Reactions to disability and strategies for dealing with it are likely to differ between people with congenital and acquired impairments, between people with unilateral and bilateral loss (one or both ears) and according to whether loss is sudden or gradual. People born with a condition have never known life without it and have had time to adapt. On the other hand, people who acquire hearing impairment later in life have had experiences not readily available to those with congenital impairment.

Some aspects of hearing loss have a more widespread impact on the individual than others. Hearing loss which affects the ability to hear speech is likely to require major changes to communication patterns. However, once again, it must be remembered that reactions to any life experience differ between individuals.

> *I don't try to hide my disability any more. I've had to learn to be honest and tell people how they can best communicate with me. Some people can't be bothered so I've become very selective about my friends. I tend to stick to people who are prepared to accept me with my disability and who cooperate in communication.*
>
> Jonathan

People who are deaf. Deaf people who use sign language as their primary means of communication do not see themselves as having a disability, so their attitude to people with other disabilities is similar to that of hearing people. Deaf people prefer to socialise with members of the Deaf community and/or those people with whom they can communicate.

Acquired loss. Acquired hearing loss is likely initially to lead to feelings of shock and grief, to anger and annoyance. There may be a period of denial and depression and a tendency to withdraw. People may feel isolated because of difficulties in communication. They may experience embarrassment and a loss of self-esteem. They may become bitter. Some people exhibit aggression because of their frustrations. However, others work out effective coping strategies and practise continuing self-help. Such self-confidence and independence helps when it is necessary to articulate needs. This assertive approach, especially in difficult hearing situations, will alert hearing people to the individual needs of hearing-impaired people and will gain respect for hearing-impaired people. A sense of humour, too, is an asset.

> *In the playground, I never really felt part of the group. It was as though there was an invisible fence between me and the other children. I had problems all through school.*
>
> Max

In older people there are often feelings of anxiety, insecurity and nervousness as a hearing loss may involve major changes to life and learning new ways to communicate. A period of denial often occurs as the person tries to maintain an appearance of 'normality'. In many cases, the person may actually be unaware of his or her hearing loss. The most common form of hearing loss in old age (presbycusis) involves gradual loss of the ability to hear high-pitched sounds and the ability to tell sounds apart. Speech becomes difficult to interpret when there is background noise. Soft consonants such as 's', 'sh' and 'ch' are difficult to separate in conversation, and without consonants, language becomes disjointed and misunderstood (Gething, 1990).

People who have a hearing impairment often become fatigued from the strain of concentration when trying to hear and to lip-read. They become tired with the concentration of listening in less than ideal conditions and may need to withdraw temporarily to 'switch off'. Communication requires greater effort on everyone's part. Without effort, understanding and patience there can be frustration, isolation and withdrawal of the person. On the other hand, the need to keep conversations succinct and simple also may be frustrating as it denies the person access to complex discussions about abstract issues which may be difficult to convey in simple terms. It also may make conversations strained and seemingly artificial if the other person is not used to conversing with someone who is deaf or hearing impaired.

I'm not only isolated from other people and experiences, but from ideas and vital knowledge. I've never found a solution for this and try to pick up a lot by reading more.

Jonathan

A person's self-image and the way he or she functions in society can be very much affected by attitudes of other people. The expectation that a person can hear influences the way others interpret behaviour and responses. Thus, a person who does not respond to a question or who responds inappropriately could be labelled as rude or slow-thinking, but not as hard of hearing. This can result in experiences such as being made to feel inadequate when giving the wrong money in a shop. Such experiences make the person feel cautious and nervous when faced with similar situations, thereby reinforcing a sense of inadequacy.

Since I had first started school, I had known I was different from the other children. For some reason I felt isolated from the others. The teachers didn't help – hey thought we were stupid, disobedient children. I used to try and work out why I was different and I felt totally confused. I felt I had done something very, very bad but I didn't know what. I was always being punished.

Anne

Sexuality

I seemed to be able to attract boys but something always went wrong. I couldn't talk on the phone. Any boy wanting to ask me out had to talk to my mother. Imagine how they felt about that!

Emily

While there is no reason for a hearing impairment to affect sexual functioning and reproduction, it has important effects on the social side of sexuality. A person growing up with deafness or a hearing impairment may find it difficult to take part in the peer group activities that are so important to teenagers in developing their knowledge of the appropriate male and female behaviours, such as the subtleties of flirting. Fashions in dress, language and behaviour can vary greatly from group to group. These rules are only vaguely defined and rarely written down. Whether a person with a hearing impairment uses speech or sign language, conversation may be difficult and inhibits the sort of intimate conversations that are usually part of forming a relationship. Some people find it easier to choose a partner who also is deaf or has a hearing impairment. Marriages of two people who are deaf or have a hearing impairment are more common than for other forms of disability.

Being a parent

Most deaf children (around 90 per cent) are born to hearing parents (Neisser, 1990).

> *I have got to thank Mum and Dad for the encouragement and support they have given me all the way through. They always encouraged me to look around, to look beyond my deafness and to do what I wanted.*
>
> Peter

The impact of a child's hearing loss on the family will depend on whether the loss is accepted or rejected. There is a greater likelihood that deaf parents will accept their child's deafness and such a child will accept his or her impairment and grow to become a member of the Deaf community. Generally speaking, hearing parents express more concerns about integrating their children who are deaf or hearing impaired into the hearing community, seeking treatments to 'cure' their child's hearing loss (for example, cochlear implants).

Family

> *At home my hearing problem was never discussed. It wasn't done to express anger or frustration. I used to go behind the garage and smash things or walk for miles to relieve my feelings. My parents said I should have a more positive attitude. My father was very involved with his work and I think it's only recently that he has realised what my brother and I were going through as he's recently had a hearing loss himself.*
>
> Anne

As with other disabilities, parents may have difficulty in accepting that their child has a hearing impairment. Some may experience grief, be overprotective, or conversely, be unrealistic in their high expectations of the child.

When the hearing loss is acquired later in life, it can place strain on hearing members of families who must now adjust to the needs of their hard-of-hearing relative. The impairment may create communication difficulties, particularly if the loss is sudden. Repetition becomes irritating and can lead to impatience and even anger. There is need for understanding and patience. There is the possibility of a period of dependence before the person becomes adjusted. A parent may, for the first time, be dependent on children to do such everyday things as answer the telephone.

How families react in such situations often reflects existing relationships within the family. If a supportive, understanding and accepting atmosphere already exists, then the changes required to accommodate a child or an adult with a hearing impairment will be much easier to accept. This may not be the case in a situation where family relationships are strained and communication is poor.

Community living

Members of the community should be aware of the needs of people who are deaf or hearing impaired. Organisations must provide appropriate services. Assistive listening devices in public buildings such as banks, post offices, senior citizen centres, hospitals, nursing homes, schools, lecture rooms, libraries, shops, theatres, cinemas and courts can eliminate many frustrations experienced by people with a moderate hearing impairment in everyday activities. Volume-controlled phones in public places are a high priority need.

An effective solution to communication problems for people who are deaf is to have a sign language interpreter. If there is an important meeting or event which is equally important to both deaf and hearing participants, it is vital that a sign language interpreter be provided. This means that the person who is deaf has full access to information. In a smaller context, ensure that the person is positioned so that they have a full view of the speaker, other participants and visual displays.

An interpreter's role is to facilitate effective communication between deaf and hearing persons and to accurately convey one person's message to another person. When working with an interpreter, it is important to remember to the following points:

- Speak directly to the person who is deaf (not to the interpreter). Avoid phrases such as 'Tell him/her . . .'. Do not be put off if the deaf person is looking at the interpreter and not you. Still keep your attention directed to the deaf person.
- Do not make asides that you do not want communicated to the deaf person. It is the role of the interpreter to interpret everything the person would otherwise hear.
- Avoid asking the interpreter for his or her opinion.
- Speak clearly at a rate that is natural for you. The interpreter will tell you if you need to change your speed.
- Remember that the interpreter will be a little behind the 'speaker'. Don't keep stopping to let the interpreter catch up. In situations where you are waiting for a response from the deaf person it will be necessary to wait until the interpreter has passed on the question before you get a response. So don't keep talking! Give the deaf person a chance to say something.
- If you have a group of people with one deaf person and one interpreter, ask individuals in the group to indicate by raising their hands when they are speaking so the deaf person can keep track of who is saying what.
- Be reassured that what you say will be interpreted faithfully, without anything added or deleted. All information will remain strictly confidential. These are requirements of interpreters as outlined in their code of ethics.

Deaf people may require the use of sign language interpreters to help them access services. Some services (such as in education, mental health and employment) employ staff with an understanding of Deaf culture and sign language (or Auslan). Access to tertiary education where notetakers or interpreters are required is often restricted by limited availability.

Access

The provision of access to community activities and services enables people who are deaf or hearing impaired to contribute to the community. The problem is that for so long these people have been seen as not having anything to contribute, but once access is provided this is shown to be wrong. The community is gradually becoming aware of the need to provide access through the implementation of such programs. The gradual change in the community's attitude towards deafness is reflected in the popularity of sign language classes. The desired result is that deaf people are perceived not as a disabled group with medical problems but as a linguistic group with its own community and culture.

Access to community life and opportunities is greatly enhanced for people who are hearing impaired if assistive listening systems are available. Many public places such as churches and cinemas have such devices installed. The international symbol for deafness (a white ear and bar on a blue background) is displayed where access is available (see Figure 9.4). Many public phones now incorporate hearing aid couplers but as yet very few teletypewriter (TTY) phones are available in public phones. Many public facilities have a TTY to enable phone access to users. A national TTY relay service funded by the Commonwealth government enables phone calls to be linked to ordinary phones.

Some countries have legislation to ensure access is available in public places for people with hearing impairment. In Australia work is ongoing in this area and better access is needed. As yet, legislation such as the Commonwealth *Anti Discrimination Act 1992* has not been enforced in this regard. At the time of writing, a case has been before the Human Rights and Equal Opportunities Commission (HREOC) under the *Disability Services Act* in which it was found that Telstra (the national telephone provider) had discriminated against people who use TTYs by not providing TTYs to subscribers who are deaf in the same way that a telephone is provided to all other subscribers. Organisations such as the Australian Deafness Forum, Better Hearing Australia and Self Help for Hard of Hearing People (SHHH Australia Inc.) promote understanding of communication strategies, as well as encouraging the provision of assistive listening systems in public places.

Access to the community is provided either through technology (exemplified by subtitles on television), and/or interpreters which enable deaf and hearing people to communicate in an optimal manner. Subtitles on television enable people who are deaf or hearing impaired to access what is said on television. The Australian Caption Centre is a national non-profit organisation established in 1982 to facilitate television access for people who are deaf or hearing impaired. Subtitles are accessed by a decoder machine with subtitled programs indicated in the television guide by means of an 'S' symbol. Monthly schedules of captioned TV programs are

Figure 9.4: The international symbol for deafness

available. Sales tax exemption for the decoder is available to people who can provide a certificate from a doctor or from an Australian Hearing Service audiologist. The Australian Caption Centre also subtitles videos and films. Foreign films with subtitles in English are a boon for people who are deaf and hearing impaired.

Access to generic services can be made easier if staff have an understanding of how to communicate with their clients who are hearing impaired. The ACCESS 2000 staff training program distributed by the Deafness Forum teaches simple communication strategies for working with hearing impaired people. The Hearing Help Card used by some people gives communication hints. The Better Hearing Hospital Disc Program raises staff awareness in assisting people who are hearing impaired. Access to generic services may be facilitated by:

- deafness awareness training for staff. The purpose of such training is to educate staff about people who are deaf or hearing impaired and the implications of hearing loss including how to communicate effectively;
- provision of a sign language interpreter;
- use of captioned videos;
- written materials which are simple, uncluttered and with illustrations. Do not assume that a deaf person must have developed excellent reading skills as a means of compensating for his or her impairment. For deaf people who use sign language, English may be their second language. This, combined with not being able to hear spoken language, means that deaf people's reading may not be at a high level. Written material should be kept clear and straightforward;
- the provision of TTYs and employees who know how to use them;
- knowledge of communication strategies;
- staff participation in sign language classes;
- the provision of any other available technology that is relevant;
- the provision of assistive listening devices in public places.

Education

I went to deaf school for a year and then left to go to the local school. My mother didn't want me to use only sign language because it would stop me from being in the other world, the world of hearing people.

Alison

Most children who are hearing impaired now attend regular classes in mainstream schools. Children with multiple disabilities may attend a special school or special class in a mainstream school. The choice depends on the extent of hearing loss, place of residence and the back-up systems which are available.

Children (and adults) take in a huge amount of information by listening. If a child with a hearing impairment is to gain access to this information, it must be presented through other senses: through sign language, pictures, diagrams, mime, touching and so on. If the hearing impairment is detected early in life (up to four years of age), an early intervention program can be implemented to assist the child in achieving developmental milestones. Such programs have a wide range of benefits including assisting the child in developing communication skills, knowledge of social rules and ways of getting along with peers. By doing so, they prepare the child for school.

Sometimes parents have difficulty in deciding what form of education is best for their child with a hearing impairment. A special school has the advantage of expert teachers who can lip-read, use and teach sign language. As other children are hearing impaired, the child is less likely to feel isolated because it is easier to communicate with other students. On the other hand, a mainstream education provides the opportunity to mix with children who live locally. Thus, friendships can be formed which can be maintained after school hours. Attendance at a special school usually means considerable travel with friends not available for play during holidays or out of school time. Children with a hearing impairment are likely to find some subjects at school more difficult than others. For example, limited use of the English language and of the ability to think in abstract terms can hinder the understanding of subjects such as the social sciences and history. Again, this is not due to a lower level of intelligence, but to the lack of access to information. In the case of Deaf students, this means the absence of sign language interpreters or teachers who can sign fluently.

People who are deaf or hearing impaired have been successful in tertiary education, often with the support of interpreters, note takers and specialised equipment. However, because of communication difficulties, students with impaired hearing have to devote more time and energy to study than others. Such students find tutorials particularly difficult because they may not hear all the discussion which takes place (Mitchell, 1986). They also may have to alert their teachers to lecturing styles which assist (rather than hinder) learning. For example, it may be necessary to ask a lecturer not to continue talking when his or her back is turned during periods of writing on the whiteboard. Many lecturers are more than pleased to provide the student with a copy of overhead material. Australian universities are now required to have an Equal Opportunity in Education (EOE) policy which includes strategies to assist people with disabilities in their learning.

> At university I did engineering. In my four years of lectures I never heard a word! . . . The only special attention I received was that a meeting was arranged with all the tutors involved in the laboratories. This was done for safety purposes, with machinery and so on. In terms of safety, the tutors had to be aware of my hearing impairment.
>
> Peter

Employment

> I left school and went nursing. I had terrible trouble because I had difficulty in taking accurate instructions. The crunch came when I had to go to the operating room and, of course, with people wearing masks, I couldn't lip-read. I had to leave.
>
> Emily

The above vignette is several years old and records an experience of a person with a disability in the days when government had taken few steps to ensure equality of access to employment and education. Today, organisations have a legal requirement under the *Disability Discrimination Act 1992* to ensure equality of access. Hopefully, knowing about such legislation would make Emily more confident and assertive about standing up for her rights. Responsibilities for ensuring access lie in the hands of both the organisation and the person with hearing impairment. Despite changing legislation, some people still try to hide their impairment from employers and workmates. As a result, they do not get the

Figure 9.5: A young boy using a technical aid which assists him with his schoolwork

assistance they need and may appear to be inefficient (Mitchell, 1986). Even when the job itself presents no problem, poor communication with fellow workers may lead to frustration and dissatisfaction. Office lunches and after work get-togethers can prove to be so stressful for people with a hearing impairment that they choose to exclude themselves from future activities. Colleagues may interpret this behaviour as anti-social, thus detracting from positive work relationships. However, as said earlier in this paragraph, it is the responsibility of both sides to find strategies to maximise the effectiveness of communication. Both the person with hearing impairment and his or her workmates should take steps to overcome barriers. Some of these strategies are suggested later in the chapter.

People with severe hearing impairments are found in a wide range of occupations: lawyers who appear in court, counsellors who spend a lot of time talking to clients and machine workers are examples of people in occupations where others rely on their hearing but where people with hearing impairment have made successful adaptations. The advent of electronic mail and TTY telephones has opened up many employment opportunities for people with hearing impairment as have many other technological devices.

It is important not to stereotype people according to what you think are appropriate jobs for them. For example, it is a myth that people who are deaf or hearing impaired can tolerate noisy environments better than can hearing people. It is rare for a deaf or hearing impaired person to have no hearing at all. Depending on the type of loss, a hearing impaired person may find it uncomfortable to work in noisy areas. Extremely high noise levels can further damage the person's remaining hearing. People who wear hearing aids are more sensitive to high noise levels because hearing aids amplify all noise.

Deafness awareness training is available for staff in service provision and the workplace. This training educates people such as service providers, workmates and employers about people who are deaf or hearing impaired, the implications of hearing loss and how to communicate effectively.

PERSON TO PERSON

Appropriate language and behaviour

Hearing impairment is generally a hidden disability. It is not obvious to others that the person has a disability. In fact, we tend to assume that other people *are* able to hear. Even when a hearing aid is obviously used, people assume that the wearer is able to hear clearly because of it. It is not generally understood that such devices have limitations. As a result, people are less likely to made accommodations in their interaction with a deaf or hearing impaired person than they are with people having other disabilities.

It is not appropriate to force your way of communicating on to someone with a hearing loss; ask how she or he prefers to communicate. Do not isolate people with hearing impairments, include them in conversations and activities. If a person who is hearing impaired is involved in a conversation or communication session (such as a lecture or small-group discussion) ensure that an assistive listening system, such as an audio loop or FM system, is provided.

Strategies for interaction

To communicate effectively, it is necessary for both parties to make certain adjustments. People who are deaf or hearing impaired have 'rules' to follow and

Table 9.5: Strategies for successful interaction

Person with hearing impairment or who is deaf and can lip-read and/or speak well	Other person
Pay attention.	Get the person's attention by tapping lightly on the shoulder or waving hands gently within vision.
Let the other person know what you need in order to take part in the conversation effectively.	Ask what you can do to facilitate the conversation.
Stop the person if you have not understood.	Speak naturally, do not exaggerate lip movements, do not speak too slowly or too fast. Do not shout or mumble. When speaking, do not have objects in your mouth such as gum, cigarettes or food.
Do not interrupt, let the conversation flow for a while and you are likely to understand it.	Use simple language, rephrase your message if it is not understood, avoid unnecessary words or long sentences.
Focus on all cues, lip-reading and interpreting gestures and facial expressions.	Move into the light, do not stand with your back to a window or bright light, keep your face out of the shadows.
React to show whether or not you have understood.	Give cues: use your hands and facial expressions.
If you are too tired to concentrate, let the other person know and suggest putting off the conversation for a while.	Be patient, take time to make sure you have been understood, be prepared to repeat yourself.
Do not be afraid to ask the person what he or she has said.	Look at the person as you talk, do not look away or cover your lips, do not eat or smoke, do not walk around the room.
	When talking to a group of people which includes someone with a hearing impairment or who is deaf, take steps to communicate your message so that this person is included.
	Do not shout into a hearing aid.

Table 9.6: Some suggestions for communicating with someone who is deaf or hearing impaired and cannot speak and/or lip-read

---

- Get the person's attention.
- Use simple language.
- Give clues and be patient.
- Use fingerspelling.
- Write down what you want to say.
- Use a combination of speech, writing and signing.
- Use a sign language interpreter.

---

adjustments to make. The same applies to those without an impairment. Do not assume that a person wearing a hearing aid is able to hear as well as others do. Hearing aids amplify sounds, they do not make sounds clearer. Their main application is to enable people to play a fuller part in spoken communication. The extent to which they are successful varies from one individual to another. Although hearing aids are helpful, they have limitations and the person may still rely on lip-reading. In noisy surroundings, such as a party or where an air-conditioner is operating, a hearing aid is not likely to be useful as it amplifies all sounds, not just speech.

Other strategies are available for communicating with people who do not use speech and lip-reading as the primary means of communication. Learn and use finger spelling. Sometimes it is necessary to write down what you want to say. Use a sign language interpreter. Sometimes, a combination of speech, writing and signing is the most appropriate.

I must have been lip-reading unconsciously for as long as I can remember. Sometimes I got things wrong and in a group I made a fool of myself by making inappropriate comments. I could never have a relaxed conversation; it was always a strain.

Max

MORE INFORMATION ABOUT HEARING IMPAIRMENT AND DEAFNESS

Anatomy

To understand the effects of hearing impairment it is necessary to know something of the structure and function of the ear. Figure 9.6 illustrates the main sections of the ear: the outer, middle and inner.

The *inner ear* consists of the pinna, external auditory canal and the tympanic membrane (eardrum).

The *middle ear* is a cavity containing three small bones, the malleus, incus and stapes, commonly called hammer, anvil and stirrup. The malleus is firmly attached to the tympanic membrane on the outer side and the stapes to the oval window (fenestra ovalis) on the inner side. The bones are connected by small joints which allow movements of the tympanic membrane to be transmitted to the inner ear.

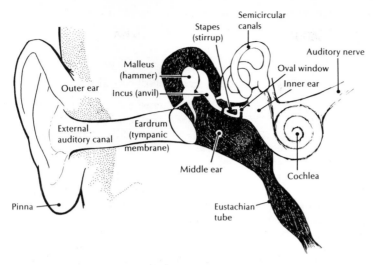

Figure 9.6: The ear

The cavity of the middle ear is connected with the nasal passage by the eustachian tube to equalise air pressure inside and outside the ear. Equalisation of these pressures is essential for effective hearing.

The inner ear starts at the oval window which connects with the middle ear. It contains the semicircular canals (which are mainly concerned with balance), cochlea and the origins of the auditory or acoustic nerve where sound waves are changed to nerve impulses.

The mechanism of hearing

Sound is transmitted in waves which vary according to the type of noise. A low-pitched noise produces long slow waves (low frequency). A high-pitched noise produces short rapid waves (high frequency). The pitch of the sound, therefore, is detected by its frequency and is measured in hertz (or the number of cycles per second). The quantity of the sound is its loudness or amplification and is measured in decibels.

Sound waves pass down the external auditory canal to strike the tympanic membrane, making it vibrate and so set up oscillation in the bones of the middle ear. This movement is transferred via the oval window and the cochlea to stimulate the hairlike endings of the auditory nerve. These stimuli pass down the auditory nerve, through the internal auditory canal to the hearing centre in the temporal lobe of the brain, where they are registered as sound and appreciated according to their frequency and amplitude. Storrs (1973) notes that the human ear is a receiving mechanism of exquisite fidelity. It is able to receive frequencies ranging from 20 to 20 000 hertz, but is tuned particularly to receive human speech which occurs at frequencies of 500, 1000 and 2000 hertz. Interference with any part of this mechanism will result in impaired hearing or deafness.

The mechanism of hearing can be divided into two main components: *conductive,* involving conduction of sound waves through the outer and middle ears; and *sensori-neural,* involving the transference of sound through the inner ear, the change to nerve impulses and their passage to the brain for interpretation.

Definition

In terms of the World Health Organization (1980) classification:

- *Impairment* refers to damage to the mechanism of hearing which involves the outer, middle and inner ear, auditory nerve and hearing centre in the brain. The extent of any damage to the ear will determine the extent of the hearing loss and this in turn will largely determine whether someone is 'hearing impaired' or 'deaf'. There are four broad types of impairment which lead to hearing loss:
  - *Conductive.* Damage to the outer and/or middle ear (such as deformity, build-up of wax, accident or trauma to bones in the middle ear).
  - *Sensori-neural.* Damage to the inner ear and cochlea (this can be due to ageing, noise, illness, heredity, accidents or damage from ototoxic drugs (these are known to have a toxic effect on the cochlear or vestibular organs – these drugs include amino-glycosides and some diuretics)).
  - *Mixed.* Both conductive and sensori-neural damage (a combination of the above).
  - *Central.* Damage to auditory pathways in the central nervous system (caused brain damage or tumours).
- *Disability* refers to lack, loss or reduction of the ability to hear and interpret sounds.
- *Handicap* refers to difficulties in communication which may be compounded by social and environmental factors and result in disadvantage in areas such as education, employment, leisure and recreation.

Causes

Impairment may result from congenital causes, heredity factors, infection, trauma, degeneration and exposure to noisy environments or industry.

Genetic or heredity factors. Impairment may affect some members of several generations or the entire family of a single generation. The loss usually becomes evident after birth and progresses to profound disability. Only about 10 per cent of deaf children are born to deaf adults (Neisser, 1990).

Congenital hearing loss. The major congenital cause of hearing loss is maternal rubella or German measles, particularly during the first trimester (three months of pregnancy). Maternal rubella at this stage nearly always results in total hearing loss in the child. If the infection occurs later in pregnancy there is a fair chance that some hearing will be present at birth. However, this may deteriorate as age advances, with severe or profound disability occurring by the end of childhood. Maternal toxaemia and marked prematurity may also result in hearing impairment.

Acquired hearing loss. This may result from trauma, infection, degenerative or environmental causes:

- *Trauma.* This can cause severe head injury and fracture of the base of the skull which damages the structure of the ear or the auditory nerve.

- *Infection*. This can occur after birth and usually results in bilateral suppurative otitis media which destroys the middle ear and causes complete deafness. Once common, this source of impairment has now almost disappeared because of antibiotics. Severe meningitis and encephalitis are other infections which can cause impairment. They are still a cause of sudden, severe loss of hearing.
- *Degenerative hearing loss*. This can accompany advancing age, where the most common cause of hearing loss is presbycusis, which is a sensori-neural loss. It involves gradual loss of ability to hear and differentiate high-frequency sounds. Other causes of degenerative hearing loss are cardiovascular disorders such as hypertension and atherosclerosis which impair blood supply to the sensori-neural areas. Arthritic changes in the small joints in the middle ear reduce their mobility and can result in conductive deafness. One type of arthritic change, otosclerosis (which results in a bony overgrowth in the middle ear) causes conductive deafness. This condition can be greatly improved by surgery. Tinnitus, which may vary from a low roar to a high-pitched ringing noise, is often associated with hearing loss.
- *Environmental or industrial deafness*. This results from frequent exposure to loud noise which causes slowly progressive hearing impairment. Continuous exposure to loud music may have similar effects. This deafness results from damage to the more sensitive high-frequency nerve receptors, resulting in degeneration. It may therefore, be regarded as due to traumatic and degenerative causes and is a sensori-neural deafness.

Incidence and prevalence

The Australian Bureau of Statistics (1988a) estimates that 7.4 per cent of the population under 60 years of age has a hearing loss, with 0.3 per cent of these people having a severe congenital or profound hearing loss. Stopford (1988) reports that one in five people in the United Kingdom have difficulty with hearing, although level of impairment is not specified. Boyd and Otos (1981) report that around 8.5 million people in the United States seek medical attention for hearing loss, with three million of these having a major hearing loss.

In 1978, the Australian Bureau of Statistics estimated that between two and three children are born deaf for every 1000 live births (that is 200–300 per 100 000 of the Australian population). More recent figures are not readily available.

Johnston (1989), reports that there may be a Deaf signing population in Australia of at least 10 000 people. Hyde and Power (1991) report that 14 000 people in their study were described as 'Deaf users of sign language'.

In Canada, one in every 1500 babies is born with some degree of deafness. Overall, 2.5 million Canadians (out of a population of around 30 million) has some form of hearing impairment. Of these people, one in 40 has an impairment which creates a barrier to everyday oral communication. In Canada, 30 000 people are classified as being profoundly deaf, 200 000 people cannot use an unmodified telephone and 400 000 use hearing aids. Deafness and hearing loss is the most common disability in North America (Canada and the United States), largely because of the ageing population (Statistics Canada, 1992). Hearing impairment is also the fastest-growing disability in North America and this increase has been attributed mainly to noise pollution. In the United States there are 184 000 people who are classified as having deafness in both ears, 498 000 as having hearing impairment in both ears, and 493 000 as being affected in at least one ear (LaPlante & Carlson, 1996).

Approximately one New Zealand child in 1000 has an onset of deafness on or around birth and by the age of five years, prevalence rates are 1.7 to 1.8 per 1000 children. For the adult population, it is estimated that in New Zealand 462 500 people have a hearing loss of greater than 25 decibels (The Review Team to Consider Hearing Impairment Among Maori People, 1989).

Age. Generally speaking, hearing loss increases with age. Around one in ten people have a hearing loss in the general population, but the prevalence is one in three for people aged 65 years and over. The processes of ageing result in a gradual loss of acuity in hearing. Hearing loss is the most common disability of old age. Loss associated with ageing is gradual, but usually has become noticeable by the time the person has reached 65–70 years of age.

People of Australian Aboriginal backgrounds. Aboriginal infants and children are known to be at high risk for hearing disorders resulting from otitis media (middle ear infection). As yet, there are no published data available about the prevalence or severity of this form of conductive hearing loss. Between 20 and 50 per cent of Aboriginal children have significant hearing impairments which affect their education. Reports suggest that in Sydney nearly 30 per cent of Aboriginal school children (as compared with 4 per cent of non-Aboriginal children) have educationally significant hearing impairments. Ear infections may be left untreated because of lack of access to medical and audiological services and result in permanent moderate to severe hearing losses in adulthood.

The Review Team to Consider Hearing Impairment Among Maori people (1989) concluded that hearing loss among the Maori population is likely to exceed that for the general New Zealand population. Although no precise national statistics are available, the Review Team reached this conclusion following analysis of socio-economic indicators and regional statistics. It argued that otitis media and its complications were the major causative factors of hearing impairment in the Maori population.

People of non–English-speaking backgrounds (NESB). In Australia this population has a higher prevalence of industrially-related disablement, including deafness, as compared with the population as a whole. However, until recently, little evidence was available to confirm this. (Note: From 1 July 1991 the Australian Hearing Services has gathered statistics for hearing impairment among Australian Aborigines and people of NESB.) Among people who migrated to Australia, it is likely that prevalence of severe hearing impairment or deafness is less than the rest of the population, as prior to 1987 deafness was classified as a contagious disease by the Australian immigration authorities and people were denied entry. However, many people who are hearing impaired migrated to Australia with their parents at a very young age, before their impairment was diagnosed, or were born here but have parents who speak little or no English. Issues for people of non–English-speaking backgrounds who acquire a hearing loss in adulthood can be compounded by disadvantage resulting from limited knowledge of the English language and lack of awareness of available services. Different cultures approach the issue of hearing impairment in culturally specific ways.

People with hearing loss and an additional disability. People who have a disability are more likely to have a hearing impairment than members of the general population. The 1988 survey conducted by the Australian Bureau of Statistics (1988b) revealed that over 240 000 people in NSW had a hearing loss and an additional disability.

Diagnosis

The general diagnosis of hearing loss is not difficult to make. Unfortunately, many people do not realise the extent of their disability because its development has been slow and gradually progressive. The two fundamentals of diagnosis are early detection and accurate assessment.

Early diagnosis involves routine checks of all children during the first year of life and again immediately before school entry. These checks should be followed by routine annual checks on all children and also adolescents, regular examination of adults working under excessively noisy conditions and thorough examination of hearing after head injuries or severe intracranial infection. Any suspicion of hearing loss, *at any age*, requires full and complete medical examination. Regular, thorough examinations should be conducted if a history of family deafness exists.

Accurate assessment is necessary once hearing loss has been established. This means immediate referral to a specialist (otologist) to determine the degree, type and the sound frequencies involved.

Several methods are available to measure hearing and hearing loss. In very young children (six months to two years of age), visual reinforcement audiometry may be used. According to Pillon (1995), in this technique a child is exposed to animated toys that appear in a window as sounds are presented through a speaker or earphones. The child can be tested for hearing, once he or she has learnt to anticipate the toys' appearance by turning the head towards the window on hearing a sound. Computers can be used to assess hearing in children who are unable to make voluntary responses to sound. The computer is used to measure the brain's response to sound (auditory evoked potentials, AEPs). In older people and those who are able to make voluntary responses to sound, the person is asked whether he or she can hear sounds of differing frequencies (hertz) and decibel strength which are presented through earphones.

Early diagnosis and accurate assessment offer the best chances to minimise the effects of hearing impairment and deafness on development and everyday life.

Treatment

Some conditions respond well to surgery, usually conducted by an ear, nose and throat (ENT) specialist. Partial sensori-neural hearing losses cannot be treated medically or surgically, but a cochlear implant can assist those who have lost most or all hearing.

Supports and services

In Australia, children to the age of 21, pensioners, part-pensioners, war veterans through the Department of Veterans Affairs, and holders of a Commonwealth Seniors Health Card are eligible for services provided by Australian Hearing Services. These include free hearing testing, free hearing aids and continuing maintenance and battery supply for an annual fee. Other people are required to use services provided by private audiologists, audiometrists and hearing aid retailers where fees are charged on a commercial basis.

Rehabilitation programs are covered by voluntary organisations such as speech reading classes run by Better Hearing Australia or support groups run by Self Help for Hard of Hearing People.

Aids and equipment

A range of equipment and aids is available to assist deaf and hearing impaired people in their communication with others.

Hearing aids. These amplify sounds, enabling the wearer to hear environmental sounds and speech. Ability to understand speech using a hearing aid depends on the type and degree of hearing impairment. In some cases the aid will amplify sound but may not make speech any easier to understand. In a noisy environment, the aid will amplify background noise, making it difficult to understand conversations. Despite these limitations, a hearing aid, when appropriately fitted by an experienced professional, can be the first and best avenue of assistance to a person with a hearing loss. Aids are worn behind the ear, in the ear, in the arm of spectacles or on the body. In-the-ear aids are popular and audiologists prefer to prescribe them for young children, as they can be finely tuned more easily and can be adjusted if a child's hearing changes over time (Pillon, 1995). The operation of a hearing aid should be monitored regularly to ensure that its wearer gains optimal benefit from it. Some hearing aids are fitted with a telecoil or direct audio input facility, enabling the aid to be used with other equipment in certain situations.

> *I had been given a hearing aid in primary school. It was a big, cumbersome body aid and when I wore it, the children teased me. In high school, my mother enlisted the aid of the headmaster to make me wear it. I can remember being marched in front of the class, where he informed the children that I had to wear the aid. I wore it for a while and then took it off because I saw it as just another barrier.*
>
> Anne, who went to school in the 1960s. (Hearing aids have become more compact since then.)

Programmable hearing aids. Some digital hearing aids can be programmed to suit a person's hearing loss. A remote-control handset enables the wearer to adjust the setting if there is difficulty in adjusting the aid manually.

The bionic ear or cochlear implant. This is the latest technology, enabling profoundly deaf people to hear sound. An external ear processor is attached to an electrode implanted in the cochlear, and the auditory nerve is stimulated to respond to environmental sounds. Pillon (1995) notes that the benefits of cochlear implant surgery are controversial, especially with young children. According to Pillon, benefits vary greatly between individuals. Fragomeni (1994) describes a cochlear implant as having three main parts: the implant, a speech processor and a unit containing a microphone, cable and transmitter. The implant is implanted surgically, the speech processor is worn on a belt around the waist and looks like a pocket calculator, and the microphone looks like a behind-the-ear hearing aid. Sounds are picked up by the microphone and sent to the speech processor for

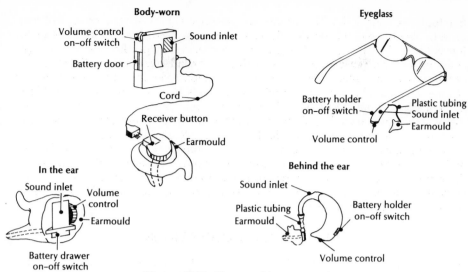

Figure 9.7: Types of hearing aids

Reproduced with permission of the publisher from L. Gething (1990). Working with older people. Sydney: W. B. Saunders/Baillière Tindall (Harcourt Brace & Co)

amplification. Sound is digitised and, via the transmitter, stimulates electrodes in the implant. These electrodes then activate the nerves in the inner ear, creating the sensation of sound which is sent to the brain for interpretation.

Assistive listening devices. In addition to hearing aids, people with hearing impairment require other assistive devices to enhance their independence and quality of life. Costs vary but many people spend several hundred dollars a year on extra equipment and services. Some of these items are:

*   telephone aids (such as volume control, hearing-aid coupler, gliding and tone caller) and teletypewriter (TTY) phones which enable those unable to hear on the phone to communicate using a keyboard;
*   TV listening aids (infra-red systems, induction loop systems, subtitled TV decoders);
*   group listening aids (personal FM systems, hand-held microphones and conference microphones);
*   visual alert systems (flashing alarms for doorbells, clocks, fire alarms, telephones, baby cry alarms etc). There also is a 'Shake-awake' alarm clock which vibrates under a person's pillow.

In auditoriums and meeting rooms, the installation of assistive listening systems such as an audio loop, FM system or infra-red system provide audio access for people who are hearing impaired.

Additional costs

Costs vary from country to country depending on government subsidies and grants. However, costs may include those for hearing aids (purchase, fitting, maintenance, batteries and repair) and audiological services. In some countries, hearing aids are free for those aged under 21 years and for pensioners. In Australia, the current cost for a behind-the ear-aid supplied through a hospital is $620 to $950. In general, this is lower than the price charged by an audiologist in private practice or by a commercial hearing aid supplier. The high cost of hearing aids reflects the inclusion of a high service content which is not charged separately. In some cases, fees are covered by medical insurance, but this rarely covers all costs. Currently, a cochlear implant costs about A$17000. Government funds are available to assist some people but others have to pay the full equipment cost. In Australia most medical insurance covers hospital and medical costs, but not equipment costs.

Access to higher education involves costs for interpreters, transcription of tapes and use of note takers. Once these costs were borne by the student, but now it is the responsibility of the educational institution to make education accessible for all students; however, it still requires assertiveness on the part of students to make complaints so that their needs are met.

RESOURCE ORGANISATIONS

All care has been taken to ensure that all information is correct at the time of publishing. However, responsibility for the accuracy of this information is not accepted by the writer. The list of resource organisations contained in this chapter is not intended to be exhaustive – it provides national organisations only. The reader is referred to local community directories for further information and for local branches of national organisations. Inclusion of services and organisations should not be taken as a recommendation.

Australia

Australian National Hearing Services
National Head Office
126 Greville Street
Chatswood NSW 2067
Ph 02 9412 6800

Better Hearing Australia (National Office)
183 Wakefield Street
Adelaide SA 5000
Ph/TTY 08 232 2996
Fax 08 223 1692

Deafness Forum Ltd
National Secretariat
7B/17 Napier Close
Deakin ACT 2600
(PO Box 60
Curtin ACT 2605)
Ph TTY 06 281 3156
Ph 06 281 3934
Fax 06 281 4309

Deafness Resources Australia
Ground Floor, 33 Argyle Street
Parramatta NSW 2150
Locked Bag 5380
Parramatta NSW 2124
Ph 02 9893 8139
Ph TTY 02 9893 8036
Fax 02 9893 8172

Self Help for Hard of Hearing People Inc
(SHHH)
1334 Pacific Highway
Turramurra NSW 2074
Ph TTY 02 9758 6449
Fax 02 9449 2381

Canada

Canadian Association of the Deaf
Suite 205, 2435 Holly Lane
Ottawa ON K1V 7P2
Ph 613 526 4785
TTY/TDD 613 526 4785
Fax 613 526 4718

Canadian Cultural Society of the Deaf Inc
Suite 144, 11337-61st Avenue
Edmonton AB T6G 1M3
TTY/TDD 403 436 2599
Fax 403 430 9489

Canadian Deaf and Hard of Hearing
Forum
Suite 205, 2435 Holly Lane
Ottawa ON K1V 7P2
Ph 613 526 1584
TDD 613 526 2498
Fax 613 526 4718

Canadian Deafened Persons Association
   (CDPA)
Suite 810, 199 Graydon Hall Drive
North York, ON M3A 3A7
Ph 416 922 3532
TDD 416 391 4627
Fax 416 922 8552

Canadian Hearing Society
271 Spadina Road
Toronto ON M5R 2V3
TTY/TDD 416 964 0023
Fax 416 964 2066

New Zealand

Deaf Association of New Zealand (Inc.)
Ground Floor, 3 Totara Avenue
(PO Box 15-770)
New Lynn, Auckland 7
Ph/TTY 09 827 0314
Fax 09 827 0316

Hearing Association of New Zealand
   (National Office)
98 Remuera Road
Auckland 5
Ph 09 522 0801
Fax 09 522 1622

National Foundation for the Deaf Inc
Suite 3, 2nd Floor
93 Dominion Road
Auckland 1003
(PO Box 99261)
Newmarket, Auckland
Ph/TTY 09 638 8885
Fax 09 638 8834

United Kingdom

British Deaf Association
38 Victoria Place
Carlisle, Cumbria CAI 1HU
Ph/TTY 0228 48844
Fax 0228 41420

Deaf Self Help Society
Wilton House
5 College Square
North Belfast BT1 6AR
Ph/TTY 0232 236581

Royal National Institute for Deaf People
   (RNID)
105 Gower Street
London WCIE 6AH
Ph 071 387 8033
TTY 071 383 3154
Fax 071 388 2346

United States

Better Hearing Institute
5021-B Backlick Road
Annandale VA 22003
Ph 703 642 0580
National Information Center on
   Deafness
Gallaudet University
800 Florida Avenue NE
Washington, DC 20002 3695
Ph 202 651 5051

National Information Center on
   Deafness
Gallaudet University
800 Florida Avenue NE
Washington DC 20002 3695
Ph 202 651 5051

Self Help for Hard of Hearing People
   (SHHH)
7910 Woodmond Solte 1200
Bethseda MD 20814
Ph: 301 657 2248
TTY: 301 657 2249
Fax 301 913 9413

FURTHER READING

Ackehurst, S. (1989). *Broken silence*. London: Collins.
Fragomeni, C. (1994). Kristopher's new world. *Disability Today*, 4 (1), 26–9.
Freeland, A. (1989). *Deafness: the facts*. Oxford: Oxford University Press.
Fritz, G. & Smith, N. (1985). *The hearing impaired employee: an untapped resource*.
   London: College-Hill Press.
Gething, L. (1990). *Working with older people*. Sydney: W. B. Saunders. (Chapter 14).
Jacobs, L. (1988). *A Deaf adult speaks out*. Washington, DC: Gallaudet College Press.
Johnston, T. (1989). *Auslan dictionary*. (A dictionary of the sign language of the Australian
   Deaf community). Melbourne: Deafness Resources Australia.

Hyde, M. & Power, D. (1991). *The use of Australian sign language by Deaf people.* Brisbane: Griffith University.

Landau, E. (1994). *Deafness.* New York: Twenty First Century Books.

Lane, H. (1993). *The mask of benevolence: disabling the Deaf community.* New York: Vintage Books.

Lee, R. (1992). *Deaf liberation.* Middlesex, UK: National Union of the Deaf.

Lewis, N. (1987). Deaf Culture. *CHIPS,* 12, September.

McCall, R. (1991). *Hearing loss: a guide to self help.* London: Hale.

Maclean, A. (1990). *Deaf people in the workplace: a guide for employers.* Melbourne: Victorian School for Deaf Children.

Moore, M. S. & Levitan, L. (1993). *For hearing people only.* New York: Deaf Life Press.

Neisser, A. (1990). *The other side of silence: sign language and the Deaf community in America.* Washington, DC: Gallaudet University Press.

Orlans, H. (ed.) (1989). *Adjustment to adult hearing loss.* College Hill Press Inc.

Padden, C. & Humphries, T. (1988). *Deaf in America: voices from a culture.* Harvard University Press.

Rosen, F. (1989). *Hearing loss: the invisible handicap.* Sydney: SHHH Australia Inc.

Sacks, O. (1989). *Seeing voices.* London: Picador.

Saunders, J. (1992). *Tinnitus: what is that noise in my ear?* Auckland: Sandalwood Enterprises.

Slater, R. & Terry, M. (1990). *Tinnitus: a guide for sufferers and professionals.* London: Chapman & Hall.

Taylor, F. & Bishop, J. (1990). *Being Deaf: the experience of deafness.* London: The Open University.

Thompsett, K. & Nickerson, E. (1992). *Missing words: the family handbook of adult hearing loss.* Washington, DC: Gallaudet University Press.

Walker, L. & Rickards, F. W. (1992). *Report to the Department of School Education, Victoria.* Melbourne: Deafness Studies Unit, The University of Melbourne.

Weir, G. (1987). *How to live with a hearing loss.* Sydney: Deafness Resources Australia.

Youngson, R. M. (1991). *How to cope with tinnitus and hearing loss.* Oxford: Isis.

CHAPTER 10

IMPAIRMENT TO THE FUNCTION OF THE SPINAL CORD

Spinal cord injury can occur in a variety of ways. Road accidents and sporting injuries are the most common single causes of acquired spinal cord injury and can result in paraplegia and quadriplegia. The second most common form of injury is other accidents such as falls or crushes. Spinal cord injury also can occur as a result of birth trauma and from congenital malformation of the spine. It also can occur as a result of other non-traumatic illnesses or neurological conditions such as vascular lesions, infections and clots.

Acquired, congenital and degenerative spinal cord injuries require major adaptations to lifestyle. Although their causation is different, many of the issues which apply for people with acquired spinal cord injury are also relevant for those with degenerative or congenital injury. They experience similar reactions and processes. Critical differences are:

- the immediacy of traumatic injury;
- the effects of experience and age of onset of disability.

While many people find it easier to adjust over a longer span of time, a response of one person who acquired his injury suddenly is as follows:

> *Both being born with a disability and acquiring one later in life have positive aspects and difficult adjustments. To be born with a disability, you always wonder what it would have been like without it. To acquire a disability, you always mourn what you've lost. Because it's all I have known, I would say that it's 'better' to acquire a disability – at least you've had a wider range of experiences without restrictions and barriers.*

> John, who acquired his disability
> in his early twenties as a result of a motor accident

PARAPLEGIA AND QUADRIPLEGIA

Paraplegia and quadriplegia are two major physical conditions which result from injury to the spinal cord. A vital factor is the area of the spinal cord which receives damage (impairment) and the extent of damage. Generally, the higher the injury, the more extensive are the effects on functioning (disability) and on the individual's lifestyle.

- *Paraplegia* results from damage to the spinal cord below the neck region. It involves paralysis from the chest or waist downwards, with little or no feeling or movement in the lower limbs and lower part of the trunk.

- *Quadriplegia* (sometimes called tetraplegia) results from damage to the spinal cord in the neck region. It affects the arms and hands as well as the legs and feet, so paralysis involves all four limbs. At a higher level, it will also affect breathing.

Paraplegia and quadriplegia may occur from sudden trauma or may result from gradual deterioration. This chapter focuses on injury resulting from sudden trauma.

Spinal cord injury does not affect the brain. Thus, there is no mental or intellectual impairment. With appropriate care, the life expectancy of a person is not affected (Australian Federal Government, 1993d).

LIVING WITH PARAPLEGIA AND QUADRIPLEGIA

Although acquired spinal cord injury occurs most commonly in young adult males, it occurs in both genders and all age groups. It is important to keep this variation in mind when considering the implications of this disability. Every person has individual needs and preferred ways of having them met. People with physical impairments are no exception. The information below is general. The individual concerned should always be consulted and each situation assessed individually.

I'm still the same person as far as my mental approach. I've always been positive, aggressive, determined. Quadriplegia is just a physical handicap.

Michael, who acquired quadriplegia after a football accident at 29 years of age

Having a disability requires learning new routines and adapting to alternative ways of doing things. A person who acquires a spinal injury must relearn everyday tasks such as toileting, showering, dressing and eating. The person also must learn new skills such as using a wheelchair, avoiding pressure sores and using hand controls for driving a motor car. For people with quadriplegia, the relearning process may involve getting accustomed to using adaptive aids for eating, writing, operating household appliances and anything that previously would have required full use of both hands.

Sensation and pressure sores. For most people there is loss of sensation below the level of the lesion (which can be complete or incomplete for both paraplegia and quadriplegia). This makes the person with spinal cord injury vulnerable to pressure sores and further injury. Pressure areas can be prevented by maintaining a good diet and by avoiding:

- skin damage (bruises/burns);
- excessive pressure on bony areas as a result of body weight;
- over-drying of skin (careful selection of soap is important, as some soaps can exacerbate this problem while others can relieve it);
- creases in clothing and bedding;
- ill-fitting shoes and clothing;

- prolonged contact with heat (car heaters, radiators, hot water bottles, electric blankets, and so on);
- incorrect lifting or positioning techniques.

Fitness. A high level of fitness is required for the person to maintain independence. This is particularly important for people who use manual wheelchairs and who must transfer (lift themselves into their wheelchair). Physiological complications can prevent a person from reaching an acceptable fitness level without extreme and constant effort. Without such a level of conditioning, the person becomes unable to maintain everyday activities. Injuries also become more common and further debilitate the person. However, a balance is required since regular and frequent exercise of small muscle groups (arms, shoulders and joints) can lead to chronic injuries and overuse. People with spinal cord injury need a high fluid intake and a balanced diet with plenty of fibre. Without this, bowel and bladder problems can occur (Australian Federal Government, 1993d).

Temperature sensitivity. There may be a loss of the ability to retain heat and to maintain temperature control. This is particularly important in quadriplegia where perspiration mechanisms are often impaired. It is important for service providers to be aware of this potential danger for the person unable to handle fluctuations in climate and room temperature.

> *Even the weather is a concern. If it's too hot we must be in air-conditioned places, too cold and our muscles tighten and arms won't move.*

> Michael

Continence. In most cases, damage to the spinal cord results in incontinence, making it necessary to use new methods of control. There are many ways that people manage bladder and bowel incontinence and the one used will depend on gender and the physical abilities of the individual.

For bladder management, males and females both mainly use indwelling catheters inserted into the urethra or they use supra-pubic catheters (which pass through the abdomen to the bladder, and for which surgery is required) which are connected to a drainage bag. Males have the option of wearing a condom-like device known as a uridome which is connected to a drainage bag. This option is used if the bladder can be trained to empty by a reflex action when full. Another option for both genders is to perform self-catheterisation a number of times during the day. This gives the freedom of not needing to wear a drainage bag. All options have their good and bad points. A major problem is risk of urinary tract infections, so high levels of hygeine and a high consumption of fluids are essential.

For bowel management, people try to maintain a regular routine, usually every second day. This is usually done by taking laxatives the day before and using enemas or suppositories the next day. Bowel management is very important as bowel accidents are a major cause of inconvenience, frustration and embarrassment.

Day-to-day management and receiving paid care. Acquiring a severe disability is likely to mean many changes to the way in which a person conducts daily living activities. Rehabilitation is likely to involve relearning many commonplace activities such as eating, dressing, driving a car and so on. For many people it also involves coming to terms with the need to use help and assistance provided by others. This process requires the person to accept the fact that he or she is no longer able to independently carry out activities which were once done with little thought or were taken for granted. Assistance may be required in such things as dressing, showering, toileting, driving, feeding, exercising, shopping and socialising (Batterham, 1986). Someone else may be required to help with the most personal and private bodily and personal functions. For example, menstruation is a time not particularly enjoyed by some women, but for a woman who requires assistance, very intimate and personal hygiene tasks associated with menstruation may cause considerable unease and embarrassment.

As most people with disabilities are living in the community, the issue of employing people to assist with everyday activities is important. Such care is important to enhance quality of life and potential for the person with a disability and to enable family and friends to carry on their own lives. Paid assistance is regarded by people with disabilities as a human and civil right which should enable the user to participate in every aspect of life such as home, work, leisure, travel, school, political life, and so on (Quad Wrangle, 1990). It involves assistance in carrying out those activities of daily living which, because of functional limitations, people are unable to adequately perform themselves (Ross, 1988). A person may use the services of a single carer or may need access to several carers in order to cover the range of skills required and to provide a service spanning many hours per day. High-need clients are the people who tend to require a high number of service hours and a package of assistance (Quad Wrangle, 1990). Services vary from one state and country to another, but generally involve a paid worker coming to the person's home for a set number of hours per week to provide assistance. Systems of payment differ. In some services, such as the Home Care Service of NSW, the government administers payment for the provision of care, however the client should have a major role in regard to the selection and direction of the worker. This service provides general housekeeping, personal care, live-in housekeepers, handypersons and relief care (Australian Quad Wrangle, 1988). Other systems, such as attendant care, give responsibility to the person with a disability (the client) to select and pay the carer with funds usually provided to the client by the government or a service organisation. It is argued by people with disabilities that, in many cases, subsidies do not cover the cost of care and the client is required to make up the deficit from elsewhere.

Using paid care not only requires acceptance of the need for help and the need to revise views about personal privacy and taboos in regard to bodily functions, but also creates many new issues surrounding using the services of someone else. The person with spinal cord injury previously may have had little experience in employing people and in establishing and maintaining an employer–employee relationship. Batterham (1986) provides a practical and useful guide for people with disabilities who wish to use paid care. She points out that, since people are individuals, each employer–employee relationship will be different. Some people with disabilities like to establish a close relationship with their carers while others prefer to treat it as a business relationship. Issues of power and control are important in that a large part of having paid care is to enable the person with a disability to feel more whole and more able to contribute to society. This will not happen if the carer is doing everything for the person, including making decisions. Batterham says that burnout is also an important consideration. The care relationship is very intimate and occurs over many hours during a day. It easy for people to become tired of each other. The decision then has to be made as to whether to terminate the relationship or to find other ways of overcoming the burnout.

Also important is how the carer fits into the family network. The presence of an external person will affect relationships between family members.

> *My husband is my husband, my lover and my friend. My attendants can be friends but they are paid employees and I've made a rule never to forget that.*
>
> Batterham (1986, p. 37)

Personal adjustment

> *Prior to my accident I was a headstrong, independent person. After my accident it took me a long time to become confident to assert myself due to the way I saw myself, not knowing what I would do with the rest of my life, and the way I felt people saw me with such a severe disability. Since studying, being involved in community committees and becoming employed, my self-esteem, attitude and the way I perceive myself has changed. I'm a much more confident person now.*
>
> Matt

The impact of traumatic spinal cord injury can be sudden and severe. One day the person is fit and well, the next he or she is dependent on others. A stay of four to eight months can be expected in hospital. After that, there may be a period in a nursing home or rehabilitation centre. Even more time is needed to recover from mental trauma and to learn new skills for mobility and independence. An identity crisis is a common experience, where the person is forced to take into account losses and changes in order to develop a new self-image which incorporates disability (Stewart & Rossier, 1979). The time to make these changes varies from person to person. A few people never seem to recover emotionally, while others rapidly start to reconstruct their lives, learning new skills and forming new goals.

The person who sustains traumatic injury or unexpected degeneration of the spinal cord undergoes the typical grieving processes that are associated with sudden major loss of any type. This is also true for the individual's family circle and local community.

> *Initially I was frightened, in hospital, not knowing what to expect. It was very hard to take in what was happening. I spent a few months in the acute ward, then in the sub-acute ward, where therapy began. I was still in a state of shock, and had no bladder or bowel control. And during that time my new wife of three months left me, saying that she couldn't handle the situation. It was hard – she could walk away, I had to face the problem.*
>
> Michael

Because spinal cord damage is irrevocable, grief is an expected and healthy reaction and, when properly understood and supported, can lead to acceptance and a positive approach to disability on the part of all concerned. The various steps towards acceptance can be very protracted and some people may never reach this point.

Typical reactions to acquiring a disability were described in Chapter 1 and are illustrated in the following quotes:

- *Shock/disbelief.* 'This can't have happened to me.' The person's life has been overturned. Stress and anxiety result from the trauma of the accident, from the use of lifesaving devices, and from confusion and uncertainty about the future. The person feels disoriented and frightened. Support and reassurance from family members and professionals is essential.
- *Denial.* 'I'll get better and everything will be OK. It can't be that I'll stay disabled.' After the initial shock, the person may retreat into a state of refusing to believe that trauma has occurred or that the injury is permanent. In its initial stages, denial is usually regarded as healthy as it gives the person time to overcome initial trauma and anguish. However, if it continues for too long, it can become counterproductive and can interfere with treatment.
- *Bargaining.* 'If I work very hard I should be the same as before.' The person may dream of a miracle cure or insist that with sufficient effort he or she *will* be able to walk again. Families, in their efforts to be comforting, may unwittingly reinforce denial.
- *Anger.* 'Why has this happened to me? I won't be disabled. I'll show them all that they are wrong.' This comes with the realisation of severe and permanent disablement. The person feels unfairly treated by life or that he or she is being punished unfairly. Often anger is directed at significant people around the person. It is important that professionals and family members do not take the anger personally. It should be tolerated as part of the healing process, but should not be encouraged.
- *Despair/depression.* 'It's all hopeless. I just want to die and it can never be any good.' This stage occurs when the person becomes aware of and accepts the full extent of injury. Feelings of lack of control over the environment and of helplessness are crucial factors (Seligman, 1992, 1975). Depression may occur at any time during the healing process and may recur over a period of many months. Counselling and support are important components of the healing process.
- *Acceptance.* 'I am disabled, I am OK. Life still goes on and it's up to me to make the most of it.' This stage heralds the acceptance of injury and of accompanying disability. In most people it occurs between one and two years after injury. However, acceptance is not always constructive. While some people reach the stage of accepting their disability and of wanting to make the best of life, some harbour bitterness and resentment, others accept their fate passively and yet others aggressively attack life, trying to prove that they can do all the things they could before the accident, and more.

These are dynamic stages of reaction and may fluctuate. However, it is important to be aware of them in order to understand that expressions of anger or frustration towards a person without a disability do not necessarily indicate a personal attack, but are likely to reflect a stage in the bereavement process.

Barry (1989) lists a series of additional psychosocial issues experienced by people with spinal cord injury. Immediately after the injury, there is a total dependence on care givers. Some people experience difficulty in accepting loss of control and in establishing trust. These reactions, along with sudden changes in interpersonal relationships and roles, can lead to a drop in self-esteem. The person may feel guilt after observing the effects of the injury on family members and may assume personal blame for the accident, especially if someone else was killed.

Close relationships may be seriously impaired. The person may withdraw from relationships. Other people may be afraid to come close either physically or psychologically. It is important that professionals are aware of such reactions. Barry comments that, before they commit themselves to therapeutic long-term relationships, professionals should examine their own attitudes to helplessness and to other feelings experienced by a paralysed person.

Most people work through their trauma and losses and return to the community, many resuming fulfilling and productive lives. It is important not to think that a person who uses a wheelchair must be frustrated or suffering. Maybe this person felt like that once, directly after the accident, but now he or she wants to get on with life.

> *I have the attitude that this has happened and you have to get on with it, but there will always be frustrations and part of yourself that you never come to terms with or like.*
>
> John

Psychological impacts of spinal cord injury are not restricted to coming to terms with initial injury. Fuhrer (1995) argues that health conditions such as pressure sores and recurrent infections result in increased depression and stress. He reports a study undertaken in Texas between 1989 and 1992 which found that levels of depression and stress were greater among people with spinal cord injury as compared with people without this disability. He also found a significant relationship between perceived stress and reports by people with spinal cord injury of the number of health conditions they had experienced over the period. In the sample, 56 per cent of people with spinal cord injury had experienced at least one urinary tract infection, 58 per cent reported pain, 48 per cent reported spasticity, 44 per cent reported that they had problems with their teeth, 23 per cent reported pressure sores, 22 per cent reported energy decline over the period, 22 per cent reported strength decline and 23 per cent reported slowly healing sores. A significant correlation emerged between the number of conditions reported and the person's perceived stress in terms of feelings that life is unpredictable, uncontrollable and overburdened.

Body image and self-esteem. Disabilities, particularly visibly obvious ones, have the potential to undermine self-confidence. People with acquired spinal cord injury have lost certain qualities that have helped them feel positive about themselves. This may be due to the fact that they are in wheelchairs and feel less attractive; or because they once prided themselves on some specific ability (for example, their physical prowess on the football field) which has now been lost; or that they gained recognition from a particular role (perhaps being a skilled tradesperson) and they are now prevented from going back to their jobs.

Losing qualities like these causes reassessment of one's worth as a person and can lead to self-doubt. Again, there is no simple solution to this problem, but a number of strategies have been adopted by people which do tend to help. These include:

- thinking about what makes a person valuable as an individual;
- being careful about making comparisons between yourself and others;
- not living in the past or mourning for what might have been.

I was so tall before, I feel I will never get used to looking up at people. It was initially hard to rebuild any level of self-confidence and self-esteem, but this changes over time as your life takes shape and good things start happening.

John

Gender. Of people who acquire traumatic spinal cord injury, 80 per cent are men. Until recently, research and writings have focused on issues for males with spinal cord injury with the neglect of the needs and experiences of women. Crisp (1987) argues that personal characteristics such as age and gender have an important effect on experiences and how the person adjusts. In particular, he argues that the dual minority status of women with disabilities exposes them to different forms of discrimination and creates additional issues in regard to adjustment.

Personality. Considerable literature has been devoted to the concept of the 'paraplegic personality'. However, such writings should be examined critically as they are in danger of promoting stereotyping. Weller & Miller (1977) concluded that patients at New York Hospital tended to be young, emotionally insecure, rebellious and at a peak of physical and sexual activity. According to the authors, these men also tended to display low self-esteem and aggressive behaviour, to have low levels of education, and to come from broken families. Lindemann (1981) developed a similar description and added that a person with spinal cord injury is likely to have previously worked in a physically active job and to be more interested in sport and mechanical activities than in academic pursuits. Professionals should exercise extreme caution in applying such stereotypes. They are based on generalisations and do not apply to all people. Each client must be treated as an individual with his or her own needs and experiences.

One way in which information about personality can be useful is in looking at those characteristics which can be used to differentiate between people in general and which may influence response to treatment. Crisp (1984) explored the different reactions of people with spinal cord injury who display *internal* and *external loci of control*. People with an external locus of control believe that events in life occur as the result of fate, chance, or due to the will of a more powerful being. That is, events are outside one's own control. On the other hand, people with an internal locus of control believe that events happen because of their own actions. Crisp found that internals are more likely to accept responsibility for vocational, leisure, home and other aspects of living, whereas externals tend to be less productive and to perceive more problems at work and socially. Externals also perceived a greater need for external assistance such as advice, repairs to equipment, job retraining, and access to buildings. These findings suggest that, to maximise effectiveness, rehabilitation strategies should be varied to suit the locus of control of the client. For example, externals may require highly-structured programs while internals may resent such restrictions and may function better when able to set their own goals (Trieschmann, 1979). Consistent findings have emerged from a recent Canadian study of variables affecting independent living for people with spinal cord injury. Boschen (1995) reported that locus of control was an important factor related to successful independent living.

Sexuality

The popular image is that people with disabilities are asexual beings. This view can often affect the expectations of people who acquire spinal cord injury. It may take some time for the person to realise he is still a man or she is still a woman, despite not being able to carry out some of the traditional roles associated with that gender. A man may no longer feel physically strong and may no longer feel masculine. He may no longer be able to have an erection or to ejaculate. In the past, the view of asexuality also affected the behaviour of many professionals who assumed that sexuality was not an important issue for someone learning to live with an acquired disability. This view is now changing. Sexuality and finding new ways of sexual expression are now regarded as important components of rehabilitation and readjustment.

> 'You are now a vessel of your husband's passion', the doctor declared. Well, I couldn't stop laughing. I only wish I'd known before the accident, the things I know now.
>
> Danielle

In order to resume sexual intimacy, changes are usually required. These may mean changes for the person and partner in their expectations and attitudes towards sexual intimacy and positions used during sexual intimacy. It also may involve learning new techniques of expression. Any degree of loss of sensation or movement may change the enjoyment of a sexual relationship. Counselling and education are available to assist people in making adjustments.

For both men and women, changes in sexual function can be associated with a fall in self-esteem and feelings of being less attractive. Furthermore, many misconceptions exist within the community about the sexuality of people with physical disabilities, which can affect how a person views him or herself. Thus, it is very important that this aspect of a person's being is addressed fully during the relearning process.

Generally, less attention is paid to sexual readjustment in women than in men with spinal cord injury (Jurisic, 1993). Any discussion of a woman's needs still tends to be based on cultural stereotypes (Crisp, 1987). For example, focus is placed on equipment to aid a homemaker rather than a wage earner or an active sexual partner. The emphasis in our culture on beauty and fashion-conscious dressing can have negative effects on the self-esteem of women who feel unable to live up to perceived expectations of others. Some women with disabilities feel compelled to live up to their ideal of femininity in order to prove they are 'normal' (Orr, 1984).

A woman may find that the tendency of others to treat her as being asexual influences the quality of health care she receives. Orr (1984) cites the surprise demonstrated by some medical practitioners when a woman with a disability requested contraceptives, and their reluctance to provide them, indicating a belief that there was no need for such protection. Orr also cites surprise exhibited by members of the general community when a woman with a disability marries a man without a disability, leading to comments such as 'He must be wonderful'. She also says that, should a woman with a disability be lesbian, this is interpreted as a matter of desperation rather than preference.

Being a parent

People with physical disabilities have the same emotional needs as other people and can maintain loving, sexual relationships. They also produce children and become loving and successful parents. Campion (1992) has published a guide for women with physical disabilities to assist them through their pregnancy.

Having a physical disability does not mean that a person cannot sustain a relationship or produce children. For some men, complications arising from paralysis can result in lowered fertility. It is impossible to predict who will be affected. In men, chronic urinary tract infections and long-term use of indwelling catheters, along with loss of temperature control in the scrotum, are thought to contribute to decreased fertility. It must be remembered that spinal cord injury does not affect the body's ability to produce sex hormones. There are various aids to assist men with spinal cord injury to achieve and maintain an erection if a specific injury prevents it. Inability to ejaculate does not mean inability to father children. Methods have been developed by which sperm are artificially removed and given to the mother. Current in vitro fertilisation programs may offer solutions for those couples who wish to have children.

For women, there is no loss in ability to conceive or bear children. A woman with a spinal cord injury is likely to have a healthy reproductive capacity but those with quadriplegia may need assistance for breathing at delivery. Having a severe physical disability may increase the risk of complications during pregnancy. This may result in the pregnant mother spending many months in bed in order to maximise the chances of a successful birth.

In addition, because of the added weight of pregnancy, a woman may be unable to lift herself (transferring) in her usual way. Once the child is born, the mother may be unable to lift her baby or carry out routine tasks such as changing nappies (diapers). For tasks such as these, she may need to obtain assistance or to find new ways of doing things. This may mean that parental responsibilities are shared according to the roles most appropriate for each person's capabilities.

If the baby cried when friends were there, they'd pass him to me but he'd keep on crying until the housekeeper took him. I could rationalise it by saying that housekeepers come and go, so eventually he would come to me – but it still hurt.

Danielle

Ageing with acquired spinal cord injury

Although the average age of a person with spinal cord injury (SCI) is around 30.7 years (SCI Care System, 1994), the population of people with this impairment is ageing. However, life expectancy is still below that for the general population. Not only is the population of people with spinal cord injury ageing, but more people are acquiring this impairment in their later years. Falls are now one of the major causes of SCI because of the high number of older people who are injured in this way (White et al., 1994).

Not everyone with spinal cord injury ages in the same way. The age at which he or she became injured, life experiences, health, fitness, lifestyle, all affect how a person deals with old age. White et al. (1994) cite as important the strength of relationships with partners, children, parents and friends, as well as the amount of physical and emotional trauma experienced at the time of the injury. White et al. also point to historical factors which influence ageing with spinal cord injury. Treatment and therapy programs have changed over the last 20 years. In the 1960s and 1970s people were pushed to do as much as possible. This put a great strain on their bodies which, as a consequence, have aged a little faster than the bodies of those who received their injury in the 1940s and 1950s.

According to White et al., people growing older with spinal cord injury experience changes and challenges typically associated with ageing, as well as those associated with having their injury. Particular issues include: care of the skin, which can become more prone to pressure sores with loss of moisture and elasticity; bones and muscles which become more prone to fatigue, pain and injury; arthritis; osteoporosis (within six months of their injury, many people with SCI develop osteoporosis regardless of their age); increased possibility of urinary tract infections; bowel cancer; kidney failure and kidney stones. Researchers are also looking at why older people with SCI tend to have more frequent infections than others. They suggest that this occurs because people with SCI have made life-long use of antibiotics for urinary, respiratory and skin infections, making those drugs less effective in their bodies.

Family

Spinal cord injury results in abrupt changes in lifestyle and relationships. Given that most people who acquire a spinal cord injury are aged between 18 and 25 years, the person who was once seen as young, strong and independent may, at least temporarily, seem dependent and in need of help. Supportive counselling is important, even after the person has returned to the community. Clients and their families must be helped to work through the stages of grief and to come to terms with changes.

> *I had my accident when I was young, and if it wasn't for the support of my parents (especially my mother who looked after me when I went home), I dread the thought of where I would have ended up. Without their support, I am sure I would be dead.*
>
> Matt

If the individual with a disability is dependent on the personal care of others for most of the activities of daily living (feeding, toileting, dressing, transferring between wheelchair and bed and so on), physical as well as emotional factors come into play. The sheer physical demands on carers, if they are also family members, can produce additional and sometimes intolerable strains on relationships and family functioning. Wives who are expected to be also mothers, lovers and carers are particularly at risk of breakdown.

Parents, partners, siblings and friends may find it difficult to accept the injury and that it is still the same person that they know. They also may experience the stages of bereavement outlined above, with some people never coming fully to terms with the injury.

> *Father couldn't deal with the situation at all and 11 years later the relationship remains very superficial. I feel he doesn't look at me as a man – more an object of pity.*
>
> John

Long periods of hospitalisation and time away in rehabilitation centres may strain family ties, especially when the institution is a long way from home. Major readjustments may be required to roles and responsibilities. It may seem to the family, at least at first, that the person who was once the major breadwinner now relies on others for assistance in everyday activities. Carers at home may have long hours of work with little time for recreation or pursuit of interests. Marriages can break up. However, the ways members of a family deal with the changes imposed by spinal cord injury reflect the strategies they have developed for dealing with life in general. Many people with spinal cord injury readjust well and have fulfilling lives, as do their families.

Friends may feel uncomfortable about visiting the family and have difficulty in coming to terms with the changed person.

> *As in all walks of life, friends drift apart. But, after my accident many friends kept away. Maybe they couldn't accept my disability. You really find out who your friends are, but I realise that they have their own lives to live.*
>
> Matt

> *Some people don't seem to look at the whole picture – they just look at the chair, for example. To them, any everyday achievement is seen as 'wonderful'. However, my friends seem to treat me as a person. They don't look at the wheelchair first. Many are open with me and seem to have benefited (in knowledge) from my experiences.*
>
> John

Figure 10.1: Specially adapted wheelchairs allow these men to compete in major sporting events

Photograph reproduced with permission of People with Disabilities Participation Division, Australian Sports Commission.

Community living

*After my accident a vocation was a dream. At the government rehabili-
tation centre I was taught to type, to use a switchboard. It was still a
dream – what about transport to/from a job? The highlight was when
they accepted me for driver training. Driving helped me look for work
again.*

Michael

A person who uses a wheelchair has to check before setting out to a place
whether it is wheelchair accessible. Despite legislative requirements, many theatres,
restaurants, government departments, solicitors' and dentists' offices, shops and so
on have steps. Even if you ring up in advance, there is no guarantee that the person
on the other end of the phone will be able to tell you if the place is accessible.
People without disabilities often do not notice the odd step that might bar the way
for someone using a wheelchair. Even places designed to be accessible are not so
to all people with disabilities. For example, an attempt to make lifts accessible by
placing controls lower on the wall outside a lift, may be unsuccessful if the controls
are still too high to be reached by someone using a wheelchair and if some strength
is required to push the buttons in. Similarly, heavy doors which open outwards at
the top of a ramp reduce the benefits of the ramp which has been installed to
provide wheelchair access to a building.

Thus, although legislation has been passed in many countries requiring new
buildings to be accessible, people with disabilities still cannot gain access to all the
places they would like to go. Additionally, floors may be slippery and toilets (even
though they are specially designed) may not be at the right height or the seat may
be loose. Many multi-storey buildings do not have adequate facilities for evacuating
someone using a wheelchair in an emergency. The first facility in a building which
stops in an emergency is the lift (elevator) and people are expected to use the fire
escape. Trying to assist someone down 20 flights of stairs can be dangerous for all
concerned.

In order to participate fully in the community, people with physical disabilities
require:

- affordable transport, both public and private;
- physical access;
- positive attitudes on the part of the general public which is combined with a
  realistic approach to physical limitations;
- personal care to compensate for limitations at home, in the workplace and in
  leisure activities;
- affordable adaptive equipment.

Access for people who use wheelchairs for mobility involves the concept of
continuous accessible pathways. People must be able to:

- reach their destination in their vehicle or by public transport which makes
  provision for wheelchairs;
- enter the building;
- move easily within the building to all the relevant areas including toilets;
- be able to fully participate in activities once within the building.

Architectural requirements for public buildings, the development of hoists and
hand controls for private motor vehicles, special parking arrangements, a limited

Table 10.1: Architectural access requirements

- Set down and pick up points for taxis (or parking for private vehicles) should be undercover if possible, located conveniently near the building to be visited and with no unavoidable steps or kerbs between the parking point and the building entrance.
- Kerb ramps should not slope more than 1:8.
- Entry ramps should not slope more than 1:14 if they are longer than 1.5m.
- If there is no level or ramped entrance through the front door, an alternative passage should be indicated with clear directions.
- No barriers (such as single steps or doors which are difficult to open) should be present to make entry difficult. Temporary barriers can occur due to building repairs and so on. On these occasions, there should be a designated access route which is clearly marked and provides safe access.
- Doors should be wide enough for people using wheelchairs (760mm minimum opening).
- Doors should have lever handles or push plates (not knobs) which can be reached by people using wheelchairs.
- Doors should open at least 90 degrees to permit the passage of a wheelchair user.
- Lifts should be available to take a person to all public floors of a building.
- Lift call and operating buttons should be at a suitable height for people using wheelchairs.
- Lifts should be of adequate size to take people using wheelchairs and for them to turn within the lift.
- There should be sufficient room in corridors to enable the person to use his or her wheelchair and allow someone to pass (minimum width 1.2m).
- There should be room between furniture and equipment to enable a person using a wheelchair to pass through.
- Enquiry counters should be low enough to be convenient for a person who uses a wheelchair.
- Toilets should be designed specifically for people with physical disabilities, with adequate turning space for wheelchair users, adequate space beside the toilet pan, support rails and cubicle doors which, once open, can be closed by someone in a wheelchair.
- Washroom fixtures (basins, taps, soap, towels, mirror, and so on) must be within reach of people in wheelchairs.
- Tap levers must be suitable for use by people with limited hand function.

supply of accessible taxis and expanding computer access networks mean that people with the most severe physical disabilities can now make more use of services provided for people who do not have disabilities.

Access

Access to buildings and accessible transport are two of the most frequently-mentioned areas of concern for people with physical disabilities. A vital precondition of full participation in community life is absence of architectural barriers in the built environment so that the same access is available to public buildings, places of employment, shopping centres and recreational facilities as for people without disabilities.

> *When I'd like to go somewhere, like the movies, I have to check whether it's accessible. I don't like having to depend on people to lift me. Access to me means the ability to do things, go places independently in a spontaneous way without the need to pre-plan, coordinate, check and organise every part of the activity.*

Matt

Double disadvantage

Particular issues arise from the double disadvantage associated with having a disability and minority group membership for residents of rural and remote areas, people of Aboriginal backgrounds and people of non-English-speaking backgrounds. These issues are concerned with modifications required to lifestyle, availability of equipment and assistance, and the ways in which the individual and family react to the presence of disability.

Residents of remote and rural areas. Spinal cord injuries and other forms of trauma can result from working in manual jobs at isolated locations. Spinal cord injury may require major lifestyle modifications; for example, a farmer may be required to sell up and move to an urban location. The highly physical nature of farming and other work in country areas presents a major barrier to someone who wishes to return to the same job. However, increased mechanisation provides opportunities for people to return to their previous occupations. For example, Pearce (1993) concluded that it is possible to modify a farm successfully to accommodate a person' desire to continue to work.

The severity of injury can be worsened by the length of time it takes to receive urgent medical attention that may be situated some distance away. Distance also creates problems in gaining access to the latest equipment and technology (see the section titled 'Equipment' later in the chapter). Isolation and distance add to the demands on families that have a dependent person with a disability (Schaefer, 1985). Mostly, such care is assumed by women who undertake this responsibility in addition to those associated with running a farm and caring for children. Many women in Schaefer's study reported feeling stretched to the limit. They were parents, full-time carers, part-time therapists, as well as being wives, farmers and employees.

People from Aboriginal backgrounds. In many Aboriginal communities, the issue of physical disability is a recent phenomenon. Previously, seriously-injured people would not survive long. As a result, many communities have not developed support mechanisms outside the extended family (Ziersch, 1990). Within many Aboriginal cultures people are reluctant to seek help outside, believing that responsibility lies within the family group. This can place considerable demands on principal carers.

People of non–English-speaking backgrounds. Attitudes towards physical disability are culturally determined and can create barriers for independent living and community integration. Families from Mediterranean and Middle Eastern countries often seem to experience particular difficulties with the effects of physical disability.

In their country of origin, young men who suddenly become both unemployed and physically dependent, lose status and this attitude is frequently transferred when the family moves to a new country. As a consequence, people with disabilities are often 'locked away' within the family circle. Families whose cultural tradition is to protect their young women can become overprotective when faced with injury and permanent disability. This tends either to stifle initiative or promote rebellion. Both reactions are likely to be counter-productive to achieving independence and integration. Cultural traditions which emphasise the role of wives as carers with sole responsibility for the smooth running of households can impose emotional and physical burdens on families which have a member with a physical disability, as these families are less likely to use external supports.

Education

Rehabilitation centres provide education for adults who acquire disability and for school leavers who need special skills for the workplace. A person who acquires a spinal cord injury must learn to look after everyday functions such as controlling incontinence and avoiding pressure sores as well as learning new ways of doing things. Many people go back to education in order to learn new skills and to create new employment opportunities.

> *I decided counselling was right for me, and I enrolled in a course to qualify for university. At the age of 40, some nine years after my accident, I started my university studies.*
>
> John

Employment

People with spinal cord injuries are being successful in a wide variety of occupations. Some people are able to continue in their original trade or profession by learning new ways to carry out their jobs. Others retrain in rehabilitation centres for new occupations which often concentrate on computing and office work and which may not appeal to everybody.

When assessing the vocational potential of a person with spinal cord injury, many factors are taken into account. These include: physical ability to work away from home, bladder and bowel management, education level, motivation, level of family support and availability of transport (Poor, 1975).

Organisations of people with disabilities are working hard to change employer attitudes, since these can act as major barriers to finding satisfying employment. Some employers use lack of toilet facilities or access to the building as an excuse for not employing people using wheelchairs. With recent legislation such as the Australian *Disability Discrimination Act 1992*, and the *Americans with Disabilities Act 1990,* such excuses are illegal. Generally, only small changes are required to make a workplace accessible. It is important to ask people with disabilities about their needs, not just to assume that they cannot manage.

Some people with disabilities have set up their own businesses where others with disabilities work for full wages. These businesses are able to be flexible to allow for the needs of their employees with disabilities. They have been successful in areas such as computer coding, printing and marketing.

A person who has acquired spinal injury and who is making a compensation or insurance claim may be advised by a lawyer not to return to work until the claim has been settled because, if the claimant is working, the amount of compensation that the court awards may be decreased. In some legal systems, settlement can take many years.

Going to work may incur many additional expenses for someone who uses a wheelchair. In addition, pensions and benefits may be lost. This means that a well-paid job is required to offset costs so that the person is not actually worse off than when receiving social security benefits.

Employment is an area where gender may affect reactions to, and the consequences of disability. Research by Brintnell et al. (1992, 1994) suggests that participation in major life roles is compromised for women following injury. Women reported a greater impact of their injury (as compared with men) in regard to satisfaction with their financial situation and general health, and a greater reliance on spouse's income. Women in the sample reported disruptions in their social networks that resulted in the compromise or loss of their working role. The researchers concluded that the loss of social networks associated with employment had an important effect on women's lives, especially those who previously worked in skilled or professional occupations. Compromise of the working role meant that women stood to lose a range of roles (for example, friend, workmate, employer, employee) that contributed significantly to their sense of identity, level of self-worth and well-being.

Accommodation

A number of factors deserve consideration. Many people are injured in their late teens. Before this they probably were living at home with their families. It is important to consider whether the individual will be able to return comfortably to this environment and whether the family will be able to deal with changed circumstances. Moving back home out of a sense of obligation or because there is nowhere else to go can create further issues in acceptance of disability that both the individual and family have to work through. Furthermore, moving back home may require home modifications which entail considerable expense. Additional modifications may be required later as the person progresses in rehabilitation and moves toward being able to leave the family home. Modifications may simply mean renovation to the bathroom to remove the hob from the shower, lower the vanity basin and install hand rails. On the other hand, it may be that the bathroom is too small to allow wheelchair manoeuvrability and so substantial renovations may be required. Doorways in the home may be too narrow to allow passage of a wheelchair and an access ramp may be needed to replace steps at the front door. Some wheelchairs require more space to manoeuvre than others and major obstacles may be that all bedrooms and bathrooms are too small and are not on the ground floor level of the house. It may be necessary to raise a kitchen bench or sink and to remove cupboards to permit wheelchair access.

A ceiling hoist in the bedroom takes away much of the strain involved in lifting and transferring, however a mobile hoist may be needed for the bathroom or for an emergency lift if the person takes a tumble from his or her wheelchair. The style of sling will vary depending on the individual. Other requirements will be a shower chair and/or commode chair.

Environmental control also must be considered. Central heating and air conditioning may be essential because of the loss of control over body temperature caused by spinal cord injury.

The person may decide not to move back into the family home. Alternative forms of accommodation include various types of group home which offer permanent or transitional housing. These forms of living generally facilitate a community lifestyle where the person shares a house with people of a similar age. Living in the same home can have many benefits, including subtle exposure to peer influence whereby an individual who has been living with a disability for some years can provide very real examples of living skills to someone with a recently-acquired disability. Factors to be considered by members of a group home include rental costs, household costs (including food), availability of support staff, compatibility with other residents and individual responsibilities within the household. Independence is a major consideration for the individual. Those who have received a compensation settlement should be able to employ their own support staff and, consequently, have a great deal of control over this aspect of their lives. Others may rely on an attendant care scheme or home care service for assistance. In both cases, the individual will have to develop skills in 'managing' carers.

Computerised environmental control units assist a person's independence by facilitating use of the telephone and by switching on and off lights, television, stereo, CD players, and so on.

In selecting accommodation, it is important not just to consider issues such as wheelchair accessibility and home modifications which enhance independence. Location is also very important. There is no point in 'escaping' the isolation of the hospital or family home environment if the individual is simply changing these for an environment where he or she cannot move beyond the front door. Ideally, the home should be located near local amenities and near accessible public transport. Accessibility of shops, public venues and footpaths also are important.

PERSON TO PERSON

A wheelchair can be isolating and can set the person apart. The behaviour of friends may change. It is important to accept the person as an individual, not the occupier of a wheelchair.

> *Some people give you that sympathetic look and avoid you because they don't know what to do. Most people want to help. They are becoming more aware. Early on, glares upset me. Now I see that it was partly my fault. Today I say 'Hi, how are you?'.*
>
> Michael

It is important for other people to be aware of the major adjustments required for someone who has had a spinal cord injury. Forced changes in lifestyle can be difficult to accept and it is important that other members of the community understand this and do not make things worse. Reactions and behaviours of people within the community can be offensive and negative. People without disabilities should be aware that a common response after spinal cord injury is anger (an attempt to fight back or gain control in situations of attack, threat and frustration). These reactions should not be taken as a personal affront by the person without a disability, but should be placed within the context of the person with a spinal cord injury going through the processes of readjustment and coming to terms with having a disability.

There are no simple rules of thumb for dealing with difficult situations. Sensitivity, understanding of the grieving process, openness and, above all, treating the person concerned as an adult whose power and control have not been diminished will all assist.

Each person is an individual. It is important to remember that a person has already developed a particular personality and particular ways of coping with life in general. As with any group of people, some have developed more effective strategies than others. If a person's coping mechanisms are not what is generally regarded as 'adequate', then the impact of disability can be overwhelming.

> *Communication is my main concern. You have to get away from the little things that get you down. You have to get back into the community. It is hard the first time. I remember looking up, then looking down. I felt they looked at me as if I were a cripple.*
>
> Michael

Avoid the temptation to use labels. Contrary to popular belief there is no such thing as the typical 'paraplegic' or 'quadriplegic'. Such generalities are stereotypes which provide the temptation not to treat each person as an individual with his or her own needs and experiences.

> *The biggest message still to be learnt by members of the community is that people with disabilities are individuals. They need to know that, like them I have many interests and needs.*
>
> John

Appropriate language and behaviour

People with spinal cord injury are not usually sick and do not usually have intellectual or sensory disabilities. When interacting with someone with a spinal cord injury, engage in conversation in exactly the same way as you would with other people – speak to the person directly and not through any companion, ask before providing assistance and allow the person to be in control of the situation.

> *Some people are a little cautious at first and even wonder if physical disability equals mental disability. I just try to act myself and, once people get to know me (and have a joke), they disregard the chair.*
>
> John

Pity will usually be viewed as being offensive. A person may require assistance because he or she simply does not have sufficient muscle power to perform some tasks. In these cases, the person will ask for help and should be allowed to direct operations. He or she understands the functioning of his or her own body better than anyone else. Accidents and embarrassment can occur when assistance is unwarranted and is initiated without attention to directions from the person with the disability.

Focus on the person, not the chair or injury as topics of conversation. Few people wish their disability to be the initial or only topic of conversation. Remarks such as 'What happened to you?' or 'What's wrong with you?' are conversation stoppers and send the message that you have only seen the disability and not the person. Do not ask about the person's disability or how he or she acquired it until you know the person well.

When meeting people for the first time they sometimes don't know what they should say to me. Sometimes, the first thing people ask is 'What happened to you?'. If they haven't had much experience with people in wheelchairs, they usually ask about my electric wheelchair, its batteries and how fast it goes. I answer their questions and finish off with telling them: 'It does the job, it gets me around.'

Matt

Strategies for successful interaction

Because people with quadriplegia depend heavily on others for physical assistance (often of the most intimate kind), it is helpful if the person with the disability and his or her carers, family, friends and acquaintances can establish good channels of verbal communication. Some basic principles of communication which have proved successful are:

- Be open – clearly state your own feelings and thoughts in order to help the other person understand you.
- Be prepared to listen – this helps you to understand the other person's point of view.
- Be willing to work with someone else – even if total agreement is impossible, a working compromise may leave both parties satisfied.
- Be prepared to admit when you are wrong – saying you are sorry eases a multitude of hurt feelings.

Handling a wheelchair

All chairs differ and it is important to consult the person for handling and storage instructions. Be aware that, while the wheelchair is *not* part of the person, it is integral to his or her functioning and personal space. Holding on to, leaning against, or moving the wheelchair interfere with these. A good rule is: if it would not be appropriate to touch, hold or put your arm around that person, then the same can be said for their chair.

Carers are at risk of back injuries. It is important for someone involved in providing care to learn safe methods of lifting and transferring the person to and from the wheelchair. Equipment such as slide boards and hoists is available to assist. It also is important for people who have regular contact with someone who uses a wheelchair and may require assistance to obtain expert advice on how to manoeuvre the wheelchair, how to dismantle it and how to put it into a car. No single set of guidelines can be given as wheelchairs differ. However, it is important to ensure that both the user and the person giving assistance are protected. For example, never attempt to take a wheelchair down a flight of steps or on an escalator. When assisting a person in transferring into a car, take care to avoid hitting his or her head or arms on the side of the vehicle.

As there are many types of wheelchair, an important role of the professional is to select the chair that suits the needs of the client. Repairs and servicing are also important issues. In Australia, the National Roads and Motorists Association of NSW provides a free repair service.

Table 10.2: Strategies for successful interaction

Person with spinal cord injury	Other person
Ask for assistance when required.	Do not assume assistance is needed – ask.
Make your need known to people who offer help.	Accept the person's right to refuse help.
Be firm but polite, insisting on your rights to privacy, independence and access.	Find out how to push a wheelchair; for example, how to get it up and down steps, how to tip it backwards, how to use the brake, not to lift by the armrests (they can pull out) or the wheels.
Be precise when instructing another person; for example, explain exactly where and how to hold the wheelchair and its parts.	Talk to the person at his or her level of height; that is, sit down if appropriate.
Be open about your access needs, give examples and ensure that other people understand your requirements.	Do not talk about the person as if she or he is not present.
You have the right to refuse to discuss personal matters.	Find out about wheelchair-accessible places in your area.
Remember that you are entitled to be in control of the situation.	Do not ask personal questions about the disability or its origin until you know the person well enough.
A sense of humour can alleviate feelings of discomfort all round.	Do not be embarrassed. We all go to the toilet. Do not be uncomfortable about cutting the person's food into small pieces.
	Do not rush the person.
	Do not be sensitive about using words such as 'walking' or 'running'. People in wheelchairs use the same words.
	Do not hold on to the wheelchair of a stranger. It is part of the person's body space.
	Do not try to move the person or his/her wheelchair without permission.

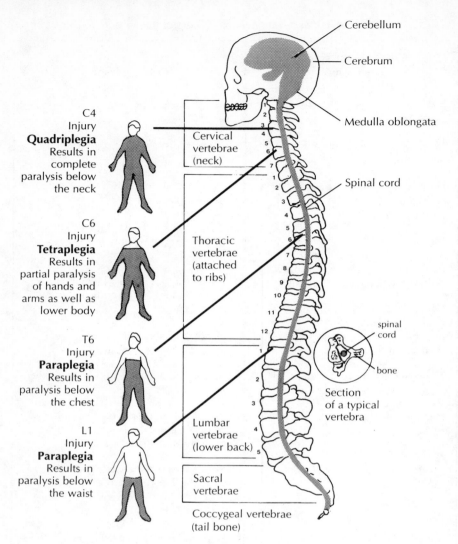

Figure 10.2: Level of injury and extent of paralysis

MORE INFORMATION ABOUT PARAPLEGIA AND QUADRIPLEGIA

The spinal cord forms part of the central nervous system. It runs through a chain of bony rings known as vertebrae. This vertebral (or spinal) column protects the spinal cord which works rather like a telephone cable by sending messages of feeling and sensation to the brain which converts them into responses such as movement. Nerves going to the brain carry messages of sensation – pain, touch and temperature – and are called sensory nerves. Nerves going from the brain carry instructions to the muscles and are called motor nerves because they initiative movement. Thus, the spinal cord is the sole link between the brain and the nerves going to and coming from all areas of the body: The spinal cord and nerves transmit all the body's messages of sensation to the brain and carry all the brain's 'movement' messages to the muscles. The spinal cord controls almost every muscle in the body. It also transmits messages of sensation (heat, cold, pain) from the body to the brain. If the spinal cord is damaged, therefore, the communication is cut between the brain and the body area served by the part of the cord below the damaged area. It should be noted that nerves are not always completely broken, so that sometimes a person has some function below the level of damage. Spinal cord tissue does not regenerate. This means that any injury to the spinal cord is permanent.

Definition

Following the World Health Organization (1980) definition, in the case of spinal cord injury:

- *Impairment* refers to damage to the spinal cord.
- *Disability* refers to lack, loss or reduction in sensation, body function, movement, bladder and bowel control.
- *Handicap* refers to reduction in the ability to use transport, and to perform tasks such as dressing and toileting. The extent to which these tasks become associated with handicap is influenced by the physical and social environment.

Depending on the extent of the damage, a person will be either partially or completely paralysed from the point of damage, or lesion, downwards. Table 10.3 and Figure 10.2 summarise the effects of level of injury on disabilities induced by spinal cord damage and their impact on everyday functioning.

Causes

The delicate fibres of the spinal cord can be injured in a number of ways. Spinal cord injury, however, is primarily an everyday injury. It can be caused by:

- road traffic accidents;
- diving accidents;
- sports accidents;
- accidents in the home;
- accidents at work, and so on.

> *I am 34 years of age, and am a C5/6 incomplete quadriplegic due to a football accident four years ago. I was just married for the second time, and my wife, and my five-year-old son Jason (from my first marriage) were at the game. Semi-conscious, I kept saying not to move me. All I felt was effervescence around my neck . . . a bubbling sensation. I didn't know where my arms or legs were. This effervescent feeling lasted three weeks. Today I have no feeling below my chest, partial feeling between my chest and neck, and little in my left hand.*
>
> Michael

It is not exclusively trauma that can cause damage to the spinal cord. Viruses, and viral infections (such as transverse myelitis or infection of the nerve covering),

Table 10.3: Expected levels of function associated with location of spinal cord injury

Expected levels of function		
Level of lesion	**Movement**	**Level of independence**
C1–3	Head and neck only.	*Self-care*: totally dependent, yet capable of directing own personal care. *Mobility*: chin-controlled electric wheelchair. *Other equipment*: respiratory apparatus. environmental control unit.
C4	Movement of head and neck and some movement of shoulders.	*Self-care*: sometimes splints to keep wrists stable. *Other activities*: able to type using mouthstick and typewriter. *Mobility*: chin-controlled electric wheelchair on flat ground; ramps of low gradient. *Other equipment*: environmental control unit to operate appliances.
C5	Movement of head and neck. Good shoulder control. Some movement in elbow and forearm.	*Self-care*: with use of splints, able to feed self, drink from adapted cup, clean teeth and shave when set up with adapted extended comb. Dressing top half of body is possible. *Other activities*: typing with typing splints or sticks. Writing with splint. Able to drive a car (rare). *Mobility*: manual wheelchair very difficult, using capstan knobs on handrims. Hand-operated electric wheelchair usually preferred.

Table 10.3: *Continued*

Expected levels of function		
Level of lesion	**Movement**	**Level of independence**
C6	Head and neck movement. Good shoulder control. Some movement in elbow and forearm. Some movement in wrist. During an extended period following the injury, the individual is usually able to develop some type of grip (although fairly weak) simply by using the natural movement of the wrist, bringing the fingers together. After a period of time during which the finger tendons shorten a little, allowing them to remain bent, utensils may be 'threaded through the fingers' avoiding the need for a palmar band (though that will usually be necessary during the time in hospital).	*Self-care*: using a palmar bank, able to feed and clean teeth. Uses adapted cup for drinking and shaving mitt for razor. Dressing top half of body and lower half with assistance. Transfers with minimal assistance from wheelchair to bed, bed to commode. *Other activities*: able to drive car using hand controls, typing, writing, using telephone – initially with aids. Domestic duties – basic tasks possible. *Mobility*: independent using manual wheelchair with capstan knobs on handrims (occasionally choose to use a hand-controlled electric wheelchair for long distance travel).
C7	Head and neck movement. Good shoulder control. Full elbow movement. Full wrist movement. Movement in fingers.	*Self-care*: should be independent in all activities, dressing, feeding, cleaning teeth, shaving and transferring on/off bed, commode (from wheelchair) toilet and in/out of car. *Other activities*: able to drive car using hand controls. Able to type, write, use telephone without aids. *Mobility*: independent using manual wheelchair. Possible also to negotiate curb.

Table 10.3: *Continued*

Expected levels of function		
Level of lesion	Movement	Level of independence
C8–T1	Head and neck movement. Good shoulder control. Full elbow movement. Full wrist movement. Movement in fingers. Movement in thumbs.	Totally independent in all activities
Below T1	The person's level of function is affected by limitations of a wheelchair and the effects of limited balance, to a greater or lesser degree, depending on the lesion level.	

cysts and growths on the cord can cause permanent damage. Life expectancy is not appreciably lessened, except with the higher lesions where breathing is affected.

Incidence/prevalence

In Australia, about 400 new cases occur each year. Generally speaking, the incidence of paraplegia and quadriplegia are about the same. The most common vertebral sites for injury are at C4–C6 and T12–L1 level. Data on the United States population suggest that about around 200000 people living in America have spinal cord injury, and between 7600 and 10000 new people become injured each year. (SCI Care System, 1994; White et al., 1994). In the United States there are 44000 people who have quadriplegia, 99000 who have hemiplegia, and 59000 who have paraplegia (LaPlante & Carlson, 1996).

Age. Most traumatic spinal cord injury occurs in young people (over 60 per cent are aged less than 30) and males (over 80 per cent). This situation arises because most traumatic spinal cord injury is caused by transport (about 60 per cent), sporting and diving accidents. Other frequent causes of spinal cord injury are falls in general and work accidents, with around 98 per cent of these injuries happening to men. For both women and men the highest rates of spinal cord injury occur between the ages of 15 and 24 years. Rates are also relatively high for both genders between 25 and 34 years and then drop off until the age of 65 years and over.

Gender. As said above, paraplegia and quadriplegia are far more common in males than females. Around 80 per cent of people with spinal cord injury are male. Causes differ between the genders – women more likely to have acquired their impairment through spinal infection, disease and 'other accidents' than through sporting or transport accidents.

Treatment and rehabilitation

Treatment at the scene of the accident is crucial for traumatic spinal cord injury. As well as the priorities of maintaining breathing, controlling bleeding and removing the person from imminent danger, emergency staff must take appropriate action to immobilise the spine to ensure that no further neurological damage is caused.

Once a person has passed the acute state, rehabilitation begins to involve every facet of life. During these stages, a wide variety of professionals including nurses, physiotherapists, occupational therapists, social workers and psychologists assist in addressing the person's needs. Issues to be addressed include where the person wishes to live, his or her vocational options and recreational possibilities. With so many changes to accommodate, considerable attention must be paid to retaining as much of the person's previous lifestyle as possible. Features such as the area where he or she used to live, previous occupations and goals should be taken into account when designing services.

> *I was in hospital for ten months, having physio and OT (occupational therapy). I really enjoyed physiotherapy, because I had the sports orientation to build up my body. In the OT sessions I was frustrated because without fine control I couldn't do much. At times I wanted to suicide, to push myself downstairs. It was frustrating, too, for family and friends. They couldn't understand how someone as fit as Michael could now be paralysed. Why Michael? . . . He used to run eight miles every morning.*
>
> Michael

Training in mobility and self-care is designed to make the person as independent as possible. The person is taught how to use a wheelchair and specialised aids. Attention is given to finding new ways of dressing, toileting, eating and sexual expression. Also important is developing understanding of a new body and how to protect and use it. For example, it is important to learn to take precautions because the body is no longer able to take them itself because of loss of sensation. (Many people report stories of having been scalded by bath water or badly sunburnt because they could not feel the heat on their skin.)

The person also must be taught ways of avoiding pressures which result from lying or sitting in one position for a long time. Some people experience involuntary muscle spasms which can be disconcerting and uncomfortable. It is necessary to learn to accept these and to find new ways of dealing with potentially embarrassing situations.

Supportive counselling relationships are important throughout rehabilitation and after a person has returned to the community. Clients and their families need to work through denial, anger, depression and suicidal thoughts in order to come to terms with the changes that have occurred in their lives. Considerable work occurs outside the rehabilitation setting. Social workers and community health nurses work with the person and family in the home environment to assist in readjusting to employment, education and family life.

Later in rehabilitation, learning to drive a motor vehicle is possible. Adaptation of vehicles is expensive but most people say the cost is well worth it as it provides independence and freedom.

Equipment

It is important to understand that, even with the most advanced technical equipment, most people with severe physical disabilities will rely on other people (usually called care attendants or personal care attendants) for many of their normal daily living activities. With appropriate resources, a person with a severe disability is able to achieve a level of independence which would have been unimaginable a decade ago.

> *Apart from my electric wheelchair, electric bed and air mattress, I use a number of home environmental control devices which are both push-button and voice activated. They have aided me more than I expected and have given me more independence than I thought. I can turn lights on and off and appliances like my radio, TV, computer, printer and so on. Also, I have a timing system to automate my house, like turning on the radio in the morning, the TV off at night, lights on before you get home, just to mention a few.*
>
> Matt, 32 who has quadriplegia as a result of a diving accident

There are very few personal recreation or everyday items which can be used without some form of adaptation to take into account incongruities in balance and stability and to maximise ease of use and dexterity. Modification usually is costly.

Even items such as clothing require modification. Some of the issues to be considered in designing and buying clothing include that: it can be easily put on or taken off while sitting, is easy to manage during toileting, will not cause irritation to the skin, can be easily washed and cared for, suits a person's temperature needs, allows ease of movement while pushing a wheelchair or walking on crutches, looks good on a person while he or she is sitting down and will not wear out from 'wheel wear'.

Many service providers have yet to fully realise that equipment designed for urban areas is not necessarily useful elsewhere:

> *. . . the provision of a shower chair to a not-so-old (Aboriginal) woman choosing to leave a nursing home and live in the dry river bed with her family. Needless to say, there isn't a shower or an ablution block, as on some camps. Access to a town camp house, not so far away, was considered satisfactory by the woman herself, but was regarded as inadequate by the many professionals deciding what was best for her.*
>
> (Harrison, 1993)

In rural areas, limited availability of information about the latest technology, together with high transport costs can result in serious disadvantages for people wishing to use equipment and to get it serviced. Distance increases the costs and delays associated with obtaining appropriate equipment. Often equipment which is appropriate in the city is of little use in the country. Furthermore, modifications can be expensive. There tend to be long waiting lists for equipment, aids and appliances in remote and rural areas (Gething et al., 1994).

Factors to be considered in design of equipment include temperature range and climate, terrains to be covered and the environment in which the equipment is to be used. Other important factors are whether the equipment can be serviced locally and whether spare parts are readily available.

If a part in my wheelchair needs to be replaced, the chair must be sent to Sydney for repair. This can take weeks and in the meantime I am stuck at home, unable to get around without my chair.

Malcolm, who lives in a remote part of NSW

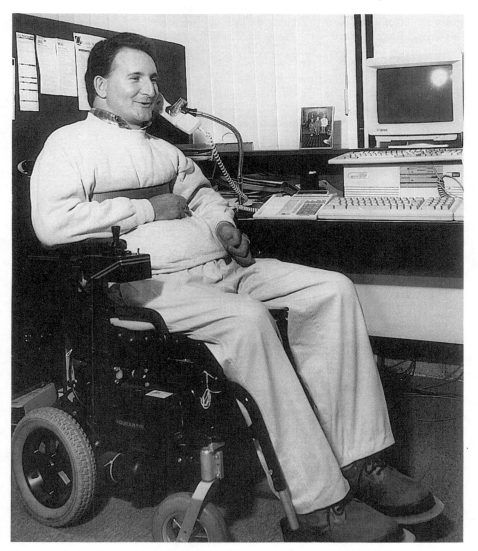

Figure 10.3: An electric wheelchair, a computer and modified telephone equipment enable this man with quadriplegia to work

Photograph reproduced with permission of the Australian Quadriplegic Association.

Services and supports

Services for people with spinal cord damage are of relatively recent origin. Generally speaking, it is only in the last 45 years that people have survived spinal cord injury or disease.

Over the decades there has been a gradual change in patterns of survival from low-level paraplegia in the 1950s, high level paraplegia in the 1960s, low-level quadriplegia in the 1970s and, finally, high-level quadriplegia in the 1980s.

Associated with each advancement has been the evolution of a medical milestone: limited antibiotics in the 1950s, full-spectrum antibiotics in the 1960s, improved respiratory care and cardio-pulmonary resuscitation (CPR) in the 1970s, and emergency medical services at the accident scene in the 1980s. Medical treatment and the question of survival have therefore tended to dominate thinking about spinal injuries.

The independent living movement had its beginnings for people with severe physical disabilities in the 1960s. Associations were formed by small yet determined groups of people with spinal cord injuries in order to support their rehabilitation process and look at issues of independent living, accommodation and employment opportunities. Services include:

- counselling and peer support;
- transitional accommodation;
- information and advocacy;
- equipment and engineering services;
- independent living skills training;
- pre-vocational training and employment;
- spinal advocacy service;
- nursing information or consultation.

The rights of people to live outside institutions and to take their place in the community are now recognised in both government policy and in the practices of many voluntary organisations.

Additional costs

People with a spinal cord injury are often financially disadvantaged. 'A "user pay" world' which was published in the Spring edition of Australian *Quad Wrangle* (1989), points out the heavy and unavoidable costs of living in the community with a physical disability such as paraplegia or quadriplegia. It also stresses the individual nature of disability and its associated costs. As indicated above, there are many direct, indirect and hidden costs. Direct costs include purchase of equipment and services, modification of the home and motor vehicle; while indirect costs include income foregone. Hidden everyday costs include the need to buy special types of clothing and expensive models of everyday items (such as radios and televisions) in order to obtain appropriate features (such as feather-touch control and programmable operation), along with the need for extra appliances and electricity.

Pensions and social security payments rarely cover these expenses. Contrary to popular belief, most people with paraplegia and quadriplegia have not received substantial compensation payments. About 20 per cent receive some form of compensation.

RESOURCE ORGANISATIONS

All care has been taken to ensure that all information is correct at the time of publishing. However, responsibility for the accuracy of this information is not accepted by the writer. The list of resource organisations contained in this chapter is not intended to be exhaustive – it provides national organisations only. The reader is referred to local community directories for further information and for local branches of national organisations. Inclusion of services and organisations should not be taken as a recommendation.

Australia

Refer to your local telephone directory for state addresses of organisations.
For NSW, addresses are as follows:
Australian Quadriplegic Association
PO Box 397
Matraville NSW 2036
Ph 02 9661 8855
Fax 02 9661 9598

PARAQUAD
33–35 Burlington Road
Homebush NSW 2140
Ph 02 9764 4166
Fax 02 9764 2391

Canada

Canadian Paraplegic Association
Suite 320, 1101 Prince of Wales Drive
Ottawa, ON K2G 3W7
Ph 613 723 1033
or 204 957 1784
Fax 613 723 1060

Spinal Cord Society of Canada
Unit 32, 120 Newkirk Road
Richmond Hill ON L4C 9S7
Ph 905 508 4000
Fax 905 508 4002

United States

PVA (Paralyzed Veterans of America)
National Spinal Cord Injury Association
801 18th Street NW
Washington, DC 20006
Ph 202 USA 1300

National Spinal Cord Injury Association
Suite 29, 245 Concord Avenue
Cambridge, MA 02138, USA
Ph 617 441 8500

New Zealand

Paraplegic & Physically Disabled
  Association
PO Box 1352
Christchurch

United Kingdom

SIA (Spinal Injuries Association)
76 St James Lane
London N103DF
Ph (0181) 444 2121

FURTHER READING

Alsop, L. (1988). *Mothers with disabilities: their needs.* Canberra: Office on the Status of Women.
Australian Quadriplegic Association Ltd. (various dates). *Quad Wrangle.*
Dickson, H., Martens, D., Dever, L. & Tonkin, J. (1993). *Spinal injuries handbook.* Sydney: The Prince Henry Hospital.
Ducharme, S. H. & Gill, K. M. (1997). *Sexuality after spinal cord injury: Answers to your questions.* Baltimore: Paul H. Brookes.
Krotoski, D. M., Nosek, M. A. & Turk, M. A. (1996). *Women with physical disabilities: Achieving and maintaining health and well-being.* Baltimore: Paul H. Brookes.
Lawrence, A. (ed.) (1989). *I always wanted to be a tap dancer.* Sydney: Womens' Advisory Council.

White, G. W., Gutierrez, R., Gardner, S. & Steward, J. (1994). *SCI and aging: a state of body and mind*. Kansas: The Research and Training Center on Indpendent Living, the University of Kansas.

Whiteneck, G. (1989). The management of high quadriplegia. *Comprehensive Neurological Rehabilitation*, Vol. 1, New York: Demos Publications.

Whiteneck, G., Charlifue, S., Gerhart, K., Lammertse, D., Manley, S., Menter, R. & Seedroff, K. (1993). *Aging with spinal cord injury*. New York: Demos Publications.

CHAPTER 11

INTELLECTUAL DISABILITY

People with intellectual disability find it more difficult to learn than others. Intellectual disability may be present from birth or may result from an accident or illness during childhood or adolescence.

Intellectual disability is *not* an illness, but rather a slowness to learn, process information and function. It means a reduced ability to learn, but not an inability to learn. People with intellectual disability can and do learn a wide range of skills. Intellectual disability cannot be 'cured'; however, with appropriate education, training and support, most people with intellectual disability can lead independent or semi-independent lives.

Intellectual disability often is confused with other disabilities. The most common of these is psychiatric disability, which, unlike intellectual disability, can occur at any point in someone's life and in most instances can be treated. Learning difficulties (such as dyslexia and brain injuries from accidents) also are disabilities commonly confused with intellectual disability. These require different expertise, support and services.

Each person's abilities differ according to the level of impairment, life experiences and the extent to which the person is able to make the most of his or her abilities. Given the opportunity, a person with intellectual disability will have the same types of interests as his or her peers without disability. Whereas once people with intellectual disability of all ages were given childlike activities, it is now realised that they prefer to do and are capable of activities appropriate to their ages. This recognition gives people with intellectual disability greater dignity in society.

Historically, people with intellectual disability have been disadvantaged in their search for acceptance; and their struggle for social justice and for a more equitable, progressive and enlightened approach within service provision. For many years it was a common belief that anyone who was different in some way from the community at large should be kept segregated. The belief that people with intellectual disability were a problem to society largely stemmed from the social conditions of early industrialised society. If you were capable of making your living you belonged in society, if you were not then you did not belong.

> There's bigoted so-and-so people today that complain that if they've got handicapped people moving into their street they lower the prices of the houses. They could find out themselves one day – they could even have an intellectually handicapped child some time.
>
> Sean, who is middle-aged

Society is now taking a more mature view of people who are different from the norm and about what people with intellectual disability have the right to expect from their lives. Society is starting slowly to come to terms with accepting people with intellectual disability as citizens with a right to dignity and equal opportunities.

203

LIVING WITH INTELLECTUAL DISABILITY

People with intellectual disability may experience difficulties with abstract thinking, decision making, short-term memory, learning and literacy/numeracy skills, body image and awareness, coordination and mobility skills, ability to concentrate and maintain interest in an activity for a length of time (Duckworth, 1987).

People with intellectual disability have the same types of goals, dreams, hopes, aspirations, emotions and needs as the rest of the population. Because of their disability they may display limitations in learning, speech, self-care, movement, independent living, employment and relationships. Support may be required to reduce the restrictions that disability could otherwise impose on life. For example, a person with intellectual disability may have difficulty reading the paper in order to find out what jobs are advertised and may need longer time to complete a task, such as filling out a form.

Delayed development

This occurs whether the intellectual impairment is congenital or acquired early in childhood (see later in this chapter). Even physical behaviour such as crawling and rolling that is not generally thought of as being 'intellectual' is likely to be achieved more slowly. In many cases, it is the mother who first notices that her child is not reaching the usual milestones and realises that the baby may have an intellectual disability. In some cases, there is very little delay in the first year of life, but gradually the child drops behind other children of the same age. Generally speaking, children continue to develop in roughly the same pattern as other children; it is just that the development takes longer. It is important not to assume that a child or adult has reached his or her full potential.

Personal adjustment

Because competence and the ability to make money are so highly valued in our society, people who do not have these particular skills tend to become devalued citizens. Devaluing is expressed in the ways that others treat a person. When a person realises he or she is somehow regarded as not of equal worth, or not respected as an equal citizen by others, he or she is likely to lose self-esteem and confidence. Once many people, especially those with a mild intellectual disability, were ashamed of their disability and afraid of ridicule, but the advent of advocacy services and strategies to empower people has done much to remove these feelings.

> *I've now accepted that I'm alright. If people look at me – well and good. It doesn't worry me any more. It used to worry me. But it's their problem. Not mine.*
>
> Mark

People with mild intellectual disability form one of the largest hidden disability groups. Some people will try to cover up their disability rather than seek support needed to do the activities they want to do, such as learning literacy and numeracy skills.

> *It is an immense degree of achievement when so many little barriers must be overcome before any progress can be made – truly amazing. I*

have seen Erin give so much of herself, much more than I would be willing to give, just for the acceptance. It makes me very humble.

Mollie, Erin's mother

Sexuality

No group of women with disabilities has been as discriminated against in terms of their reproductive rights as women with intellectual disability (Traustadottir, 1990). Sexuality is still a controversial issue and myths about these women still exist. Today sterilisation is illegal in many countries without the full knowledge and consent of the person with a disability. Many people with intellectual disability are capable of maintaining a relationship. Many are happily married and quite a few are parents. The factors which influence success are the same as for other people and include age of marriage, level of income, emotional stability of partners and role models provided by parents (McCarthy & Fegan, 1984). Nowadays, people with intellectual disability are taught about sexuality, contraception, pregnancy and parenting so that individuals are able to make informed choices. People with intellectual disability have the same range of emotions and the same rights to relationships as any other person in the community (Schwier, 1994).

Each person's self-image is inseparably tied to his or her gender. Adolescence can be a time of great confusion for a teenager, especially if he or she is not prepared and informed about sexuality (Fegan & Rauch, 1993). Many parents and members of the community have difficulty in coming to terms with sexuality in an adolescent with a disability. Sexual intimacy, marriage, homosexuality and having children are issues that often have been overlooked. This may have resulted in the widespread belief that people with disabilities do not have sexual feelings.

Today, people with intellectual disability are taught about sexuality in the same way they learn about other life skills. They are encouraged to get to know their own bodies and are taught about pregnancy and contraception. The responsibilities of parenthood are also explained so that both men and women can decide whether they feel they could cope with its demands.

Learning about sexuality is a complex process that occurs gradually and usually unconsciously. It includes many skills and much knowledge. Learning about one's own body is just one important part. Others include social skills, such as when and who to hug (and when and who not to hug), how to greet people and to talk politely; what behaviour is public and what is private; how to make decisions, and so on. Other learning centres around understanding and coming to terms with feelings and reactions. Adolescents also need to learn about sexually transmitted diseases and methods of protection against these and against unwanted pregnancy (Maksym, 1990). An adolescent will learn some of this information by observing others. In other cases, a parent or adult may need to teach the social skills that the adolescent seems to be having difficulty in learning by himself or herself. An adolescent should also be taught about issues associated with sexual abuse (what it is and how to cope).

Violence and sexual abuse toward people with intellectual disability

Recently, a considerable body of literature has reported that violence and sexual abuse are not uncommon experiences of people with intellectual disability. These have occurred within the family, in the community, and within institutions. Sexual

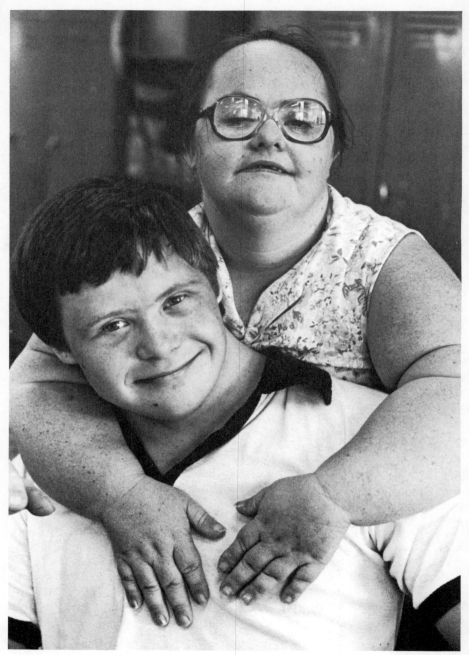

Figure 11.1: Friendship and warm relationships are an important part of life

abuse may include any unwanted or forced sexual contact, unwanted touching or unwanted displays of sexual parts, and threats of harm or coercion in connection with sexual activity (Roeher Institute, 1992). The Roeher Institute reports that figures indicate that 39–68 per cent of girls and 16–30 per cent of boys with intellectual disability will be sexually abused before they reach the age of 18. Risk factors for sexual abuse include: emotional deprivation, social isolation, dependence on the abuser, vulnerability to incentives, feelings of helplessness and powerlessness, ignorance of what is happening, sexual repression and curiosity, coercion, and learned compliance. Education about sexuality and appropriate sexual behaviours for people with intellectual disability provides an important means of empowering to help them deal with potential abuse. Also important is education for professionals (police, social workers, and so on) and care givers to assist them in identifying possible cases of abuse and in helping the victim.

> *A guy tried to feel me up. I pushed him away, I told but they (the staff) didn't listen. They say it isn't true, but it is true. Jack is his name and he's still working there.*
>
> Maureen, quoted by the Roeher Institute, 1992

Being a parent

Whether or not both parents have an intellectual disability, they may choose to have children. There is no reason to expect their child will have intellectual disability. Llewellyn (in Johnston, 1993) points out that parents with intellectual disability are adults first, parents second and people with disabilities third. As do all parents, they compare their children with others, feel concerned and feel proud. But often they have had very different life experiences from other parents. These experiences may have led to low self-esteem and a general lack of assertiveness. They also may have included others talking for the person and making decisions for them (Booth & Booth, 1994).

People who come in to contact with parents with intellectual disability have a responsibility to ensure their rights as parents are not denied. Parents with intellectual disability have a right to respect for their preferences and abilities as do other parents. They require information in non-ambiguous, direct, short statements. It is often necessary to repeat the information, perhaps over several visits. It may be useful to ask the parent to explain to you what they think a piece of information means as a way of assessing whether they have understood. It is important to ensure that the parent is not denied the right to be the adult who takes responsibility for their child.

> *I've got a boyfriend and we plan to get engaged at Christmas. I want to have children later. My mother said I can't have children because I will not be able to look after them. But I think I will be able to care for them.*
>
> Linda

Family

The effects of intellectual disability are different for every family and very much affected by the available services and attitudes of those around. Many families experience grief when they first become aware that their child has intellectual disability, others experience guilt or anger. These are common emotions experienced by parents and families and are discussed in more detail in Chapter 1. Many people come to terms with these feelings and come to accept their family member's disability. Others report that, even though they have largely come to terms with the disability, important life milestones bring reminders of the previous sense of loss. Milestones such as going to school, having close friends, getting a job, getting married and having children seem a lot more difficult for their son or daughter to achieve.

> *Erin has few friends but is friendly with everyone. She is beginning to attend various camp activities for fun and independence. She has come a tremendously long way, but the road ahead for her is long and stony. She has taught her mother a great deal about life's priorities and choices, tolerance, acceptance and achievement.*
>
> Mollie

If a child has severe intellectual disability, it is likely that he or she may have a second disability, such as epilepsy, cerebral palsy, speech or physical impairment. Having a family member with high support needs affects the family psychologically, emotionally, financially and in practical day-to-day issues. How the family deals with these issues is affected by the types of outside support and what supports are culturally acceptable to that family.

> *Sometimes I think that I'm OK and then something small happens and I burst into floods of tears. I wonder if it is something you ever really accept. There's always a scar on your heart.*
>
> Ellis, J. & Whaite, 1987, p. 12

Disability affects the whole family and each family member reacts differently. Some adjust to their member with a disability readily, some may feel ambivalence. For example, they may love their sibling but fear ridicule from friends. Until recently, most research has concentrated on stress and burden experienced by the family, however researchers now acknowledge that many families value and accept their member with a disability and function effectively as a unit (Marsh, 1992). Unfortunately, in some cases there has been a tendency for professionals to regard such families as being in a state of denial and not adjusting to their child's disability. In reality, the opposite has occurred. Families are different, and the way they adjust to having a member with disability reflects strategies and behaviour patterns already established within the family group (Turnbull et al., 1993).

> *The nurses and resident doctors at the hospital only see the torment and grief that a family experiences when told of a disability. They see the hopelessness and the pain. They don't see that the future can hold joy and happiness.*
>
> Mollie

Recent studies in America have shown that many of the assumptions that we make, such as those related to stress and hardship, are not based on facts. Some of the positives stated by parents about having a child with a disability include that families had 'a greater sense of purpose in their lives', had their 'sensitivity enhanced', 'showed a higher well-being' and 'had learnt more about themselves from their family member with a disability than they had from their other children'.

Much of the impact that disability has on the family reflects the manner in which parents were informed of their child's condition and the ready availability of appropriate services and community supports. These are discussed later in the chapter.

People with intellectual disability, with appropriate support and family and community acceptance, lead satisfying and full lives in the community. Support and lobby groups are available to assist families with a member with intellectual disability. *The power of positive thinking* (Roeher Institute, 1989) describes experiences associated with setting up and running five mutual support groups. It tracks the development of these groups in their attempts to build personal relationships of trust and commitment and to develop individual strengths and initiatives. Major goals of these groups were to secure and deliver services, find a means through which to lobby for government change, create a climate of friendship and support that helps to achieve personal development and growth; and provide emotional support that encourages self-esteem and a sense of dignity.

Community living

Legislation has sent the clear message to the community that segregation is not acceptable. That is, it is no longer appropriate for organisations to provide 'cradle to grave' services and supports for people with intellectual disability which segregate them from the rest of the community in all aspects of their life. The philosophy is that, with the appropriate amount of support and services, people can achieve a higher quality of life by living in the community and by having a life similar to that of all other citizens. This is their right.

People with intellectual disability are not sick, therefore it is wrong to see them as patients who need to be institutionalised. They need special support to learn. This is difficult to achieve in the environment of an institution where the nature, size, and staffing ratios greatly limit teaching new skills.

Many larger institutions (particularly in urban areas) have now closed down and most people with intellectual disability live in the community. Many schemes and services are available to assist them in finding and being successful in open, competitive employment (as opposed to segregated 'sheltered' employment). However, attitudes and beliefs in smaller communities are very slow to change and sometimes there is reluctance to close large institutions and 'sheltered' employment services. Years of segregation are difficult to overcome as they have denied many people in mainstream society the opportunity to get to know people with intellectual disability as individuals. Fear and inaccurate beliefs are often the result.

Legislation such as the *Americans with Disabilities Act 1986*, the Australian *Disability Services Act 1986* and the *Australian Discrimination Act 1992* sends messages to the community and to service providers that people with intellectual (and other disabilities) are entitled to the same rights and have the same obligations as others in society. Clearly, practices which are discriminatory are no longer permissible. This formal acknowledgment of change builds on a gradual movement which has been occurring in the community for some time. However, attitudes and behaviours prevalent in the community often deny equity and equality. People with intellectual disabilities have to deal with the effects of attitudes and behaviour of other people. An important skill they must learn is how to deal with situations in which others do not respect their rights. There also may be feelings of being treated unfairly by life in general – 'Why am I so slow when other people seem able to think so fast?'.

> *Because I can't read it limits my understanding with other people. They're talking to me and I hear what they're saying but I sort of can't grasp sometimes what they're telling me.*
>
> Sean, who has intellectual disability

Other people (either unthinkingly or deliberately) may create situations which arouse frustration and anger in the person with intellectual disability who does not know how to counteract it. The result may be feelings of uncertainty (because the person is not sure what is going on), of inadequacy (because of other people's impatience), of helplessness and resentment (because someone has tried to trick you, but you are not quite sure how). Most people with intellectual disability are aware of being degraded or exploited.

For example, a common complaint from people with intellectual disability is that they find themselves the brunt of teasing and ridicule. This behaviour still persists, despite awareness education which has taken place in schools. It is important that the community (especially schools) continues to work to address such negative behaviour, as children with intellectual disability will never feel fully accepted in regular schools until other children become more tolerant and accepting of those who are different in some way.

Pity and feeling sorry are common reactions of others which ignore the many capabilities of people with intellectual disabilities and overlook their potential to contribute to society.

People with intellectual disability are not 'happy innocents', untroubled by the world and not responsible for their behaviour. They experience frustration and difficulty living in a world designed by people without disabilities. People with intellectual disability can learn to be responsible for their own actions and are subject to the same laws as others. Consequently they have the same rights as well as the same responsibilities as all other citizens. There are now actively politicised groups of people with intellectual disability who are advocating better understanding and acceptance from the community. Self-advocacy groups encourage people to speak up for themselves and are breaking down the barriers between people with intellectual disability and others.

The following strategies encourage community integration and the breaking down of fears and myths:

- Participating in community activities with only one or two people with intellectual disability, rather than the 'bus load' approach. This gets away from the 'us' and 'them' situation and allows people to be in a position where everyone can learn.
- Providing people with intellectual disability with training and support to develop skills to be independent.
- Opening up opportunities in the community for people with intellectual disability, such as through employment training and job support agencies.
- Educating the community so there is a greater understanding and a more positive attitude towards people with intellectual disability.
- Inclusive education, where a person with an intellectual disability attends classes with appropriate support levels in a local school.

Figure 11.2: Sporting activities are enjoyable and help build self-confidence
*Photograph reproduced with permission of People with Disabilities Participation Division,
Australian Sports Commission.*

- Giving appropriate support to enable the person with intellectual disability to have choices in regard to doing things in the community. Part of this involves questioning our own preconceptions about what a person's capabilities may be.
- A commitment from all levels of government that everyone has a right to be part of the community and should be given the appropriate supports to achieve this. This commitment has come through legislation, but needs to be supported by community education.

After class finished, the ballet teacher took Erin's hand and moved towards me. All I could think was 'OK, here it comes' but she was only concerned about Erin's small stature. She said she would be pleased and proud to include Erin and not to worry about the opinions of the other parents. Erin had been given a chance to prove herself – and she did. Incidents like this make all the work and worry seem worthwhile.

Mollie

Rights and responsibilities of people with intellectual disability

Rights for people with intellectual disability are the same as those for everyone else. Today, people with disabilities and their families are supported by legislation and policies of normalisation, integration, and anti-discrimination (see Chapter 2). They are now aware that they can claim entitlement to the same opportunities, services and benefits as other citizens. Rights include the opportunity to learn, work, be accepted by others, develop relationships, live in the community and participate in its activities, make choices and be involved in decisions affecting one's future, and to be provided with appropriate training, assistance and support to meet one's needs.

As people with intellectual disability are subject to the same laws and consequently have the same rights as others, so must they also have the same responsibilities. Members of the community must learn that they are not doing the person with the disability a favour by accepting behaviour that would not be tolerated in their peers without a disability. People have to learn that they must pay for items, wait in queues, and take part in other practices accepted as part of everyday life by other people.

Rights services and grievance services

Agencies are available where people with intellectual disability can go to learn about their rights and about where to go for legal advice. Disability complaints services assist people to gain access to appropriate mechanisms for their particular grievance.

Advocacy services. Two major forms of advocacy are available: self-advocacy and citizen advocacy. The aims of *self-advocacy* are to provide an avenue for meetings and interaction between people with intellectual disability so that they can help each other, learn more about their rights and become more responsible in the community. Self-advocacy works to enable people to develop skills and confidence so that they can speak for themselves and make their own decisions. A further aim is to make people in the community more aware of the needs, rights and abilities of people with intellectual disability. This movement provides assertiveness training for people with intellectual disability. Activities include community education, lobbying, self-help, development of self-respect, helping one another deal with the negative impacts of labelling, publication of newsletters, recreational and social activities, training people with intellectual disability in self-advocacy, networking, learning and teaching about rights.

Citizen advocacy is a program where people with and without intellectual disability (proteges and advocates) are matched with each other on a short- or long-term basis. This relationship has benefits for both parties, but is particularly designed to provide an advocate who will assist the person with an intellectual disability in overcoming devaluation and inequality and in achieving opportunities to share in freedom of choice and quality of life generally available to other citizens. By doing educational work in the community and raising the self-esteem of their members, advocacy groups help the community to focus on ability, not disability.

> *I found out about Citizen Advocacy when I was overcharged on an electricity bill. I got an advocate and he helped me sort out the bill. I was being overcharged by five times. I'm now a member of a self-advocacy group and I go around talking to people to urge them to stand up for their rights.*
>
> Jean

Access

For people with intellectual disability, access is usually a matter of acquiring the skills necessary to be able to gain access to services in the community (generic or mainstream services). In addition, workers in generic services need education on how to communicate with the person with intellectual disability.

People with intellectual disability may need support in the process of gaining access to services. This may involve help in getting to the service, training in filling out forms, explaining what is being said and prompting people to have the confidence to ask questions. The degree of support should be the minimum needed to obtain access as independently as possible. In the jargon this is often written as 'the least restrictive alternative'. It is preferable to teach each person the skills necessary to overcome access problems rather than to have people reliant on direct help. For example, this may mean teaching a person how to interpret a bus or train timetable rather than simply accompanying him or her on every journey.

If the person with the intellectual disability is from a non-English-speaking background or a non-majority culture, appropriate access steps need to be taken such as provision of language interpreters and of culturally-appropriate service provision.

Education

Early intervention programs assist children from birth to around five years of age. Intervention at this age greatly enhances a person's capabilities in later years. During preschool and school years, special assistance is available to integrate children with intellectual disability into local schools. Therapy services are also available to help children who have difficulties which impede overall development and learning. Such services include physiotherapy, speech therapy and occupational therapy. After childhood, programs are available to aid transition from school to employment or adult life. Living skills programs prepare the person for the daily tasks of living within the community.

The philosophy underpinning programs is that the first five years of life are crucial for the child's later development. Opportunities and experiences missed during this period affect individuals throughout their whole lives. Early intervention programs are concerned with two basic issues: identification of children in need of early intervention and selection and implementation of appropriate interventions. The target population for early intervention programs usually is families with children who are aged from birth until they enter the school system and who already have a developmental delay or disability, or require specialised services without which it is likely that developmental milestones will not be achieved and/ or a handicap may result.

Early intervention generally involves a number of agencies and it aims to promote the optimal growth and development of infants and preschoolers with disabilities and/or delay to assist them in maximising their potential, to enable and empower families who have a child with a developmental delay or disability, to encourage acceptance and support of families with children who have disabilities (thus enriching the community); and to promote the most efficient and effective use of community and government resources.

Early intervention programs are based on two important premises: that it is important that identification occurs as early as possible and that the whole family

Figure 11.3: Listening to music at kindergarten

is involved. Key elements that families may expect if they use the early intervention system are:

- support and comprehensive information on their child's disability or developmental delay and the range of servicews, supports and options available;
- interdisciplinary team assessment which involves the family;
- an individual family service plan and an individual program for each child.

At three or four years of age, the child may go into an integrated preschool and then will start school at five or six years of age. Many parents find this a difficult time. They have to weigh up the advantages of integrating their child into a mainstream or regular class as compared with attending special classes within a regular school or of having their child attend a special school, usually some distance away. Children who attend special classes or special schools are usually taught life skills such as dressing, washing, cooking and shopping. These programs assist the child in developing into an independent adult. Physiotherapy (physical therapy), occupational therapy and speech therapy also may continue for the child.

Community centres and technical colleges cater for young adults with intellectual disability who have left school but require further training in specific skills. Courses also are available in some countries through television open learning programs. Courses are available on topics such as basic literacy and independent living skills, such as cooking and budgeting.

Accommodation

Programs are provided by government and non-government organisations, with an emphasis on community-based integrated options rather than large residential institutions. People with intellectual disability have individual needs for accommodation just as they have individual needs in other areas of their lives. Although community perceptions are that most people with intellectual disability live in residential institutions, this is not the case. Most people with intellectual disability live at home with their family (Racino et al., 1993). However, like other young adults, young people with intellectual disability also need opportunities to move out from home and to live independently with friends or in the community. These living arrangements may be organised by the family or with support from a government or non-government organisation. They can include flatting with a friend with a disability or a non-disabled flatmate, or sharing a house with several other people. In each of these options, the person with intellectual disability may live entirely independently, semi-independently, or with considerable support, depending on his or her support needs (Halpern, Close & Nelson, 1986).

Accommodation for some people with intellectual disability will comprise living with around four to six other people. For others, particularly those who are medically frail or who require a level of intensive care, a community-based accommodation option comprising ten or twelve people may be needed. Regrettably, many people with intellectual disability continue to live in large residential institutions or nursing homes due to the lack of resources available to accommodate them in community-based options.

Providing sufficient community-based living accommodation is perhaps one of the greatest challenges facing governments in many countries around the world.

Employment

Employment opportunities range from competitive employment placement and training schemes, supported employment, Independent Living Skills centres, and Community Access Services for people with high support needs. This means that people with intellectual disability are no longer limited to working in sheltered workshops. However, employment for people with intellectual disability often remains part-time, poorly paid, and not protected by industrial awards. For people with intellectual disability to have the same opportunities for employment as others in the community, this employment must be:

- paid work;
- at full award rates or pro-rata award rates;
- in the open labour market or supported employment;
- under an industrial award or agreement and which can include contractual and self-employment opportunities (Baume & Kay, 1995).

For some people with intellectual disability, enrolment in an employment preparation program may be appropriate. These programs have as a defined goal assisting people with a significant disability to achieve employment within an agreed period of time.

In times of high unemployment, people with intellectual disability find it difficult to compete with others for the few jobs that are available. Some employers set aside jobs for people with intellectual disability. The fact that these employers continue with their programs suggests that they are satisfied with these employees.

However, it is important not to stereotype people with intellectual disability in terms of the type of work they enjoy and are good at. Some employers have said that people with intellectual disability will perform conscientiously jobs that others are too impatient to do, but it is easy for such people to get locked into boring tasks.

> *After 19 years it is really monotonous. I don't really like it. I'm stuck doing the same thing all the time. I think I could do something else if they gave me the chance.*
>
> Mark

Some countries have developed and implemented programs which assist people with intellectual disability in gaining and keeping competitive employment. Government-funded subsidy schemes and training programs are increasing the number of people with intellectual disability who receive wages equivalent to those received by others in similar jobs.

In the recent past, a common form of employment was activity centres or sheltered workshops. Recent legislation such as the *Australian Disability Services Act 1986* heralds the downscaling of such forms of employment in many countries. However, many still exist. Those that had reputations similar to the workhouses of the Victorian era have largely closed in many countries, but in many of those remaining, often little training is provided, work is repetitive and pay levels are low. Workers may be warned that they will not be allowed to return if they leave to try their fortunes in open employment.

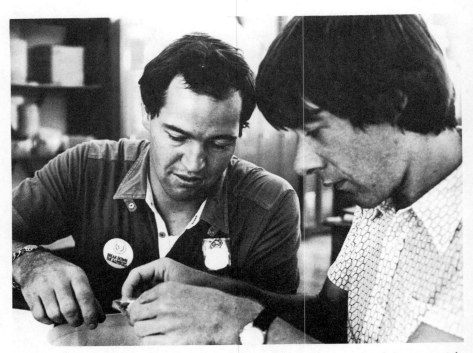

Figure 11.4: A man with intellectual disability learning skills during a work experience program

I worked in sheltered workshops for a while, but I did not like it. You had to work hard and you didn't get much money. I would not work in one again.

Linda

Other centres provide positive experiences and training for their workers, however few pay their employees at standard full rates. Workers are encouraged to develop a variety of skills that will be useful in outside employment.

Governments in many countries are carefully scrutinising the conditions for workers in sheltered employment. Considerable attention is being given to rates of pay and worker rights. These changes have been resisted by some employing organisations, many of which are registered charities or organisations representing people with disabilities. Such changes represent major challenges to ingrained attitudes and beliefs and are argued to be financially expensive and to decrease profits.

In these situations unpaid work often may be a more satisfactory solution. Many community groups are pleased to receive extra help and the person with intellectual disability has the chance to gain useful skills and to make new friends.

PERSON TO PERSON

Appropriate language and behaviour

When referring to people with intellectual disability, remember that they are people first regardless of their disability. Do not refer to, or treat, adults with intellectual disability as children. Each individual has a right to participate in the life of the community by working, shopping, going to school, playing sport and so on.

People with intellectual disability have been given many labels which carry negative connotations. Names such as 'feeble minded', 'backward', 'subnormal', 'dull', 'slow', 'fool', 'idiot' and 'imbecile' have been used over the years. More recently, terms such as 'mentally retarded', 'mentally handicapped', 'mentally disabled', 'developmentally delayed' and 'developmentally handicapped' have been in vogue. However, these are stigmatising and offensive to people with intellectual disability. Therefore, they should be avoided. These terms are no longer appropriate and should *never* be used. Instead, use the term *person with intellectual disability*. Person first, disability second.

Many myths still exist about people with intellectual disability. It is important to correct these serious misconceptions.

Attitudes towards people with disabilities, even from the enlightened, tend to describe the way non-disabled people feel towards people with disabilities. For example, often people have said to me as Erin has grown older, 'Congratulations, you have done such a good job'. It makes me really angry, because, sure I have worked hard, but can you imagine how much harder my little daughter has had to work to achieve the standards which are seen to be only ordinary, or average.

Mollie

The intellectual disability is secondary to the person being an individual with the right to be an equal and participating member of society.

Strategies for successful interaction

Give people time. One of the most important strategies to remember is to allow the person enough time to either formulate a response or to complete what he or she is doing. Our impatience often will lead us into 'helping' someone to get his or her money to pay for something, find a bus pass, set the table or think about a choice. It is frustrating for people with intellectual disability when others take over in a situation where they could have done something for themselves with more time.

Remember you are generally not there to do things for people, but to enable them to do things for themselves. To make this a positive experience for everyone you should be aware of:

- the way people learn;
- a person's life experiences that may affect his or her reaction to new experience. If, for instance, someone's life to date has been in an institution, she or he may be afraid at first, or inexperienced in ways we take for granted;
- treating everyone with the same respect for privacy, and so on as you would wish to be given yourself.

Some strategies for successful interaction are suggested in Table 11.1.

It is not often that people without intellectual disability are required to use their intelligence to its full extent, but they may feel drained after a period of intense concentration. A person with intellectual disability may have to concentrate very hard to understand another person. If we are not prepared to explain or repeat ourselves when necessary, the person with intellectual disability may not be prepared to put in a lot of effort to understand us. Speak in a straightforward manner and give the other person plenty of opportunities to show that he or she has understood. Then you will both enjoy a successful interaction.

The dignity of risk

Overprotection is a reaction which can stem from feeling sorry and from devaluing a person's abilities. Families are especially likely to display this caring, but restrictive reaction. An important concept which is becoming increasingly recognised is the *dignity of risk* or allowing a person to take risks and learn from the consequences. Parents tend to experience this dilemma with all their growing children, not just the child with intellectual disability. Sometimes things might go wrong, but by talking about what has happened and sharing the information, the person develops skills, feelings of capability and independence. People with intellectual disability should be given opportunities to do the things their peers do, by both parents and service providers. At first the concept may be alarming for the person who feels personally responsible for a person with intellectual disability. People must be allowed to take risks, make mistakes and learn from the consequences. Thus, after someone has acquired the skills necessary to catch the train to and from school or work, the time comes to step back and let the person assume responsibility. Sometimes things can go wrong but, by asking what happened and sharing more information, the person with intellectual disability can come to feel able to try again. The important feature of such learning is that the person has the skills to be able to determine whether the plan has been a success or has failed and has options which he or she can then pursue. Thus, the person knows that if he or she has missed the bus stop, it is important to get off at the next stop and find a phone to

Table 11.1: Strategies for successful interaction

Person with intellectual disability	Other person
Interrupt if necessary and ask for explanations.	Use the same tone and way of talking as you would to anyone of the same age.
	Speak in a straightforward manner, choose simple and commonly used words.
Make it clear to someone if their assistance is not necessary.	Check understanding: pause occasionally so that the person with intellectual disability can ask for an explanation.
Ask the person to repeat what he or she has said if you have not understood.	Get eye contact and talk to the person, not above, below, or about him or her.
	Give only one instruction at a time so as not to confuse people with too much information at once.
	If possible, demonstrate what you mean by using actions.
Be willing to ask when you do need help.	Try another way of saying something if the person does not understand, and keep trying.
	Remember there are many other ways to communicate than just words!
	Have patience and wait for the person to finish speaking, do not finish people's sentences.
Be willing to explain what your needs are.	Do not shout. Unless someone has a hearing impairment they can hear the same as anyone else.
	Do not talk abnormally slowly. Do not use patronising language or gestures.
Be patient with another person when he or she is trying to find out about your views or needs.	Even if a person with intellectual disability takes longer to complete a task, there is no need to take over.
	Do not make assumptions about a person's capabilities. People's abilities are very diverse.

call from. Such measures should be trialed and potential mishaps anticipated and taken into account.

Legal aspects of duty of care

When people are learning to access their wider community the question will sometimes be asked: 'What if something happens to a person in my care because I am letting them, or encouraging them, to do something new?'

People working with persons with intellectual disabilities have a duty by law to take 'reasonable steps' to prevent harm that was 'reasonably foreseeable'. They should look at the benefits gained by the person doing the activity and assess how to minimise any risks. Common sense will usually tell what is reasonable risk taking and what is negligence. If there are any doubts, the matter should be discussed with others and the skills and information that have been given to enable a person to make his or her own choices should be recorded.

Remember, people cannot be locked up or restrained from doing things that are within the law for others. It is the worker's duty to help people to gain skills needed to do safely whatever they want to enhance their quality of life and to empower people with sufficient information to make choices. You may not always agree with a person's choices but it is not part of duty of care to make moral judgments or to stop him or her from being free to make mistakes. Mistakes are part of growth and life experiences. They should not be denied to anyone nor looked upon as undesirable. It should be noted, in the unlikely event of a worker being sued for negligence, the benefits of encouraging independence and development would be taken into account.

MORE INFORMATION ABOUT INTELLECTUAL DISABILITY

Definition

Intellectual disability refers to a substantial limitation in intellectual functioning compared with people of the same age and in the same situation. A range of personal skills and capabilities is taken into account when assessing intellectual disability. The more severe the disability, the more likely the person is to have associated physical disabilities, difficulty in functioning independently, difficulty with communicating and difficulty in social interaction. There is a wide range of intellectual disability and each person must be assessed and considered on his or her own terms. (Australian Federal Government, 1993a).

Applying the World Health Organization (1980) definition of impairment, disability and handicap is not straightforward in the case of intellectual disability. This is because the source of impairment is not always clear. For this reason, the term 'intellectual disability' rather than 'intellectual impairment' is used.

- *Impairment* in many cases is associated with brain damage due to a variety of causes, but in others the source is unknown.
- *Disability* is reflected in a slower rate of learning and understanding.
- *Handicap* is reflected in reduced opportunities for employment, attitudes of others which affect self-esteem and restrictions which result from overprotection.

The American Association of Mental Retardation (1992) proposed the following definition:

Mental Retardation [sic] refers to substantial limitations in present functioning. It is characterized by significantly sub-average intellectual functioning, existing concurrently with related limitations in two or more of the following applicable adaptive skill areas: communication, self-care, home, living, social skills, community use, self-direction, health and safety, functional academics, leisure and work. Mental retardation [sic] manifests before age 18.

(AAMR, 1992, p. 18)

This definition has been argued to represent an advance in thinking in that it replaces a previous definition which focused on a deficit model of intellectual disability with a support model which places greater focus on the needs of individuals (Reis, 1994; Smith, 1994). It should be noted that the United States has yet to adopt terminology changes already in everyday use in Australia and Canada. Although, the revised AAMR definition reduces the focus on deficit, its continued use of the outdated phrase 'mental retardation' is an example of how inappropriate language can serve to reinforce the continued use of a no longer appropriate view of disability (see Chapter 2 of this book).

Members of the community often confuse the terms 'intellectual disability', 'mental retardation', 'developmental disability' and 'learning disability'. The term 'intellectual disability' is now the preferred term. In Australia, 'developmental disability' is a broad term used to refer to permanent severe disabilities attributable to intellectual and/or physical impairment which emerge before 18 years of age. It extends beyond intellectual disability to include conditions such as cerebral palsy and many forms of epilepsy. A developmental disability slows progression towards adult intellectual functioning. The term 'learning disability' is a more specific term and can occur in people within all levels of intellectual functioning, including those classified as above average. It refers to limitations in a specific area. A person with a learning disability may have difficulty in processing auditory information accurately. In extensive psychological testing, such a person would have one or two very low scores mixed with a majority of average or above average scores. In contrast, a person with intellectual disability will characteristically score below average on a range of tests (Makas, 1981); however, it must be remembered that such a person will show a range of scores, like anyone else.

Multiple disability

There may be a combination of other disabilities occurring with intellectual disability: people with intellectual disability may also have a physical disability and use a wheelchair, be hearing or vision impaired, have epilepsy, a psychiatric disability or cerebral palsy. For example, it has been reported that up to 30 per cent of people with intellectual disability in Canada have an accompanying disability such as epilepsy and/or cerebral palsy. The more severe a person's disability, the more likelihood of multiple involvement. However, for most people with intellectual disability, the impairment is mild and there is no evidence to suggest that they are any more likely to have other disabilities than members of the general population.

Causes

Anyone can have a child with intellectual disability and in many cases the cause is not known. Some of the most common causes are:

Genetic/inherited. Intellectual disability may reflect heredity factors or chromosome abnormalities such as in Down syndrome which is often referred to as Trisomy 21. This is one of the most well-known and largest single causes of intellectual disability. It is caused by an extra chromosome – 47 instead of the usual 46. The reason for inaccurate cell division is not clear but it has been linked with the age of the parents. When the mother is 20 years of age, the risk is less than one in 1200. This rises to one in 50 by the time the mother is 45 or the father is 55 (Stopford, 1988). Advances in medical procedures such as amniocentesis enable diagnosis in the first 12 weeks of life. People with Down syndrome have a characteristic appearance: short height, slanting eyes, flat broad face, and large protruding tongue. The degree of intellectual impairment varies from mild to very severe. It may be accompanied by other impairments such as congenital heart defects, visual defects (myopia and cataracts), hearing impairment and frail skin and lungs causing susceptibility to colds and bronchial infections.

Congenital. Intellectual disability may result from brain damage at/or before birth due to factors such as:

- *Infections.* These may result from drug- or diet-related problems in the mother. Both viral and protozoal maternal infections can have adverse effects on the fetus. Viral infection includes cytomegalovirus (CMV) and rubella. CMV infection is common but usually produces few, if any, symptoms unless a woman has a primary infection in early pregnancy when the virus passes readily to the fetus. The central nervous system is affected more frequently with rubella and there is a substantial risk of intellectual impairment. Protozoal infection such as toxoplasmosis is a common human infection, usually with few clinical symptoms. If it occurs during pregnancy, the fetus may be severely infected, leading to chorioretinitis, hydrocephaly or microcephaly at birth and subsequent profound intellectual impairment.
- *Brain damage.* This may occur during birth as a result of trauma, lack of oxygen or prolonged labour. It may also occur before birth as a result of alcohol (fetal alcohol syndrome) or drug abuse on the part of the mother.
- *Metabolic disturbances.* These include phenylketonuria (PKU), and hormone deficiencies such as hypothyroidism. PKU is an inherited disorder occurring in about one in every 10 000 births. Affected babies without treatment almost invariably develop severe intellectual impairment. To be successful, treatment must be commenced within the first few weeks of life. At one time, 1–2 per cent of all institutionalised people with intellectual impairment had disorders associated with PKU. This figure is much lower today and will continue to fall because of testing newborn infants in the first six days of life (the Guthrie test). In the event of a positive test, appropriate treatment with the necessary follow-up is instituted immediately. Hypothyroidism is a hormone deficiency which occurs in one in 5000 newborn infants. Some degree of intellectual impairment is likely to ensue if treatment is not commenced within the first few weeks of life. Testing of all infants is now carried out in most countries.
- *Unknown prenatal influences.* This explanation is used to account for unexplained disabilities which existed at or prior to birth. Other conditions, such as being born too early, may originate in the prenatal period.

Acquired. Intellectual impairment may result from malnutrition in infancy and early childhood; from the inability of the infant's body to use and/or eliminate products; and sometimes from severe neglect by care givers in early years (deprivation). It also may occur as a result of an illness such as encephalitis, an accident or poisoning in early childhood, and from gross brain disease after birth. It also may occur gradually as a result of lead poisoning.

Incidence and prevalence

People with intellectual disability form one of the largest single disability groups in the community. Approximately 3 per cent of the Australian population has some form of intellectual disability. Over three-quarters of these people have a mild intellectual disability with low support needs. The remainder require varying degrees of support, reflecting their level of disability. Intellectual disability is nine times more prevalent than cerebral palsy. It affects 15 times as many people as legal blindness. The most common known single cause of intellectual disability is Down syndrome, which affects one in 600 births.

In Canada, approximately 750 000 people (or one in 1000) have some form of intellectual disability requiring a limited degree of support to function in the community. A further three to four people per 1000 in the population require more extensive support.

In the United States, around 7.2 million people have an intellectual disability.

No race, class, age group or culture is exempt: intellectual disability occurs across the community.

Gender. Studies have shown that males are more likely to have intellectual disability than females. However, with Down syndrome, girls are marginally more at risk than boys.

Other variables. Although there is evidence that there are higher numbers of people with intellectual disability among lower socio-economic groups, this should be seen as a circular phenomenon. Two of the causes of intellectual disability (malnutrition in infancy and early childhood and being neglected in early years) are more likely to happen where there are fewer services to aid parents and less money is available. The latest evidence shows that, apart from Down syndrome which is a chromosome abnormality, women who delay their child-bearing years to mid-thirties and after are not more likely to have a child with intellectual disability. This finding is contrary to previous medical opinion and popular belief. However, labour with a first child is more difficult at an advanced age.

Life expectancy and ageing. The average life expectancy of someone with Down syndrome is 61.5 years. Other people with intellectual disability have the same life expectancy as the rest of the population – around 77 years for men and 82 years for women (NSW Office of the Aged, 1987). Lubin & Kiely (1985) report that advances in medical treatment and technology have increased life expectancy among people with intellectual disability, largely as a result of the fall in mortality rate during the first year of life. Decreases since the middle of this century in neonatal deaths, the development of antibiotics and improvements in health care and social service programs have are now having an effect on the ageing population. The increase in the number of older people with intellectual disabilities exceeds the increases of older people in general and for those occurring as a result of the post-war 'baby boom' and migration. These demographic changes have many implications which are yet to be addressed by governments; including catering for the needs of older parents with dependent adult children with disabilities, and developing strategies for maintaining quality of life for older people with disabilities who become frail and unable to live independently (Sutton et al., 1993). A late-life move into an institution may result in frustration for a person who has never lived in one; or for a person who has experienced deinstitutionalisation and has enjoyed many years of life in the community. As Seltzer, Krauss and Janicki (1994) have said, changes in the demography of the older population are a 'dynamic, new social phenomenon' which is expected to place new demands on economic and social resources within the community.

Dual diagnosis. Some people with intellectual disability also have a form of mental illness. The likelihood of having a mental illness is higher than that for the general population (Matson & Barrett, 1993). Most people with intellectual disability do not, however, have mental health concerns. Recent evidence suggests that most individuals with Down syndrome over the age of 40 have neurological changes associated with Alzheimer's disease. This disease affects only about 10 per cent of people in the general population aged over 65 years, but is common in people with Down syndrome. Once people with this form of intellectual disability rarely lived past 40 years of age. Now, more than half will reach 50 years (McCleary, 1995). Dementia is surfacing as a new issue for these people, who tend to display features of the disease at earlier years than other members of the population. The course of the disease also is shorter: McCleary found that adults with Down syndrome live seven to eight years after the onset of Alzheimer's disease as compared with 12 to 15 years for people in the general population.

Diagnosis

Unless a family has a child with Down syndrome, which is recognisable from birth, it may be that they do not know their child has intellectual disability until he or she fails to reach accepted milestones. It may be that parents have been aware for some time that something is different before a formal diagnosis is made (Bowman & Virtue, 1993; Ellis & Whaite, 1987). Even after diagnosis, the extent of the disability may not be clear for several years, so that a family cannot make plans for schooling or the future. There may be conflicting viewpoints about what the family should do, what intellectual disability actually means and about which services are needed or available. The family may be subjected to many of the myths in society, such as 'Your child will never be able to do anything'; 'Your child is sick and can/can't be cured', through to 'Your child would be better off in an institution'. Naturally this is very confusing and distressing for parents. Parents suddenly have to become experts on something they may never have thought of before and have to wade through a very complex and diverse system to find the supports that they need.

> A young doctor pronounced the sentence – Down syndrome. He was terribly nervous and had obviously rehearsed his speech a thousand times before speaking to us. Well, he botched the job, because it sounded like a sentence of life for our whole family – there was utterly no hope. I've often thought back to those moments and I've decided that there is no right or correct way of telling people this kind of news.
>
> Mollie

Assessment

Modern identification that a person has intellectual disability is based on a variety of tests which determine a person's capabilities and the level of support required.

Once the widespread method of assessing intellectual functioning was in terms of IQ (intelligence quotient). This score was derived from the administration of an instrument such as the Stanford Binet Scale or the Wechsler Intelligence Scales. It placed the person in a category of functioning which was used to indicate whether he or she was average, or above or below average (and by how much). It was derived by comparing a person's chronological age (years and months of age) with his or her mental age (the typical age of people who have equivalent levels of mental functioning). An IQ score was derived by placing chronological age and mental age into the following formula:

$$IQ = MA/CA \times 100$$

Average functioning was said to be reflected in IQ scores of around 100 points, with most of the population falling between 70 and 130 points. Half the population fall above and half below the score of 100.

Over the last 20 years, there has been growing dissatisfaction with the concept of IQ. This approach is now regarded as less important than evaluating skills and ability to adapt to the environment. People learn throughout their lives: we no longer talk of people having a mental age which is different from their chronological age, although in certain aspects of their development they may have reached the same milestones as could be expected from a child of a certain age. A 40-year-old has had 40 years of life, not five years of life and should not be compared with a child.

It is important to remember that achievements can change with time and circumstances, and that potential is not limited to categorisation. Many factors such as home environment, education, training, age, physical health, and availability of services can influence a person's level of functioning.

Assessment is usually undertaken as a basis for determining the level and type of services and supports that are required and, as such, is extremely important. There can, however, be drawbacks to the assessment procedure. For example:

- Assessment reflects nothing more than the individual's abilities in a series of tests *at the time of testing*. Abilities can change over time and in new circumstances. For instance, someone assessed as 'having a severe disability' while living in an non-stimulating environment (such as an institution) will almost certainly develop new skills with appropriate support in a house in the community.
- Assessment classification does not predict an individual's potential to learn new skills when given the opportunity to do so. Assessments can easily become self-fulfilling prophesies: little is expected of someone with the label 'having a profound disability', therefore he or she is not given opportunities to learn new skills and the label may then may be reinforced.
- Assessments do not take into account many facets of the whole person. They do not include abilities in areas such as creative expression.
- Assessments give people one label which is supposed to sum them up, whereas on closer acquaintance with a person with intellectual disability, it becomes clear that he or she is just like the rest of us; not so good at some things, good at other things, and very good at yet others.

Therapy

Intellectual disability is not a sickness – people are mostly healthy and well – it is not appropriate, therefore, to talk about treatments. People with intellectual disability do not need medication, physiotherapy or speech therapy for their intellectual disability. This is not to say people with intellectual disability do not need therapy services or medication, but it will be for a second disability such as epilepsy, a speech or physical impairment and not as a treatment for the intellectual disability.

Special learning techniques

All people with intellectual disability can learn skills for living and working in the community. Even people with high support needs can be taught complex tasks. People with intellectual disability take longer to acquire skills. From the time of diagnosis throughout life they will continue to learn, but will need help. The handicap of disability can be greatly reduced by applying specially-designed learning techniques. These techniques break down a task into small steps which are taught in a consistent way that makes learning of complex tasks possible. It may take more time initially to teach people to do things for themselves, but not only do people then have the dignity of being able to do things independently – time is saved as the person no longer has to be helped to bath, dress, go out to the movies, use a telephone, and so on.

Equipment

Sometimes special equipment or modifications assist learning. These may be very simple modifications such as marks on the stove, cassette player or washing machine which indicate where to turn the dial. Other more sophisticated equipment (such as computers) assist in the acquisition of new skills (for example, using bank teller machines). Special recipe books which clearly illustrate recipes with pictures enable people who may not be able to read to cook. Any aid, equipment or appliance is useful if it makes it easier for someone to learn.

Services and supports

Much of the impact of having a child with intellectual disability is related to availability of support services that assist the family and child at home and choices when the person is ready to leave home. Often services are missing and their lack has an effect on the family. For example, unavailability of a work placement once the person has left school may mean that a parent cannot go to work, but must stay at home to care for the son or daughter. Many parents worry about what will happen when they die, especially when the person with the intellectual disability has high support needs.

Having said this, however, things are improving! Doctors and other first points of contact who initially detect intellectual disability are slowly becoming more aware of the appropriate services to which to refer people to find facts (not fiction). Services are starting to evolve to meet the real, rather than presumed, needs of consumers.

Respite care. Respite care is designed to give families, carers and dependent people with intellectual disability a chance to experience time away from each other. This is particularly important as it may be difficult to organise the usual babysitting, child care, family holidays or other 'time away' experiences that other families have. The needs of all parties must be considered when making a selection. Facilities include centre-based respite care as well as host family programs. Flexible models of 'brokerage' care are now available. In these models, the government provides the family or person with funds so that they are able to choose and pay for the form of care that they use. One problem with this approach is that cases arise where the provided funds do not match the costs of services desired by the client.

Additional costs

There are many hidden costs involved in having intellectual disability. During childhood, the costs of treatment such as speech and occupational therapy may have to be met by parents. School-age children with intellectual disability (especially if they display challenging behaviours) may be excluded from after-school care or holiday programs and the family may have to find the money to have a much needed break or to enable parents to continue in their jobs.

After they have passed school age, people with intellectual disability and their families may have to pay for day care services, so that instead of the more common pattern of the financial burden becoming less for parents as children grow up and start to work, the pattern reverses.

RESOURCE ORGANISATIONS

All care has been taken to ensure that all information is correct at the time of publishing, however responsibility for the accuracy of this information is not accepted by the writer. The list of resource organisations contained in this chapter is not intended to be exhaustive; it provides national organisations only. The reader is referred to local community directories for further information and for local branches of national organisations. Inclusion of services and organisations should not be taken as a recommendation.

Australia

National Council on Intellectual Disability
Unit 3, 36 Botany Street
Phillip ACT 2606
(PO Box 521)
Mawson ACT 2607
Ph 02 9282 5624
Fax 02 9282 5639

Canada

Canadian Down Syndrome Society
Suite 206, 12837 78th Street
Surrey, BC V3W 2V3
Ph 604 599 6009
Fax 604 599 6165

New Zealand

IHC New Zealand Inc
PO Box 4155
Wellington
Ph 04 472 2247
Fax 04 472 0429

United Kingdom

British Institute of Learning Disabilities
Frankfurt Lodge, Clevedon Hall
Victoria Road
Clevedon, Avon BS21 7SJ
Ph 0275 876 519
Fax 0275 343 096

United States

The ARC
Suite 300, 500 East Border Street
Arlington
Texas 76010
Phone 817 261 6003
Fax 817 277 3491

American Association on Mental
    Retardation
Suite 846, 444 North Capitol Street NW
Washington DC 20001-1512
Ph 202 387 1968
Toll free: 800 424 3688
Fax 202 387 2193

FURTHER READING

American Association on Mental Retardation (1992). *Mental retardation: definition, classification and systems of supports* (9th edn). Washington DC: American Association on Mental Retardation.

Fegan, L. & Rauch, A. (1993). *Sexuality and people with intellectual disability.* Sydney: MacLennan & Petty.

Fulwood, D. (1993). *Chances and choices: making integration work.* Sydney: MacLennan and Petty.

Fullwood, D. (1993). *Here, there and everywhere: integration in our community.* Sydney: NSW Council for Intellectual Disability.

Miller, N. B. (1994). *Nobody's perfect: living and growing with children who have special needs.* Baltimore, MD: Paul H. Brookes.

Powell, T. H. (1993). *Brothers and sisters: a special part of exceptional families* (2nd edn). Baltimore, MD: Paul H. Brookes.

Pueschel, S. M. (1990). *A parent's guide to Down syndrome.* Baltimore, MD: Paul H. Brookes.

Schleien, S. J., Myer, L. H., Brandt, L. A. & Briel, B. (1995). *Lifelong leisure skills and lifestyles for people with developmental disabilities.* Baltimore, MD: Paul H. Brookes.

Seltzer, M. M. Krauss, M. W. & Janicki, M. P. (1994). *Life course perspectives on adulthood and old age.* Washington, DC: American Association on Mental Retardation.

Sutton, E., Factor, A., Hawkings, B. A., Heller, T. & Seltzer, G. B. (1993). *Older adults with developmental disabilities.* Baltimore, MD: Paul H. Brookes.

Turnbull, H. R., Turnbull, A. P., Bronicki, G. J., Summers, J. A. & Roeder-Gordon, C. (1989). *Disability and the family.* Baltimore, MD: Paul H. Brookes

CHAPTER 12

MENTAL ILLNESS AND PSYCHIATRIC DISABILITY

A mental illness is a disorder of the functioning of the mind. It can happen at any time to anyone. Mental illness is one of the most misunderstood and feared experiences within our community. Negative reactions and inappropriate behaviours on the part of others can profoundly influence quality of life and achievement of rights for many people with mental illness. Some people argue that stigma and prejudice are worse than the actual illness or disability. Thus, any steps that can be taken to reduce stigma and prejudice would have major implications for reducing the negative consequences of mental illness.

The causes of mental illness are controversial and the subject of considerable research. It is likely that a number of factors work in combination, including genetic inheritance, family environment, life stresses, life events, cultural background and physical illness. Some forms of mental illness appear to be caused by chemical imbalances in the brain (Australian Federal Government, 1993b).

The terms mental illness and psychiatric disability are often confused. The following definitions clarify the distinction:

- *Mental illness* is a clinical term used by psychiatrists to refer to a cluster of psychological and physiological symptoms which cause a person suffering or distress and which represent a departure from a person's usual pattern and level of functioning.
- *Psychiatric disability* refers to the range of functional difficulties which are often linked with past or current mental illness, associated institutional dependence, the adverse effects of medications used to treat mental illness, and other treatments.

In other words, a person who has a mental illness or who has had one in the past, does not necessarily have a psychiatric disability. This chapter focuses on mental illness. Mental illnesses can be divided into two broad groups: neuroses and psychoses. *Neuroses* or neurotic disorders involve an exaggeration or distortion of common feelings, thoughts and behaviours. Neuroses are given names such as anxiety, phobia, obsession and neurotic depression. A person who has a *psychosis* or psychotic disorder is out of touch with the real world. He or she may have delusions (such as believing that others are plotting against him or her) or hallucinations (such as hearing voices). The person may have difficulty in making sense of what is going on around him or her and may react inappropriately (Australian Federal Government, 1993b).

This chapter focuses on psychosis. It begins with a general overview of issues for people with mental illness and then focuses on three types: schizophrenia, manic depression and depression.

229

LIVING WITH MENTAL ILLNESS

People with a mental illness have the same goals, hopes and desires as other people; however, attitudes of others often make them question their own feelings of self-worth and self-esteem. The onset of mental illness can be a life-changing experience which is highly disrupting and threatens feelings of safety and continuity in life.

Personal adjustment

The experience of mental illness can be frightening and confusing because of the nature of the symptoms and the way they can affect an individual. An episode of mental illness can have the following effects for a person:

- *Fear*. The experience of mental illness in general can be frightening and confusing because of the nature of the symptoms and the way they affect an individual.
- *Disbelief and anger*. 'Why is this happening to me?' This can be experienced by the individual and by his or her family and close friends.
- *Sense of personal disintegration*. The experience of mental illness can undermine feelings of safety and order in a person's life, it can be highly disruptive to any sense of flow and continuity in life (especially if the illness tends to recur).
- *Low self-esteem*. After an episode, the person often has little confidence in himself/herself, even in carrying out what were once simple day-to-day activities.
- *Confusion*. The nature of the illness itself, along with the disruption it causes can result in confusion.
- *Isolation*. The person may withdraw from the company of others.
- *Depression*. This can follow an episode of mania or schizophrenia.

Smith (1993) reports the following reactions described by people who had experienced mental illness:

'. . . I had episodes of depression . . . (and) . . . became after some time insecure, nervous, lacking in confidence and unable to concentrate or put my soul into anything.'

'. . . I feel isolation, alienation, desolation and despair . . .'

'. . . I feel depressed, frightened and lonely . . .'

'. . . I lose my self-confidence and become extremely indecisive; I feel more incompetent, clumsy, inefficient than usual . . .'

Mental illness can be a devastating experience. However, nothing is more devastating and disabling for someone recovering from a mental illness than stigma. Until this stigma is eliminated, prejudice will persist which will inevitably be expressed as discrimination. Further, this discrimination often means that people are denied opportunities that will enable them to resume their previous lifestyle. What others do not understand is that complete recovery after an episode of mental illness is now more likely than ever before. People are able to lead as full a life as anyone else in the community.

I think attitudes towards mental illness are slowly becoming more positive. Ridiculing people with disabilities is never likely to be totally eradicated as it has been going on for a long time. Although you can pass laws about such things, you can't change human nature.

Marcus, who has schizophrenia

Ways in which people deal with mental illness vary considerably, however the following strategies often help people to adjust:

- decreasing stress/avoiding high-stress situations;
- taking medication regularly;
- setting reasonable, achievable goals;
- monitoring symptoms and seeking help when they reappear;
- planning or organising activities for each day.

Sexuality

When people are in a psychotic state they can be vulnerable to sexual exploitation. For example, they may be taking strong medication which makes it difficult to understand and resist what is happening. When experiencing psychosis, a person may place himself or herself in dangerous situations that he or she would not normally wish to be in.

People in a manic state may experience a heightened sex drive and do things that they would not usually do. They may experience embarrassment and shame afterwards, as well as the possibility that they may have contracted a sexually transmitted disease, or may be pregnant.

Being a parent

People with a mental illness who have children often feel at risk of having their children taken from them if they become ill. Most people with a mental illness, as for others in the general population, are not in danger of harming their children, but they have to face the stigma and fear associated with mental illness.

Family

My Dad died when I was 14, so I can't relate to him as an adult. But I am pleased he wasn't around to see me going in and out of mental hospitals. I love my Mum dearly and, despite sometimes disagreeing, we get on quite well.

Marcus

As well as having a debilitating effect on the individual, the effects of mental illness can disrupt family life and relationships. Horsfall (1987) argues that having a family member who is mentally ill can influence the emotional and mental health of all members. Support for families is essential. A number of common reactions have been recounted by families. Some of these reactions are:

- *Guilt and confusion.* Families experience concern over what is happening to their family member. Parents may blame themselves for the illness and wonder where they went wrong in rearing their son or daughter.
- *Fear.* This comes from lack of knowledge about the disorder and what it means for the individual.

- *Social isolation.* This is commonly due to the individual's perceived inappropriate social behaviour and his or her sometimes unpredictable behaviour. Stigma associated with having a member of the family with a mental illness can result in social isolation for both the family and individual.
- *Stresses on interpersonal relationships.* Illness in a family can create numerous interpersonal stresses. Not only does presence of illness demand changes to previous relationships, but the changing nature of the illness can be disruptive. The return of the person with mental illness to the family after a period of hospitalisation can create stresses for all.

Many families are unsure as to how they should act or respond to the ill family member. They are afraid of being overprotective, but at the same time are afraid of being too demanding. For example, families find it difficult to ask the person to get out of bed, help with the daily chores or have a shower. This, in turn, can hinder the person's independence as she or he is not being given the opportunity to do tasks for himself or herself.

A primary focus in working with individuals with mental illness and their families is to assist them to exercise choices, including decisions about independent living, relationships, and so on. Provision of accurate information is an important part of the process. This helps those involved to come to understand the illness and to anticipate the effects it may have on the individual.

Community living

During the nineteenth century, people with a mental illness were usually admitted to mental institutions and 'treated' using a diverse range of physical methods. For the rest of society, these people tended to be forgotten – 'out of sight, out of mind'. Mental illness was traditionally seen as a social problem rather than a medical one (these attitudes have remained relatively unchanged in our society). It was not until the 1960s that recognition came that some behaviours of many people with a chronic mental illness who had been institutionalised for a long period were exacerbated by the experience of institutionalisation. As a result, services were established within the community to provide care and assistance to people with a mental illness. Now, long-term hospitalisation occurs only for those very few people who cannot be assisted effectively by community services.

The report of the National Inquiry into the Rights of People with Mental Illness (Burdekin Report, 1993) investigated the human rights and fundamental freedoms afforded to people affected by mental illness. It concluded that people affected by mental illness are among the most vulnerable and disadvantaged in Australia: these people experience widespread, systematic discrimination and are denied the rights and services to which they are entitled.

> *People like myself, with or without family support, literally 'fall through the cracks of the system'. We try to lead as normal lives as possible, only to have a psychiatric episode and find ourselves having to rebuild our lives again. We live in a virtual wages/poverty income cycle and, because of not knowing if we could become ill again, try to obtain as cheap a rent as possible in order not to lose our accommodation due to an episode and having to go on benefits for a time.*
>
> Frances

Access

Just like everyone else in the community, people who have a mental illness have a right to access to all kinds of services. However, for reasons outlined above (including prejudice and stigma) equality of access does not occur. The Australian *Disability Discrimination Act 1992* made discrimination in delivery and receipt of services illegal; however, major changes are required in community attitudes before the objectives of this legislation are achieved.

The devastating nature of mental illness is likely to be compounded for people who experience difficulties in gaining access to appropriate services. Two such groups are those who come from non-majority cultures (such as those from Australian Aboriginal cultures) and people who live in remote areas. It can be said that these groups of people experience *double disadvantage*.

Double disadvantage

People of Australian Aboriginal backgrounds. Hunter (1992) describes how historical factors and those associated with being Aboriginal can combine to create reluctance to use mental health services. He argues that factors such as mistrust (as a result of past segregation, prejudice and mistreatment) mean that a person with a mental illness is not likely to come to a service unless the illness is severe. Thus, many Aboriginal people who could benefit from treatment do not receive services. By the time the person presents for a service, she or he is likely to be very disturbed. The person is likely to find himself or herself in a strange environment with people from another culture. These experiences can exacerbate signs associated with mental illness.

Another factor underlying the reluctance to use services and to complete courses of treatment is the reluctance (until recently) of service provision agencies to take into account beliefs and mores of Aboriginal cultures. Increased knowledge and understanding of Aboriginal people and their cultures, and the involvement of Aboriginal people in service provision, are essential prerequisites to enhanced service provision. Some of the issues which services providers should consider are as follows:

- Aboriginal elders once treated mental illness, but in many places elders are disappearing (Munro, 1993). Before attending a government agency, an Aboriginal client may have already sought the help of a traditional healer (Hunter, 1993).
- Traditional beliefs among Aboriginal cultures may link serious illness and disability with supernatural forces (Ziersch, 1990).

Once again, it must be reiterated that people are individuals. Individuality applies to people with disabilities. It also applies to Aboriginal people. There are many Aboriginal cultures within Australia; and within these cultures individuals vary.

The Burdekin Report (1993) found Aboriginal and Torres Strait Island people who live in isolated areas were further denied access to adequate mental health services. Remote residence is a source of double disadvantage for both Aboriginal and non-Aboriginal people with a mental illness.

Residents of remote and rural areas. Burdekin (1993) found that isolation and social factors within small-scale communities were likely to exacerbate mental health problems. In rural areas, psychiatric services were found to be more inadequate than other health services. Lack of facilities in rural and isolated areas meant that people were often transferred to city hospitals or given inappropriate care in a local hospital. Fanning (1993) reports that isolation and distance can impose special stresses for someone caring for a person who has times of being difficult to care for.

Education

The onset of some serious mental illnesses, particularly schizophrenia and manic depressive disorder, frequently occurs during adolescence and early adulthood. Consequently, some people have their education interrupted at a crucial time. If, and when, they recover from the illness or episode of mental illness, they may need support in resuming their education. Universities usually have a disability consultant who will help. TAFE (Technical and Further Education) colleges in NSW are also starting to provide support for people with a mental illness.

Employment

Prejudice and ignorance can deny a person access and opportunities to return to the community, employment and social activities.

> *I have applied for many jobs, but as soon as I say that I have a mental illness, I am told the job is no longer available.*
>
> Jane

It is important to remember that, given effective treatment and support, complete and ongoing recovery after many forms of mental illness is the usual outcome.

> *After I went back to work when I had been in hospital, no one asked me anything. They didn't want to know me.*
>
> Edward

Many people who have experienced a mental illness are able to return to work with little or no change in the work environment. However, others experience ongoing changes in functioning which require environmental modifications. Mancuso (1993) states that common functional limitations experienced by workers with a mental illness include difficulty in maintaining concentration over time, screening out external stimuli, maintaining stamina throughout the work day, managing time pressures and deadlines, initiating interpersonal contact, focusing on multiple tasks simultaneously, and responding to negative feedback.

According to the Washington Business Group on Health (undated), a *reasonable accommodation* in the workplace involves any modification to the job or workplace that enables an employee with a disability to perform the essential functions of the job, without placing undue hardship on the employer. Examples of reasonable accommodations which can be made to assist in reducing the difficulties cited by Mancuso (1993) include schedule modification to allow more frequent breaks or more flexibility; job modification such as job sharing or reassignment to another position; modifications of the physical environment such as providing an enclosed office or positioning the worker as far as possible from noisy machinery; changes in policy such as extending additional paid or unpaid leave or allowing the employee to work at home; provision of assistive technology such as software that allows a worker to structure time and receive prompts during the work day; and having a supervisor or co-worker available to provide support when required (Washington Business Group on Health, undated).

PERSON TO PERSON

Appropriate language and behaviour

It is important to remember that each person is an individual and that mental illness affects people in different ways.

The way in which you approach a person with a mental illness is no different from the way in which you approach any person. Basic skills of empathy, good listening, tolerance and patience are the primary requirements for interaction with anyone. Sensitivity to the privacy needs of the person (for example, do not interview someone where others may overhear your conversation), and providing assurance of confidentiality will assist the person to feel more comfortable, and so feel more able to talk with you.

Friends, workers and family members can be most helpful by accepting the person and, if appropriate, gently encouraging him or her to gradually regain former skills and to cope with any stress.

Determine from the person what his or her needs are, both at the present time and in the longer term, and make an agreement to work together to devise the most appropriate strategy for the issue at hand.

Be particularly aware of the need for clear, concise communication. For example, if the person feels anxious it may take him or her a little longer to respond and remain focused with you. Remember, mental illness does not affect the person's intelligence, but he or she may experience difficulty in concentrating for longer periods.

Strategies for successful interaction

Table 12.1 gives some suggestions for people to assist them in interacting successfully with each other. Some of these strategies refer specifically to a situation in which someone is experiencing an episode of illness. It is important to remember that on most of the occasions where interaction occurs between people with and without a mental illness, no special behaviours are appropriate other than those that convey the dignity and respect that we hopefully show toward all people and that we ask to be shown towards ourselves.

SCHIZOPHRENIA

Most people have heard of the term schizophrenia, but very few people have much knowledge of what schizophrenia is and what can be done for it.

Schizophrenia is a major disorder that affects approximately one in 100 people and is diagnosed by a cluster of signs and symptoms. A sign is something that can be observed by another person; a symptom is something that is experienced by the person.

Schizophrenia is *not* a 'split' personality. This is a different, very rare disorder called 'dissociative disorder', whereby parts of the mind split off from other parts, forming a number of new personalities. This does not happen with schizophrenia.

Table 12.1: Strategies for successful interaction

Person with a mental illness	Other person
In anticipation of/during an episode	*In anticipation of/during an episode*
Understand how your illness affects you and what helps you to lessen its influence.	Remember that each person is an individual and that mental illness affects people in different ways.
Make sure others know how to assist you in the event that an episode occurs, in case you are not able to give directions or instructions to others.	Learn about the features of the person's illness and how best to assist when you are needed.
	Do not treat the person as if he or she is stupid. If you receive an unclear response, tell the person you do not understand and ask him or her to repeat it more clearly.
	Give one direction at a time and make sure this is understood.
	If you are speaking with someone who is agitated, speak calmly. If this is unsuccessful, phone your local community health centre or crisis team.
At all times	*At all times*
Have tolerance and understanding for yourself and others.	Have tolerance and understanding.
Remember that the mental illness is one part of your life, it does not mean that you cannot live a fulfilling and successful life.	Remember that there are many effective ways in which mental illness can be controlled and alleviated. As a result, it is highly likely that the other person is functioning as effectively as you are.
	Challenge within yourself common myths and stereotypes about people with a mental illness.

People with schizophrenia will often complain of the difficulty of knowing what is real and not real and can be overwhelmed and confused by feeling that too much is going on around them that they cannot sort out. At times, people with schizophrenia may act in an unusual way, but more often they will behave just like other people.

The symptoms of schizophrenia include hallucinations (false perceptions), delusions (mistaken beliefs) and difficulties with thinking, feeling and behaviour. When people have an hallucination they hear, see or smell things that are not seen, heard or smelt by other people. Hearing voices when nobody is in the room is a very common symptom of schizophrenia.

A delusion is a mistaken belief that others do not share. These ideas often come on quite suddenly and are quite unusual, so that workers, friends and family readily recognise that they are unlikely to be really happening. After recovery, a person with schizophrenia will be surprised at what he or she believed when ill. It is a little like waking up from a dream or nightmare.

A person with schizophrenia may complain of difficulties with speaking, may make up unusual words, or others may find the person's speech difficult to follow. Emotional responses and expressions may change from one time to the next.

The exact cause of schizophrenia is not known but there are several medical hypotheses. (Research in this area is highly active.) Stress and tension make the symptoms worse and may possibly trigger off an episode. There is evidence to suggest that relapses can have a direct relationship to stress. This is the stress-diathesis hypothesis which proposes a personal vulnerability or sensitivity to a diverse range of environmental stressors.

While people with schizophrenia possibly have a vulnerability which may run in families that increases their risk of developing schizophrenia, families are not to blame for either the development or onset of schizophrenia.

Many people recover from schizophrenia completely, but others may continue to have some difficulties and may have either frequent or infrequent relapses. Although it is not known what causes schizophrenia, and a complete cure is not available, relapses can often be prevented and life difficulties overcome.

There is a tendency for symptoms of schizophrenia to decrease over the years. For some, schizophrenia is a life-long concern, but much can be done to control the disorder and enable the person to live a reasonably happy, fulfilled life.

There are a number of modes of treatment, the primary one of which includes the use of medication. It is important to note here that empirical studies, clinical evidence, and the self-reports of clients, families, and carers attest to the value of professionals working jointly with the clients and their carers to minimise the effects of the illness.

MANIC DEPRESSIVE (BIPOLAR MOOD) DISORDER

This describes a disorder where extreme mood levels are experienced. Approximately one to two people in 100 have this disorder. Mood can change from very high to very low (mania and depression-bipolar) or can involve changes to low moods only (depression alone-unipolar).

People can have severe bouts of feeling extremely unhappy for no obvious reason, for weeks or months on end. Between episodes a full and productive life is common. Among the symptoms people recount experiencing with depression are feelings of tiredness and of being weighed down, terrible sadness, overwhelming anxiety, bodily symptoms such as constipation or diarrhoea and changes in sleep patterns. There is often an inability to concentrate, agitation or slowness, feelings of worthlessness and reduced interest in all activities.

Some of the symptoms people recount with mania are the 'seeing of the world through rose coloured glasses'. People can be irritable, and insensitive to others, not wanting to sleep and feeling 'terrific'. They may experience a fast flow of ideas, lack insight and have increased sexual activity, increased spending, and experience a reduced sense of danger.

As with schizophrenia, there may be a genetic susceptibility to develop the disorder, and again, families are not to blame for either the cause or the development of the disorder.

Medical treatment for manic depression (bipolar mood disorder) often involves the drug lithium carbonate which is a 'mood stabiliser'. People who experience depression are more likely to be prescribed anti-depressant medication.

With both manic depression and schizophrenia it is important to note that a central task for the affected individual is to learn how to manage the disorder. It also is important for the person to accept that he or she is not responsible for the condition. This is no different from the person who has diabetes or arthritis. Bipolar and unipolar mood disorders do not inevitably become long-term, however they may do so.

DEPRESSION

The word 'depression' is used to describe a whole range of experiences varying from feeling 'blue' or 'out of sorts' or 'caught in a rut' to overwhelming 'black despair'. Most people have experienced the depression which is a response to grief, loss or other life experiences. Most people have felt overwhelmed by situations or have felt too tired or too fed-up to keep going. These reactions have been experienced by most of us. However, many people also have experienced a more severe form of depression which is a disorder and interferes with their everyday life.

Around 5 per cent of the adult population at any one time suffers from a depressive disorder of some sort. Yet, depression is widely misunderstood. It is often ignored or untreated. People do not recognise their symptoms, are afraid to seem 'weak', or are too depressed to take action. But, depression can be treated successfully. Most people can start feeling well again in a few weeks.

The causes of depression relate to one of more of these factors:

- *Biochemical functions.* Hormonal or chemical imbalances in the brain influence mood and can cause depression. Illness, infection, alcohol or other drugs can also lead to depression.
- *Genetic pattern.* The tendency towards depression can run in families.
- *Personality type.* People who are highly self-critical, very demanding or unusually passive–dependent may be prone to depression.
- *Environmental stresses.* Problems at home or work, loss of, or separation from a loved one and so on, can cause depression.

Depression is characterised by the following:

- Disturbance in sleep pattern. Some people will sleep all day and are unable to sleep at night while others may awaken in the early morning and be unable to get back to sleep.
- Feelings of unreality and confusion.
- Feeling anxious, nervous and being upset easily.
- Feeling unworthy and desperate.
- Poor concentration span.

- Social isolation and feeling inadequate in social situations so that holding a conversation can be a trying ordeal.

- Lack of hygiene as it feels too much of an effort to look after oneself.
- Inability to work.
- Obsession with death and harming oneself.
- Uncontrollable feelings and sinking feelings.
- Obsessive and neurotic behaviour.

Everyone experiences some or all of these symptoms at some time, but when they are severe and lasting so that pain and problems outweigh pleasure much of the time, then it is time to get qualified help. A thorough assessment is necessary to work out a program of treatment. As with most illnesses, treatment is most effective when begun early.

MORE INFORMATION ABOUT MENTAL ILLNESS

The causes of many forms of mental illness are unclear, and explanations are often contradictory. Some individuals may be predisposed to experiencing a mental illness but this does not mean that they will necessarily experience one.

Definition

The World Health Organization (1980) definition is not used here as, unlike other conditions discussed in this book, it is usually not possible to trace disability and handicap to precise forms of impairment.

The NSW *Mental Health Act 1990* defines mental illness as:

A condition which seriously impairs, either temporarily or permanently, the mental functioning of a person and is characterised by the presence in the person of any one or more of the following symptoms:

(a) Delusions.
(b) Hallucinations.
(c) Serious disorder of thought form.
(d) Severe disturbance of mood.
(e) Sustained or repeated irrational behaviour indicating the presence of any one or more of the symptoms referred to in paragraphs a) to d).

(Schedule 1, *Mental Health Act 1990*, p. 123)

These disorders can be severe, debilitating and long-lasting. In addition, symptoms can worsen without active intervention. The three disorders discussed in this chapter are schizophrenia, manic-depressive (bipolar mood) disorder and depression. These are the three major disorders identified by the DSM-IV (*Diagnostic and Statistical Manual*), the most commonly used diagnostic tool in Australia.

Incidence and prevalence

According to Burdekin's (1993) Report of the National Inquiry into the Human Rights of People with Mental Illness, at any one time approximately 1.5 per cent of the Australian population will have a major mental illness (including 1 per cent with schizophrenia) and approximately one in five adults have, or will develop, some form of mental disorder during their lives. It has been estimated that at any one time in NSW, between 18 per cent and 23 per cent of the population have a significant psychological disorder. It is estimated that only 3 per cent of those who become ill ever come to the attention of specialist mental health services (Burdekin, 1993). The majority of those who experience mental illness do not have a disability. Only a minority have a severe, chronically disabling disorder.

It has been estimated that there are 6 879 000 people with a 'mental or emotional disability' in the United States. According to LaPlante and Carlson (1996), in the United States there are 235 000 people who have been diagnosed as having schizophrenia, 150 000 as having affective psychoses and 259 000 as having depressive forms of mental illness.

A characteristic of mental illness or psychiatric disorders is their episodic nature. Most people will have one or more episodes of mental illness and recover. Less than 7 per cent of those affected have symptoms for a year or longer.

Mental illness is believed to occur in all societies, regardless of gender, ethnic background or socio-economic status. How it is perceived differs between societies and reflects cultural beliefs.

Age. Mental illness usually has its onset early in life, with the median age of onset being 16 years with 75 per cent of people having experienced symptoms by 24 years of age and 90 per cent by 39 years of age (Rey, 1992).

Gender. Figures from the United States indicate, that over the lifespan, 22 per cent of women and 19 per cent of men are likely to experience a major form of mental illness – thus women are more likely to experience a mental illness.

> *Although, like many people who experience mental illness, I can iden-*
> *tify periods in my childhood when I was very depressed and had bleak*
> *thoughts about myself, such as that I was dying from cancer, it was not*
> *until my late teens that things really began to go haywire for me.*
>
> Nancy

Diagnosis

Psychiatric diagnosis involves identifying clusters of signs and symptoms, usually according to one of the standard diagnostic tools. The most widely accepted diagnostic classification system is the American Psychiatric Association's *Diagnostic and Statistical Manual of Mental Disorders*. The current version is DSM-IV. The manual sets out more than 300 mental disorders with descriptions of the features of each one. The *Diagnostic and Statistical Manual* is constantly under review and over the years huge changes have been made in the description of what constitutes a mental disorder.

Some people with a mental illness are happy to have a diagnosis or a label attached to their illness as it gives them a feeling that they are not alone in having those symptoms. Other people object to being labelled in this way as it makes them feel stigmatised and disempowered. Others say that the labels take no account of cultural differences.

Treatment

Medication. The majority of people with a mental illness will be treated within their own community, most likely from their local community health centre, or by their general practitioner. Very few people will require hospitalisation but if they do, they probably will be admitted to a special unit in a general hospital.

Medication has saved me from a life of misery. Despite the sometimes very uncomfortable side effects, anti-psychotics and anti-depressants have made my life tolerable.

Marcus

Medications are one of the treatment options available to a person with a mental illness. These can have side effects, one of which is lethargy, making it difficult for people to get out of bed and function in the mornings. Medications can cause fine tremors and restlessness which make detailed work difficult. They can cause weight gain which can be embarrassing and distressing, especially for people on long-term medication. Thus, as well as having to deal with the disorder itself, people also must deal with the side effects of the medication. It is no wonder that some people find compliance with medication so difficult.

The tablets iron-out my crippling mood swings and they make a big difference to the way I think. I used to ruminate a lot, going over and over the same things in my mind, progressively becoming as tightly wound up as a clock spring. In order to release the tension, I'd often hurt myself or do something dangerous. That doesn't happen to me any more thanks to the drug, but it does have side effects – my mouth gets very dry, especially in the mornings, and I drink a lot, sometimes my hands shake a bit and I've put on weight since I moved on to a higher dose.

Marcus

The most common side effects of medications used to treat mental illness are:

- muscle spasms, especially in the back, neck and eyes;
- fine tremors;
- cogwheel rigidity of joints and muscles which can contribute to an 'unusual' gait;
- sleepiness;
- restlessness;
- blurred vision;
- constipation;
- urinary retention;
- dry mouth.

Medication helps me to cope with each day as it comes. Sometimes, the side effects are unpleasant, but at least my life is more manageable.

Jane

Psychotherapy. This usually involves talking with a trained professional about problems and issues. Counselling may take place on a one-to-one basis or in a group setting.

Behaviour management. This aims to assist in modifying behaviour in order to change behaviours which are not helpful for the person. Another aim is to assist the person in acquiring skills which are adaptive and useful.

Social management. The aim of this aspect of treatment is to help the person come to terms with changes that may be required to their lifestyle. It also assists the person in dealing with situations that are experienced as stressful and difficult to deal with.

Services and supports

The issue of service provision for people who are mentally ill has been highly controversial and politicised. Government and non-government agencies are highly aware of the need for change. Many are now using recommendations made in the Burdekin Report (1993) to direct changes in their organisations. Recent legislation has specified the required features of service delivery and non-government service providers are now obliged to conform with the provisions of Acts such as the NSW *Disability Services Act 1993*. Most service provision for people with a mental illness occurs within the community. The services available within the community extend from 24-hour accommodation services through to social networks and self-help groups.

Community health centres. These are staffed by people from many different disciplines, providing a range of services that can be tailored to each person's particular needs. Not only are community health centres a treatment option, they also provide access to rehabilitation and support services as well as being a meeting place for the community.

Extended hours and crisis teams. These operate out of community health centres and extend the hours of service and the range of services provided by the community centre during the day. Services may include assessment, treatment, crisis support and other services to assist the person with a mental illness and his or her family members and/or carer(s).

Self-help and support groups. Mental illness can affect anyone (and often affects people in many different ways). Self-help and support groups have been found invaluable by both clients and families.

> *I became involved in a self-help group. I met other people who also experienced a mental illness. We wrote articles about our experiences, we published a quarterly newsletter and we gave out information on treatment options and drug side effects and how to cope with these.*
>
> Nancy

Supported accommodation services. These include permanent or transitional accommodation. Support provided involves teaching living skills, counselling, group therapy and fostering the independence of clients.

Advocacy groups. These provide information, advocacy and lobbying for the rights of people with a psychiatric disability.

Additional costs

The costs of mental illness can occur both for the individual and for the community. The individual faces financial costs associated with medication and treatment, as well as possibly a reduced ability to work. Low or irregular income limits a person's buying power and access to housing. There are 'hidden costs', which include stigma, low self-esteem, limited social contact and lack of contact with family and support networks. Community attitudes to mental illness can preclude people from employment, education and other aspects of life. As well as the enormous costs for the individual, mental illness can have hidden and practical costs for the community. These include cost of hospitals and community facilities, cost of benefits payable and loss of tax revenue if the person is unable to work.

RESOURCE ORGANISATIONS

All care has been taken to ensure that all information is correct at the time of publishing; however, responsibility for the accuracy of this information is not accepted by the writer. The list of resource organisations contained in this chapter is not intended to be exhaustive – it provides national organisations only. The reader is referred to local community directories for further information and for local branches of national organisations. Inclusion of services and organisations should not be taken as a recommendation.

Australia

ANAMH – Australian National Association
 for Mental Health
Tweedie Place
Richmond Vic 3121
Ph 03 9427 0373
Fax 03 9427 1294

Australian Psychiatric Disability Coalition
 Inc
Building 3, Room 10
 Pearce Community Centre
Collett Place
Pearce ACT 2607
Ph 06 286 2022
Fax 06 286 2922

National Community Advisory Group
C/- NCAG Liaison Officer
(PO Box 355)
Woden ACT 2601
Ph 06 289 8293

Canada

Canadian Mental Health Association
3rd Floor, 2160 Yonge Street
Toronto ON M4S 2Z3
Ph 416 484 7750
Fax 416 484 4617

Canadian Psychiatric Association
Suite 200, 237 Argyle Avenue

Ottawa ON K2P 1B8
Ph 613 234 2815
Fax 613 234 9857

Schizophrenia Society of Canada
Suite 814, 75 The Donway W
Don Mills ON M3C 2E9
Ph 1 800 809 4673
Ph 416 445 8204
Fax 416 445 2270

New Zealand

Aotearoa Network of Psychiatric Survivors
PO Box 46-018
Herne Bay Auckland

United Kingdom

National Association for Mental Health
15/19 Broadway
Statford London E15 4BQ
Ph 081 519 2122
Fax 081 522 1725

United States

National Mental Health Association
1021 Prince Street
Alexandra VA 22314-2971
Ph 703 684 7722
Ph 1 800 969 NMHA

244   PERSON *to* PERSON

FURTHER READING

Aboriginal Medical Services Cooperative (1991). *NSW Aboriginal mental health report.* Sydney.

American Psychiatric Association (1994). *Diagnostic and statistical manual of mental disorders* (4th edn). Washington DC: APA.

Ammer, C. (1991). *Getting help: a consumer's guide to therapy.* New York: Paragon House.

Australian Health Ministers Conference (1992). *National Mental Health Policy.* Canberra: Australian Government Publishing Service.

Brown, R. (1994). *The second son of God.* Sydney: Fast Books.

Burdekin, B. (1993). *Human rights and mental illness: report of the National Inquiry into the Human Rights of People with Mental Illness.* Sydney: Human Rights and Equal Opportunity Commission.

Hunter, E. (1992). Aboriginal health awareness: an overview. Parts 1–3. *Aboriginal and Islander Health Worker Journal, 16.*

Kass, F. I., Oldham, J. M. & Pardes, H. (1992). *Complete home guide to mental health.* New York: H. Holt.

Lundy, A. (1990). *Diagnosis and treatment of mental illness.* New York: Chelsea House.

Mental Health Consumer Outcomes Task Force (1991). *Mental health statement of rights and responsibilities.* Canberra: Australian Government Publishing Service.

National Health Strategy (1993). *Help where help is needed: continuity of care for people with chronic mental illness.* Canberra: Department of Health, Housing and Community Services. Issues Paper No. 5.

NSW Department of Health (1991). *Leading the way: a framework for NSW mental health services, 1991–2001.* Sydney: NSW Government.

Rey, J. M. (1992). The epidemiologic catchment area (ECA) study: implications for Australia. *Medical Journal of Australia, 156,* 200–3.

Smith, D. W. (1993). *Schizophrenia.* New York: F. Watts.

Spender, L. (ed.) (1995). *Mental health rights manual.* Redfern: Mental Health Coordinating Council Inc, Redfern Legal Centre Publishing, Ltd.

CHAPTER 13
MULTIPLE SCLEROSIS

I feel it is important for people to realise that MS is not the curse it is made out to be. Not all people with MS are paralysed or confined to bed for life. In some people it affects only a finger or a toe. MS is not something to be scared or ashamed of.

Melinda

Multiple sclerosis (MS) is a progressive disease which has many signs and symptoms. As a result, individuals with MS can vary greatly between each other and any particular individual can vary over time in the level of disability associated with the impairment. The majority of people with MS do not use wheelchairs. For others, the use of a wheelchair can enhance their mobility.

Currently there is no known cause of MS, but it is a topic of considerable research. MS is not a fatal disease, people with this condition can expect a lifespan near that of the general population.

Multiple sclerosis is a chronic, progressive disease of the central nervous system (CNS). The job of the CNS is to convey messages through nerve fibres in two directions – from the brain to the rest of the body and from all parts of the body back to the brain. Healthy nerve fibres are insulated by myelin, a fatty substance which aids the flow of messages. In MS, the myelin breaks down and is replaced by scar tissue. This distorts or blocks the flow of messages. The effect of demyelination is to delay or confuse messages transmitted along the nerve pathways.

MS may result in cognitive impairment, but is not connected to intellectual disability or mental illness.

LIVING WITH MULTIPLE SCLEROSIS

The majority of people with MS are able to continue their lives with only minor changes to accommodate occasional exacerbations (Cristall, 1992). Multiple sclerosis poses many implications for people in their everyday lives. Three features to remember are:

- The *level* and *area* of impairment is different for each individual. The disability and handicap experienced are therefore different for each individual. Some of the effects of MS such as fatigue or short-term memory loss are not visible to others.
- Multiple sclerosis is an *acquired* condition. People with MS (as well as those near to them) will need to re-evaluate their lifestyles, ambitions and goals. Again, this process will differ for each individual, whether he or she is a person with MS, a spouse, partner, child or carer.
- Multiple sclerosis is a *degenerative* condition. People must not only come to terms with their current level of impairment, but must also be prepared for some future deterioration of functioning capacities. Periods of remission, with

the uncertainty of how long improvement will last, may make adjustment to this disease particularly difficult.

Some of the consequences of MS include:

- A person with MS may experience patches of numbness, pain or temperature sensation. Others may feel tingling sensations similar to 'pins and needles' .
- Some people become unaware of internal signals such as those usually provided by a full bladder. This can result in loss of bladder control.
- The body may provide wrong information about the position of the limbs, causing clumsiness and upset balance. In severe cases, paralysis occurs.
- Difficulties with sight are common among people with MS. Double vision, blurred vision, and inability to focus are frequent experiences, but these symptoms (unlike some others) often disappear or improve.
- Hand, arm and leg movements can be affected, resulting in slowness and/or staggering of gait, difficulties in hand–eye coordination, shaking of the hands or head, or stiffness in many body movements.
- Speech may be impaired, resulting in hesitation or a slurring of words.
- Fatigue is a common symptom. Many people with MS must be moderate in their activity levels because overtiredness can bring on other symptoms.
- Heat intolerance is another common experience for people with MS. An increase in body temperature will often aggravate symptoms temporarily, whether brought about by hot weather, a hot shower, exercise, an infection, or some other cause.
- People with MS may have problems with short- or long-term memory and concentration, while some will experience swings in mood or personality changes.

I've had MS for 22 years. It was diagnosed about eight or nine years ago. Originally I lost the sight of my right eye, which took about six months to come back. I'd been going though quite a few traumas at that time. Then there was numbness in my left leg.

Ellen

The combination and severity of symptoms of MS vary from person to person. In broad terms the disease may follow one of three patterns for each individual, as shown in Table 13.1.

Table 13.1: Patterns of MS

Pattern	Characteristics	Frequency
Benign	Mild symptoms, full remissions, little or no increasing disability.	20–30% of people with MS
Relapsing/ remitting	Nearly full remissions; long periods of stability; may result in increasing disability over time.	40–50% of people with MS
Chronic/ progressive	Gradual onset, progression despite treatment, major disability in 2–10 years.	20–30% of people with MS

Personal adjustment

Many people who acquire MS experience similar stages of bereavement as others with disabilities. However, one major difference is that people with MS cannot be sure of the outcome of their disability. Some live for many years with only minor impairment while others become seriously limited in their functioning (Mairs, 1986). Some people with MS experience years of knowing something is wrong before their disability is finally diagnosed. Even when the disability has been diagnosed, its future directions and path are uncertain. This can be a source of disruption, anxiety and uncertainty for the person.

> *I could cope with the symptoms I had, but where was it going to lead? For weeks after the diagnosis, whenever I went to bed with tingling in my legs I would lie awake worrying that I wouldn't be able to walk in the morning.*
>
> Alex

Because the disability is often hidden, the person may try to conceal it from others, delaying his or her own acceptance of the diagnosis and trying to minimise the impact it has on life. There are three strategies used by people with an invisible disability, acquired disability, or a disability which is not obvious to others in its early stages. These strategies are outlined in Chapter 1 and were used by Robinson (1988) to describe reactions of people with MS. These strategies are:

- *Passing or efforts to pass oneself off as not having a disability* by attempting to maintain social invisibility. This strategy was first discussed by Goffman (1965) and is an option for many people in the early stages of MS, but usually becomes difficult to maintain. It requires redesign of one's life in order to conceal the disability and may involve collaboration with another person in the deception. This strategy is particularly likely to be adopted when employment could be jeopardised by letting others know about the presence of MS.
- *Normalisation* was first mentioned by Davis (1963) and refers to a strategy to maintain a 'normal' identity or self-concept and to carry on life as usual, with the disability treated as a 'normal' but not dominant part of life. The person's reference group is the non-disabled community rather than people with disabilities. This strategy may be difficult to achieve when the disability becomes visible to others who are unwilling to treat the person as 'normal'.
- *Dissociation* was discussed by Miles (1979) as a strategy where a separate disability-related lifestyle is developed. The primary reference groups for beliefs and behaviours are others with MS rather than the community at large. This stage involves withdrawal from the general community. It may help the person feel safe and may protect a fragile self-image by limiting contacts to people who know about MS and are likely to be understanding.

It can be difficult to adjust to the range of losses that result from being diagnosed as having MS. Resentment can be experienced (at least until the person comes to terms with having a disability) and may recur during times of frustration.

> *And what about my job prospects? What about planning for the future? Not knowing was the worst.*
>
> Alex

When a person is diagnosed as having MS, it usually comes as a great shock. This is to be expected and it is typical and natural for mixed emotional feelings of anger, sadness and grief for the loss of good health through illness.

I had read a story in my local newspaper about the fact that a large percentage of people with optical neuritis, or swelling of the optic nerve (the same condition the neurologist determined I had) have MS. I was horrified. The only thing I had ever heard about MS was people ending up in wheelchairs.

Phillip

The way in which people react to MS does not necessarily relate to the severity of their condition. Someone who is mildly affected may be psychologically devastated, whereas someone who is severely disabled may appear to manage well emotionally.

Finding out I had MS was the beginning of a long, major freak-out. I never learnt anything about the disease. I never told anyone I had it. I denied it to myself, going through dreadful depressions on my own, crying about it for months and months every year. I was crying over the death of a close family member. The death was my own death. For 13 years I couldn't even say the term 'MS', least of all what it stood for. 'Multiple sclerosis' sounded too heavy and serious for a shattered victim to admit, even to herself. I was angry that such a healthy woman, through no fault of her own, should be afflicted with such a foul disease. I was embarrassed and humiliated. I would have preferred to have cancer, a brain tumour; something, anything; which would kill me.

Alex

Individual reactions can also depend on a person's past experience with life, values, the work he or she does and whether a change in employment would be necessary. Personality also plays a large part, together with self-image, family stability and community support. Because multiple sclerosis is an acquired condition, the major reactions of individuals concern the changes that will occur in their lives as a result. Some of these changes are:

- *Social role.* Isolation may result if the person is no longer able to maintain employment or an active social life because of disability and, in particular, because of fatigue. Sometimes people become fearful of going out, especially if they have bowel or bladder problems. They may also be embarrassed by having to use a walking aid.
- *Family role.* A person with MS may no longer be the major breadwinner or be able to care for children. A spouse's role may change from that of partner to that of carer. These role changes can place additional stress on a marriage or a relationship and may result in feelings of guilt and worthlessness.
- *Physical functions.* Grief can be experienced each time the condition leads to the temporary or permanent loss of physical capacities.
- *Financial.* Income levels may fall as a result of not working. The cost of medication, appliances or household modifications can lead to financial problems.

- *Attitudes*. Individuals may feel that they are useless and a drain on their loved ones. Others may feel sorry for them and relate to them differently.
- *Body image*. Changes in the body often lead to psychological adjustments. The person has to learn to become accustomed to the new unfamiliar self.

For a while the person may become inward-looking and difficult to live with. He or she may blame everything on the MS, get upset easily and get angry over small things. Sleep disruptions, tension, depression, stress and fatigue may also occur. Some people with MS experience other mental or emotional symptoms such as inability to concentrate, rapid mood changes, poor short-term memory and faulty problem-solving (Cristall, 1992). These changes affect the person and everyone around.

Many of these symptoms of MS remain invisible to the general public. It may not be evident that individuals have a disability and that they may experience symptoms that drastically reduce or affect their ability to function at maximum levels. Such symptoms may be due to:

- Nerve scarring (demyelination) causing structural changes in the brain which can, in turn, affect one's thinking and emotional responses.
- Understandable emotional reactions to having a long-term degenerative neurological disease.
- The unpredictability of MS.

Coming to terms with MS is about finding the balance between completely giving in to the disease and, on the other hand, completely denying it and refusing to accept it. An inner strength is achieved through reaching this balance and in accepting limitations, by realising new potential and creating a new purpose and meaning in life.

> *In a way, it's a better life. Its been a learning time for me. I've grown a lot. I've learned to be a lot more assertive. I was always afraid of hurting people's feelings, but I'm not like that any more.*
>
> Ellen

Sexuality

The first symptoms of MS usually appear in early adulthood. The person may be married, have a partner, or have young children. Thus, the spouse, children and other relatives are likely to be profoundly affected. These effects may include sexuality and changes in roles both within the family and outside.

In general, MS does not affect sexual performance. However, some people may feel that changes in their body make them less sexually attractive. Sexual performance may be influenced by psychological reactions such as self-esteem and body image so that it is important for the partner to be supportive. Problems associated with sexuality may be reinforced unwittingly by health professionals who treat the person as asexual and as lacking the feelings and needs of people without disabilities (Campling, 1981).

Sexual sensation rarely completely disappears, although a loss of sensation may lead to a reduction in pleasure. In men, erections may become less strong, shorter or even absent, as a result of impairment in the relay of nerve impulses from the brain down the spinal cord. Localised stimulation which does not rely on spinal cord transmission can overcome this change.

Fertility is not affected. Menstruation and the ability to have children are unaltered in women.

Being a parent

Women with MS are as capable as others of bearing and raising children. Because diagnosis tends to occur in young adults, many people may have already begun to establish their lifestyle. If a person already has an occupation, children and a partner, she or he will have to come to terms with the disability and to incorporate it within her or his lifestyle. Children may take time to understand the changes in their parent and in the way he or she carries out the parenting role.

Family

> *MS has not made too much difference to our family. I used to be scared by all the aids for the disabled person, but now I realise they just help Mum get around better.*

Melinda, who is in her teens

As with other forms of disability, families differ in the ways they react to news that a family member has a severe disability. They also are likely to go through the stages of adjusting to bereavement and loss. Myths and fears about MS are still widespread. Sometimes these fears are compounded by the information (or lack of information) provided by health professionals.

Initial family reactions are likely to be shock and fear. Longer-term reactions are likely to have a major bearing on the way a person learns to deal with the disease.

> *My parents' reaction was the worst – they were so worried. All the doctor told me was that it was multiple sclerosis and that I should stay out of the sun and avoid hot baths. We didn't know anything about the disease and that's what scared me and my family the most.*

Phillip

> *I knew when there were problems, Mum had to go into hospital. I sometimes took it out on my friends and was irritable. I always regretted it afterwards, but I feel you should express your fears and emotions openly, rather than bottling up what you feel and making yourself miserable.*

Melinda

Some people with MS become more dependent and marital relationships may undergo changes. Family members may feel guilty or become overprotective of the person. Some family members may worry about future financial security if the person with MS is the major breadwinner. Because of changed circumstances, the other parent may be required to return to the workforce after an absence of many years.

An initial reaction of children may be anger and resentment when they find that routines that once seemed to be permanent have been suddenly upset. The child may find that she or he has more responsibilities than before and, as a result, has less free time. The parent with MS becomes focus of attention and everything else seems to have been set aside (Cristall, 1992). Parents seem to be constantly preoccupied with the disorder. Cristall points out that sometimes family members seem to be arguing with each other all the time, but they are really arguing with the disease, not with each other. In other families, people may hardly speak to each other and seem to retire into themselves. These are all different ways of reacting to the initial shock and major life changes required by the diagnosis.

As with other disabilities, all members of the family are likely to have to work through feelings of anger, guilt and helplessness. These are natural reactions and most people work through them to come to a stage of acceptance.

Community living

The fact that MS is often a hidden disability and that there are wide variations (both within and between individuals) can be confusing for members of the general community who may find it difficult to understand why a person seems fine on one occasion but tired and lethargic on another. They may wrongly try to explain such differences in terms of personality ('she is a moody person'). They also may be reluctant to make allowances for the person's special needs.

Because of negative images associated with MS in our society, people often react with fear when they meet someone they know has MS. Others are thoughtless and rude, forgetting that the individual is a human being and does not enjoy being stared at or made to feel different.

> *People are cruel. When they used to call Mum names, I got mad and wanted to hit out and hurt them too. But people with MS soon seem to accept this and write it off, and so did I. Now I feel I would like to educate people. People do tend to stare, but this cannot be helped. If you smile at them, it does make you feel better.*

> Melinda

These reactions indicate more about people in our community than about the person with MS. There is an urgent need for community education to inform people about disabilities and about ways of behaving appropriately towards people with disabilities.

> *Far too many people only look towards a wheelchair, and never try to talk to the person inside. They treat people with disabilities as inferior or talk over them, not to them.*

> Phillip

Inappropriate stereotypes and myths interfere with quality of life for people with MS. They can mean that for many adults with MS, hard-earned achievements (such as a good job) disappear. It also means that milestones and important life experiences taken for granted by others are denied to the person with MS.

Each person's access to community support groups or facilities is influenced by the attitudes and behaviour of staff employed at venues. If staff are cooperative and understanding, arrangements can often be made to meet the needs of people with disabilities. On the other hand, if staff are uncooperative or overly solicitous towards individuals, the outcome can be ruined. Overall, it should be remembered that people with disabilities are individuals and therefore have individual needs regardless of their disability.

Access

The majority of people with MS can maintain an active and independent role in family life by making adjustments to their lifestyle and physical environment. In many cases, however, environmental and/or psychological barriers prevent full participation in community activities. In terms of people with disabilities, an 'accessible community' is one in which the transportation systems, physical environment, communications systems, technological systems, political, cultural, bureaucratic, corporate and social institutions, value systems and employment practices are open and available.

The interrelationship of these systems is something that people without disabilities take for granted. For example, going to the movies and to dinner with friends requires little organisation for people without a disability. For those with a physical disability, however, arrangements must be made around such issues as:

• What transport is available? This includes access to and from public transport depots such as train stations, bus stops and ferry terminals.
• If private transport is used, is adequate parking available near the event?
• Is the cinema equipped for wheelchairs – that is, no stairs and space in the theatrette?
• Are there accessible toilets available?
• Does a person using a wheelchair need to transfer from the wheelchair to sit among friends?
• Are there any particular difficulties in reaching a restaurant, manoeuvring within the restaurant or using the toilet facilities?

Specific issues that may need to be considered for people with MS are:

• the time of day and whether fatigue will prevent or hinder participation;
• whether the venues are air-conditioned.

Relatively small issues can become logistical nightmares. For those who use wheelchairs, the positioning of automatic bank teller machines and public telephones, the occurrence of slight inclines or the absence of lips in kerbing can all lead to access difficulties.

Many councils, shires or municipalities have access committees which examine ways of improving the general access of the local area. Public facilities developed in this way include libraries, sporting venues, parks and pathways.

Employment

Many people with MS can maintain demanding positions in the workforce. For some, employment options may be limited or people may need modifications to their work sites or work programs. However, attitudes of employers can form one of the major barriers to continued satisfying employment.

Change of employment is not usually necessary, at least in the early stages. Qualifications and the ability to do a job are more important than diagnosis in determining career and employment issues. Many people work until the usual retirement age. Some changes may be required to take account of symptoms. For example, fatigue may mean the person is able to work fewer hours or that hours of work need to be more flexible. Nowadays, more flexible working arrangements make continuing employment feasible for many people. Work site modification, part-time employment, job sharing and retraining have proved useful strategies. Other people use special aids and adaptations.

In some cases, a person may need to review his or her current type of work and make a complete change. Occupational therapists can advise on suitable retraining for learning new marketable skills.

Employer misunderstanding can create major problems. In can be difficult to convince someone that you are still a valuable employee.

PERSON TO PERSON

Appropriate language and behaviour

As with other forms of disability, an open and honest approach is usually best in the long run. Concealing disability from others can become time consuming and can come to dominate life. It also can result in misunderstandings on the part of others. Often it is a great relief to all when a person feels able to disclose his or her disability to others.

> *A few months ago I started to tell close friends. They knew something was wrong, but didn't know what. One said she thought I had a serious drug addiction. One said she had noticed me swaying, and thought I was drunk, 'but Alex hasn't had a drink'. One had noticed me walking pigeon-toed, which I tend to do in an exacerbation, and walking very slowly and carefully. I thought I had kept it a secret, but my denial and grief over my MS had made friends think something else, more serious, had happened.*
>
> Alex

Strategies for successful interaction

It should always be remembered that each person with MS is an individual. Symptoms may be slight or severe, invisible or highly visible. Each person may experience any number or combination of symptoms and these may change over time.

Each person with MS develops different mechanisms to deal with the condition. These mechanisms may be internal (coming to terms with MS, stress management, re-evaluation of lifestyle and so on) or they may be external (developing family or community networks to assist).

Some people may need counselling in order to cope with this major adjustment to their lives, others may simply need the continued friendship and support of those close to them. For some people, meeting and talking to others with MS is an ideal way of understanding about problems and learning methods of overcoming them. It is also important to remember that each close family member of a person with MS may also be in need of support at some stage.

Access to community activities and facilities can depend on the provision of appropriate support. Having an attendant available to assist with personal care details can make events 'accessible'. It is important to remember that a person who has an attendant is usually capable of communicating on his or her own behalf. Comments or questions directed towards the attendant and ignoring the person with a disability are not appropriate. Table 13.2 lists some strategies for successful interaction.

Table 13.2: Strategies for successful interaction

Person with MS	Other person
Be open and honest about your disability.	Understand that each person with MS is an individual with his or her own needs. Some of these needs reflect the nature of the person's disability.
	Others reflect the nature of the person as a human being.
	Do not try to take over and do things for the person without first asking.
Explain to others about your particular needs.	Ask the individual what his or her specific needs are.
	Remember that MS affects functioning in many ways and that there are variations both between and within people as to the effects of MS.
	Ensure that an atmosphere is created in which people feel confident that their needs can be met.
	Ensure that needs can and will be met in a manner that maintains the person's dignity and privacy.

While individual interactions are enhanced by a positive approach or a willingness to understand and individual's needs, it is important to ensure that general access issues are addressed.

MORE INFORMATION ABOUT MULTIPLE SCLEROSIS

Multiple sclerosis is a chronic, progressive disease of the central nervous system (CNS). The CNS is usually defined as the brain and spinal cord, although it is linked with most nerve systems in the body. (For more information about the structure and functions of the brain and spinal cord, refer to chapters 3, 8 and 10.) The job of the CNS is to convey messages in two directions – from the brain to the rest of the body and from all parts of the body back to the brain.

Sensory nerves delivery information to the brain from the body and from the outside world. Motor nerves convey instructions to the body. This system works most of the time without conscious control or thought. Figure 13.1 shows diagrams of a healthy and a damaged nerves.

Each nerve of the CNS can be compared to an electric cable. The inner part of the nerve, the axon, carries messages, or impulses, throughout the body, like the wire-fibre in an electric cable (see Figure 13.2). The axon is surrounded by a layer of fatty substance, the myelin sheath, like the insulating cover on the electric cable. The myelin helps in the conduction of messages along the nerve as well as

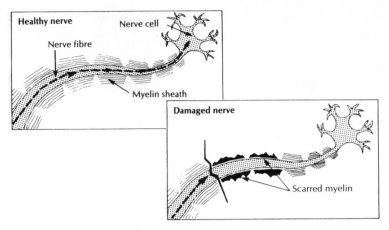

Figure 13.1: A healthy and a damaged nerve

Reproduced with permission from the Multiple Sclerosis Society of Australia (1990). Living with multiple sclerosis.

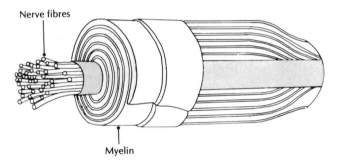

Figure 13.2: Detail of the axon

insulating and protecting the nerve. Usually, these messages travel at great speed (up to 80 metres per second).

In MS, parts of the myelin sheath become inflamed. Sometimes this inflammation is temporary, leading to brief and/or minor interruptions to the nerve signals. But if the attack on the myelin continues, the insulating coat becomes damaged beyond repair and a scar (*sclerosis*) forms, often completely blocking the nerve impulses. This is called demyelination. The term *multiple* is applied because the damage usually occurs at a number of points along the CNS. Multiple sclerosis is the most significant demyelinating disease in human beings, but it is not the only one. Other diseases that are similar to MS in their processes and effects are acute disseminated encephalomyelitis, acute haemorrhagic leuco-encephalitis, disseminated myelitis with optic neuritis, diffuse sclerosis and central pontine myelinolysis.

The symptoms of MS, which result from damage to the myelin, depend upon which areas of the CNS are involved. For instance, if the optic nerve is involved, conduction delay or block may lead to blurring of vision. Similarly, if the cerebellum or its pathways are involved, then coordination of limbs, walking or speech may become impaired.

Definition

In terms of the World Health Organization 1980 definitions:

- *Impairment* refers to damage to the myelin sheath, with the area and frequency of damage determining disability.
- *Disability* refers to loss of functions such as mobility, balance, speech or touch.
- *Handicap* refers to the consequences of disability such as difficulty in performing everyday tasks and maintaining employment.

Causes

We do not know what causes MS. It is not contagious or infectious. It does appear that people inherit a susceptibility to the disease, but not MS itself. Since the disease was first identified, a number of theories have been tested and disproved. Currently, scientists involved in MS research are working on three major theories.

The first is that MS is caused by a virus. When viruses invade the body, they take over some body cells. Most viruses, like cold and flu, cause symptoms quickly. There are however, some slow-acting viruses which can stay within the body for months or years before making their presence felt. MS could be caused by one of the slow-acting viruses or it might be a delayed reaction to a common virus.

The second theory is that the body's defence system or immune system somehow gets confused when fighting a virus and starts to attack the body's own cells. This may occur because some viruses take over parts of cells, and the immune system might attack both host cells and virus.

The third theory is that MS might involve a combination of both viral and immune system factors. When viruses invade the body, they take over body cells. Again, the body's defence system might become confused and attack both host cells and the virus.

Incidence and prevalence

There are, at present, approximately 10 000 people with MS in Australia. Around a quarter of a million Americans have this condition (Cristall, 1992; LaPlante & Carlson, 1996; Pitzele, 1985). It is difficult to predict who will get MS; however, there is a pattern as to who is more likely to develop the disease.

Age. Symptoms usually appear for the first time between the ages of 20 and 40. MS is the most common chronic neurological condition among young adults in Australia (Australian Federal Government, 1993c). Diagnosis before the age of 15 is very rare, and onset is unusual in those over 50.

Gender. There are more women than men in the MS population. The imbalance seems to vary around the world but it is anything between 12 and 20 women for every 10 men.

Location of residence. MS tends to be more common between 40 and 60 degrees north and 40 and 60 degrees south of the Equator. The incidence in

Canada, Europe and the southern parts of Australia is quite high. The closer an area is to the Equator, the fewer the cases of MS. For example, in Australia the incidence of MS per 100 000 people varies according to latitude.

- In northern Queensland approximately 11 people per 100 000 are affected;
- In New South Wales approximately 57 people per 100 000 are affected; and
- In Tasmania approximately 75 people per 100 000 are affected.

Ethinicity/race. MS is more common in white races. In the United States, for example, it is twice as common in white people as in black people. It is rare among the Maoris in New Zealand and among such races as Polynesians and Negroid peoples. In Asia it has a prevalence of one or two per 100 000 as compared with 30 per 100 000 in Western nations (National Association of Multiple Sclerosis of Australia, 1989).

Diagnosis

After 14 years of regular, long remissions after a bout of exacerbation which comes every two years and goes away on its own after six to eight weeks, I know that only a small percentage of people with MS are severely affected. The rest are like me. It would have been nice if some neurologist or doctor had bothered to tell me this when I was 30, before the Great Freak-out.

Alex, who was diagnosed as having MS when she was 30

The process of confirming a diagnosis of MS can sometimes be very long and difficult, with many visits to doctors and specialists (such as a neurologist) before a firm opinion can be given. Robinson (1988) refers to this process as a 'medical merry-go-round'. The period between onset and diagnosis can be very frustrating for the person and family, who may wonder whether symptoms are real or imagined; or may feel depressed, anxious, misunderstood or confused. Most of the early symptoms are quite common in other conditions as well. In fact, they are more likely to be due to these other causes than to be the result of MS. Another difficulty is that everyone with MS experiences different degrees and combinations of symptoms; no two people have exactly the same set. Furthermore, most people in the early stages will have the remitting form of the disease. Because symptoms can come and go fairly quickly, the doctor must often rely on the individual's description of what happened. Symptoms may not occur again for years.

Usually a general medical practitioner who has a suspicion of MS will refer the person to a neurologist who will conduct a full neurological examination. The neurologist, with the aid of modern diagnostic techniques, will be able to determine whether a diagnosis of MS is possible, probable or definite.

The following are cited by the National Association of Multiple Sclerosis of Australia (1989, 1990) as the most common forms of assessment:

- An examination of the cerebrospinal fluid which bathes the spinal cord and brain. This fluid shows changes in protein composition, which is common in MS, and rare in other conditions.
- An MRI (magnetic resonancing image) scan of the brain or a CAT scan (computer-assisted axial tomography), which are conducted to exclude other medical conditions. These techniques show the structure of the brain in thin cross-sections.

- An evoked responses test of nerve transmissions to assess whether there is normal nerve pathway conduction of vision and touch sensations.

Some people do not remember anything that is explained to them on first being told that they have the disease. Some medical practitioners feel that it is appropriate to have a second interview a short time later, so that the person has time to digest the information, develop a greater understanding and raise further questions and concerns.

Treatment

There is no overall treatment for MS, but symptoms can be successfully managed if they are treated individually, if and when they occur.

Many treatments have been tried with very little success. Cortisone (ACTH) can help some people, but has no effect on the course of the disease when taken on a long-term basis. In 1980 it was discovered that people with MS have some abnormal cells in their immune system. To stimulate these cells a substance called 'the transfer factor' (TF) was taken from healthy people and given to people with MS by means of a blood transfusion. This treatment was found to give only a small benefit to those who are mildly affected. Further trials into TF are currently in progress. Also currently under investigation is the drug interferon. Like TF, interferon stimulates the immune system and is active against viral infections which are strongly suspected to be important in causing MS.

In recent years there has been considerable interest in using hyperbaric oxygen in the treatment of MS. This follows suggestions by some health workers that many people benefit from it. It is administered in special compression chambers which are also used to treat divers suffering from the 'bends'. However, a number of recently-published carefully-conducted studies have failed to confirm any benefit from this form of therapy.

Recent research suggests that MS may be a disease of the immune system, so living a healthy life with a nutritious diet, exercise, rest and stress management may be important (Australian Federal Government, 1993c). One form of treatment has involved changing diet in order to avoid foods high in saturated or animal fats and to use polyunsaturated fats. However, the benefits of this have yet to be demonstrated, although these changes in eating patterns are widely accepted as beneficial for reducing the incidence of other conditions, such as heart disease.

People with MS often can do much to assist themselves by avoiding situations that aggravate their symptoms. For example, people who tire easily may relieve this symptom to some extent by taking frequent rests.

A number of medications are available for relief of some of the specific symptoms. Muscle relaxers may relieve spasms, while other medication reduces the severity and duration of acute attacks. Physiotherapy and occupational therapy can improve or maintain the individual's independence in activities of daily living.

Speech pathologists can assess and design programs for people with speech and swallowing disorders. Assistance can be given to people who have only slight communication impairment or to those who are unable to speak at all and need help in developing non-speech methods of communication.

Individual counselling and/or group therapy can help people with MS and their families manage depression, anxieties and the limitations caused by MS.

Physiotherapy (physical therapy) is important to show the person how to exercise and to improve posture to decrease stress on muscles and joints. Swimming, yoga and tai chi are forms of exercise which can be modified to suit many levels of disability. Massage is soothing and relaxing.

Services and supports

The course of MS is unpredictable; needs and disabilities change. Continuing professional assessment and treatment is essential.

The following services are available within the community for people with MS:

- Information about MS.
- Professional counselling for individuals and families.
- Professional assessment and treatment:
  - medical
  - urological
  - physiotherapy (physical therapy)
  - occupational therapy
  - neuropsychology.
- Attendant care programs.
- Support groups for people with MS and carers' groups.
- Long- and short-term supported accommodation, including respite accommodation.
- Outreach services to country areas.
- Advice and support on recreational and leisure activities.
- Community education.
- Education and training for other health professionals.

Equipment and aids

A range of equipment is available commercially to assist people with MS. Many simple gadgets are beneficial to people who lack strength in their arms or legs. Driving can be assisted in many ways by cars having automatic transmissions, power steering and, if needed, rooftop hoists for a wheelchair. Cars can be modified to accommodate the needs of people with quite a high level of physical disability. Mobility aids such as walking frames, crutches, callipers or wheelchairs can be useful, or a variety of aids may help in increasing independence. Usually, a physiotherapist or occupational therapist will be involved in the selection of equipment such as wheelchairs because the range available is extensive and individual requirements will need to be considered. The PADP (Program of Aids for Disabled People) can assist with the provision of some equipment.

Home alterations can also increase independence for people with MS. Replacing steps with ramps or creating smooth non-slip walking surfaces in place of broken concrete or pavers can increase independence and/or mobility around the home. Often doorways need to be widened to accommodate the use of a wheelchair. Switches and door and cupboard handles may need to be lowered and/or altered to allow easier use. Quite often major alterations need to be made to kitchens, bathrooms and toilet areas to enable use of a wheelchair or the presence of an attendant.

The provision of air-conditioning units in homes, workplaces and cars can be of great assistance to people with MS. Any increase in body temperature can lead to temporary aggravation of the symptoms of MS. Air-conditioning helps by maintaining a constant temperature at a level that suits the individual.

Additional costs

Multiple sclerosis is an acquired disability, with the symptoms usually appearing between the ages of 20 to 40. For many people, MS will affect their employment. They may need to come to terms with the possibility of major interruptions to their career or a reduced income at a time in life when expenses are high (for example, mortgages and educational costs for children). Also there may be the increased costs of living associated with disability. These additional costs include medication, transport, equipment and home modifications.

The symptoms of MS that cause people to reduce or stop work may not be obvious. The person may show no outer signs of having a disability but may be extremely affected by chronic fatigue and therefore must face the prospect of changing a job or a career, or taking on part-time work, all of which may reduce income. These effects are worsened if, in a two-income family, the spouse also gives up work to look after the person with MS on a full-time basis.

Financial counselling or advice may be required and there are a range of community services that can assist in this area. The organisations listed at the end of this chapter can provide more specific information.

Some people who have led independent lifestyles in the past may find it difficult to accept that they may become a person receiving social security benefits. Nevertheless, a range of entitlements is available and inquiries should be made at local offices in regard to social security and other payments. Additional assistance can also be gained from government and non-government employment services in the search and attainment of employment opportunities.

RESOURCE ORGANISATIONS

All care has been taken to ensure that all information is correct at the time of publishing; however, responsibility for the accuracy of this information is not accepted by the writer. The list of resource organisations contained in this chapter is not intended to be exhaustive – it provides national organisations. The reader is referred to local community directories for further information and for local branches of national organisations. Inclusion of services and organisations should not be taken as a recommendation.

Australia

Refer to your local telephone directory for state addresses. For NSW, the address is:

MS Society
Private Bag Q1000
Queen Victoria Building
Sydney 2000
Ph 02 9287 2929

Canada

Multiple Sclerosis Society of Canada
Suite 1000, 250 Bloor Street East
Toronto ON M4W 3P9
Ph 416 922 6065
Fax 416 922 7538

New Zealand

Multiple Sclerosis Society of New Zealand
Rosemore House
123 Molesworth Street
Thordon
Wellington
Ph 04 499 4677
Fax 04 499 4675

United Kingdom

MS Society of Great Britain
  & Northern Ireland
25 Effie Road
Fulham
London
Ph (0171) 736 6267
Fax (0171) 763 9861

United States

National Multiple Sclerosis Society
733 Third Avenue
New York NY 10017 5706
Ph 1800 227 3166
http://www.nmss.org./home.html

FURTHER READING

Benz, C. (1994). *Coping with multiple sclerosis*. United Kingdom: Optima.

Carroll, D. L. & Dorman, J. D. (1993). *Living well with MS: a guide for patient, caregiver and family*. Harper Perennial: New York.

Cristall, B. (1992). *When a parent has multiple sclerosis*. New York: Rosen.

De Souza, L. (1990). *Multiple sclerosis: approaches to management*. London: Chapman & Hall.

Frith, J. (1988). History of multiple sclerosis: an Australian perspective. *Clinical Experimental Neurology, 25,* 7–16.

Henderson, C. (1992). On the question of pregnancy. *Inside MS*, Spring, 11–13.

Kalb, R. & Scheinberg, L. (1992). *Multiple sclerosis and the family*. New York: Demos Publications.

Matthews, B. (1993). *Multiple sclerosis: the facts* (3rd edn). Oxford: Oxford University Press.

MS Society Canada (1982). *Someone you know has multiple sclerosis: a book for families*. Canada: MSS Canada.

MS Society NSW (1993). *Work issues for people with multiple sclerosis*. (Fact sheet No. 6.4). Sydney: MS Society NSW.

Rosner, L. J. & Ross, S. (1992). *MS: new coping and practical advice for people with MS and their families*. New York: Simon & Schuster.

Scheinberg, L. (ed.) (1987). *Multiple sclerosis: a guide for patients and their families* (2nd edn). New York: Raven Press.

CHAPTER 14

MUSCULAR DYSTROPHIES AND OTHER NEUROMUSCULAR DISORDERS

Muscle disease and neuromuscular disease refer to impaired function of voluntary muscle. There are various types of these diseases, of which many (but not all) are inherited. They differ in their mode of inheritance, age of onset, severity and progression. Not all muscle diseases are progressive and degenerative, some are static, some are treatable and some are curable (for example, inflammatory disease of the muscle). However, muscular dystrophies are not curable. Intellectual impairment is not a characteristic of most types. This chapter discusses a range of muscle diseases but gives most attention to Duchenne muscular dystrophy (see Figure 14.1).

In neuromuscular disease, abnormalities occur in the motor units which initiate and control voluntary movement. Discussion later in the chapter indicates that, depending on the site, neuromuscular disease may be grouped into four types, each of which has different implications for the individual. Many disorders are slowly progressive while others produce side effects which rapidly reduce the lifespan.

IMPLICATIONS FOR EVERYDAY LIVING

Age of onset, severity and life expectancy vary greatly among the types of muscular dystrophy mentioned in this chapter. However, one implication they have in common is the fact that they are inherited. Their occurrence creates dilemmas for all family members in terms of prospects of being genetic carriers and the possibility of disease recurring in future generations or future siblings.

Personal adjustment

Issues vary with the type of neuromuscular disorder and the age at which symptoms first appear. Common experiences of people with muscular and neuromuscular disorders are ready fatigue and slowness. After a period of mobility early in life, boys (who are generally more likely to be affected than girls) find themselves becoming more dependent and less mobile as their disease progresses. At the same time, their peers are venturing out into the world. Consequences include social isolation which may be compounded by the overprotectiveness of parents and limited opportunities for acquiring social skills. Difficulty in carrying out everyday tasks and in not being able to keep up with other children can result in anxiety and a fall in self-confidence.

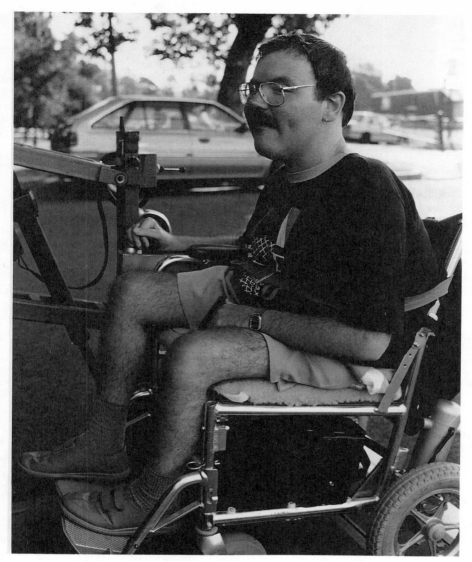

Figure 14.1: A man with Duchenne muscular dystrophy

Duchenne muscular dystrophy (DMD) occurs almost entirely in boys and is the most common form of neuromuscular disorder present at birth, but is not usually diagnosed until early childhood. Boys with DMD are aware of their short-ened lifespan; they also are aware of the constant threat of death and the tenaciousness of life; they know death will come, but do not know when. For these boys, the move into a wheelchair is an important milestone as it provides irrefutable evidence that degeneration and increased dependency are occurring. This is often the time when the boy and his family finally accept that the disease is irreversible and that death is inevitable. Such realisations are likely to be associated with grieving. Some boys react by showing passivity, others become aggressive and rebellious. Most eventually become quiet, stoic and philosophical (Lindemann & Stanger, 1981).

> *Going to school with other children that have muscular dystrophy was, in some ways fairly confronting. Seeing my school friends die at a young age was quite shocking. It didn't really encourage me to spend a lot of years studying at school or university. I couldn't see the point.*
>
> Darren, who died in his late 20s from complications
> associated with Duchenne muscular dystrophy

Corrick (1992) says that many people with muscular dystrophy go through bouts of depression, feeling sorry for themselves and what they cannot do. This is a natural part of the grieving process and in coming to terms with having a disability. The person is aware of loss in function and is grieving this. At school this may result in a fall in performance which the teacher may interpret as a decline in intellectual functioning. It is important for teachers to remember that, unlike muscle function, intelligence does not deteriorate.

Hope & Mallos (1995) discuss the stages that a boy is likely to go through in coming to terms with DMD. They cite the example of an adolescent boy who was just a few months short of turning 16 when he read that the average lifespan for a boy with DMD is 16 years. After reading this he became moody and very quiet, and when at last his birthday came, he become even more disturbed and very angry. It was a shattering experience for him.

Sexuality

> *Relationships have always been a problem. It is very hard to have a relationship with someone when you have a physical disability. It means that you are limited in being able to satisfy the other person's needs. I have gone out with a number of girls, but have not had a long-term relationship.*
>
> Darren

Usually there is little interference with sexual functioning, desires and wishes, but adults with muscle disorders may have difficulty in establishing and maintaining independent lifestyles that provide opportunities for meeting partners and for sufficient privacy to explore their sexuality. As with many people with severe disabilities, they are often reliant on a carer to assist with daily routines such as showering, shaving and dressing. This makes modesty and self-consciousness about the body difficult to maintain. Such reactions are common in adolescence when rapid body changes can create confusion and uncertainty. For the adolescent with a severe muscle disorder, body privacy may be denied.

> *My father looks after most of my daily physical needs, including lifting and bathing.*
>
> Darren

Being a parent

People with Duchenne muscular dystrophy are not only living longer, but increasing numbers of them have partners, and some are having families. All their sons are unaffected and all their daughters are carriers (Hope & Mallos, 1995).

Family

When I was four years old, my mother noticed that I had begun to walk with a waddle and was having trouble negotiating stairs. Medical tests showed that I had Duchenne muscular dystrophy.

Darren

Guilt and grief are common. In some cases, the condition is apparent at birth, while in others it appears in a child or adult who was apparently strong and healthy. In both cases, the disability will affect the whole family. The issue of inheritance is distressing and can cause tension and resentment in others in the family. Distress is particularly strong if there was no previous family history of the condition. Parents may have other children who are not yet affected and they may worry about these children's futures.

The mother is likely to play a major role in day-to-day care of the child with a disability and this may provide a constant reminder that she was responsible for the genetic inheritance (see later in the chapter). Parents may overprotect and have difficulty in punishing their child with a disability, perhaps causing resentment in siblings. Many families have to come to terms with the fact that their child has a limited lifespan. Counselling may help them to accept this inevitability.

I owe a lot to my parents. Without them and their efforts, I could not be enjoying the life that I currently do. It has been difficult for all of us, but I think we have coped really well.

Darren

Community living

My movement is fairly restricted and I must rely on others to hand me things. This does not stop me going out or doing many things. It does mean, however, that activities must be planned in advance. Special taxis for people who have disabilities have meant that I can go to work or social events without relying on others.

Darren

Changing abilities and strengths mean that the nature of equipment and assistance required by a person change over time. Community events and activities which were once easily accessible when the person was able to walk or use a manual wheelchair may become more difficult to gain access to as the disease progresses. This can lead to frustration for the family and the person. It also can lead to misunderstandings on the part of other people who do not take account of the person's changing needs and abilities. However, it is important that others do not assume that the person is unable to act independently or needs protection from the everyday experiences of life. Hope & Mallos (1995) report an incident where a boy with muscular dystrophy reported being thrilled because he was appointed as a bin monitor in the school playground. Another boy was overjoyed because he was hauled out before the school principal to be reprimanded for bad behaviour. People do not want to be patronised and are likely to do anything to avoid being seen as any more different than they already are.

Access

Access issues are similar for other people with severe physical disabilities. Community attitudes often form major barriers to integration and acceptance. In countries such as Australia, Canada and the United States, legislation outlaws behaviours which interfere with equality and equity in employment, education, receipt of services and community living. The changing nature of muscular dystrophy and other forms of muscular disorders can mean that issues related to access may change as the disease progresses. Issues associated with physical access are likely to become more pronounced as the person's abilities in regard to independent mobility decline.

Education

Many children begin their education at local preschools, playgroups or primary (elementary) schools. Their level of intellectual functioning would enable them to continue in a mainstream class, but physical limitations may make special education a necessity. Part of education may involve setting goals which are feasible for the lifetime of the person with a form of muscle disorder which shortens life expectancy.

> *I started going to an ordinary school when I was five, but after a while it became clear that I couldn't physically keep up with the other kids. It was very frustrating. So, I was enrolled in a 'special school'. It is probably a good idea to have a school where children with disabilities can have proper care ... however, it can also mean that children go from one protective area (at home) to another protective area (at school). I don't think that this helps to prepare people for life because you could so easily become a 'cotton wool' child.*
>
> Darren

Modifications may be required to the school such as installing ramps, providing wheelchair access to toilets and engaging a teacher's aide.

Hope & Mallos (1995) point out that children with muscle disorders should be encouraged to take part in sport, excursions and other activities. For example, older boys with Duchenne muscular dystrophy are often very much involved with wheelchair sports. Sometimes parents may accompany their son on a camp or extended excursion, however these times often provide a break for them and it may be possible to have a volunteer or aide go with him. Before going on a camp or excursion it is important for the teacher to find out about the boy's needs. Hope & Mallos cite the example of a boy who, while still able to walk, went on a school camp for three days. In that time he did not have a shower because he could not turn on the taps and was too embarrassed to ask anyone for help.

Promotion of physical independence is not a vital issue for children with a muscle disorder such as DMD. Loss of function from this progressive condition may mean that it can be a contra-indication to promote independence in certain activities when they are likely to be lost a short time later. Hope & Mallos (1995) use the example of swimming, stating that it does not seem to make sense to teach a young boy with DMD to swim overarm when he will lose the ability to keep swimming in this manner within a couple of years. It would seem better to devote the energy to teaching him to be safe in the water, to move about freely with breast stroke or dog paddling so that he can keep exercising for many years to come.

Employment

Adults with less severe forms of neuromuscular disorder may engage in full-time work. Most people are limited in their occupational choice by their own interests and skills rather than by their disorder. However, for many people employment options are restricted because of muscle weakness and impaired social skills. Some people are counselled to assist them in setting realistic employment goals.

Many teenage boys are encouraged to engage in sedentary hobbies and activities which help retain social, cognitive and physical skills. Muscle disorders with adult onset may cause frustration for people who find they are not able to continue participation in active sports and social activities.

PERSON TO PERSON

Appropriate language and behaviour

Behavioural characteristics associated with muscular dystrophy and other neuromuscular disorders can create embarrassment and make social interaction difficult. An odd walk or gait can evoke cruel comments and stares. Clumsy adults may be accused of being drunk. Facial weakness may result in difficulty in smiling and so denies the person an important form of non-verbal communication. Difficulty in carrying out daily activities does not mean the person is lazy or stupid.

The public image of these disorders is one of catastrophe, a view which has been encouraged by organisations who use phrases such as 'The tragedy of muscular dystrophy' in their fundraising efforts. This tragic view is especially strong for Duchenne MD and for other childhood forms of this group of disorders. However, most people and their families do not want pity. They are doing their best to get on with life and to minimise the effects of impairment. It is important for teachers, friends and other people to be well informed about muscle disease, as this will help them come to terms and understand the changes which are occurring in their pupil, employee or friend.

Strategies for successful interaction

Table 14.1: Strategies for successful interaction

Person with a neuromuscular disorder	Other person
Many people do not understand your condition. Open and honest information will help reduce anxiety and promote successful interaction. Ask for help when needed and give clear instructions. Explain what is needed, how and why. Give the other person time to comply with your request. Try not to get impatient with helpers, all people make mistakes. Be as independent as you can – it is often better for you to do things for yourself than to let someone else do everything for you.	Take care not to bump or startle a person who is unsure on his or her feet. Allow the person enough time to do what he or she is able to do. Ask how best you can help. Talk to the person with a disability, not to his or her carer. Be aware that many muscular dystrophies are progressive and abilities can decline. Place things in reach, let the person feel useful by helping himself or herself. Make sure walking areas are clear. Slow your pace to enable the person to keep in step. Lend an arm for support or an arm to lift. Do not rush. When they first hear of the condition, many families experience shock. Give information in stages to avoid information overload and misunderstanding.

MORE INFORMATION ABOUT MUSCULAR DYSTROPHIES AND OTHER NEUROMUSCULAR DISORDERS

Definition

Normal functioning of the central and peripheral nervous systems results in smooth, efficient and coordinated muscle action whereas any abnormality will

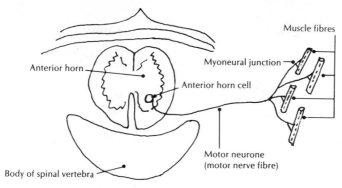

Figure 14.2: Motor unit

Reproduced with permission from The Muscular Dystrophy Association of NSW.

produce muscle malfunction. In neuromuscular disease, abnormalities occur in the motor units which initiate and control voluntary movement. Figure 14.2 shows that a motor unit consists of a nerve cell (anterior horn cell) in the spinal cord, myoneural junctions, the motor nerve which extends from this cell and the group of muscles activated by this nerve. Depending on the site, neuromuscular disease may be grouped into:

- Myopathies which occur with damage to the muscle fibres.
- Myasathenic disorders which arise from damage to the nerve/muscle (myoneural) junction.
- Peripheral neuropathies which develop when motor nerves are affected.
- Spinal muscular atrophies which result from anterior horn cell damage.

When damage or disease affects one part of this nerve unit, the remaining parts cannot function efficiently. Differing effects may account for varying degrees of severity seen in different individuals. Many disorders are slowly progressive, while others produce side effects which rapidly reduce the lifespan. Of the four categories listed above, myopathies and myasthenic diseases are directly related to the muscles and are called *myopathies*, while the latter two arise from involvement of the nerve cell or nerve fibres and are called *neuropathies*.

According to the World Health Organization (1980) definition:

- *Impairment* refers to damage or disease of the motor nerve units which initiate and control voluntary movement.
- *Disability* reflects the type of impairment and varies between types, with effects being displayed in muscle functioning, mobility, lifespan, ready fatigue, vision, hearing, and so on.
- *Handicap* reflects limitations in independence and in carrying out everyday activities resulting from disabilities associated with neuromuscular disorders and with barriers and limitations imposed by a society which does not take the special needs of people into account.

Myopathies

These include muscular dystrophies and myotonias.

Muscular dystrophies

Duchenne muscular dystrophy (DMD) used to be called 'pseudohypertrophic muscular dystrophy'. It usually affects males (and females in rare exceptions). It is the most common form of muscular dystrophy at birth and the most severe. Age of onset is early, but diagnosis is rarely made before two years of age. Before diagnosis, parents may have noticed that the child has an unusual gait, falls easily, has difficulty in getting up from the ground and in climbing stairs. Muscle weakness is progressive so that a wheelchair is required by the time the boy reaches his early teens. Death usually occurs in the late teens or early twenties, most commonly being the result of respiratory infection, respiratory muscle failure or cardiac involvement. Medical advances through use of antibiotics have resulted in an increased life expectancy with some people living into their early thirties. Another factor which has increased lifespan is corrective surgery which prevents scoliosis from contributing to respiratory impairment. In addition, in recent years a substantial proportion of young men with DMD have had mechanically-assisted breathing. At first they are able to stay alive by using a ventilator only at night during sleep. Without use of a ventilator at night, death occurs usually within weeks or a few months of developing symptoms of hypoventilation. However, eventually the time arrives when ventilation is needed in daytime and even continuous ventilatory support may be required. People with DMD tend to have the following associated medical features: joints which are restricted in their range of movement (contracture), scoliosis or curvature of the spine, and impairment of the heart and lung. Characteristically there are large, bulky calf muscles, and sometimes enlargement of other muscles. This is sometimes called 'pseudohypertrophy' (which Emery, cited by Morgan (1996) says results from excess fat and connective tissues), although true hypertrophy is at least partly responsible for the muscle enlargement (Morgan, 1996).

Becker muscular dystrophy (BMD) is also a disease of males, but is less severe and less common than DMD. Its resemblance to DMD reflects association with defects of the same gene. A rule of thumb for distinguishing between the two is whether the boy can still walk at 16 years. BMD is more variable in its course than DMD with some people able to walk at an advanced age and some living a full lifespan. The heart is less often affected and serious impairment of breathing is less frequent. Scoliosis is rarely a problem. Many people experience cramps, otherwise pain is not a feature of Becker muscular dystrophy.

Limb girdle muscular dystrophies are a heterogeneous set of diseases, both genetically and clinically. There are now eight different genetic types, of which seven have a known chromosomal location and in four of these the gene which is defective has been identified (Morgan, 1996). Although most are autosomally recessive, there are dominant families and sex-linked families (see later in the chapter). These dystrophies affect the muscles acting on the shoulder and elbow joints and on the hip and knee joints. Clinical heterogeneity is reflected in variation in the extent to which upper and lower limbs are affected.

Facioscapulohumeral muscular dystrophy (FSHD) affects the muscles of the face, upper arms and shoulders in both sexes. As with all muscular dystrophies, weakness is selective. It also may involve muscles associated with hip and knee movement and muscles in the front of the lower legs. This results in foot drop, a tendency to trip up easily and inability to walk on the heels. Other complications are lordosis (exaggerated curvature of the lower spine) and awkward gait. Most people are not diagnosed until teenage years. The course varies, with some people in wheelchairs in their teens while others are able to walk independently until middle age. Some people with FSHD use a wheelchair as they get older, but the majority do not. A normal lifespan can be expected. A distinctive feature of this form of muscular dystrophy is facial weakness, often making smiling difficult. In all but mild cases, people with FSHD are unable to raise their arms above the shoulder and have weakness in bending and straightening the elbow. Unlike most other muscular dystrophies, FSHD is usually asymmetrical in that some muscles are stronger on the left of the body while others are stronger on the right. Severity varies greatly, even within a single family. The heart is not affected, but deafness is common in cases of early onset. Changes may occur in blood vessels at the back of the eye, but this does not usually affect vision.

Myotonic muscular dystrophy (MMD) is also called Steinert's disease and dystrophia myotonia. It is the most common muscular dystrophy of adulthood and, overall, has the highest prevalence of the muscular dystrophies across all age ranges. It is characterised by weakness and inability to release the hand from a firm grip (myotonia), but can also result in difficulty in walking, stumbling after sudden movement and difficulty in climbing stairs. As with other muscular dystrophies, there is a distinctive pattern of muscle wasting. First to be affected are muscles in the face, neck, hands, forearms and feet. This dystrophy is *multisystemic* in that it can affect many parts of the body in addition to the voluntary muscle system. Other features can include heart problems, cataracts, testicular atrophy, respiratory problems, difficulty in swallowing, gastro-intestinal tract problems, mental disorders, excessive sleeping, excessive output of insulin and abnormal carbohydrate metabolism. Visible signs of the disease are usually present by 20 years of age, but some people do not have clear symptoms until they are 50. The course varies widely, with some people being so mildly affected that they are barely aware of the disorder. Considerable controversy has existed about MMD over the years. As early as 1918 the phenomenon of 'anticipation' was noted. That is, the onset was earlier and severity of disability became more severe as the disease went from one generation to the next. The influence of this phenomenon was disputed for many years, but since 1980 it has become widely accepted as real and is believed to reflect the nature of the mutation that occurs. Another piece of interesting information about MMD is that all affected people of European origin alive today are believed to be descended from one or a very small group of individuals who had the mutation in the sixteenth century or thereabouts.

Myotonias

In these conditions, the voluntary muscles are slow to relax after contracting, particularly after long periods of rest or as a result of cold or fatigue.

Myotonia congenita occurs in two forms (recessive and dominant) which vary in the age at which symptoms become apparent and in severity of the progression. The dominant form is called Thomsen's disease. It used to be thought that myotonia congenita was always autosomal dominant (see 'Heredity' below), as first described by Dr Thomsen. However, investigations of a large number of families in Germany over 20 years ago by Professor Becker found two forms of the disease, with the recessive form being more frequent. People with myotonia congenita have myotonia without the weakness which is characteristic of myotonic dystrophy.

Paramyotonia congenita is a rare condition which is triggered by cold and results in prolonged muscle spasms giving the face a still expression and making the hands clumsy. It is said to be paradoxical in that repetitive slow activity makes it worse rather than better. Contractions last longer than in other forms of myotonia.

Some people with paramyotonia congenita experience a type of periodic paralysis in which there is an episodic severe weakness lasting for hours or even days.

Myasthenic disorders

The best known of these disorders is *myasthenia gravis* which is characterised by weakness which varies within a day and even within an hour. It is made worse by muscle usage and improved with rest. Emotional stress and infection also will increase symptoms. Signs that may be present include progressive weakness during sustained effort, nasal speech, difficulty with swallowing, weakness of jaw closure and weakness of neck extension (leading to jaw propping and head droop). The smile has a characteristic snarling quality. Ability to raise the arms, elbow extension, hip flexion and finger movement are commonly affected. It is considered to be due to failure of transmission at the myoneural junction (see Figure 14.2), although the exact nature of this condition is unknown. The disorder is thought to be related to the thymus gland and a breakdown in immune tolerance. It is sometimes as-sociated with thyroid hyperactivity, rheumatoid arthritis and pernicious anaemia. It usually appears between the ages of 15 and 50 years, predominantly in women. Symptoms tend to fluctuate in intensity with relapses precipitated by severe muscular exertion. Muscle wasting may occur in longstanding cases, but there are no signs of central nervous system involvement.

Neuropathies

Spinal muscular atrophy (SMA) refers to a group of disorders where muscles weaken and waste because of genetically-determined degeneration of motor neurones in the spinal cord. It is one of the most common neuromuscular disorders of childhood and affects the brainstem but not intellectual functioning. There are several varieties, differentiated on the basis of which muscles are affected most severely. As it is commonly used, the term spinal muscular atrophy usually refers to proximal spinal muscular atrophy which affects predominantly the proximal muscles of the limbs, these being the ones closest to the centre of the body. There have been many attempts to put forward a logical categorisation of proximal spinal muscular dystrophies and the classification generally preferred now is one based on severity of disability. The proximal spinal atrophies, according to this classification, are separated into types 1, 2, 3 and 4 with 1 being the most severe. People with type 1 SMA are never able to sit, those with type 2 SMA can sit but cannot walk, people with type 3 are able to walk and type 4 is related to adult age of onset.

Type 1 SMA is often called Werdnig-Hoffmann disease and type 3 is called Kugelberg-Welander disease. Classification is usually closely associated with age of onset and length of survival. For example, babies with type 1 SMA are nearly always affected by the age of six months and die by two years of age. However, there are exceptions and occasionally two siblings with type 1 SMA, each with age of onset in the first six months of life, will have very different lengths of survival. Babies with type 1 SMA are sometimes affected before birth, the mother having noticed diminution of fetal movements. More often, the baby appears well until a few weeks or months of age when he or she fairly quickly and obviously becomes floppy and immobile. Eventually paralysis affects nearly all of the voluntary muscles and is likely to result in breathing and feeding problems. Death is due almost invariably to respiratory muscle failure. Diagnosis is not difficult and the parents must be informed of the baby's prognosis. Doctors and parents generally agree that every effort should be made to keep the baby comfortable without going to extraordinary lengths to prolong life.

Types 2, 3 and 4 proximal SMA present a spectrum of severity from profound to relatively mild disability.

Hereditary motor and sensory neuropathy (HMSN) occurs in the peripheral nerves. There are four types, with varying ages of onset and severity. Mild forms may result in high arches and some weakness in the feet. More serious forms result in weakness in foot muscles, high arches, hammer toes, unstable ankles, foot drop in walking and 'stork legs'. Most people remain able to walk.

Causes

The following explanation of heredity and genetics is taken with permission from a fact sheet prepared by Dr G. Morgan and published by the Muscular Dystrophy Association of Australia (Inc.) (1990–91).

Heredity

A hereditary characteristic is one which is determined by the genetic material put together when a sperm and an egg join at conception. This is true of both 'normal' characteristics and hereditary disorders. The genetic material from the sperm and the egg produces inherited characteristics by directing the body to make certain proteins. Normal variations in these proteins produce the everyday variability that we see in people. Inability to make an essential protein, because of a defect in the genetic material, may cause a hereditary condition or disease. Such conditions are also called inherited conditions or diseases, genetic conditions or genetically-determined conditions. Examples are the muscular dystrophies of which there are about ten types with three modes of inheritance.

Inheritance

Inheritance refers to the various ways in which variations in the genetic material produce the typical range of human characteristics. Defects in the genetic material produce genetic diseases and conditions. A brief explanation follows of what genetic material is, how it is organised and how it works.

DNA (an abbreviation for the chemical deoxyribonucleic acid) is a long, thin molecule which is like two pieces of string wound round each other. This chemical structure is called a double helix and contains thousands of pieces of information about the chemical structure of proteins and tells the body how to make proteins. Our hereditary characteristics come from the ability of our DNA, though the genetic code, to direct the cells of our bodies to make proteins.

A *gene* is a length of DNA which encodes the structure of a particular protein. It is a recipe for making that protein. For example, the insulin gene is a recipe which enables the cells of the pancreas to make insulin. Most proteins are encoded in each of two genes, one from each parent. Exceptions to this rule include genes on the X chromosome, of which females have two and males have one. The dystrophin gene is an example, it is paired in females but single in males.

All the genes in each cell of the human body are packaged in 46 *chromosomes* (23 from each parent). Since 46 chromosomes contain about 120 000 genes, a chromosome is much larger than a gene.

Genes are located in matching positions on each pair of chromosomes. Like DNA, chromosomes are long, thin, string-like structures. When a cell divides to

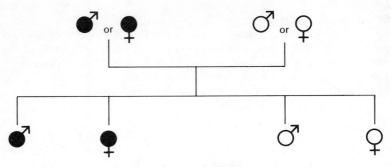

Autosomal dominant
One parent has MD

Each child has a 50% chance of developing MD
(e.g. facioscapulohumeral MD and myotonic MD).

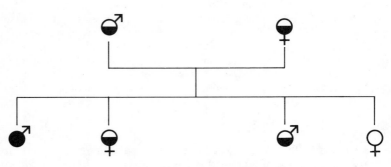

Autosomal recessive
Both parents are carriers

Each child has a 25% chance of developing MD
(e.g. limb girdle MD, SMA, juvenile forms of SMA)
and it can affect both sons and daughters. Two children will be carriers.

Figure 14.3: Patterns of inheritance in neuromuscular disease

make two new cells, the chromosome divides into two identical parts so that each new cell can have a full set of chromosomes, identical to those of the parent cell.

Chromosomes occur in pairs, one from each parent. They vary in size and are numbered by scientists in decreasing order of size. Chromosomes in the first 22 pairs look alike. However, those in the twenty-third pair look alike in females but not in males. They are called the *sex chromosomes*. The 22 pairs which are not sex chromosomes are called *autosomes*.

All human eggs contain an X chromosome. Sperm contain either an X or a Y. The sex of the baby is therefore determined by the father's sperm. The baby is female if the sperm contains an X and male if it contains a Y. The sex chromosome constitution of a female is described as XX, that of a male is XY. The fact that females have two X chromosomes and males have only one is responsible for the characteristic patterns of inheritance and conditions due to defects in genes in the X chromosome.

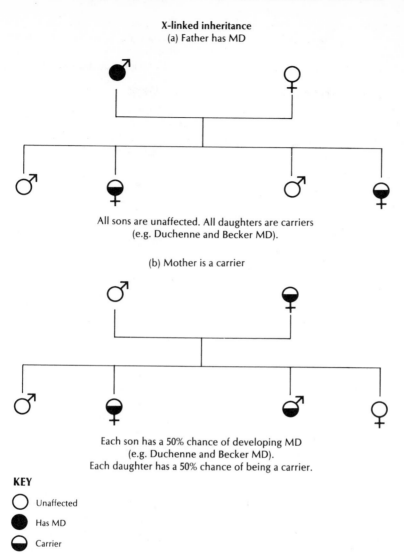

X-linked inheritance
(a) Father has MD

All sons are unaffected. All daughters are carriers
(e.g. Duchenne and Becker MD).

(b) Mother is a carrier

Each son has a 50% chance of developing MD
(e.g. Duchenne and Becker MD).
Each daughter has a 50% chance of being a carrier.

KEY

○ Unaffected

● Has MD

◑ Carrier

Figure 14.3: *Continued*

Genetic diseases can be caused by a variety of gene defects, including defects in one or both members of a single gene pair, with the combined influence of a large number of gene pairs and chromosomal rearrangements disturbing hundreds of thousands of genes. Muscle diseases of genetic causes are nearly all due to defects in one or both members of a single gene pair. This sort of inheritance is called *monogenic* or *unifactorial* or *mendelian*, the last of these terms deriving its name from Gregor Mendel who demonstrated this form of inheritance in peas, starting his experiments in 1856 and reporting them in 1865.

Nearly all muscle diseases of genetic causes are medelian in their mode of inheritance. The gene defect or defects may be of various types. One base in the DNA of the gene may be replaced by another (*point mutation*) or a part of it may be missing (*deletion*) or rearranged (for example, *inversion*). When a previously normal gene becomes defective, this change is called a *mutation*. Defective genes are called *mutant genes*. When there is evidence that a gene defect in a person is not present in either parent, a new mutation is assumed to have occurred.

Genes involved in the causation of muscle diseases of mendelian inheritance may be on the X chromosome (called *X-linked genes*) or on one of the autosomes (called *autosomal genes*). There are no known muscle diseases due to defects in Y-linked genes. Inheritance may be dominant or recessive, as described below, so that the medelian modes of inheritance other than Y-linked are:

- autosomal dominant.
- autosomal recessive.
- X-linked dominant.
- X-linked recessive.

Figure 14.3 displays common forms of inheritance in neuromuscular disease. *Autosomal dominant* disease occurs only when one member of the gene pair is defective, despite the presence of a normal gene. Examples are facio-scapulohumeral muscular dystrophy (FSHD) and myotonic muscular dystrophy. Every time a person with the gene defect produces offspring, the offspring has one chance in two of inheriting the defective gene and being affected. It is a new 50 per cent chance for each offspring, so it cannot be predicted that half of an affected person's offspring will be affected. Any combination of affected or unaf-fected offspring is possible. A typical family tree for an autosomal dominant condition shows people affected in succeeding generations and often in several branches of a family. Sometimes, though, an affected person has no known affected relatives. This may be due to a new mutation or to very mild undetected disease in a parent. Autosomal dominant disorders are often associated with a very wide spectrum of severity. Generally, severity of handicap in an affected parent is not predictive of severity in an affected offspring. In the case of myotonic muscular dystrophy, there are special considerations in relation to this, such as the phenom-enon of 'anticipation' (see above). Presymptomatic and prenatal diagnosis are possible for some autosomal dominant disorders, including myotonic muscular dystrophy.

The location of the gene for FSHD was discovered in 1990, but the nature of the gene defect is not yet known. The possibility of genetic heterogeneity – that is, that there is more than one gene in which defects can cause FSHD – cannot be ruled out (Morgan, 1996). Myotonia congenita has two patterns, one of which is autosomal dominant and the other recessive. In dominant cases, the child of an affected person has a 50 per cent chance of having the disease, while in recessive conditions there is a 25 per cent chance.

Autosomal recessive disease occurs when both members of the relevant gene pair are defective. If one of the gene pair is defective and the other is normal, the individual is not affected. He or she is called a *carrier*. If an individual is affected with an autosomal recessive disease, it is assumed that he or she inherited one defective gene from each parent and that both parents, therefore, are carriers. Nearly all cases of proximal spinal muscular atrophy are autosomal recessive, as are the great majority of cases of limb girdle muscular dystrophy. The typical pedigree of an autosomal recessive disorder shows only one branch of a family affected in only one generation; that is, in a single set of brothers or sisters. Among those brothers and sisters there may be only one affected or there may be two or more, but other branches of the family are not affected. Previous generations are not affected and the risk to future generations is close to negligible. The exception to this is where a recessive condition is seen in more than one branch of a family (for example, in second cousins) or in succeeding generations. This can be explained in one of three ways. Either the gene is a very common one (which is not so of any of the conditions being considered here), or the parents of an affected person are related (for example, cousins), or the parents are unrelated but each has a family history of the same recessive condition. Cousin marriage increases the probability of both parents having the same defective recessive gene.

Most cases of limb girdle muscular dystrophy are autosomal recessive. Spinal muscular atrophy and the infantile and juvenile forms of SMA are usually autosomal recessive. Type 1 SMA is autosomal recessive which means a 25 per cent recurrence risk for each offspring of the parents. The chromosomal location of the gene has been known since 1990 and prenatal diagnosis can be offered to the great majority of parents who want it. Most other forms of SMA (2, 3 and 4 proximal) are also autosomal recessive and most are caused by defects in the same gene as that involved in type 1 SMA. However, some are autosomal dominant. In a family with an isolated case – that is, with only one affected person – it may be possible to know which mode of inheritance applies. In cases which are autosomal recessive, it is sometimes possible to offer prenatal diagnosis. A gene defect associated with proximal SMA was described in 1985, but it is not present in all cases and its precise relationship to the disease process is not yet understood.

X-linked inheritance is exemplified by Duchenne muscular dystrophy and Becker muscular dystrophy. A male with a defect in his single dystrophin gene is affected. A female carrier, with one defective and one normal dystrophin gene, is unaffected except in rare instances. The son of a carrier female has a 50 per cent probability of being affected. The daughter of a carrier female has a 50 per cent probability of being a carrier. The daughter of an affected male is an obligate carrier because she receives his single, defective dystrophin gene. The characteristic pedigree shows affected males related to each other through unaffected carrier females. However, the mutation rate is very high and the potential exists to make genetic counselling very effective, so that female carriers and possible carriers usually are able to avoid having affected sons. In NSW, between 80 per cent and 85 per cent of affected males are isolated cases. In the absence of genetic counselling, the expected incidence of isolated cases is 33 per cent. Genetic counselling for families with DMD and BMD creates a heavy workload. A boy or man with DMD or BMD may have a few female relatives who are obligate carriers and several who are possible carriers. The great majority of these will want genetic testing to determine their carrier status. Most of those who are carriers or who have a high probability of being carriers request genetic testing to determine whether they can be offered prenatal diagnosis. The advent of DNA diagnostic testing has made an enormous difference over the last decade to the quality of the genetic testing and counselling which can be offered.

In 1987 the cause of Duchenne and Becker dystrophies was discovered. The gene was sequenced and found to encode the structure of a protein which was not previously known to exist. It comprises a miniscule proportion, about 0.002 per cent of muscle protein. It was given the name dystrophin. People with DMD generally have no detectable or a minute amount of dystrophin, people with BMD usually have dystrophin in a diminished amount, usually with an abnormal molecular weight.

Incidence and prevalence

Emery (1991) reports results of a survey of 150 studies across the world. He states that a conservative estimate would be that one in 3500 of the population has an inherited neuromuscular disease which is disabling and presents in childhood or later life. He cites incidence figures for specific conditions. For example, for Duchenne muscular dystrophy the incidence appears to be about one in 3500 male births, for Becker muscular dystrophy the incidence at birth appears to be about one in 700 births. According to Corrick (1992), muscular dystrophy affects 250 000 Americans.

Diagnosis

Several techniques are used in the diagnosis of neuromuscular disorders. When a physician suspects that something is wrong with the muscles or suspects a particular muscle disease because of characteristics such as the particular pattern of muscle weakness, he or she usually proceeds to a sequence of tests as follows:

- In myotonic dystrophy, weakness and wasting in the jaw, face and neck muscles are taken into account as is frontal balding which is often found in men with this condition. Enlarged calf muscles are an important indicator in diagnosis of Duchenne MD. Fatigue in the muscles is an important indicator of myasthenia gravis.
- *Serum creatine kinase* (SCK) blood testing is used in the diagnosis of Duchenne and Becker MD. Creatine kinase is a chemical which leaks out of muscle fibres in these conditions and is found in increased amounts in the serum of the blood. For Duchenne MD, the SCK enzyme test can also be used to identify about 70 per cent of women who are carriers.
- *Muscle biopsy* involves the removal of a small piece of muscle for examination to obtain evidence of degeneration. For DMD and BMD, a recent advance is a method of assessing the level of dystrophin within muscle tissue. Dystrophin is a protein produced by normal muscle fibres under direction from the gene. If the gene is abnormal, this direction is faulty and the production of dystrophin falls. Hence, the level of dystrophin in the muscle will enable a diagnosis to be made. Research is now disclosing specific defects in other proteins so that in previously unclassifiable muscular dystrophies, testing for those proteins is becoming part of the pathologist's repertoire. This is a very new field which is developing fast.
- *Electromyography* (EMG) involves examination of electrical activity generated by a muscle when it contracts. A needle picks up changes in electrical potential which occur across the muscle fibre membrane when it contracts. The electromyographer learns to recognise patterns which are characteristic of primary muscle disease, primary neuropathy, myotonia and inflammatory muscle disease. When an EMG is done, the electromyographer usually measures nerve conduction velocities as well. If the nerve conduction velocities are slowed, this indicates peripheral neuropathy. If the EMG indicates neurogenic disease, but the nerve conduction velocities are normal, this is a strong indication that the pathology is at the level of the anterior horn cells.
- *DNA diagnostic testing* is usually done for the purposes of genetic counselling when a diagnosis already exists. However, it can also be used for genetic counselling. For example, if the medical specialist has noted that a young boy

looks as if he has DMD and has a serum creatine kinase level consistent with that, the decision may be made to send blood for DNA testing. Dystropin gene deletion provides a firm diagnosis. Muscle biopsy then would not be really essential, although most people would still go on to this form of test because they would say that absence of dystrophin is the 'gold standard' for diagnosis and, if the dystrophin is not entirely absent, the amount of dystrophin may be a pointer towards prognosis. The same applies in myotonic muscular dystrophy, where an EMG (which is quite painful) or a muscle biopsy are not really required when a blood specimen will tell the specialist whether the mutation is present or not.

Treatment

Antibiotics have been a major factor in increased life expectancy of people with Duchenne muscular dystrophy. Myotonias can be relieved by drugs, but these do not affect the underlying disease process. Many people with myotonia find it helpful to acquire the habit of 'warming up' after long periods of immobility. Myasthenia gravis can be relieved by medication taken orally or by injection.

Genetic counselling and testing are vital for families with a history of muscular dystrophy. DNA testing is conducted with some muscular dystrophies to determine the probability of carrier status and is used in prenatal diagnosis. Amniocentesis enables chromosome study to identify the sex of the unborn child, but is rarely used nowadays as more modern and reliable methods are available. If the fetus is male, there is a 50 per cent chance that he will be affected if the mother has a 100 per cent probability of carrier status. However, usually the mother's probability falls below this. Examination of the occurrence of muscular dystrophy within the family tree also is important.

Exercising is an important form of treatment for muscle diseases such as Duchenne muscular dystrophy. No amount of exercise will improve or strengthen muscles in an affected person, but stretches and exercise will help ensure that the length of muscles is maintained. Exercise followed by excessive soreness of muscles is detrimental and best avoided (Hope & Mallos, 1995).

Foot surgery may be used to make it easier or more comfortable for a person to stand or the relieve pain along the outer border of the foot when resting on the footplate of a wheelchair. Back surgery may relieve scoliosis (sideways curvature of the spine which occurs in most people with Duchenne muscular dystrophy). Scoliosis often affects the ability to use two hands together because of the need to use one arm to prop the body from falling sideways. Scoliosis changes the shape of the chest, so that breathing is increasingly impaired (Hope & Mallos, 1995).

Services and supports

As there is no cure, treatment focuses on slowing disabilities associated with muscular dystrophy. Physiotherapists (physical therapists) work to retain functioning in the muscles and joints while occupational therapists advise on posture, sitting positions and activities. If a wheelchair is required, an occupational therapist can recommend whether a manual or powered wheelchair is more appropriate. A wide range of services are available in the community which are designed to enhance quality of life and opportunities for people with muscular dystrophy and neuromuscular disorders. Active sport and leisure clubs and associations exist for people with disabilities. Participation in sport is important to encourage fitness,

Figure 14.4: A man with Duchenne muscular dystrophy and the computer which enables him to gain access to part-time employment as a member of a university research team

team building, feelings of competency and self-confidence. Computer information networks exist in many countries which can be used to gain information about services and facilities available for people with disabilities. For example, NICAN (which can be accessed through disability organisations and local and state libraries) provides an Australia-wide directory on many issues. One of these is sport, recreation and tourism for people with disabilities.

Equipment

Orthotic aids such as braces, callipers, surgical boots and wheelchairs (manual or electric) aid mobility and independence. Aids such as hoists become increasingly important for the family as the person with a neuromuscular disorder grows from being to a child to a teenager and to an adult. Many parents have back problems as a result of lifting and moving their adult son or daughter. Ceiling hoists help relieve this strain. Hoists are used to lift the person out of bed, on to a chair, into a bath, and so on.

Additional costs

Costs are associated with the need for specialised equipment, home modifications and specialised transport. Hidden costs may result from the decision of a parent to stay at home rather than to continue in paid employment. Everyday costs such as for laundry are likely to be higher in a family with a member with a severe physical disability. Emotional costs for the family may stem from watching the gradual deterioration of a loved person or for the demands placed on them by ongoing and seemingly continuous care of a dependent person.

RESOURCE ORGANISATIONS

All care has been taken to ensure that all information is correct at the time of publishing; however, responsibility for the accuracy of this information is not accepted by the writer. The list of resource organisations contained in this chapter is not intended to be exhaustive – it provides national organisations only. The reader is referred to local community directories for further information and for local branches of national organisations. Inclusion of services and organisations should not be taken as a recommendation.

Australia

A series of state organisations operate. Consult your local telephone directory for your local or state organisation. For NSW the address is:

Muscular Dystrophy Association of NSW
GPO Box 9932
Sydney 2001
Ph 02 9360 3438
Fax 02 9360 3098

Canada

Muscular Dystrophy Society of Canada
Suite 900, 2345 Yonge Street
Toronto ON M4P 2E5
Ph 416 488 0030
Fax 416 488 7523

United Kingdom

Muscular Dystrophy Group of Great Britain and Northern Ireland
7–11 Prescott Place
London SW4 6BS
Ph 0171 720 8055
Fax 0171 498 0670

United States

Muscular Dystrophy Association Inc
3300 Eastsunrise Drive
Tucson Arizona 85718-3208
Ph 520 529 2000
1 800 572 1717
Fax 520 529 5300

World wide web

http:\\www.webnet.com.au\mda

FURTHER READING

Corrick, J. A. (1992). *Muscular dystrophy*. Venture: New York.
Emery, A. E. H. (1994). *Muscular dystrophy: the facts*. Oxford: Oxford University Press.
Hope, M. & Mallos, T. (1995). *Duchenne muscular dystrophy: a guide for teachers*. Sydney: Muscle Diseases Clinic, Prince of Wales Children's Hospital.
Muscular Dystrophy Associations of Australia (1990). *Fact sheets*. (A series of fact sheets about muscular dystrophies, myotonias and spinal muscular atrophy.)
Muscular Dystrophy Association of NSW (undated). *My friend has muscular dystrophy*. PO Box 10, Strawberry Hills, NSW 2021.
Muscular Dystrophy Association of South Australia (undated). *Facts about Duchenne and Becker muscular dystrophy*. 251 Morphett St, Adelaide, SA 5000.

Muscular Dystrophy Association of South Australia (undated). *The myotonias.* 251 Morphett St, Adelaide, SA 5000.

Ringel, S. P. (1987). *Neuromuscular disorder: a guide for patient and family.* New York: Raven Press.

CHAPTER 15
SHORT STATURE

Sometimes I feel different from other people, and sometimes they make me feel different from them. In some ways, it has affected my childhood, but not that much.

Michael

I don't class it as a disability because if I put my mind to it, I can do most things.

Miriam

In general, a person with short stature is an individual who is under 150 cm (4'10") tall and shorter than average for his or her ethnic background. It should be kept in mind that there are communities of short-statured people in countries such as Malaysia, New Guinea, India, Mexico, the Philippines and central Africa where the range of typical height would be different from that for Western countries. The incidence of people under 150 cm tall is greater in these communities, where such levels of height would not be considered as unusual.

The terms 'dwarf' and 'midget' are often used to describe people of short stature. These terms are used by members of the general community and by professionals (as can be seen from titles in the reading list for this chapter). However, many people with short stature prefer to be described as 'little' people, rather than as dwarfs or midgets.

Most children who are shorter than their peers at a given age exhibit a slow-growth pattern and are merely lagging behind their contemporaries. Eventually they will catch up. A few children remain small, with their body parts usually proportional. Others will remain small but their body parts will be disproportionate. The term 'short stature' is most frequently applied to these people (Crandall & Crosson, 1994).

LIVING WITH SHORT STATURE

Social and psychological implications of restricted growth are based on the tendency of people to use cues of stature and physique to make assumptions about the age and mental maturity of others. People of short stature may find that they are not treated as adults. Many find that others take a protective and patronising attitude toward them, regardless of their age.

In many Western countries where the ethos is 'the bigger the better', people with short stature are treated as being inferior in their abilities and worth (Ablon, 1990). During childhood and adult life, the taunts and thoughtless comments of others serve as a reminder of a person's height and can create or compound a poor body image and lowered self-esteem.

Depending on the type of short stature, there may be medical accompaniments. The most common of these are headache, backache, earache, weakness

Figure 15.1: Modifications might not suit everyone

in the legs, respiratory problems, and concave or convex curvature of the spine (scoliosis). Surgery or a brace may be used to correct curvatures and to alleviate pain.

There are also physical implications associated with height, reach and comfort. The built environment is designed for the average population in terms of reach and step. Furniture, vehicles, placement of door handles, light switches and public telephones are all designed with people of average height in mind. Everyday activities may be made troublesome for people of short stature if adjustments are not made to the size and height of equipment and fittings. Many families with a member with short stature find it easier to redesign the whole house around this person (see Figure 15.1).

> *I got the fittings in my kitchen lowered because I got tired of kicking a stool around, especially when I was pregnant.*
>
> Miriam

Personal adjustment

Most people with short stature do not regard themselves as having a disability. However, for a person with short stature, both as an adult and child, adjustments have to be made in social, emotional and physical terms.

The way in which people react to their stature and their own self-image is highly individual and is greatly influenced by family reactions and social experiences. Others often categorise a physically small adult as a child and do not allow (or expect) that person to behave in an adult manner. Some people with short stature seem to wage a constant campaign against being treated as younger and less mature. A few people with short stature succumb to expectations and adopt an 'eternal child' role. However, these people tend to be few in number. Most people and their families get on with life and learn to adjust to living with short stature.

> *I applied to the Air Force because in their advertisement they didn't mention a minimum height. The principal of my school heard what I was trying to do and called me in for a talk. He told me I would have to be honest about my 'dwarfism'. The word hit me hard and I started to fully realise what it was like to feel different. It was a lonely time.*
>
> Brian, who has achondroplasia

Adolescence is a difficult transition time for many teenagers. It is an extended period of physical change where growth spurts and an emphasis on body image may create additional difficulties for an adolescent with restricted growth. Feelings of isolation and the awareness of being different may become more pronounced. Difficulties may be encountered in handling social relationships and in sexual development.

> *To be accepted is one thing, but to be able to take part is another. This was brought home to me in adolescence. My peers were growing into the physiques of men and sport was very much the scene. My place on the playing field was the touchline, or for swimming, it was the spectator seats.*
>
> Brian

Adolescence is the time for discarding the dream that the disability might go away.

> *I suddenly realised that I was going to be just the same as I had always been – very small, funnily shaped and unable to walk. It seemed at that moment that the sky cracked.*
>
> Campling (1981, p. 23)

Sexuality

There is some variation in sexual development between the types of short stature. If the hormones of the pituitary gland are affected, as in pituitary hormone deficiency, this may prevent mature sexual development. If only the human growth hormone is missing, the person may mature sexually and be able to have children.

However, there is nothing to prevent people with short stature from having sexual relationships. One of the possible psychological implications of this condition is not seeing oneself as a sexual being or as attractive to others.

Being a parent

As discussed later in the chapter, many forms of short stature result from genetic transmission or mutation. Genetic counselling is important for people if they are thinking about becoming parents. Women with most forms of short stature usually bear children by caesarean delivery.

Family

> *Being part of a large, close family gave me security. My parents did not stop having children when I was born and I am the second eldest of five. I am the only one with short stature.*
>
> Brian

For most parents, the desire to have tall, healthy children is a natural expectation. They take great pride in watching their children grow into full-sized adults. Having a child with short stature may be perceived by parents as robbing them of this right.

> *It wasn't until the morning after her birth that the doctor informed us our daughter was short statured . . . his words took hold of our lives and we felt the world crash in around us, leaving us in the grey light of reality. We felt angry and confused. Somehow our daughter's dwarfism was our fault. We grieved for the perfect little girl we dreamed of, the girl who was not meant to be.*
>
> Crandall & Crosson (1994, p. xvii)

Common reactions cited by Crandall & Crosson (1994) include:

- *Confusion* – on hearing the news, parents do not understand what is happening and feel overwhelmed.
- *Denial* – parents find it difficult to believe this is happening to them and to their child; they may not tell their own parents and other family members or may try to hide their child's disability by wrapping him or her in blankets.
- *Anger* – as parents begin to acknowledge the diagnosis, they may feel helpless, lash out at others and be angry with doctors because they cannot cure the child. Some may be angry at their god or look for someone to blame. They may blame themselves. This anger can affect relationships with family and friends. Some relationships never recover.
- *Fear of the unknown* – parents have many questions about their child's disability and what he or she will be able or not able to do in life. If the baby is diagnosed in utero, this may lead to exaggerated fears of what he or she will look like.

> *I thought I was going to give birth to an alien and was so happy when my little boy was born. He is wonderful and doesn't look anything like I imagined.*
>
> Crandall & Crosson (1994, p. 10)

- *Grief* – this is a healthy part of the acceptance process where parents mourn the loss of the child they dreamed they would have.
- *Powerlessness* – parents feel helpless and unable to change the situation. They must rely on the judgments of total strangers.
- *Disappointment* – this is felt as a result of the birth of a less-than-perfect child.
- *Guilt* – this occurs as a result of parents blaming themselves for their child's short stature. The parents may go over their lives and try to find some event or action that could have affected the child's genes or appearance. Parents who

were unaware that they were carriers of a gene associated with short stature may also feel guilt.

- *Rejection* – this may be felt for a fleeting moment towards the child, but can cause feelings of guilt for a long time.
- *Acceptance* – when parents realise that life will go on and will be all right. Things are not as bad as they once seemed.

Professionals have an important role to play in assisting parents and the family to work through these reactions. Trauma may be unwittingly exacerbated by a professional who lacks sensitivity in how he or she treats the parents. Some professionals have difficulty in breaking difficult news to parents and experience discomfort and embarrassment when doing so. They may have problems in maintaining eye contact and in giving clear information. They may use euphemisms and indirect references such as 'your baby is going to be short'. These behaviours add to the confusion and stress experienced by parents. Often the mother is not allowed to see her baby for some time after the birth. This denial creates further ambiguity and stress (Ablon, 1988, 1990).

The attitude the doctors adopted was extraordinary. It was not the attitude you would expect from medical people. It was as if to say: 'Well, this is your problem, go away and look after it'. We knew nothing and . . . felt very isolated at first.

Michael's parents

It also is important to consider how grandparents might be feeling. They may desperately want to help, but cannot. They may feel left out and not consulted. Some may experience denial and may refuse to visit the baby. Others might overwhelm the new parents with unsolicited advice. Grandparents, like other members of the family, need correct and accurate information about the child's diagnosis and what can be done to get on with life.

Parents of children with short stature may be overprotective and anxious. This reaction generally stems from a loving concern for their child's social and emotional welfare and the need to provide shelter in a society that sees their child as different. However, it also can serve to make the child dependent on the family and can reduce opportunities to develop the social skills and confidence necessary for a full and satisfying life. It also may be a source of resentment among siblings. A balance between love and support, on the one hand, and allowing freedom on the other, is as essential for a child with a disability as it is for any other child.

In our home an individual is not measured by height, weight or other physical description . . . but rather by the stature of a person's inner worth, their compassion, gifts, abilities and personality.

Family of a 16-year-old with achondroplasia cited
by Crandall & Crosson (1994, p. 78)

Parents should also be aware of the effects that short stature may have on siblings of the child. Many families are able to deal with teasing and ridicule from outside, but siblings may feel strongly about the way they see their brother or sister being treated by others at school for example, or about how their own friends behave.

Some families may be made up entirely of people with short stature. This may be a result of a decision to adopt children, but many forms of short stature are inheritable and short stature is passed on from parent to child.

We decided to have children . . . we understood the likelihood of having children the same as ourselves which didn't worry us, as that's what we are – we can cope . . . now my mother is the odd one out living with the four of us.

Miriam

Community living

I was not shielded by my family from the curiosity, staring and ridicule of strangers. I was accepted as being the same among my family and friends, but when moving to a new area, it took quite some time before the boy that I was then could go out and about without something happening to drive home my difference.

Brian

As mentioned above, it is often the attitude of other people which makes short stature a handicap in social and emotional terms. Not only do many people take a protective and patronising attitude toward a physically small adult, but they often believe the person's capabilities and intelligence are restricted.

People's reactions? Some become overly rude, some poke fun. Most times people are very good. It doesn't worry me very much at all. It's only every now and then it annoys me. Children don't worry me because they don't understand.

Brian

Access

It has often been said to me that being a healthy, active short-statured person cannot be considered as having a disability. This has always been said by non-disabled people. The fact that a lot of day-to-day things are out of my reach (getting on and off a chair is an effort) is not the only tag that classifies me as disabled. Short stature is made into a disability by the attitude of the majority of non-disabled people toward those who do not conform to the so-called norm.

Brian

Social situations involving crowds can be physically threatening for someone very much smaller than the average. Everyday activities such as shopping in supermarkets with high shelves or trying to use a public telephone may be difficult and annoying without the assistance of others. Modifications will be necessary if a person with short stature wishes to drive a car or buy ready-made clothes. Restrictions on employment choices and opportunities may exist for people of short stature. While it is easy to say that a person should be realistic about height and physique and that certain jobs are not suitable, it does not make it any easier to accept these limitations (see Figure 15.2).

Figure 15.2: No modifications were needed to enable this person with short stature to teach in primary school

Sometimes my daughter has whimsical ideas about what she wants to do – like being a flight attendant. I have to bring her down to earth and say 'don't forget you're not as big as other kids, you may have difficulty' . . . But I never stop her. I tell her if she wants to do it, she should try it.

Miriam

Education

Children with short stature show the range of intelligence and aptitude for learning typical of the rest of the population. Most attend regular schools. Modifications may be required to the classroom to accommodate a child who finds desks are too far from the floor. Access to library shelves and other resource material may be difficult.

Generally, only those with severe disabilities need to spend any time in special schools. Children with osteogenesis imperfecta ('brittle bones') may attend special schools. Interruptions to school attendance may occur for these children because of frequent hospitalisation.

Often the biggest problems at school are social rather than educational. In primary and secondary years, teasing, name calling and feelings of being left out of activities because of small stature may cause behavioural problems both at school and at home.

It was hard starting high school at first. Some of the students tried to be smart in front of their friends. But, after the first couple of weeks, they got used to me.

Michael

Employment

Honesty about yourself and a sense of humour are the two important factors in a job interview if you are to put the other people at ease.

Brian

A limited number of vocational areas is closed to people with short stature. Occupations with average height requirements or those that may aggravate existing medical conditions are unsuitable. However, the most restricting barrier is the attitude of employers who believe that the person with short stature has limited capabilities.

Required modifications to the workplace are usually minor and can be easily made. Adjustable seating, a smaller desk or a stool and set of small steps might be all that is needed to make a person comfortable and work areas accessible.

PERSON TO PERSON

Appropriate language and behaviours

There is no reason why communication between people of at least average height and those who are much shorter than average cannot be the same as with other people. The range of intelligence, abilities and personality types is the same. There is no reason to treat a person differently simply on the basis of stature.

While a sense of humour can overcome many embarrassing or uncomfortable situations, it should not be used as a form of mockery.

> *Some people are okay, others are taken aback and some fluster. Some even get down on their knees to be my height – that makes me feel worse. I tell them to get up – because I'm looking up at people all the time, I'm used to it.*
>
> Miriam

Strategies for interaction

Table 15.1: Strategies for successful interaction

Person with short stature	Other person
Be assertive about your rights and need to be accepted as a mature adult.	Do not communicate with the person in a patronising or condescending manner.
Ask for any form of assistance if it is required.	In situations requiring height and reach, assistance might be needed. Ask the person if you can help, but remember he or she has the right to refuse.
Discomfort in social situations can often be overcome by using humour or by trying to make other people feel more at ease.	Be aware that a person with short stature might feel discomfort in social situations involving crowds.
	A sense of humour can often put people at ease and overcome embarrassment in social situations, but not if used insensitively.

MORE INFORMATION ABOUT SHORT STATURE

Definition

In terms of the World Health Organization (1980) definition:

- *Impairment* varies depending on the type of short stature, but is referred to as below-typical height for a community group and may be accompanied by other forms of impairment.
- *Disability* reflects limitations in carrying out everyday tasks and functioning associated with the characteristics of short stature.

- *Handicap* refers to difficulties such as in gaining access to employment and public facilities which do not cater for people of below average height, and prejudice and inappropriate behaviour on the part of others.

The Little People's Association of Australia (1981) and Crandall & Crosson (1994) describe the following major types of short stature. This list is not intended to be exhaustive, but illustrates the types of short stature.

Short-limb short stature

There are over 100 types of short-limb short stature.

Achondroplasia. This is the most common form of disproportionate short stature and is recognisable at birth and after the twenty-fourth week of gestation, using ultrasound. The limbs are generally affected more than the trunk. A prominent forehead and depressed nasal bridge often produce a characteristic facial appearance. The person also is likely to have short fingers, bowed legs, swayback and prominent buttocks and abdomen. Intelligence is not affected.

Pseudoachondroplasia. This is usually recognised at two to three years of age, when a waddling gait becomes apparent and the child begins to show disproportionate short stature. Facial features are not affected.

Diastrophic dysplasia. This is characterised by short limbs, club feet, and broad hands with short fingers and thumbs. There also may be dislocation of the knees. Spinal disorders also may be present. 'Cauliflower ears' may develop in the first few weeks of life. In about half of these children, cleft palate occurs.

Multiple epiphyseal dysplasia (MED). This is associated with abnormal development of the articular centres of the long bones. The spine is not affected. The condition may not be recognised until early childhood when the child does not seem to be growing a fast as other children. The hands may appear short and stubby. Joint deformities and stiffness are common features of this condition.

Spondylo-epiphyseal dysplasia (SED). This affects the spine and epiphyses (growing ends of the bones). Some forms can be present at birth and result in extreme growth restriction, others develop later in childhood.

Osteogenesis imperfecta (OI). This condition is characterised by 'brittle bones' which remain brittle throughout life. It usually results from bone collagen deficiency. There are four major types: OI type I, II, III and IV. OI type II is lethal. Most people with OI have type I or type IV which usually have their onset in childhood. OI type III commonly becomes apparent in the newborn period, with multiple fractures occurring. All people with OI are at risk of fractures, although the fracture rate decreases at puberty There are many disability issues. In OI type III, there is progressive deformity and growth retardation, and those affected frequently need mobility aids. Some children undergo an operation called 'rodding' in which rods are inserted into the long bones to provide additional strength and to help prevent fractures.

Other types. Other major types of short stature result from hormone insufficiency and from growth failure prior to birth.

Causes

It is impossible to describe a typical condition of short stature as over 100 different types have been identified, the causes of which are complex. Depending on the type, there may or may not be associated medical concomitants.

Achondroplasia is due to an autosomal dominant gene and the affected person has a 50-50 chance of passing this gene to offspring. (For a more detailed discussion of inheritance, please refer to Chapter 14 'Muscular dystrophies and other neuromuscular disorders'.) Pseudoachondroplasia also is genetically transmitted and is inherited in an autosomal dominant fashion like achondroplasia.

Diastrophic dysplasia is due to an autosomal recessive gene. There is a 25 per cent chance with each pregnancy that the child will receive the gene from both parents who are carriers and will be affected. Multiple epiphyseal dysplasia (MED) is due to an autosomal dominant gene and 50 per cent of the offspring of an affected person are likely to have the condition. Spondylo-epiphyseal dysplasia (SED) is due to an autosomal dominant single gene.

Osteogenesis imperfecta (OI) in most cases is due to autosomal dominant gene mutations, although in occasional families, OI results from autosomal recessive inheritance.

Hormone failure

Pituitary hormone deficiency. This occurs in approximately one in 15 000 children as a result of abnormal functioning of the pituitary gland. It can be detected in the first year of life. These people have average proportions, but are smaller than other people. There are many types of hormone deficiency. The type of deficiency depends on the presence or lack of each of the seven pituitary hormones, one of which is the human growth hormone. In some cases, growth can be achieved with injections of growth hormones, thus early detection is important.

Hypothyroidism. Slow growth, sluggish behaviour, tongue enlargement, facial changes, thickened and puffy face and skin are manifestations of low thyroid gland function, as are neurological abnormalities. Screening is carried out at birth in all states of Australia and in most developed countries; however, the condition can develop later in life.

Nutritional short stature. Ongoing malnutrition prevents children from reaching their full growth potential. The body becomes weak and frail and usually shows signs that muscle or bone tissue is wasting. Malnutrition is the most common cause of growth failure around the world, primarily due to a lack of protein and other basic nutrients in the diet. A well-balanced diet will help prevent or overcome its effects.

Primary growth failure

Prenatal intrauterine growth failure. This is indicated when a full-term baby is unusually small. Such children develop into small, but well-proportioned adults. Specific causes have not been found for this type of restricted growth. It is sometimes linked to chronic placental insufficiency.

Secondary growth failure

Disorders that impair growth. These may include systemic diseases of the kidneys, liver, heart, bowels or lungs. Treatment of underlying conditions can often lead to growth improvement.

Incidence

Estimates of the number of people of short-stature vary from one study to another. Ablon (1990) states that the reported prevalence for the United States varies between one and five per 100 000 people. Numbers vary because definitions vary. The most common form of short stature is achondroplasia, and its minimum incidence is one in 27 000 births. The frequency of OI in the population is approximately one in 10 000 individuals.

Most babies with short stature (85–90 per cent) are born to parents of at least average height.

Diagnosis

Depending on the type of short stature, diagnosis may involve a detailed recording of pregnancy, family history, a thorough physical examination, a review of X-rays and sometimes taking urine or blood samples. The specific diagnosis will determine the likely course of treatment. Genetic counselling is always advised and clinical genetics consultation will usually be necessary as part of the diagnostic process.

Treatment

Management of the various types of short stature is specific to each type. For most types, specific recommendations can be given which enhance quality of life and prevent complications. Some people require little or no treatment while others may require surgery. Treatment may include physiotherapy, and mobility aids are useful for some people. An occupational therapist may assist with home modifications and activities of daily living.

Services and supports

Self-help groups and national associations provide support and advice to people with short stature and their families. Members can benefit from newsletters, conferences, booklets, professional directories, pen-pal networks and other activities.

RESOURCE ORGANISATIONS

All care has been taken to ensure that all information is correct at the time of publishing; however, responsibility for the accuracy of this information is not accepted by the writer. The list of resource organisations contained in this chapter is not intended to be exhaustive – it provides national organisations only. The reader is referred to local community directories for further information and for local branches of national organisations. Inclusion of services and organisations should not be taken as a recommendation.

Australia

OI Association of Australia
PO Box 401
Epping NSW 2121
Ph 02 9869 1486

Short Statured People of Australia
(formerly Little People's Association of
Australia)
82 Mintaro Avenue
Strathfield NSW 2135
Ph 02 9642 5046

Canada

Canadian Osteogenesis Imperfecta Society
C/- 128 Thornhill Crescent
Chatham ON N7L 4M3
Ph 519 436 0025
Fax 519 627 0557

New Zealand

Little People's Association of New Zealand
O/S International Correspondent
Sutton Road RD 43
Waitara Taranaki

United Kingdom

Little People's Association
O/S International Correspondent
  Coordinator
61 Lady Walk, Maple Cross
Rickmansworth Herts WD3 2YZ

United States

Little People of America Inc.
PO Box 9897
Washington, DC 20016
Ph 1 888 LPA 2001

FURTHER READING

Ablon, J. (1988). *Living with difference: families with dwarf children*. New York: Prager.
Ablon, J. (1990). Ambiguity and difference: families of dwarf children. *Social Science and Medicine,* 30, 870-87.
Crandall, R. & Crosson, T. (eds) (1994). *Dwarfism: the family and professional guide*. Irvine, CA: Short Stature Foundation and Information Center Inc.
Glauser, H. C. (undated). *Living with osteogenesis imperfecta: a guidebook for families*. Tampa, Florida: OI Foundation, Inc., 5005 Laurel Street, Suite 210, Tampa, FL 33607, USA.
Sillence, D. O. & Barlow, K. K. (1991). *Osteogenesis imperfecta: a handbook for medical practitioners and health care professionals* (2nd edn). Sydney: IMS Publishing.
Van Etten, A. M. (1988). *Dwarfs don't live in doll houses*. Rochester, NY: Adaptive Living, PO Box 60857, Rochester, NY 14606, USA.

CHAPTER 16

SEVERE VISION IMPAIRMENT AND BLINDNESS

The word 'blindness' conjures up images of a world without light, of darkness and of helplessness. In reality, very few people who are classified as blind experience a life of total darkness and certainly not one of helplessness. Most people who are blind see light, others see shape while others have sufficient vision to enable them to move around with the aid of a dog, cane or sonic device. Others need no assistance at all for mobility.

Not all people with vision impairment are classified as blind. There are many causes of severe vision impairment and blindness and levels of impairment differ greatly. As with other disabilities, the extent to which the impairment affects a person's life depends on many factors. For example, implications of the disability are very different for someone who was born with a visual impairment as compared with someone who acquired disability after several years of sight. Other important factors are whether the impairment was acquired suddenly or is the result of gradual deterioration; and whether the person has no sight at all or has some level of useable vision. These, together with personality factors and factors which reflect the different ways we, as individuals, adapt to our worlds, further reinforce one of the major messages of this book: that each of us is an individual and it is important not to make assumptions about a particular person or disability type, or to stereotype people with disabilities as all being alike.

For most people with a severe visual impairment, onset is slow and begins between 60 and 65 years of age. This chapter looks at issues arising for people across a wide range of ages.

Some of the issues surrounding life with a vision impairment or with blindness are discussed below. However, first it is important to differentiate between these two forms of disability.

The term *vision impairment* is more commonly used today than *blindness*. Most people have some vision. Of those classified as legally blind in Australia, 95 per cent of people have some residual or remaining vision. The term legally blind is used to describe people eligible for the Disability Support Pension/Blind and the Aged (Blind) Pension which is provided by the Department of Social Security.

LIVING WITH VISUAL IMPAIRMENT AND BLINDNESS

Personal adjustment

People born with a form of vision impairment or blindness (*congenital*) have never known life without it. Their disability has influenced the way they have received their education and has always influenced the way they receive information from their environment. On the other hand, people who *acquire* vision impairment or

296

blindness later in life have had experiences not readily available to those with congenital impairment. For example, they may have attended a regular school, learnt to read, have concepts of colour, space and distance, and have a clear sense of their own body image.

As a child I had minimal object perception, but quite good colour perception; but now I have light perception only.

Rachael

The way in which the impairment is acquired also is important. Sudden blindness or vision impairment (as a result of an accident, for example) demands rapid changes to life and adjustments to lifestyle. Gradual acquisition (for example, through gradual deterioration) also requires changes to lifestyle, but these generally occur more gradually and the person has more time to adjust.

I believe it is better for a person to have experienced life in both situations, that is with and without a disability. It is impossible to 'throw the dice of life again', but my opinion is that it is better to acquire a disability later in life than earlier on as you will have had a chance to do things that otherwise you may not have been able to do.

Angus

As well as the practical implications of sight loss, people with vision impairment can experience the frustration of being able to see some things and not others. This can also be confusing for relatives, friends and visitors. For example, somebody with macular degeneration may be able to see something as small as a pin on the floor, using his or her peripheral vision, but will not be able to read. Such things can lead to distress, conflict and accusations of being a fraud.

It is important to recognise that limitations upon activity which are imposed by new vision loss are often compounded by other physical factors. Some of these may be related to the cause of the vision loss. Diabetes, for example, often carries with it other serious physical impairments. In most cases of vision loss in older people, compounding factors are characteristic of the general process of ageing.

Acquiring realistic expectations about future competencies is one of the most important aspects of adjustment to vision impairment. One of the best ways to establish this is to have early success at life-relevant tasks. A rehabilitation specialist may work with a person in setting achievable goals. By encouraging the person to work at tasks of increasing difficulty, the worker hopes to engender a feeling of effective functioning in the person. The perception of self-efficacy has an important motivation role in that it can encourage the person to strive for further successes. On the other hand, if the person withdraws from tasks for long periods or is placed in situations in which he or she feels incompetent, self-confidence will be lost.

Changes in sight after the age of 40 years are a typical part of ageing and most people need to adjust to these. By the age of 70, almost everyone needs glasses for reading. It becomes more difficult to see clearly at a distance and to focus on near objects. Many people need light to see well as they get older. Night driving becomes dangerous (Gething, 1990). These are all typical changes with ageing. However, in more severe cases of sight loss many adjustments and changes may be required to the person's lifestyle and activities. This may result in lower levels of confidence about going about everyday activities and a loss of independence. The person may feel reluctant to go out and feels safer at home, in a familiar environment.

A range of emotional responses are possible when a person becomes vision impaired. Some people take it very much in their stride, adjust their lives accordingly and move on. Others find it more difficult to accept. They may have to reappraise their whole life. Individuals may question who they are and how they think about themselves. In the absence of first-hand input from other people with a vision impairment about their experiences, a person with a new vision loss might accept stereotyped views of 'blind' people that are current in society. This may carry with it the connotation of someone who is generally perceived by sighted people to be helpless, worthy of pity, and unable to do very much to help himself or herself or others.

These stereotypes can initially limit a person with a new vision loss by causing him or her to have low self-expectations. Feelings of helplessness may also arise from the initial stages of sight loss, when simple everyday tasks may become difficult. This combination of negative views about capabilities of people who are vision impaired, combined with the experience of finding daily tasks difficult in the initial stages, can lead to depression and loss of self-esteem. Coupled with this may be anxiety because the person is searching for unambiguous information about the impairment and professionals feel unable to commit themselves to a definite prognosis.

There may be uncertainty about the future and particularly about what the person might be able to do. Not knowing about possible options can create considerable anxiety. A whole range of painful feelings can follow, including feelings of worthlessness and uselessness. Some people may even wish they were dead and away from it all. At this stage, it is critical for a person to gain some positive information about possibilities. The person may or may not want to act on it immediately, but it is imperative for him or her to know what options are available and what ways there are of moving forward.

> *Before I became blind, I was involved in many sports and was working as a labourer. My car accident meant that I could not participate in these sports or this kind of work any more.*
>
> Angus, who became vision impaired after a car accident

Sight loss impairs the individual's ability to interact in a visual way with the environment and hampers the performance of even the simplest of everyday tasks. Inability to drive a car represents a significant setback, particularly for a person with acquired disability who has been used to having this form of mobility and its associated freedom. Vision impairment and blindness can have major effects on daily routines and on a person's independence and flexibility. Most people without a disability take for granted their ability to go where, when and how they want to go. For those who are blind or vision impaired the choice is limited if they do not have skills necessary for travelling with little or no sight.

Myths and misconceptions abound about the concepts of getting 'old' and 'being blind'. Many older people internalise inaccurate beliefs and myths. These, combined with visual loss, make it difficult to cope successfully with the changes that are required. Negative feelings of older people with vision impairment may reduce their motivation and make them resistant to rehabilitation services.

Some people with an acquired disability become less able to carry on activities outside the home which once were simple everyday events. Now these activities not only take more time but serve as reminders of vision impairment and provide a source of frustration. Not only is the person's confidence in the ability to control his/her world shaken, but a certain propensity toward social isolation may develop. Furthermore, by not practising activities, a person's skills may become 'rusty', further decreasing feelings of confidence.

Falling confidence can particularly be a problem for an older person who has acquired a vision impairment as a result of the ageing process. This person finds himself or herself no longer able to do things the way they were done before. It may no longer be possible to drive a car; the person may be restricted to reading large-print books, and so on.

Ability to read is one of the most notable of the daily functions drastically reduced by vision loss. Reading plays a large role in modern life and many people with vision impairment say that inability to read is one of the most difficult aspects of their impairment. Some people have mastered braille, a system of writing in which raised dots on a page represent letters and words. But not all written materials are available in braille and not all people with a vision impairment are able to read it.

Strategies for receiving information

Sight is the sense we use to confirm information gained from other senses. Loss of sight means the person has to rely on information gained in other ways. It is widely believed that people with vision impairment automatically develop greater acuteness in hearing, touch and smell. This is not the case. The ability to make maximum use of other senses has to be learned.

Adaptations may be required to assist communication. Vision impairment means missing many non-verbal cues. Although the voice plays a large part in conversation, much is communicated on the visual level. When these cues are unavailable, the quality of the exchange is jeopardised.

Vision impairment also results in the loss of access to detailed information such as reading printed text, or locating items in a work situation or at home.

> *Access to information will always be difficult as alternative formats are not always available. Portability of adaptive technology is not possible at the present time. Perhaps in the future lap-tops and closed circuit television with scanners will be hand-held. Until then, dream on!*
>
> Angus

Two strategies may be used to assist the person in receiving information – these are vision enhancement (see Figure 16.1) and sight substitution techniques. Which one is used depends on whether the person has remaining vision or not. Some people are able to use a combination of these two.

Vision enhancement

This involves maximising the use of any remaining vision. It can be achieved through appropriate use of lighting, colour and size. For two major reasons, people with a vision impairment (and particularly older people) require higher levels of illumination. Firstly, less of the light entering the eye actually gets to the retina and secondly, some people require a short viewing distance which increases the likelihood of head shadow being thrown on to whatever is being observed. Good lighting avoids glare, is bright and is tailored to the task and the individual. There are a few exceptions to the lighting principle. Some people with cataracts do not find it useful and, in some less common eye disorders, moderate to high levels of

Figure 16.1: Enlarged print on a computer screen enables this man to do his job
Reproduced with permission of the Royal Blind Society.

light can cause discomfort. Nevertheless, a majority of older people and those with a vision impairment require more light to attain best vision.

Important ways to provide light to assist with tasks are as follows.

Whole-room lighting. This can be provided by daylight, by ceiling, floor-standing or wall-mounted electric lights or by a combination of these various sources. Its purpose is to maintain sufficient background light for seeing to take place and for objects and surfaces around to be visible at a distance. The level of light should be even from area to area and from one room to another, since many people with a vision impairment are unable to adapt or adjust quickly to changes in light levels. Even light levels are particularly important where there are potential obstacles such as furniture, stairs or steps.

Local lighting. This is for specific tasks and is designed to provide a relatively high level of light selectively on a visual task and from the appropriate direction. Adjustable reading lamps are ideal for this purpose.

Natural light. This is often overlooked as a source of lighting. Natural light with glare eliminated by venetian blinds can aid a person's ability to carry out detailed tasks. To make most use of it, the person should sit with his or her back to the window to allow light to fall on to working material.

Colour contrast. This means increasing the difference in colour between an object and its background so that the object becomes more visible. Contrast will often be the main ingredient in improving the visibility of objects and their detail. There are many ways of manipulating contrast in everyday life so that a person can see better. Some examples of contrasts are:

- contrasting edging strips on steps, especially outside the home;
- light switches and wall sockets which contrast with walls;
- dark food on a light plate and vice versa;
- a dark cup to hold light fluids and vice versa.

Size. This can be used to assist people with a vision impairment by increasing the apparent size of objects in the environment and of detail in visual tasks. The principle of apparent size can be put to use in one or all three of the following ways: relative distance, magnification, optical magnification and enlargement.

- Relative distance magnification entails making something appear to be larger by bringing it closer to the eye. This is probably the simplest of all aids to vision. Close viewing cannot strain or harm the eye in any way, although there is a limit to the smallest distance at which the lens of the eye can bring an image into sharp focus on the retina. When focusing on near objects for long periods, the muscles of the eye will tend to fatigue like any other muscle in the body. If this happens it is only necessary to close the eyes for a while until the muscles recover. Relative distance magnification works very well for such tasks as watching TV.
- Optical magnification depends on using lenses which come in a range of sizes and can be mounted in different ways, depending on the purpose for which they are to be used. Some important points to remember:
  - Big is not necessarily best. The bigger the magnifier, the smaller the degree of magnification. The highest-powered magnifiers are relatively small in diameter.
  - Cheaper magnifiers may produce distortions, particularly around the edges of the lens.
  - The lens must be held the correct distance from the task for it to be in focus. Some magnifiers incorporate a stand so they can be easily used at a predetermined distance.
  - Magnifiers are task-specific.
- Enlargement works by increasing the actual size of an object or the critical detail in a visual task. Large print is probably the best example of this.

Sight substitution techniques

These techniques may be useful for a person with vision impairment who has no useful remaining vision or where the vision is useful for some tasks but not for others. Where possible, substitution would include hearing, smell and touch. A planned rehabilitation program is usually required and would include developing other senses to the best of the person's ability. For some people substitution may not be possible because of other disabilities such as hearing loss. Sight substitution techniques include marking equipment such as stoves or microwaves with raised dots or other tactile material; alternative formats – adaptive technology, talking books and newspapers; and (for some people) braille.

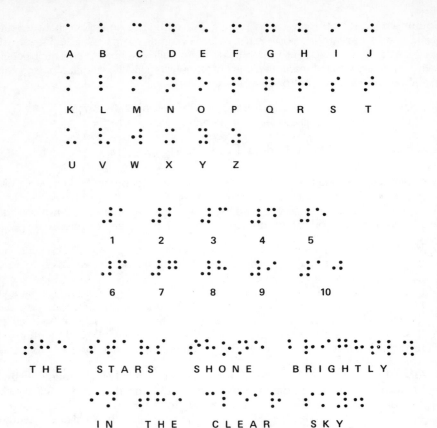

Figure 16.2: A braille key

Braille is a system in which characters are represented by raised dots. It is produced by a special machine and read by running the fingers over the page. A sample page is displayed in Figure 16.2. Not all people who are blind or vision impaired learn braille because it may not be suitable for their lifestyle or they may have reduced sensation in their fingers. Braille versions of many items are available, including computers and scrabble boards. Most organisations for visually impaired and blind people have a library of braille books which were originally published in print form.

The Kurzweil reader gives people with vision impairment access to materials that others can read using their sight. It has a voice synthesiser which converts the printed word into electronic speech. Other aids and equipment available for use by people with vision impairment are described later in the chapter.

Sexuality

Vision impairment does not interfere with sexual functioning and reproduction. It may, however, create difficulties in meeting and getting to know a partner. Many people with vision impairment can be mistaken as being sighted in a brief encounter. The other person may interpret them as being rude if they do not respond to an outstretched hand or a friendly smile. Eye contact is usually very important in the early stages of a relationship. For example, without eye contact, flirting is difficult. It also is difficult to make the first move. Without sight, a person cannot tell who looks attractive and whether the other person already has a partner.

In large groups of people, say at parties, it is often difficult for a person with vision impairment to work out who is speaking and when to join in the conversation. People with severe congenital visual impairment need to be taught appropriate social skills, such as looking at a person when speaking to them, standing upright and maintaining appropriate body posture. There is no other way that these people can learn such culturally-accepted behaviours as they cannot directly observe them. These conventions are important and may act as a barrier for the person in getting to know others and in attracting a partner.

Toleno (1994) discusses the strategies she used to help herself find her sexual identity. She argues that, as a child, she was taught that feeling herself and other people was unacceptable. Because of this, she was denied access to one of the major ways available to a person who is blind to find out about the world. It also created difficulty in understanding about her sexuality and gender. She argues that coming to accept her sexuality was an important step in coming to feel whole and complete. In her article she discusses how she learnt the skill of flirting. She realised that visual cues were of no use to her. However, with practice she learned to use verbal cues to take the place of methods of visual attraction that are commonly used to start a relationship.

Being a parent

In addition to the typical responsibilities associated with parenting, a parent who is blind or vision impaired may have other dimensions to consider. Knowing where a child is and what he or she is doing is achieved by focusing on the development of good verbal communication skills between parent and child. Participating in or taking children to activities involves extra planning and preparation. Approaching the activity in another way, examining how it is going to be done, how to get there, and what to expect on arrival are all examples of planning issues which must be considered to ensure that both parent and child feel confident and are likely to enjoy the activity.

Family

I consider myself extremely lucky for my ability to make friends and keep them. These friends, along with a super-supportive family are the most important tools that any person with a disability could ask for.

Angus

For all people (whether with or without a disability) attitudes towards independence or dependence largely result from influences of the family, friends, employers, and other important people. Family attitudes are important in determining how a person who is blind or has a vision impairment views his or her own capabilities. The more difficulties parents have in accepting their child who is vision impaired, the harder it will be for the child to accept him/herself and to understand realistic limits imposed by blindness or visual impairment. Parental attitudes and interactions with the child are of central importance in moulding the child's immediate and future attitudes toward vision impairment, toward him/herself and toward the environment. Similar factors apply to the adjustment of someone with acquired impairment.

Attitudes of other family members also significantly influence how the individual perceives him/herself and have an effect on the development of life strategies. Vision impairment, like any other disability, affects more than just the individual. It has implications for the whole family, especially parents, siblings and grandparents. All members are required to make adjustments. People vary widely in their reactions and in the ways they adjust to new situations. Some family members will find the challenges easier to deal with than will others.

> *My parents took quite differing views of how to handle my acquired blindness. My mother tended to blame herself; however, she was supportive both emotionally and physically. It also was my mother who was the main motivating force that pushed be towards such organisations as the Commonwealth Rehabilitation Service and the Royal Guide Dogs for the Blind. My father tended to lack patience. In reflection, I am sure that Dad would not have realised how hard it was for me not being able to be independent.*
>
> Angus

The origin of the vision impairment can have an impact on the way parents react. Was the vision impairment congenital or did it occur later in the child's development? Was it an acquired loss from a traumatic accident, or the result of a later onset visual diagnosis, such as retinitis pigmentosa (a major cause of deteriorating vision in adolescents)? Important factors are: when in the child's life the vision impairment was diagnosed, the degree of impairment and its prognosis.

Some of the emotional responses experienced by parents and family members on the birth of a child with a congenital impairment include feelings of guilt, grief, resentment, anger, shock and denial. Some parents may feel a sense of powerlessness in the face of confusing or contradictory information and what may be a large group of concerned people who regularly invade their lives or their home. All parents have expectations and fantasies about their child before birth. There are hopes and dreams about who the child will resemble, what she or he will achieve, and what part she or he will play in the family. The birth of a child with a disability (particularly if unanticipated) is likely to shatter all these dreams.

> *After the loss of sight in my second eye I think it was traumatic for (my family). My parents, in fact, wanted to move from the country to the city to take care of me while I was undergoing rehabilitation; I don't know whether they thought I would need constant care.*
>
> Angelo

The reactions of some families may be influenced by negative associations and stereotypes to which they may have subscribed for many years. Such stereotypes and beliefs must be challenged when families are faced with raising a child who is blind or vision impaired.

Although members of the medical and health professions have become more sensitive to the needs and feelings of family members, insensitive and extensive questioning may reinforce feelings of guilt and grief, rather than allay anxieties and negative reactions. The parents, in turn, can subject those same professionals or themselves to intense and angry cross examination. 'What did I do wrong? What did I take during the pregnancy? Why didn't the doctor notice earlier and why couldn't he or she have done something?' Mothers particularly blame themselves and fathers can often imply criticism of their partners. The extended family may become involved in a process of fault finding. The parents may have a sense of shame about revealing that they have a child with a disability, and may try to hide the news from other family members.

These types of responses can become harmful to the growth of self-esteem in the child. Guilt and anger are common reactions in the grief process, and the extent to which they affect family relationships or individual members will depend on the presence of other unresolved issues. For example, strong guilt may be experienced by the mother who sees her child's disability as a punishment from some previous misdemeanour.

However, it should be noted that there are various forms of support and counselling available to assist parents, and other family members. Many parents report as helpful supportive networks of people who share the same experiences. From these networks they often gain a bonding to others whom they feel have similar experiences. These groups can also become involved in advocating for needed services, thereby becoming a positive influence for the child as well as the parent. Other parents may benefit from individual or couples counselling to help them in their adjustment process.

Children who are blind or vision impaired, have many advantages when they grow up in a family with other children. The child can be part of family activities and games which the other children play. Siblings are usually quick to recognise that their sister or brother with vision impairment needs auditory or tactile information, or some modification/adjustment to their play activities. Many adults who are blind or vision impaired express appreciation that they were able to play with their siblings at home and join in with other children in the neighbourhood. In a group they were able to venture into areas or to participate in activities which perhaps their parents may not have permitted them to do on their own.

However, like parents, sometimes siblings may respond to the child by overprotectiveness. A brother or sister may insist on always leading a blind or vision impaired sibling around or actually preventing the child from mixing with peers by monopolising his or her attention. Parents may find these behaviours easy to ignore, without realising that they tend to reduce the opportunities for the child with a disability to develop independence.

Sometimes, siblings may react negatively to a brother or sister who is blind or vision impaired, especially if they perceive their brother or sister is receiving more attention than themselves. Rivalries may occur and siblings may develop attention-seeking behaviours which affect family life. Sighted siblings may also view medical appointments, hospital and school visits as additional or special attention given to their brother or sister. Parents can counter this by trying to balance attention and time spent with each child as much as possible. Siblings should be encouraged to express their concerns, fears, irritations and other feelings with their parents to enable a broader understanding of the issues, and correction of misperceptions and beliefs. In the same way that parents may benefit from support groups, sibling support groups may be an avenue for meeting other children of a similar age to discuss feelings with others seen to have similar experiences.

After the family has progressed through the early years and learnt to manage the medical, rehabilitative and educational systems, the next major challenge it to allow the child who is blind or vision impaired to begin to separate from the parents and to develop and test his or her independence. The tasks of adolescence relating to independence, development of sexuality and identity are made more complex by the presence of a vision impairment. Overprotectiveness is a common response of families to the demands of an adolescent seeking more independence. Often negotiations are required to achieve compromise solutions between parents and the adolescent. Both parents and the young person will need to take risks, but these can be structured so as to engender confidence in both the parents and the adolescent. Training in mobility and the general tasks of daily living can assist the adolescent in the development of necessary skills, while offering reassurance to parents.

Family expectations regarding what are seen to be the likely achievements of their child will affect outcomes. Parents who do not believe that a person with a vision impairment can learn to travel independently or cook for him or herself will not encourage or facilitate their child's learning of such skills. Alternatively, parents who deny the extent of the vision loss may encourage their child to believe he or she is ready for difficult tasks when he or she is not. The young person is then put under stress to prove him or herself. Role models can be helpful for families seeking some guidance as to expectations. Competent adults who are blind or vision impaired can help to allay the fears of parents and young people.

The person who loses sight as an adult also needs a great deal of support and has many adjustments to make. He or she may go through long periods of depression. It may be difficult for the family to understand or to act appropriately. For example, blindness resulting from diabetes may fluctuate, sometimes it is worse than at other times. If the family does not understand this, they may think the person is 'faking' or being manipulative.

Community living

As with other disabilities, often the greatest handicap facing the person is the attitudes of others. Vision impairment and blindness tend to be perceived within our society as overwhelming and tragic, so that disability is the first and sometimes the only characteristic used to describe a person. Others see the blindness or vision impairment, but not the person. They may believe that people with vision impairment are completely helpless, incapable of performing the simplest tasks, have no interest in or knowledge of everyday affairs, are unable to speak for themselves and have to be addressed through a third person.

These reactions and beliefs may reflect the fact that most people rely on sight as their major way of obtaining information about the world. Therefore, any thought of loss of sight is met with dread and fear. People do not realise that it is possible to deal with the world successfully without the full use of sight.

Many changes have occurred in our society. Most people now are fully aware that people with disabilities are human beings who have feelings, thoughts and reactions. But quite often, others think these must be different than those for everyone else – feelings, thoughts, and experiences that characterise others are assumed to be impossible for someone who cannot see. As a result, people who are blind and vision impaired may be treated as objects, as something different from the rest of the human race. This can lead to severe frustration for these people. Sighted people often assume that help is needed and insist on helping, regardless of what the person wants. Many members of the community are not knowledgeable about how people deal with their vision impairment. Such ignorance may

Figure 16.3: Eye contact is not necessary for these two people to enjoy their conversation

engender fear which – fed by personal experiences such as power blackouts, wearing blindfolds, or walking down a dark alley – are misrepresentations in that such experiences do not accurately represent the state of having a vision impairment.

> *My girlfriend and I have been together for almost nine years. Our relationship started just before my car accident. She never once questioned our relationship or our possible future together because of my disability. I think it has never crossed her mind.*
>
> Angus

Access

This is an important issue which extends well beyond the physical environment. Public buildings should have prominent, easy-to-read notices stating the name of the building and the nature of the activities therein. The entrance should be clearly identified. Good overall lighting assists the person, as do contrasting signs which give directions and clearly marked danger areas.

Access to information is important to keep open channels which allow participation in the community. Providing such access involves making material available in various formats, including large print, audio tape, machine readable format (for example, computers with large print displays or speech synthesis capabilities). Radio for the Print Handicapped is a medium through which those who are blind and vision impaired can access news and other information. Access will be further improved through technological advances, such as the production of 'talking newspapers'.

Mobility and independent travel

For most people with a visual impairment, loss of sight will be a gradual process. Despite the frustration and difficulties experienced, the majority will continue managing in their own homes and will feel in control of their lives. Generally people will work out their own answers to the practical problems posed in getting around the house as sight diminishes. Help from a mobility specialist may be required if the person moves to a new environment.

> *I was really proud the first time I went down to the local shopping centre and bought fish and chips! I rang up my parents to tell them.*
>
> Angelo

People with a vision impairment can be independently mobile inside and outside the home, no matter how limited their vision is. Some people maintain enough vision for safe travel. Other people require specialist training to help them travel safely outdoors. Training will include developing the other senses where possible, to help with orientation and learning how to use mobility equipment. For the majority of travellers with vision impairment, a cane is the favoured mobility aid. The cane is used as an extension of the person's arm and is moved from side to side in an arch about the width of the user's body. The idea of the cane is that it detects information in advance, so that the user can stop at obstacles and take appropriate action without injury. Used with skill, the cane will detect kerbs, steps and pavement obstacles. Training can involve anything from route-specific travel to generalised travel, including use of public transport such as trains, from locating correct train platforms, boarding trains and buses, and recognising destinations. It can take someone with a severe sight loss three to four months of regular tuition to become a safe outdoor traveller.

White walking sticks are used by some people for mobility. They are a means of providing support and indicate to others that the user is vision impaired. Guide dogs are used by some people with vision impairment. Their choice will depend on the person's level of vision, skill and frequency of travel.

The built environment assumes sight is present and so is not designed for people with vision impairment. Thus, frequently it is the environment that imposes limits on vision impaired people, not the skills of the travellers.

Public transport in most metropolitan areas is currently provided free to people classified as legally blind. As with any people using public transport, people with vision impairment may find travel time is greater than with private transport. As a result, such travellers may experience unnecessary delays, injury, disorientation, or dependence on sighted people for assistance. It is important that people who are blind or vision impaired have good access to, and confidence in, the use of public transport systems so that they can carry out their daily activities independently, safely and efficiently and thus maintain their quality of life. People who are blind or vision impaired require information about which platforms to use, where to find timetables, how to work out route changes, or how to arrange connections with country services. For the benefit of those with some useful vision, symbols should be clear and consistent, and signs should be of adequate size and well illuminated.

I keep my cane in my knapsack. I find it useful when I am trying to impress upon a stranger that I cannot read the train timetable – my cane helps to identify that I have special needs.

Angus

The issue of safety is also a major consideration. People who are blind or vision impaired may not necessarily be immediately aware of dangers or ways of dealing with threatening situations should they arise. Taxi transport is often a viable or preferred option; however, it increases the cost of travel.

Education

The choice of mainstreamed (integration into a regular school) or special education depends on many factors. More and more children who are blind or vision impaired are being integrated into their local schools (see Figure 16.4). A regular education enables the child to share similar experiences to sighted children and further opportunities to gather a group of friends who live in the neighbourhood.

Limited access to information can influence acquisition of skills unless special strategies are employed. It is generally accepted that 85 per cent of learning involves the use of sight. A teacher cannot draw a triangle on a board and expect a child with vision impairment to understand what it is. It must be described verbally and by using a cut-out triangle so that the child can feel the shape. The child who does not receive such additional forms of input will have more difficulty at school.

Figure 16.4: A braille machine is used by a student at school

The young child with a vision impairment must learn in a non-visual way to process information, if he or she is to understand about the world. This requires early education which emphasises use of tactile and verbal input. Ongoing assistance is available for children with vision impairments who attend regular schools. Within government schools and some schools within the private school system there are support teachers specially trained in the educational needs of children who are blind or vision impaired.

Possibly the greatest disadvantage of a mainstream class is that children may not get sufficient verbal or tactile input to facilitate the learning process; however, specially-trained resource teachers and consultants work to ensure such limitations are minimised. The advantages of a special school lie in that they teach specific skills such as learning braille and spatial awareness.

> *There were definite disadvantages in attending my local school rather than attending a special school for blind kids. As there were no special facilities for me I found that I had to work a lot harder than the other kids and there were some things which I could not follow in the classroom. Also I was not taught braille. The definite advantages were, however, that I was exposed to a wide variety of experiences both socially and academically that I felt I wouldn't have had in a special school. In short, although my early education was not ideal, given the same circumstances again, I would still choose to do it the same way.*
>
> Rachael, who has a genetic form of blindness

Many of the classes at university are of little use to the student who is blind or vision impaired, unless appropriate technology is made available. There are now many students with severe vision impairment attending tertiary institutions. They may require special provisions such as recording facilities or permission to tape lectures. Most universities and colleges have staff whose role is to facilitate learning for students with disabilities. Equal opportunity in education officers are responsible for ensuring equity of access to education and to the campus on which the student is located.

> *I found it not very productive to sit in a class where all the notes were being written on the board. I studied with very limited technological resources. I think I only attended about 20 per cent of the classes because it was not worth my time.*
>
> Angus

The student has to find new strategies for learning information.

> *Being blind has slowed down my rate of work, especially reading, writing and clerical tasks. This has meant I have had to work longer hours.*
>
> Angus

Employment

People who have a severe vision impairment are just as interested as other people in having satisfying careers, professions and jobs. There are lawyers, counsellors, computer programmers, information and training officers, composers, musicians and singers who are blind. Prevalent stereotypes exist in the community about appropriate jobs for people who are blind or have a vision impairment. There are some limits, but it is up to the individual to determine what these are. People should not be stereotyped by placement into jobs such as telephonist, dictaphone typist or darkroom technician. A wide range of technical equipment and support is available to assist people in carrying out their jobs and in pursuing study and a career.

> *When I got my first job, I was put on a three-month training period. I can remember the first day: I was terrified. I thought, 'What will I do? I can't make mistakes because they will get rid of me'. However, the people were fantastic and reacted to me quite well.*
>
> Jan

The key to successful continued employment or re-employment is to match the capabilities of the individual with appropriate opportunities. Vocational education within the general community is limited for people who are vision impaired or blind. This can reduce their expectations in relation to potential employment. It is important that people who experience severe vision loss as adults undertake an assessment of their personal potential for continuing employment or of being re-employed in another capacity. There are many opportunities for retraining which exist in the community.

Access to training and employment opportunities is often enhanced by the use of technology. The development of adaptive technology and its wider availability in the last few years have broadened employment opportunities for people who are

Figure 16.5: The advent of electronic equipment has opened up many opportunities for people with severe vision impairment

vision impaired or blind. These opportunities are generally dependent upon the use of computers which have been modified to host software which facilitates access to information through either large print or speech output. The ability of the individual to gain employment is greatly dependent upon successful completion of training in the use of the most appropriate adaptive technology device.

Accommodation

A house or apartment may require modification and this can be costly. Provision of adequate lighting and ensuring that surfaces have appropriate contrast are among the changes that may be necessary.

> *I didn't really understand, and my parents didn't either, what my degree of sight loss was. I know now that as a child I had about 2 per cent vision; but at the time I thought that I probably had about 50 per cent of normal vision. This may sound a bit strange but when you don't have any concept of what full vision is, it is hard to judge what you're experiencing in relation to what is usual. This sometimes caused anxiety in me because I wasn't really sure if difficulties I experienced were related to my blindness or not.*
>
> Rachael

PERSON TO PERSON

Appropriate language and behaviour

Listening and understanding the person's feelings are essential. A specialist worker may assist the person to realise that people with vision impairment can, and do, live independently. Exploring the key tasks that have been lost and working with the person to discover how these can be restored, paves the way to restoring power.

Adults with a vision impairment already have a history of dealing with difficulties presented by life. One helpful strategy is to explore the positive resources that were useful in past situations. This can remind the person that he or she has effectively overcome problems before and can do so again using similar strategies.

A vision impairment may impose certain limitations. Limitations are individual. Remember not to generalise. People who are blind or vision impaired come from different sections of the community and from varying age groups, so too they have different characteristics, tastes and interests.

Members of the community still do not understand the capabilities of people who are severely vision impaired or blind, underestimating skills in mobility and in carrying out everyday tasks. Most people with these disabilities can recall incidents where someone has stepped in to assist without asking first. This can be frustrating and annoying. It also can be disorienting and dangerous for a person who has been 'helped' to get to a place they had no intention of going and from where they do not know the way back. People who are blind or vision impaired do not appreciate your expressions of sympathy or your signs of amazement when they perform the ordinary activities of daily living. Remember that what is sometimes attributed to a sixth sense is often simply common sense.

Dealing with printed and written materials is difficult or impossible for many people who are blind or vision impaired. They must rely on others to read aloud to them or have the material transcribed in some way (for example, into braille, audio tape, large print, or machine-readable format). When generic service providers write a letter to a person who is blind or vision impaired, they should keep in mind that it might not be read immediately. When it is read, others might see its contents. For private messages or for pressing matters, the telephone may be a better medium. Generic services could also consider offering their message by audiotape rather than in writing. Many vision-impaired people greatly appreciate receiving mail in this form because they can enjoy it at their leisure, unassisted and in private. If a conventional letter is sent, it should be typed or written in dark ink. Use plain stationery.

Generic services should consider making commonly-used written materials available in another medium. For example, pamphlets, business brochures and timetables could be printed in braille or recorded on audio tape for the benefit of patrons who are vision impaired.

Strategies for successful interaction

When communicating with someone who has a severe visual impairment it is important to treat the person as you would any other person, only taking into consideration the fact that the person has impaired vision. Much of our everyday interaction with those around us relies on gesture, facial expression and eye-to-eye contact. Vision impairment can prevent these subtle communication forms. Some easy tips can help:

- Introduce yourself and others to the person by name.
- When first approaching the person, give your name before you start a conversation. Never play 'guess who' games as this can be extremely annoying.
- Always indicate when leaving or ending a conversation.
- Try to accompany non-verbal greetings with the appropriate words.
- In a group, it may be necessary to cue a person into the conversation by mentioning his or her name or touching the person lightly on the arm.
- People who are vision impaired do not mind if you talk about watching television or use expressions such as 'you see'.

Mobility

Associations for people who are blind or vision impaired have staff available to teach techniques for guiding. Most people with vision impairment will explain to you how to guide them. The following suggestions should be followed:

- Let the person take your arm, do not grab him or her.
- Keep your arm relaxed and by your side.
- He or she will walk about half a step behind you.
- When you come to steps, curbs or narrow spaces, identify them and guide the person across.
- When showing the person to a seat, place his or her hand on the back of the chair and state which way it is facing. She or he will do the rest.
- Do not shout, the person probably has adequate hearing.
- When getting into a car, tell the person if he or she is to sit in the front or back. Put his or her hand on the top of the door or door opening and let the person settle him or herself in.

- When guiding a person, give concise and accurate verbal information; for example, 'You are approaching steps'.

The measure of being a decent friend can sometimes be a simple task such as showing me where the nearest toilet is when we go to a hotel for the first time. The people who point me in the general direction and tell me it's on the other side of a crowded room don't understand the problem.

Angus

Some additional suggestions are:

- Do not leave the room without letting the person know, because he or she may continue to talk to an empty space. When you first enter a room, speak so the person knows you are there.
- Keep floors free of clutter. Let the person know if furniture has been moved and do not move personal belongings without first letting the person know.
- If there is a stain or smudge on his or her clothes, tell the person discreetly. Such help is usually appreciated.
- If the person with a vision impairment has a guide dog, do not feed or pat the dog without the owner's permission. You may distract the animal from its work.

It is important to remember that each person is an individual who has been shaped by a unique set of experiences and has individual qualities. All people (whether they have a disability or not) should be given the freedom and flexibility to function as independently as possible.

MORE INFORMATION ABOUT VISUAL IMPAIRMENT AND BLINDNESS

According to the World Health Organization (WHO) there are over 65 different and acceptable definitions of blindness. Following the WHO (1980) definition, in the case of vision loss:

- *Impairment* refers to some form of limitation of one or more of the basic components of the visual system. These components include the parts of the eye, optic nerve and visual centre in the brain.
- *Disability* is the lack, loss or reduction of the individual's ability to perform certain tasks such as reading, writing, travelling and so on.
- *Handicap* is associated with social and environmental factors and results in disadvantage in areas such as education, employment, leisure and recreation.

There are many causes of sight loss, all of which lead to varying degrees of vision impairment. The amount of sight that 'legally blind' people have varies considerably between individuals. In general, low vision can arise from either poor visual acuity and/or loss of visual field.

Visual acuity

Visual acuity is a measurement which reflects the eye's ability to see at both near and far distances and to distinguish detail and shape. Each eye has its own level of visual acuity. In Australia, normal vision is recorded as 6/6 which means that a person can read at 6 metres what someone should be able to read at 6 metres. The

Table 16.1: Strategies for successful interaction

Person who is blind or vision impaired	Other person
Be patient when offered assistance. When accepting assistance, express your requirements clearly and explain to the person the appropriate way to help you. Be mindful of the intentions of sighted people. Their offers of help, although sometimes misguided, are usually well meant and should be accepted or refused on this basis.	Always introduce yourself by name, even if you know the person well. Ask if the person wants assistance; do not assume that it is needed. Never grab the person as this could be very frightening. Accept the person's decision if your offer of help is declined. Always address the person directly, not through a third person. People who are blind or vision impaired can speak. If assistance is accepted, let the person tell you how and in what way you can help. When addressing a person, a light touch on the arm or back of the hand indicates where you are and that you are speaking to him or her. Do not hesitate to use words like 'see', 'look' and 'read'. People who are visually impaired use these words too.

top part of the fraction represents the testing distance in metres. The bottom part of the fraction represents the smallest line of characters that can be read on the vision chart. Therefore, if someone has a visual acuity of 6/60 this means that at 6 metres the person can read the line of letters that a fully sighted person can read at 60 metres.

In Australia, a person with vision below 6/60 in both eyes is classified as legally blind for the purpose of receiving the Department of Social Security Blind Pension and the Visually Impaired Person's Travel Pass. In the United States, blindness is defined in terms of what a person can see at 200 feet (60 metres) as compared with a person with normal vision. Under this classification, 'legal blindness' occurs when distance visual acuity is 20/200 or less (Boyd & Otos, 1981).

Visual field

A visual field refers to the width or breadth of vision. It is the area that can be seen with the eyes fixed, looking directly ahead. The normal visual field is approximately 170 degrees (an angle of 85 degrees on each side of a central line.

A visual field of less than 10 degrees may be manifested in the form of tunnel vision (like looking though a tube); that is, only a small area, directly ahead, can be seen. It also can be manifested in peripheral vision; that is, where the person cannot see ahead but can see only a small area on either side. The person who has peripheral vision has a greater potential for spatial awareness and generally has less difficulty with mobility than a person with tunnel vision. It may be difficult to identify these people as 'blind' since they appear to move around freely.

Tunnel vision often leads to night blindness, sensitivity to glare and problems with orientation and mobility. For example, a person may be trying to cross a road and can see to the other side but is unable to see a vehicle approaching unless he or she turns the head to look directly at the vehicle.

The mechanism of sight

The eye is a very complex structure and only a brief description of its structure and function can be given here (see Figure 16.6 for a diagram of the eye). It lies in the orbital socket and is cushioned in fat and protected by the eyelids. It is moved by externally-attached muscles and supplied with nourishment by arteries, with waste products being taken away by veins and lymph vessels. It is directed by nerves. The optic nerve which connects the eye to the central nervous system is not really a nerve, but a stalk of the brain (Nisbett, 1973).

Interference or damage may be repaired if it occurs in the front of the eye, but usually not if it occurs in the back of the eye, optic nerve or brain.

The *outer eye* comprises three layers. The outer layer is the fibrous layer and is made up of three parts which are directly continuous: the sclera, which is strong, tough and maintains the shape of the eye; the conjunctiva, or the white of the eye; and the cornea which is the transparent part in front of the eye.

The middle layer is the vascular pigmented coat and comprises, from behind forwards, the choroid, ciliary body and iris.

The inner layer is the nervous layer or retina, and is composed of nerve cells and nerve fibres. There are two types of nerve cells: rods and cones. Rods are sensitive to dim light, respond to movement and record black-and-white images; cones react to bright light, distinguish colours and record coloured vision. Each rod and cone is attached to a nerve fibre. These nerve fibres pass to the back of the eye

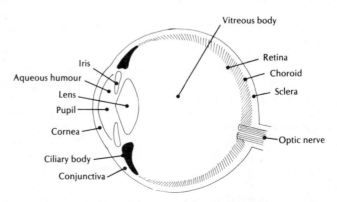

Figure 16.6: Cross-sectional diagram of the eye

to form the optic nerve which connects with the occipital lobes of the brain. Here signals from the rods and cones are interpreted into images.

The *inner eye* is comprised of the vitreous body, a transparent gel filling the back two-thirds of the eye; the lens which focuses light rays on to the retina and is concerned with visual acuity; and the aqueous humour, a small amount of liquid which provides nourishment to the front of the eye.

When the eye is functioning normally, light rays striking the cornea are refracted on to the lens and focused on to the retina to stimulate the rods and cones, thereby initiating the nerve impulses. These are transmitted by the optic nerve to the brain to be registered as a visual image. Any interference with this mechanism will result in impaired vision.

Causes

Vision impairment and blindness can affect people of all ages, and can be inherited, congenital or acquired after birth.

Inherited. Vision impairment or blindness transmitted through a genetic pattern may or may not be present at birth. For example, retinitis pigmentosa, which is an inherited, degenerative condition affecting the retina (nerve cell layer in the eye). Often the first symptom is night blindness, followed by narrowing of side vision and leading to tunnel vision (Stopford, 1988). Its symptoms may occur at any age, but are most likely to emerge in late childhood and early adulthood.

Congenital. Vision impairment is present from birth and can be the result of maternal disease such as rubella during early pregnancy, infections, lack of oxygen during birth, fetal development abnormalities, bilateral cataract, tumours, infantile glaucoma and albinism.

Acquired after birth. Sight loss during the course of life can be the result of:

- trauma – to produce vision impairment this must affect both eyes. More frequently, one eye is injured resulting in corneal laceration, detached retina and/or haemorrhage, all of which are conditions which may produce severe visual loss in the affected eye. Apart from loss of binocular vision which interferes with perception of depth, loss of vision in one eye does not require major adjustments to lifestyle;
- burns from direct sun rays, solar blindness or indirect rays (reflection from sun, snow blindness);
- burns to the face from explosions (for example, accidents with fireworks);
- burns from contact with chemicals such as strong acids or alkalis;
- infections such as keratitis and trachoma;
- tumours of either the eyes or the brain;
- glaucoma;
- systemic diseases – diabetes mellitus is the leading cause of vision loss in people aged 20 to 75 years and is described in more detail below. Onset can be sudden and reflects damage to the retina resulting from long-term diabetes and high blood pressure (hypertension);
- age-related conditions such as macular degeneration.

Eye conditions affecting children. Causes of vision impairment and blindness in children are varied, the most common being albinism, cataracts, retinopathy of prematurity, optic nerve atrophy, and a group of conditions related to brain damage or malformation. Vision impairment may be either a single disability or part of a multiple disability, as when associated with such conditions as cerebral palsy, hearing loss or intellectual disability.

Common causes of sight loss in adults. There are four main causes of sight loss in adults: diabetic retinopathy, cataracts, macular degeneration and glaucoma (Naeyaert, 1990).

Diabetic retinopathy is a condition caused by diabetes. Over a long period of time, diabetes can cause damage to the blood vessels in the eye. Blood vessels become weak and leak fluid into the back of the eye. Diabetic retinopathy can be treated by surgery, but where this is unsuccessful, damage to vision can occur, ranging from blurred vision, patchy losses of field to total blindness. A problem for people with this type of loss is that their vision does not always stay constant. As a result, a person may be able to perform some tasks visually at some times during the day, but not at others. Practical difficulties can range from reading and writing to orientation and mobility, depending on the severity of the loss.

A *cataract* is a clouding of the lens in the eye. It is most frequently seen in older people, although they can be present at birth and may also be caused by injury. In many cases an operation to remove the lens will help improve vision. However, where this is not possible, or prior to surgery, an advanced cataract can make daily activities difficult. Some examples of the effects cataracts can have on the person are:

• inability to distinguish pastel colours;
• restrictions on reading;
• discomfort in bright sunlight;
• reducing the ease of outdoor travel.

Macular degeneration is the most common cause of severe vision loss in people over 60 and, as the name implies, is a degenerative condition. It is a result of changes to the macula, a small area in the eye which is responsible for detailed central vision. Macular degeneration does not result in total blindness. It results in impairment in central vision while side/peripheral vision is usually retained. Practical implications include:

• difficulties with tasks that require central detailed vision such as reading, sewing, seeing faces;
• dim colour vision;
• discomfort in situations where light is bright or there is glare.

Glaucoma can affect people of all ages, including the very young. It is caused by a rise in the level of pressure in the eye because fluid cannot drain away as it should. The increased pressure causes damage to the optic nerve and results in vision loss. Initially, side/peripheral vision is affected, resulting in a form of tunnel vision. People with this impairment often experience no symptoms until they have lost part of their central visual field. Headaches can be an early symptom followed by blurring of vision. Glaucoma runs in families and it is important, therefore, for other family members to have regular checks (Gething, 1990). If left untreated, glaucoma will progress to total blindness. Practical implications include:

- restrictions on mobility;
- difficulty with any task attempted in poor lighting conditions;
- discomfort in situations where light is bright or there is glare.

Incidence and prevalence

The Australian Bureau of Statistics (1988) cites 12 per cent of the Australian population as having sight loss; however, the severity of this loss is not specified. In the United States 332 000 people are classified as having blindness in both eyes, 527 000 with visual impairment in both eyes and 578 000 with blindness or visual impairment in at least one eye. There are 171 000 people with macular degeneration, 407 000 glaucoma and 446 000 with cataracts (LaPlante & Carlson, 1996).

Gender. Generally, more men are blind or vision impaired than women up to the age group of 60 to 64 years; however, women outnumber men in the older age groups. This latter finding can be explained by the higher life expectancy and greater number of older women.

Age. More than 80 per cent of people retain reasonable vision throughout their lives. Serious deterioration in sight occurs in only 14 per cent of people. The 1981 Handicapped Persons in Australia Survey (ABS, 1981) reported that 3.6 per cent of people aged between 64 and 75 years had a sight loss which they regarded as handicapping, whereas 14.5 per cent of people aged 75 years and over reported this handicap. Data from the Health and Activity Limitation Survey (HALS) (Statistics Canada, 1988) indicate that approximately 10 per cent of Canadians aged over 65 years had a serious visual impairment that restricted the activities of everyday living. The Canadian National Institute for the Blind (1988) reported that, of its total client population, the age group of 0–29 years accounted for 12.7 per cent of the population, the 30–59 age group accounted for 19.9 per cent, while the vast majority (65.9 per cent) were aged over 60 years.

People of Aboriginal backgrounds. Little up-to-date statistical information is available for Aboriginal people with disabilities (McDougall, 1993a). However, it is known that Australian Aboriginal populations experience higher rates of trachoma, glaucoma, diabetes and cataracts (conditions associated with vision impairment) than those experienced by other Australians. A study carried out by the Royal College of Ophthalmologists in 1980 in rural Australia found that Aboriginal people had blindness rates of at least four times those of non-Aboriginal people in most age groups. Since this time, several highly successful treatment and prevention programs have been implemented which have targeted Aboriginal people.

Treatment

Surgery is possible for some conditions. However, if sight loss cannot be corrected, equipment can enable people with partial sight to perform everyday tasks. Considerable advances have been made in treating vision impairments associated with ageing. Cataracts can be managed by surgery. A cloudy lens may be surgically replaced by intraocular implants. Laser treatment is now available for macular degeneration and is used to slow down progression. Glaucoma usually responds to medicinal drops to reduce pressure in the eye. Surgery is used in more severe cases.

In many cases it is important to address such impairments as early as possible in order to adopt preventative measures. Therefore, regular eye check-ups are essential for someone with a family history of impairments such as diabetic retinopathy or glaucoma.

Services and supports

A range of services is available for adults and children with a vision impairment. The need for such services will vary according to the person's level of functional vision and age. It is important to recognise that a congenital vision impairment can have a significant impact on a young child's general development. Early intervention services and assessment of developmental and visual status can assist parents to understand their child's disability and the consequent implications for his or her development. Programs aimed at fine motor, gross motor, self-help, language and social skills can assist the child to attain his or her maximum potential.

Counselling and peer support. Contact with and support from other vision impaired peers reduces the sense of isolation, provides important social networks and offers an opportunity to discuss and/or explore alternative coping strategies. It also may provide an opportunity for counselling regarding any grief responses or negative perceptions regarding vision loss. Training in social skills and assertiveness may be important for some children or young people.

Services for children. The most intensive services are provided for younger age groups. Early intervention focuses on development of cognitive and motor skills, as well as on minimising the effects of the vision impairment on development and life. Services may be a mixture of home- and centre-based activities with most input being provided at the child's home. Later, contact with trained preschool teachers focuses on development and implementation of an educational program tailored to the needs of the vision-impaired child.

School age (6–18 years) children receive support through education authorities, but other supports are available from non-government agencies and may be delivered by teachers (education and rehabilitation), social workers and psychologists. Direct counselling support to the family is available along with liaison with the various education systems, individual educational programming where necessary, mobility training, communication skills (social and technical), and development of recreational opportunities.

Services for adults. School leavers are assisted in the transition from school to work or tertiary study through services aimed specifically at vocational issues. Psychologists provide psychometric, personality and vocational assessment and counselling. This is backed up by employment development officers who approach employers to open up job opportunities and support new vision-impaired employees in their jobs. Development of specific job skills and understanding of technology is provided by teachers and technical staff who develop and implement training programs on a group or individual basis. Transcription services enable print material to be transcribed into the preferred format (for example, braille, large print, tape or disk).

Older clients are offered counselling support by welfare officers and social workers who work in close liaison with rehabilitation teachers and recreation

Figure 16.7: Sports and recreation can be enjoyable and encourage social interaction

Reproduced with permission of People with Disabilities
Participation Division, Australian Sports Commission.

officers offering specific programs in daily living skills, recreational activities, orientation and mobility, braille and communication skills instruction.

Mobility training. This is vital to independence. In it, the person learns to move around the home and places visited regularly, such as the workplace, shops and neighbourhood. Also learnt are skills such as using a cane and public transport. Most people with vision impairment have sufficient sight to be able to get around without a cane or guide dog, but many use a cane to inform the general public that they have a vision impairment or are blind. Only about 2 per cent of people who are blind or vision impaired use guide dogs.

Personal assistance. This is required by some people, who employ readers to assist with work-related activities, educational pursuits or personal reading.

Equipment

Various aids and devices are specially manufactured or adapted for people who are vision impaired. Some examples are reading stands, telephones and household tools, clocks and watches (see Figure 16.8), playing cards, scrabble, dominoes, balls with bells, Rubik's cube, Monopoly, dark line writing pads, needle threaders, bathroom scales and more sophisticated pieces of equipment such as talking calculators and computers.

Figure 16.8: Using a braille watch

Low-vision aids are those tools which help people to get the most use of their vision. These aids may be optical lenses, such as magnifiers, and telescopes or non-optical devices such as lamps and large print. To determine which aids could be helpful, it may be necessary to obtain a thorough low-vision evaluation from a specialist in the field.

The following list itemises the technology used by one person:

- monocular telescope for watching television and outside activities such as football and cricket;
- lap-top computer with voice synthesis program;
- computer with screen enhancement program;
- talking calculator;
- magnifier;
- closed-circuit television;
- talking alarm clock;
- talking watch;
- cellular phone;
- talking scales (for weighing oneself);
- cane.

Without equipment, I would not be able to function in a productive way in my workplace. I know that presently I am putting back into my job and the general community as much as I took out during the rehabilitation process.

Angus

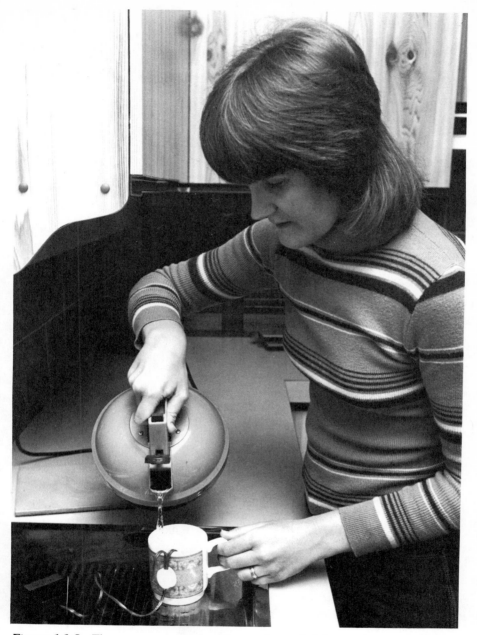

Figure 16.9: The sensor warns when the cup is nearly full, in order to avoid burns.

Additional costs

Medical conditions underlying vision impairment or blindness may require costly medication. Such medication may not be fully covered under the current pensioner health benefits scheme and may cause a substantial and regular financial outlay.

Travel and transport costs may form a significant form of expenditure. However, many people who are blind or vision impaired are eligible for a 50 per cent government subsidy on metered taxi fares. They also are entitled to a means-test-free pension if they meet the legally-blind criteria for eligibility.

Home maintenance forms another source of expenditure because some people who are vision impaired are unable to adequately perform maintenance tasks alone, or because of the extra time involved in carrying them out.

RESOURCE ORGANISATIONS

All care has been taken to ensure that all information is correct at the time of publishing; however, responsibility for the accuracy of this information is not accepted by the writer. The list of resource organisations contained in this chapter is not intended to be exhaustive – it provides national organisations only. The reader is referred to local community directories for further information and for local branches of national organisations. Inclusion of services and organisations should not be taken as a recommendation.

Australia

National Federation of Blind Citizens
  of Australia Ltd (NFBCA)
National Office, 87 High Street
Prahran Vic 3181
Ph 03 9521 3733
Toll free 1800 033 66045
Waverley Road
East Malvern Vic 3145
Ph 03 9572 1044

Vision Information Line
Ph 1800 331000 (Australia wide)
Ph 03 9822 9838 (Melbourne
  metropolitan)

Refer to your local telephone directory for state addresses of the Royal Blind Society and the Guide Dogs Association. For NSW, addresses are as follows:

Guide Dogs Association of NSW
  and the ACT
5 Northcliff Street
Milsons Point NSW 2061
Ph 02 9922 4211

Royal Blind Society
4 Mitchell Street
Enfield NSW 2136
PO Box 176
Burwood NSW 2134

Ph 02 9334 3333
Fax 02 9747 5993

Canada

Canadian Council of the Blind
Suite 405, 396 Cooper Street
Ottawa ON K2P 2H7
Ph 613 567 0311
Fax 613 567 2728

Canadian National Institute for the Blind
1929 Bayview Avenue
Toronto ON M4G 3E8
Ph 416 480 7580
Fax 416 480 7677

New Zealand

Royal New Zealand Foundation for
  the Blind
2 Titoki Street
Parnell
Private Bag 41
New Market Auckland
Ph 9 774 389
Fax 9 366 0099

United Kingdom

British Retinitis Pigmentosa Society
Pond House

Lillingstone Dayrell
Buckingham MK18 5AS
Ph 2806 363

Guide Dogs for the Blind Association
Hillfields, Burghfield Common
Reading Berkshire RG7 3YG
Ph 734 83 5555
Fax 734 83 5211

United States

American Council of the Blind
Suite 720, 1155 15th Street NW
Washington DC 20005
Ph 202 467 5081
Fax 202 467 5085

American Foundation for the Blind
Suite 300, 11 Penn Plaza

New York 10001
Ph 212 502 7657
Fax 212 501 7774

National Association for Visually
   Handicapped
22 West 21st Street, 6th floor
New York 10010
Ph 212 889 3141
Fax 212 727 2931

National Federation of the Blind
1800 Johnson Street
Baltimore Maryland 21230
Ph 410 659 9314
Fax 410 685 5653

FURTHER READING

Ainlay, S. (1989). *Day brought back my night: ageing and new vision loss.* London: Routledge.

Bailey, I. L. and Hall, A. (1990). *Visual impairment: an overview.* New York: American Foundation for the Blind.

Butler, S. R. (ed.) (1990). *The exceptional child.* Sydney: Harcourt Brace Jovanovich. (Part 5: 'Visual impairment', pp. 207–57.)

Gething, L. (1990). *Working with older people: a guide for health professionals.* Sydney: W.B. Saunders.

Hollins, M. (1989). *Understanding blindness.* Hillsdale, NJ: Lawrence Erlbaum Associates.

Resources for Rehabilitation (1993). *Living with low vision: a resource guide for people with sight loss.* Lexington, Mass.

PERSONAL ACCOUNTS OF LIFE WITH A DISABILITY

The following pages give personal accounts written by several people about their lives. The main characteristic that these people have in common is that they live with some form of disability. However, these individuals are very different.

The accounts illustrate the diverse ways in which human beings react to life experiences. They emphasise that each of us is unique and that we deal with life's events in different ways. Thus, the focus is on how people deal with life experiences, rather than on the particular disability they happen to have.

The accounts do not cover all types of disability included in this book. Rather, they take a very personal point of view to consider how a range of individuals perceive their life situations and their strategies in dealing with important events in their lives.

Although these accounts stress individuality, they also show that themes can cross people's lives. Some of these themes include the impact of initial diagnosis and how the behaviour of professionals can hinder or assist a person in coming to terms with disability; the impact of congenital versus acquired disability, the stages people tend to go through in grieving about and coming to terms with their disability, the effects of community attitudes and stereotypes on quality of life and opportunities; and how the presence of disability affects many individuals including family and friends, as well as the person with the disability.

These accounts bring to life and illustrate much of the material presented in the book. They show the reality of living with a disability. Depending on the wishes of the person, sometimes his or her real name is used and at other times this has been changed to protect privacy.

SUE

In this account Sue talks about her experiences associated with learning that she has MS. She also talks about how she tried to deal with having a disability. Readers may find it useful to read this account in conjunction with the stages of bereavement discussed in Chapter 1 and stages of adjustment to MS discussed in Chapter 13. Recently, Sue published a book about the experiences of other people with disabilities. Some of these accounts are reproduced below with Sue's permission.

I have MS the way the majority of people with MS have it – the remitting/relapsing type. However, the bad public relations MS has amongst the community, one's friends, family, former workmates and (unfortunately) some doctors, means that, in their eyes, I have the terrible, galloping and fiercely degenerative crippling MS.

Getting the incurable and mysterious MS is such a shock that you endure denial (even denying it to yourself), terrible depressions, anger and grief. But, because it doesn't kill you, you'll survive. You'll have to live with this forever.

Briefly, it started when I was 27 and had double vision for some months. No one could have guessed this was MS until, three years later, I got optic neuritis. I happened to read in the same newspaper that I worked for that many people with optic neuritis have MS. That was enough for me not to continue checking for signs of MS, but to panic and run away, leaving my job, my home in Sydney and to hide out in Tasmania awaiting the worst – the wheelchair.

For three years that didn't happen and I forgot the dreaded MS until it was diagnosed after a bout of unbalanced walking and acute fatigue. Then I had more panic and depression until I came to realise this would continue with regular exacerbations. No one tells you much about MS and it was through my experiences, amateur research and the help of a caring expert that I eventually learnt how MS affects me. Even in remission, strange things have happened to me with MS. I remember my right foot becoming like a block of concrete for a few days, intermittent bouts of incontinence, fatigue and lack of coordination. Even my writing didn't work for 12 months to the extent that I couldn't even sign my name. Tripping on something on a footpath and actually falling over is awful. Because I seemed to have lost most of my balance and have the 'drunken walk' which affects most people with MS, it was very annoying if I happened to be crossing a road and hoons in a car would yell out to me, 'lay off the piss, babe'.

MS just seems to come and go. Thank heavens it goes. With remitting/relapsing MS, something you could never even have had a nightmare about comes at its own will and then goes – pooff – on its own will, when it's ready to go. I feel as if I'm at its mercy, even though I make sure I get a lots of rest and healthy food. I have to remember I must not let myself think I'm at anything's mercy, least of all MS.

Friends offer the sympathy you'd show to a crippled dog. The understanding is not there because no one, except maybe a few neurologists, understand the many and extraordinary faces MS can show. As far as friends and some members of my family are concerned, I don't have MS because I'm not in a wheelchair. And, as far as they are concerned, I'll end up in a wheelchair.

I've had MS for more than 16 years now and I see that while getting MS (somehow, where?), was unlucky, I am very lucky it's so comparatively mild. But that doesn't erase the poor coordination, unbalanced walk, and occasional tiredness, all of which are with me without a relapse. I know now that when I have a relapse, I simply must go to bed and stay there until the relapse decides to go. So often in the past, I've tried to ignore the growing signs of fatigue and increasing inability to walk; and, of course, I have tripped, fallen, and stumbled about.

Of course I am extremely grateful that I am not in the minority who have severe MS. However, I would do anything to never have got this thing. To me, MS is a *thing*. So often, especially when I feel I am about to subside into a major depression, I glimpse at what I used to be and hate what I have become – a guinea pig for doctors' experiments and family's and friends' useless sympathies. MS has placed me into the position of being a victim – the very thing most people want to avoid.

(Susan Molloy is the author of *Handling it: you and your long-term disease*, which was published by Hill of Content Publishing, Melbourne, 1995. Some material from her book is included in this section with her permission.)

WENDY

Wendy's account provides a perspective of the life of a woman who is now in her middle age. Medical diagnosis and treatment have changed since her childhood, but she gives a picture of what it was like to grow up with cerebral palsy in the 1950s and 1960s. She also provides a view of what it is like to age with this disability, and so addresses one of the issues which is now receiving increasing attention from researchers and professionals, and which is discussed in several chapters in this book. Wendy' s account also raises some of the issues for a family with a member who has cerebral palsy.

Born at the end of World War Two in Newcastle, NSW; I was nine weeks premature and was a difficult first birth for my mother. I was born in a small cottage hospital with my delivery supervised by a local general medical practitioner. Contrary to medical predictions, I defied the odds and survived.

I was not diagnosed until the age of four years as a child with tension athtoid cerebral palsy. This delay occurred despite frequent trips to various doctors and to hospitals in Sydney where we now resided. Prior to being diagnosed, poor Mum and Dad had a terrible time. I was their first child and the fact that my legs crossed when my nappy was changed didn't mean much. At nine months I was propped up with cushions, they thought I was a bit backward. I went to many specialists who said I had all sorts of weird and wonderful things. Finally, at four years of age I was diagnosed as having cerebral palsy.

After the diagnosis of cerebral palsy I was accepted at the Spastic Centre at Mosman for education and treatment. At age seven years my parents transferred me to the Crippled Children's Society's school at Parramatta as it was much closer to home. After the usual sheltered education at a special school where I received my education mostly by correspondence, I was sent to Mount Wilga, a rehabilitation centre for employment training. My stint of 18 months there systematically eliminated every avenue I wished to pursue. I found myself in the then obligatory employment of females who were disabled: the office worker. Ironically, I was employed as a switchboard operator/typist at the headquarters of the Crippled Children's Society for the next nine years. I finally had the fortitude to go to outside employment at Balmain Hospital where life was vastly different and much more enjoyable.

People who have a disability from birth usually find maturity, life experiences and personal relationships much harder to achieve than their counterparts who are not disabled. It is an area which needs much attention to strengthen and maintain solid self-esteem, growing general knowledge and assimilation into society.

I met my husband Jack in 1968 and we were married two years later. We have two daughters now aged 22 and 18 years, respectively. Our daughters have not found it easy having a mother with a disability. There have been many activities I have been unable to share with them. The problem was greater during the high school years when it was decidedly 'uncool' to have a 'spazo' mother. This, coupled with their father having a seven-day-a-week milk run, meant no family holidays, picnics, etc, and led to rather an unusual time for both of them. Aunts, grandparents, friends and stints in the Girl Guides all provided holidays and outings, but it was not the same as family togetherness.

In the years from 1981 to 1991 I embraced university education to fill a void. Other women went to tennis and lunches. I studied. It was mainly to increase my self-esteem. I gradually worked my way through an Arts degree at the University of

New England, and then a degree in Adult Education in the Community at the University of Technology, Sydney (UTS) where I concentrated on issues for people with disabilities. The degrees led to a stint as Disability Officer at UTS and then as a tutor for some people with severe disabilities at Manly-Warringah Community College. In these jobs my emphasis always has been on self esteem. Both positions allowed me to be inventive and to think laterally about solving many problems.

Over the past four years I have watched people with cerebral palsy in my classes and have ached at their lack of self-determination, freedom and ambition. There is such a great deal of work to be done to enable them to have lifestyles that include dignity, quality and meaning.

Cerebral palsy is not an attractive or popular disability with the general public. Facial grimaces, guttural voices and flailing limbs disturb many people, but things are getting better slowly. Ironically Steady Eddy, a well known comedian with cerebral palsy, has helped dispel much of the embarrassment through his irreverent view of his own disability.

Most people with cerebral palsy would prefer the name 'The Cerebral Palsy Association' to the current name of 'The Spastic Centre'. They believe the connotations associated with the derogative term 'spazo' are offensive and demeaning.

All people with cerebral palsy that I know who are ageing are very concerned that there is no backup network for the strange symptoms we are experiencing. No organisations or medical people seem able to shed any light on the breaking down of our bodies. We do not fit into the post-polio syndrome, as it is now thought that the polio virus is re-attacking its victims. We need a support group to inform us of any progress as ageing is affecting each person in different ways. It is worrying for us, to say the least. I am now in a wheelchair because of muscle breakdown and general deterioration, but I am still driving and still am able to work part time.

Our daughters are nearly ready to leave the nest, so Jack and I will be a twosome again. He has been working in his trade as a cabinet maker for the last few years so we now have holidays and weekends together, but too late as the girls are grown and don't want to come away with us.

Life is good and, as the saying goes, 'I wouldn't be dead for quids.'

PIETRO

Like Wendy, Pietro was born with cerebral palsy and is experiencing changes in functioning associated with ageing. Pietro is 49 years old and his body is showing changes that indicate premature ageing. In this account he talks about his constant struggle throughout his life to maintain his physical abilities and emphasises that the presence of physical disability does not necessarily mean that a person has an intellectual disability.

I was born two months premature in a little village in Sicily. I was diagnosed as having infantile paralysis. My mother's friends used to tell her to drown me. Luckily, after she was told this, they were no longer her friends any more.

My babyhood was rather horrendous for my parents. Being the first born, and being a male offspring made it difficult for my parents to accept that I couldn't do all those things that a child does. As I grew I used to sit in an old wooden highchair in my grandparents' home; although I could not speak I could make myself understood. For example, whenever my grandmother forgot where she put things I was able to tell her by pointing and making loud noises until she realised what I was trying to tell her. From then on she would ask me where 'such and such' a thing was.

My father decided to migrate, either to America or Australia, to find a better life for me. He chose Australia.

I started school at the Spastic Centre at the age of four. This was when my whole world started to change. A new way of living, a new language, with different people and different surroundings. At school I learnt with the others the usual school lessons, had lunch with the other kids, and mucked around with them. The only difference was that much of my schooling had to suffer because of therapy such as physiotherapy, speech and occupational therapies. So, I planned on catching up at a later date, which I never did.

My dream at the time was to become a fisherman, like my father, and go prawning. In the winter, Dad went deep-sea fishing in any type of weather. He never took me because of the danger involved and because of the cold weather. So, one of my dreams was to one day go deep-sea fishing and to catch the big one.

I was a happy-go-lucky child. I guess I had my moods when I couldn't get my own way. I would throw a tantrum like any other kid. But on the whole I was pretty happy-go-lucky with no concerns for the future, no real goals but to go fishing and earn my livelihood that way even though I had cerebral palsy. My parents were the main source of influence on me. They encouraged independence and treated me like my sisters. I had to do my own chores, and was made to do them. In those days I did everything for myself, except get out of bed in the mornings. Mum had to drag me out! I was a healthy child, never had to take a pill or see a doctor. Now I'm a 'walking' pill box.

I left school at the age of 16 years and went to work in a sheltered workshop. That was a whole new life once again. New people, new way of life. At the workshop I was drilling holes in the components of telecommunication relay sets. At first I could drill about three or four parts a day and the expected rate was 203 an hour! I worked in the drilling department for about ten years and within that time I achieved, among other things, that 203 per hour which was approximately 16 000 parts per day.

I arrived at the sheltered workshop able to do everything for myself. I could wheel myself around, stand up, shower and shave myself, brush my hair, toilet myself – those everyday things. I was able to write with a pen, even able to use a manual typewriter. I was able to fix my own wheelchair. I was independent!

I went up hill before I went down. An occupational therapist got hold of me and started to walk me in a frame with long callipers on my legs. He said that if I had some surgery and then tried hard enough I would walk one day unaided, without callipers and without a frame. With this in mind, I gave it all I had. So the process started and I had surgery on my ankles, my knees and then my groin. This was a very painful procedure and I was laid up for three months in plaster. Then it was a very slow process to get me on my feet. We started off with callipers and a large frame. After my legs got stronger and stronger, I was able to throw away the callipers and use a smaller frame. In the end, I was using a small frame and was walking everywhere. I was able to take a few steps unaided.

My walking ability lasted about ten years, then I started to lose the use of my limbs. Walking became a chore, even my independence was going down hill. I went to doctor after doctor to find out why I was losing my independence, but no doctor was able to tell me the real reason for my physical decline. So, therefore, I had to start all over again. But this time without being able to do day-to-day things for myself, I had to rely on someone to do those things for me.

During this period of my physical decline, I lost my father with a massive heart attack. One of the reasons for my father's death was, I guess, because of my downfall. He was very proud of what I had achieved and to see me going down hill like that hurt him very much. My father's death affected the whole family, me more so, because I had three crises to contend with – my father's death, my loss of independence and having to move out of my home. The day after my father's death I was offered accommodation at the Spastic Centre because they realised that my family could not cope with me at home at the time. So, during the week I stayed at the hostel and went home on weekends. It took me a long time to adjust to a new way of living. Being surrounded by 45 other individuals and different staff members was very different to what I was used to. Even the food was different. No one can cook meals like my Mamma!

It took a long time to accept the loss of my father and my hard-earned independence. I became angry and frustrated with myself, but as time went on I realised that I had to pick myself up and make the best of it. I thought I knew what it was like to be severely disabled, like some of my friends who were stuck in a chair in one position all day. But no one actually realises until one experiences this for oneself.

Today I am 49 years old, and totally physically dependent for everything – toileting, mobility, meal time assistance, drinking, and require a lot of physical support at work and at home. These high support needs didn't happen overnight. They gradually became evident as I aged over the last 16 years. There are other consumers experiencing the consequences of ageing as I am, and I am sure there will be others in the future. Many of us are losing physical functions earlier than those in the general population, making adapting to the outside world even more difficult and frustrating.

One of the obvious problems within supported accommodation which showed its ugly head was ageing, with its loss of independence. Where previously I performed many of the day-to-day things myself, I now require assistance from staff. As I am going through the increased dependency, I am observing other residents in the same predicament. Even the more physically independent residents who were able to assist staff, now find themselves being totally dependent on staff. These changes are frustrating for both the residents and the staff, who sometimes do not understand that we are not just being lazy.

Residents are not realising that what is happening to their bodies is making them angry and frustrated with themselves. This has an effect on staff who do not understand why residents are not able to do what they had been able to do before. This is causing some animosity, sometimes friction, between residents and staff.

There is a need to take away the assumption that if a person is severely physically disabled, that he or she is also intellectually disabled. There are a number of us who have a physical disability who are becoming frustrated and annoyed because people think we are mentally deteriorating. Let me assure you that this is not the case with many of us. My physical deterioration, in my opinion, has not affected my mental abilities. I am still able to participate on committees and working parties. I am still absolutely able to be in control of my life, despite attempts by some people to discredit me and to keep me on the same level as one who is also becoming mentally dependent. It is bad enough to watch the severe loss of your physical independence without having people take away your mental independence as well. Recognition of mental independence, while acknowledging physical dependence in some of us, will enable us to age in a more satisfying and graceful manner.

It is time that service providers realise that they have an enormous responsibility towards consumers who are experiencing the consequences of ageing, such as the decrease in physical independence. The consequences of ageing mean that consumers require more staff support, extra resources and understanding by others of the effects of ageing. If service providers do not respond to this cry for help, then I am afraid that the future seems rather grim.

ROSE

The account written by Rose describes the experiences of a mother whose twin boys are profoundly deaf. She describes difficulties in obtaining a firm diagnosis and discusses family reactions and experiences following cochlear implants. The account also displays how important it is for a health professional to be well informed and sensitive when informing parents about their child's disability and prognosis.

I am the mother of twin boys who are profoundly deaf. I was fourteen weeks pregnant when an ultrasound revealed that I was expecting twins. My husband and I were absolutely thrilled, if not somewhat over-awed, and our four other children were very excited at the prospect.

The pregnancy proceeded normally and I kept well, although the extra load I was carrying made me very tired. The babies were induced ten days early due to my tiredness and discomfort. After a four-hour labour they were delivered normally. Our identical twin sons were with us, well and healthy, and were of good size.

Before we left hospital many routine tests were carried out, as with all babies. One was a hearing test which they passed.

As the months went by I took the boys to the local baby health clinic for the usual weighing and other early tests. They never performed well at the hearing tests. This was, we thought, due to the fact that they had 'glue ear' which can make hearing difficult. In every other respect they were thriving. However, at ten months I questioned the paediatrician about their hearing and he assured me that I had no need for concern.

By one year of age, the boys were babbling, but not saying any easily identifiable words such as 'mum' or 'dad'. The clinic sister became concerned and we were sent for further testing which was inconclusive. Finally, when they were 16 months old we went to the Children's Hospital for more comprehensive testing which they failed. An operation was organised to insert grommets to clear the 'glue ear'. It was hoped that this would improve their hearing. At 18 months they were tested again and were diagnosed as profoundly deaf.

We were both shocked and devastated. We had been trying for so long to get a correct and precise diagnosis of their hearing and had been given so much false hope along the way that to be told that they were both deaf was shattering. There is no history of deafness anywhere in our families.

The diagnosis was delivered to us very abruptly and insensitively and we were told the boys would probably never learn to speak.

Our whole family, therefore, entered a new world, the world of silence and deafness . . . something we knew almost nothing about. We had to make decisions, we had to decide on what path to send our boys down. We had no advice other than the brochures I had been given on the day they were diagnosed. No one came to us, no one phoned. There was a total absence of backup or support from any of the health care professionals who had brought us to this diagnosis. The sense of being totally alone was overwhelming.

The most soul destroying of all comments made to us was that the boys would probably never learn to speak. Not only was this prognosis extremely negative and devoid of hope, but more importantly (and inexcusably) so incorrect, so far from the truth. Many children who are profoundly deaf acquire speech.

The point of diagnosis is crucial. The decisions parents have to make at this point will have far reaching effects on their child and yet at this stage parents are so utterly distraught that their sense of vision can be somewhat clouded.

As stated earlier, the most soul destroying comment made to us was that our children would probably never learn to speak. This comment kept ringing in my ears for weeks. Having four other children who all hear and speak, I found the notion of two children living in our household and being unable to speak, quite impossible to contemplate.

We chose an auditory-oral program for our sons in preference to a signing program. I believe very sincerely that it was the only choice because I believe that speech is every child's right, and that as their parents we have a duty to assist them in whatever way possible to achieve this goal. As a family we daily meet this challenge.

After two years using hearing aids the boys received cochlear implants. They had been plagued with ear infections over these two years. Every time they had an ear infection the hearing aids had to be taken off and, therefore, they were not getting any sound at these times. We had to look for an alternative. The cochlear implant, a sophisticated internal hearing aid, was the answer. The implant has been wonderful for the boys. It is giving them a consistent, high quality sound and their language is improving rapidly.

Every parent prays for the perfect child. For some of us our children have imperfections. For some this is evident at birth, for others is not apparent until some time later. The diagnosis of a disability requires adjustments, particularly emotionally, on the part of the parents. The greater the disability, the greater the adjustment. The accepting, the 'taking on board', so to speak, of a disability that will be life-long, is heart rending. As far as our boys are concerned, we have endeavoured to make decisions that will see *their* best interests served. We have tried to be practical and realistic, but also have tried to maintain a 'reach for the sky' approach. That is to say, all is attainable with hard work.

Teaching a child who is profoundly deaf to speak is hard work. Teaching two is even harder. You could say that our family has become immersed in an intensive language program. We all have become acutely aware of the process by which children acquire language, the babble stage, the importance of the receptive language stage, and how both of these initial stages lay the foundations for speech as we know it. We all have been on a steep learning curve.

The boys are now five and a half and this year they have integrated for two days a week into a local preschool. Next year they will attend the local parish school and will integrate into kindergarten with the support of an itinerant teacher of the deaf and a teacher's aid.

The boys have had their implants for less than two years. They are making daily discoveries with sound. They can hear the phone ring and can answer it. They hear the door bell ring. They hear the birds singing in the trees in our garden. Their receptive language is excellent and their expressive language is improving daily. I can only describe their progress as a daily miracle.

DARREN

Darren wrote this account when he was 27. At this time he had used an electric wheelchair since he was 14 years old. His profile outlines some of the problems and adjustments that occur when someone has a disability that not only involves significant physical limitations, but also shortens life expectancy. Two years after completing this vignette, Darren died. He caught a virus while with his family on a cruise off the west coast of the United States. In the year prior to his death, Darren and those around him noticed a decline in his physical strength and abilities. He is remembered with affection by his workmates who appreciated his calm, caring and sensible approach to life.

I was a perfectly healthy baby. I walked at the right age and talked at the right age. However, when I was four years old, my mother noticed that I had begun to walk with a waddle and was having trouble negotiating stairs. Medical tests showed that I have Duchenne muscular dystrophy.

At that age I didn't understand that I had a disability. I had trouble running around and keeping up with other children, but I didn't fully understand why that was. I felt lucky that I had an older brother who would help me to get around.

I started going to an ordinary school when I was five, but after a while it became clear that I couldn't physically keep up with the other kids. It was very frustrating. So I was enrolled in a 'special school'. It is probably a good idea to have a school where children with disabilities can have proper care, physiotherapy (physical therapy) and education all in one situation. However, it can also mean that children go from one protective area (at home) to another protective area (at school). I don't think that this helps to prepare people for life because you could so easily become a 'cotton wool' child. Luckily, though, my parents, my home environment and my local neighbourhood helped to ensure that this didn't happen to me. I grew up in an area where I had a lot of 'non-disabled' friends and so I had a fairly 'normal' childhood.

Going to school with other children that have muscular dystrophy was, in some ways, fairly confronting. It is possible, with muscular dystrophy, to die of complications from the common cold. Seeing others die at a young age was quite shocking. It didn't really encourage me to spend a lot of years studying at school or university. I couldn't see the point.

So I left school after Year 11, went home, grew a beard and watched soap operas for a year. I rejected the offer of a 'rehabilitation' program. I had always been disabled so I couldn't understand the point of it. I also was not that interested in learning office skills, which seemed to be the main focus of the program.

After 12 months of being a 'house creature', I decided to get out more often. I had a friend who was a courier so, for a while, I travelled around in the vehicle with him during the day. Then a friend who worked for a disability education program asked me to give a guest lecture about my disability. I ended up being offered a permanent part-time job. So, for a number of years now, I have been a research assistant at a university.

I use an electric wheelchair and my father looks after most of my daily physical needs, including lifting and bathing, etc. Movement is fairly restricted and I must rely on others to hand me things. This does not stop me going or doing many things. It does mean, however, that activities must be planned in advance. Special taxis for people who have disabilities have meant that I can go to work or social events without relying on others.

I owe a lot of my current lifestyle to my parents. Without them and their efforts, I could not be enjoying the life that I currently do. It has been difficult for all of us, but I think we have all coped really well.

Relationships have always been a problem. It is very hard to have a relationship with someone when you have a physical disability. It means that you are limited in being able to satisfy the other person's needs. I have gone out with a number of girls, but have not had a long-term relationship.

Nonetheless I have got lots of friends. I have travelled overseas a number of times. I frequently go out socially and I work part-time. I really believe that you must live your life, do your best and experience as much as you can.

SARAH

Sarah was diagnosed with diabetes when she was in her early twenties. This vignette was written 18 months after the diagnosis. Sarah is a registered nurse who, as her profile shows, had to come to grips with daily insulin injections and the changes to lifestyle and routine that diabetes can bring.

I have insulin-dependent diabetes. Because my body produces no insulin, I must give myself insulin injections every day. I was diagnosed just over a year ago, so I am still quite new to diabetes.

I had a bad virus that put me in hospital for a week before my wedding three years ago. I never seemed to recover from that virus, I was constantly tired and depressed. Because I had a very busy job and had only recently got married, I just put it down to stress. I decided to change to a more enjoyable, less stressful and less time-consuming job. Unfortunately, this didn't seem to help, I felt tired and sick a lot of the time. I would get headaches, be extremely thirsty and I was losing weight.

One day I was showing a student nurse how to do a urinalysis. I decided to check my own. There was a colour change which meant that there was sugar in my urine. So I borrowed a glucometer and went quietly back into the room and checked my blood. My blood sugar level was 19 (4 or 5 is normal). I couldn't believe it.

I then went to see a local doctor and asked him to tell me I was wrong. He did a test and then said, 'No, you're right. You have diabetes, you will need to give yourself insulin injections every day. You are a nurse, you understand.' It was like he was punching me. Maybe it was the way he was best able to handle the situation.

My mother contacted Diabetes Australia, who suggested that I see a specialist. He was very good, he confirmed that I had 'juvenile onset' diabetes and that I would need to be on insulin injections. I was not very happy with the idea of sticking myself with needles, so he suggested that I go to a diabetes clinic.

I was stressed, exhausted and angry. I felt cheated out of a 'normal' lifestyle.

The nurse at the diabetes clinic drew up the insulin into a syringe and gave it to me to inject. I felt that I couldn't give it to myself unless my husband and the nurse left the room. After they left, I got ready to jab it in and rested the syringe on my stomach. It just slid in, it didn't hurt. As I took it out, I burst into tears.

Everyone seemed to think that because I was a nurse, I wouldn't mind giving myself injections. They just took it for granted that I would cope. I cope quite well now and, in fact, the regimen that I have chosen means that I give myself four injections every day. Some people choose to inject their insulin once or twice a day, but this usually means that they must eat at set times. I chose my regimen because it gives me more flexibility in my daily routine. I give myself one injection of long-acting insulin every night and then I inject short-acting insulin half an hour before each meal during the day.

Diabetes is a hidden disability that has meant I have had to make some changes in my life. I must always make sure I have my insulin with me and I must monitor my blood sugar levels regularly. My husband has also had to learn about diabetes. He knows what I do if I have a hypo or a hyper. He has been very supportive.

I have discovered that diabetes doesn't have to restrict my life. I have chosen a regimen that means that I don't have to stick to a set routine every day. I know the types of food I should eat and I don't find it difficult to accommodate them within my normal diet. I guess I'm getting used to having diabetes.

LIBBY

This account is extracted with permission from Susan Molloy (1995). *Handling it: you and your long-term disease*. Melbourne: Hill of Content, pp. 54–7.

Libby talks about her reactions to acquired hearing impairment. She also talks about the major changes that acquired disability had on her life and how she has learned to adapt life to take account of having a disability.

I had an attack of influenza in my twenties just after I got married and that left me with a high frequency hearing loss (not being able to hear telephone calls and that sort of thing), and that hearing loss progressed, and then about eight years ago I developed into having a profound hearing loss. I have some low-frequency hearing, but no high-frequency hearing.

Only recently have I come to terms with my hearing loss. It happened over a period of time, which I think is easier to cope with rather than a sudden hearing loss. My family found it harder to come to terms with than I did. However, I hadn't come to terms with the fact that I may need a hearing aid. But finally I did have a hearing aid fitted.

At that time I was pregnant with my first child, doing relief work in a pharmacy at a children's hospital, I was answering telephones and people would ring and say their child had been bitten by a spider and what was the antidote. I had taken on the job but had not told anyone I had a hearing problem and then I realised that by hiding my hearing aid maybe I had not been hearing exactly what the people were ringing for and maybe I was giving them the wrong information.

I remember one long-distance call where the child had swallowed sheep dip and I could not hear it and the people were getting really upset and angry. The job was a two-week locum and I realised I could not stay on. I continued in other jobs in retail pharmacy and found it harder and harder to cope. But I had a boss who understood. He kept me on for another 15 years or so, part-time, until I became such a liability that I thought I should give this up.

I became involved in a local organisation to support people with an acquired hearing loss. I was working with a woman who was a real dynamo. She had been a teacher until her hearing loss became so bad she had to completely alter her life.

Through that organisation I learnt more about what was available for hard of hearing people. I have a teletext TV that brings up sub-titles, a flashing orange light lets me know the phone is ringing, these sorts of things.

Over the last eight years my hearing has dropped. My hearing aids have become more powerful and without them I hear nothing. I'm sure one of my ears has lost any discrimination now.

It would be really hard to lose everything, it really would be. I rely on my residual hearing, and I use it as much as I can, together with lip reading.

I know people who've had loss of hearing happen very suddenly, and they've gone through great depression, being suddenly cut off from any communication. When I realised I was doing deaf I realised the hardest thing would be loss of communication. Communicating with my family is hard.

If people could just overlook the disability and look at the person they would see such a wealth of humanity there. I've turned my disability into a positive thing in my life. I'm almost cashing in on this disability. It's an extra dimension that has helped me help other people with disabilities and to feel good about my life.

I've gained a lot of support by being involved in a small self-help group with people who have similar disabilities.

Acquired hearing loss is quite different from being born deaf. I felt a terrible sense of loss, losing my hearing.

ELIZABETH

This account is extracted with permission from Susan Molloy (1995). *Handling it: you and your long-term disease*. Melbourne: Hill of Content, pp. 69–74.

In this account, Elizabeth talks about the process by which she came to accept having MS. She talks about her grief and the behaviours she adopted in an effort to cope with this.

I was diagnosed with MS when I was about 32, after a long period, about six years, and I was christened with this grand name of multiple sclerosis, which I knew nothing about. I went to the library to find out what it was and found it was not a relief finding out about it, but a death sentence. I suppose that was the only shock I had. Either I was numb, or I would not accept it.

When I was first diagnosed I was in a shocked state, it hadn't really sunk in. Then I went through that horrible stage of 'why me?' I retreated to my bed, I didn't want to eat, I kept weeping. My family told me I was beautiful and I could do whatever I wanted, but I wasn't convinced and decided I wasn't ever going to eat again.

I had to learn to live with my loss. It took me a long time to get out of my bed, I must have smelt because I wasn't having showers, I'm really, entirely, ashamed of myself, the way I handled it. I quite believe I needed to go through that stage to be able to accept the next stage, and the next stage is saying, well all right, you are the way you are, what are you going to do about it? Are you going to continue the way it is, are you going to have some sort of life? Are you going to enjoy what is left?

And I think I've enjoyed what was left. For me, it was important to be mentally and physically busy, provided I don't overload myself. I do the evening crossword every day and that is my mental physio.

It is not the end of the world. It is up to you how you manage your body. You're the only one who knows your body; no doctor does.

If people consider themselves sick, although MS is not a sickness (it is a disease) then they behave as if they're sick.

It is essential that you retain your independence, your quality of life. I accept MS now, today, better than I have done because I'm more disciplined. I know a lot more about how it affects people and how they handle it – and a lot don't. A lot of people succumb to it and really like to live it, because they probably are that kind of people. No matter what they got, they would have been exactly the same. I know a lot more about my body today and I know how I can manage my body. I'm in control. No one else is in control, least of all my MS. I hardly think of myself as having MS – it has been so long. To me, I am 'normal'.

NARELLE

Narelle is a nurse educator. She has lived with rheumatoid arthritis for many years. In this account she talks about its impact on her life and her work. Recently, Narelle had surgery for a knee replacement. She was still recovering from this surgery when she wrote this account.

Living with a disability or different-ableness, particularly one acquired from an ongoing problem like arthritis, has left little certainty in my life. Change has become a constant companion as deterioration and adjustment have become a part of living. I have had to learn to 'listen' and respond to the various imperatives of a changed and changing body. The experience is often frightening, the frustration of limitation where previously there was none can be overwhelming.

Practical day-to-day advice and assistance are often difficult to find, and in many instances even more difficult to accept as I attempt to hang on to what I have got: job, status, place in the world, and the freedom to go anywhere and do anything I want to without having to ask for, or wait for, help.

The little limitations are often what bring me crashing down. Going shopping can be a major undertaking that often requires the strategic planning of a major army manoeuvre. When I can't do it myself and I have to rely on friends (and, yes, I am lucky as I have some wonderful ones), I frequently forget to put some of the basic essentials on my list, or overlook the little luxuries that make life more tolerable; the sorts of things you see on the way round the supermarket and buy on impulse because you feel like it. I went 18 months without any of those luxuries prior to my first knee replacement.

The psychological preparation necessary to continually walk on crutches into classrooms of nurses has been the most demanding experience I have ever faced in over 25 years of nursing. I have frequently pushed myself physically much further than I should have, and have usually paid a considerable price for doing so. But, pride gets in the way, and you don't use the sticks when you know you should or you stand twice as long as your legs want you to!

The restrictions accompanying arthritis can have a devastating effect on one's confidence and self-esteem, particularly in a world where health, fitness and ability are the perceived 'norm'. Little things can be hurtful. Help is often not helpful (or wanted) as you struggle to maintain some control.

When I began to have real trouble with my feet and knees I used to come home from working eight hours on my feet and lie down with ice packs just to get rid of the pain. I refused to talk about it. I didn't want to. I wouldn't accept that it was happening to me. I was like a bear with a sore head. Grumpy and uncommunicative. It was particularly hard on my personal relationship, although I had a very understanding partner who made plenty of space for me and never pushed me into talking about it. It took me a lot of time to actually acknowledge that this was going to have a significant impact on my life. I am not sure if I have ever totally accepted the full implications of this disease and its disabling effects.

The best thing since the knee replacements has been the extra mobility and the lack of unrelenting pain in my joints. My self-esteem and self-confidence have been restored to a certain extent. I have regained some of my affect. I spent a number of years in a very flat mood. Never one thing or the other. It was difficult to be enthusiastic about anything. It had a very negative effect on my teaching. I tended to speak in a monotone most of the time. I suppose the pain killers were partly to blame.

Mind you, the sheer frustration and, I suppose, anger has not gone away completely. At times it still hits me, even with my improved mobility. It's better than it was, but it's never going to be 'better better' if you know what I mean. I will never be able to do everything that I want to and will always have to rely on others to help, and I hate that aspect of arthritis.

SYD

This account provides an across-the-lifespan view of having a disability. Syd has lived with epilepsy for most of his life. In this account he focuses on his experiences in school and employment and shows that he has been able to incorporate having epilepsy into a full and successful life. This account describes Syd's approach to disclosure, a topic mentioned several times in the book as being an important issue for many people with hidden disabilities. Syd chose to be open about his disability and he believes this has stood him in good stead during his life.

My first grand mal (tonic-clonic) seizures began at the age of 12 years and at the beginning of second year in high school.

It was 1931 and little was known about epilepsy medically at that time. The following 12 months were very traumatic and every avenue, from Chinese herbalists to chiropractors, was tried. Finally, after intense questioning, a neurosurgeon related the case to an injury I had received on the playing field the year previous to the attacks. He then wrote about his findings, emphasising the need for me to continue school studies. I placed this letter with the local headmaster who agreed I could continue, but stipulated that undue attention, apart from every care during a seizure, was not to be. The next two years when I worked towards intermediate standard were not easy and I had to learn ways to by-pass the damaged area of the brain and bring other areas into compensating sharpness. My lowered ability was the hardest to accept, but a wonderful family and many friends helped me to adjust by treating me as they would any other boy, but one who had a problem (not a disability). Here also my early education in discipline and self-respect was of paramount importance. My earlier experiences in an orphanage taught me a great deal about independence.

Respect for the straightforward approach and a refusal to hide the name 'epilepsy' earned me the offer of work immediately on leaving school The scarcity of work at that time made me realise the importance of the old saying: 'Honesty is the best policy'. After two years in assisting in the landscaping of three and a half acres of garden, my employer obtained for me a position of apprenticeship on the local golf course and after three years of a correspondence course and hard work, I became a qualified greenkeeper. It was a great disappointment to both myself and the course curator (whose relationship with me had been, and remained, virtually father to son) when the club did not retain me as an assistant greenkeeper.

However, being well-known, I had no trouble finding employment and for nine years worked in a variety of positions as a freelance employee. This broadened my knowledge and capabilities.

During the Second World War, the encephalogram became available and I was an early recipient of it. It verified the specialist's diagnosis and I was given Dilantin and Prominal on a trial basis as they had been shown to control or reduce seizures. The result was complete seizure control.

In 1947 the position of head greenkeeper became vacant at the Blue Mountains Golf Course. At my interview with the engineers I stressed my position with epilepsy and every possibility of full control. In due course I received notice for a further interview with the chief engineer who, on informing me that the position was mine, remarked that my openness gained me the position. My final 32 years in the workforce were spent with the council.

My social life has been very full. Besides caring for my mother until her death in 1972 all my working life I have been involved in associations and organisations involved in social and charitable activities. Since retirement 13 years ago, I have become involved with the Alzheimer's Association and the Epilepsy Association. I represent these organisations in interagency activities. I live alone, but am never lonely. My basic philosophy of moral fidelity and being ever mindful of the needs of others has been my mainstay, ensuring a contented mind.

To people with epilepsy, carers and potential employers alike: epilepsy is not a dirty word and, with love tempered with firmness and self-discipline, the person with epilepsy in the majority of cases can lead a happy and fruitful life.

SANDY AND DES

Sandy and Des are married and have one child. They both have severe vision impairments which they have lived with for all or most of their lives. More recently, Sandy has acquired chronic fatigue syndrome and, in many ways, this has had a more handicapping effect on her life than has her vision impairment. Sandy is a person who can personally compare the effects of having a lifelong disability versus one which has been recently acquired (see Chapter 1). This account reveals that Sandy and Des are people who have taken a positive approach to life and have found ways to adapt to their disabilities but, in many cases, the impact of disability has been exacerbated by external factors (for example, schooling and the absence of safe footpaths near their home). This account was written by Des.

Sandy's blindness is caused by a genetic condition – retinitis pigmentosa (RP). She is the youngest of three children. The eldest, a brother, is also blind, but the older sister has normal sight. Sandy and her brother Barry inherited the recessive form of the retinitis pigmentosa gene from their parents – each of whom was a carrier of this recessive gene.

When Barry was born, and his vision impairment was first diagnosed, the parents were told that it had a one in four chance of occurring in other children they might have. When the first girl was born, with no apparent vision problems, the parents were not concerned about the prospect of another child being born with the same vision impairment. Then Sandy was born, and it was then realised that there was a one in four chance at each conception of the child being affected. There was equally a one in four chance of the child having normal sight and not inheriting the recessive gene from either parent, and a one in two chance of the child being not affected but being a carrier (inheriting the recessive gene from only one of the parents).

Both Sandy and Barry were to some extent atypical of the general manner in which RP presents in that they both showed early onset signs of the condition. The more common scenario is that people might progress through life with little difficulty performing visual tasks and then experience a series of visual field deteriorations with 'tunnel vision' and 'night blindness' being the functional ramifications.

Whereas Barry was educated at a special school for blind children, Sandy had the advantage of attending her local infants and primary schools. This was only made possible through the cooperation of the incumbent school principal and a lot of extra work from her parents in reading and recording material for her on tape. At this time there were no itinerant support teachers to facilitate the integration of students with vision impairment in mainstream classes.

Sandy's experience of secondary education was, unfortunately, not as positive as that for primary school. She was forced to attend a special 'partially sighted unit' at a high school other than the one which was literally at the end of her street. However, her earlier school experience and the tremendous support she had from her parents was sufficiently positive to instil a strong sense of identity and ability to cope independently. The down side to the model of special education which was in vogue at this time was that there was no recognition of her individuality and hence a denial of the opportunity for a person's full potential to be realised.

My own situation is a stark contrast to that of Sandy. I am the ninth of ten children raised in an authoritarian environment. My Asian heritage predisposes me towards myopia because of its high incidence in the Asiatic gene pool. Every member of my family had spectacles prescribed for myopia. I attended my local school until the end of fourth class primary. Each year, when the school medical checks were done, I was prescribed progressively stronger and stronger spectacles. These worked fine for close tasks, but at no stage in my school life was I ever able to read from the blackboard. Technically, I would have been a candidate for a 'partially sighted unit', but perhaps such things didn't exist in the early 1950s.

Being blessed with a highly retentive memory actually meant that my school experiences after fourth class went to the other extreme. I was placed in classes for children of above average ability. I went to Woollahra Opportunity School and thence Sydney Boys' High School, neither of which were in my local area. Because I didn't really understand the nature of my vision problem (we all thought I was just incredibly short-sighted) and my self-concept at adolescence was not particularly strong, I found it hard to talk about the difficulties I had in coping with the school work in later years. (Up until then I had managed by listening carefully and trusting to my memory, still without ever being able to read anything from the board.) Because of my own inability to handle the issues relating to my vision impairment, I opted for 'non-participation' during my last two years of high school. The consequence was that I failed my final exams and probably disappointed my parents, even though nothing was ever said to that effect.

After leaving school, I followed my first vocation and studied art at East Sydney. I left the course without completing it to commence work as a graphic designer. At about the same time I had my first prescription for contact lenses, and with these I was able to correct my vision sufficiently to obtain my driver's licence. This achievement brought inestimable independence to my life, not to mention a huge upsurge in my self-esteem and personal relationships with the opposite sex.

Like all good things, it could not last, and I started having difficulty seeing the fine detail necessary for producing finished artwork for print reproduction. I left my job as a graphic designer after four years and relied solely on my second string – working as a musician in the then very active Sydney club scene. In 1974 I underwent surgery to repair a non traumatic retinal detachment and pathology results indicated that I had contracted toxoplasmosis. This is an infection carried by domestic cats which can be passed on to women who are pregnant with some negative consequences for the unborn child. Put simply, the infection can affect sensitive nerve cells, in my case those in the macular region of the retina. This had been the underlying reason for my abnormal low vision and continual deterioration of sight from birth (not the hereditary myopia).

With the loss of eligibility (but not the ability) to drive, and the inability to see well enough to read musical arrangements when backing floor show artists, my career as a club musician was abruptly terminated. Upon referral to the Royal Blind Society, I chose to learn touch-typing and braille. These two skills have proved invaluable to me.

My mid-life crisis led me to alternate carer paths via retraining and my extensive study/work in community welfare, counselling and education.

This brings me to my current position with TAFE NSW, where I work as a teacher/consultant for students with vision impairment – a job in which I can share with my students many of the 'tricks of the trade'. Much of the support to the students comes in the form of 'reasonable adjustment' via adaptive technology – computer software and hardware which facilitates the accommodation of students with vision impairments into their chosen courses of study. This technology is the means by which I can effectively perform my job. However, sometimes it is difficult to keep up with changes in technology. For example, I am currently confronted by the spectre of the GUI (graphical user interface) (such as Microsoft Windows and now Windows 95) which presents enormous problems for blind consumers who are reliant on speech output to access their computers. This battle still rages.

On a more personal note, Sandy and I have done a complete about face regarding our position on starting a family. Originally, we decided not to have children, based on our understanding of the genetic probabilities of our situation. That is, any offspring would be carriers of the recessive form of RP (from Sandy), but the probability of our offspring being affected would depend on whether I also carried the same gene. Our research indicated that there was a lesser incidence of RP in the Asian gene pool and the predisposition towards myopia from my side was not such a critical issue. Our original decision not to have children was largely based on our belief that we ought not to knowingly perpetuate a recessive gene.

After some ten years of marriage and, in Sandy's case, a change in career orientation which saw her voluntarily leave a highly-paid computer programming job to undertake university study and less highly-paid social science research work, we revised our thinking on the issue of children. We figured that between us we had sufficient knowledge, skills and experience relating to the issue of vision impairment and its implications for education and employment so that, if we should have a child who also had a vision impairment, we had the right resources to cope with the situation. Perhaps as a further justification, we also told ourselves that (unknowingly) we all can carry recessive genes for any number of things, so the question of inherited conditions is as much (if not more) a lottery for other couples who are not aware of any family history of inherited conditions.

We had a positive experience of childbirth and the preparations preceding it. Antenatal classes and consultations with the gynaecologist culminated in the birth of our daughter in the Birth Centre at the Royal Hospital for Women at Paddington. Samantha is now seven years old, bright, active, with no hint of any form of vision impairment.

The intervening years have not been the easiest due mainly to the fact that Sandy has had chronic fatigue syndrome (CFS) or ME for the last six years. This was probably precipitated by the fact that Samantha never slept through the night until the age of nine months, so the disrupted sleep pattern might have affected Sandy's immune response to environmental stressors. This phase of our lives also explains why there are no siblings for Samantha. When we decided to start a family, we wanted at least two children. The CFS complicated matters to the extent that, when we finally decided that we felt sufficiently able to cope with life and CFS, things just didn't work out for us, so we are resigned to the fact that we have only one child.

The important point to make here is that Sandy's blindness and my vision impairment are less restrictive or limiting factors in our life than the CFS.

When Samantha was very small, it was difficult for Sandy to take her places independently in the stroller. This was because in our area there are many streets which do not have footpaths. It is really difficult anyway for a blind person to use the white cane in one hand to negotiate whatever obstacles might be in the path, while pulling a baby in a stroller. It is not possible to push the stroller because you can't see what hazards might be in front. Thus, this whole process was further exacerbated by the lack of footpaths. The grass nature strips and gravel driveways were too rough. The stroller had to be pulled along in the gutter as close as possible to the kerb.

When Samantha started playgroup and preschool, Sandy took full responsibility for organising the programs. Sandy's highly developed communication skills enabled her to easily feel comfortable with articulating what she needed in order to participate, and she made some good friends with other mothers who offered her help with transport to and from these activities. At the commencement of Samantha's formal schooling we both requested a meeting with the school principal to learn how the school was run and discuss ways in which we could be involved. Right from kindergarten, Sandy has worked with the children from Samantha's class, helping with their reading and maths. This is accomplished by using children's story books with both print and Braille, and large magnetic letters and numbers which can be placed on a metal scone tray. Sandy also now works with primary school children who are slow-to-learn and this extra individual attention has helped these children make far greater progress in their work.

As Samantha has grown, and taken up more and more after-school activities, we have developed a stable pattern or routine in which one or other of us assumes responsibility. Sandy has also opted to become involved in the school parents and teachers association which meets monthly.

To summarise, I think that Sandy's ability to cope with the various tasks and responsibilities in her life has come from the solid foundations that her parents laid down in those critical formative years. All we hope is that between us, we can do as good a job in helping our daughter develop the personal attributes she might need to cope with whatever challenges she might face in life.

RAY

The following account is taken with permission from Ray's book. The account describes his experience of mental illness and gives a vivid picture of what it is like to live with delusions and his own version of reality. Ray also talks about the steps he has taken to come to terms with schizophrenia.

I was wandering round my home town, literally dressed in rags at times, telling my friends that aliens were invading the world. I told people I was having mental battles with these aliens on television, and I was doing strange things. For example, I would go to bed with sticking plaster all over my mouth because I thought I was talking in my sleep and revealing all my very personal thoughts. One time I was at a friend's place – there were about a dozen of us – and I was convinced they were the disciples come down from heaven. I told one guy that I couldn't be hurt. I grabbed a blunt knife and started stabbing myself in the stomach. Of course it was so blunt it hardly left a mark, but then, as an act of faith, I snatched a very sharp-pointed knife and was about to plunge it into myself when my friend, with a look of horror, grabbed the knife from me, cutting his own hand in the process.

The day I was taken to hospital I had been sitting watching a football match and went into a catatonic trance. I was watching the game and, for reasons I can't remember, contorted my body into an unusual position and refused to respond to those around me. I supposed they thought I was freaking out on drugs, but I hadn't had any for ages. I fell into a deep trance. I could hear my heart beating. It was slowing down. I felt the absence of my heartbeat and expelled all the air from my lungs. It seemed that I was drifting through a red mist toward a small light. As I got closer I could see that the light was an opening to another place, dimension if you like. I could see what I can only describe as perfect faces of about three or four men. They were beckoning to me, saying, 'Come on, you can make it'. Suddenly I was filled with fear as the thought occurred to me that I would have to die first. I started slipping away and the faces changed into ordinary men's faces with beards and long hair. I opened my eyes and gulped in air and became aware that an ambulance officer was pounding my chest. I was led away to the nearby fire station and restrained. It took about six of my strong surfie mates to hold me down. They carried me off with my pants pulled down, feeling very humiliated, to an ambulance and I was driven to hospital.

I had weird religious delusions. I believed I was the second son of God and many of these delusions recurred in all three of my breakdowns. During my first one I nominated and accepted myself as president of the world. I was surrounded by witches, warlocks, assassins, vampires, werewolves, aliens from various worlds and many different so-called gods. Clouds in the sky were, to me, gods watching with great interest. They dubbed me 'the defiant one', as I often fought with them.

It's very hard for other people to understand how the mind, bereft of reason, explains very convincingly that the delusions are actually reality.

I quite often walked in front of cars knowing they couldn't hit me because of the power I possessed. When they screeched to a halt, sometimes inches from me, I could hold up the one-way sign, a finger pointed to the heavens. I couldn't understand why some would turn pale and be shaking and others would become abusive. After all, nobody could hurt me.

It seemed to me that most of my friends deserted me. A number of my mates came to visit me once, but they didn't come again. My brothers were pillars of strength to me during those times. They would come to visit me after school regularly. Sometimes when I was a bit better we played table tennis or just talked. They stood by me thick and thin and still do.

Mine certainly has been an interesting life, incredible some might say, but true. Upon reflection I feel I have not conveyed to others the constant misery that I and many like me have had to endure. Life wasn't a challenge, nor was it something to be lived. Rather, it was an empty, miserable journey through a labyrinth of passages filled with loneliness, tears and darkness. Someone looking at my words might think this guy really feels sorry for himself, but if they only knew, if they only knew. To meet me you would not suspect past torments and terrors, instead you would see a reasonably 'together' young man.

I discovered four years ago, after a life of aimlessness and a complete disregard for ambition, that I wanted to be an inventor. At 26 years of age, discontentment and lack of purpose were suddenly replaced by inspiration. I wanted to achieve something in life. Be somebody. I had always failed in everything. School, dead-end jobs, romance, you name it, I failed it. One thing though I hadn't failed at was being a person. Most regard me as a real person. Someone you can turn to in times of trouble or need.

I've invented quite a few things and had quite a few knockbacks. However, once again when I thought I had failed as an inventor, a company has become interested in a gutter cleaner I have invented. Meetings and demonstrations of my invention went very smoothly. Last Tuesday I hired a three-piece suit for the signing of the contract! The suit cost $37, but the forecast of royalties show that they may be as high as $45 000 per year.

Over the last six weeks I haven't experienced any depression, not due to my success as an inventor, but because of the radical change in my attitudes. For years I had told myself that I was worthless, useless and unloved. I was living a lie as I know this to be untrue. Is it any wonder that I became depressed?

I've decided that I've been a martyr long enough. It's now time to turn my life of tragedy into a life of triumph. Perseverance has resulted in the discovery of the secret of the power of positive thinking. Positive, healthy thinking produces a positive, healthy mind. Mind you, I haven't discovered this overnight. It's been a series of events over the last 12 months that have gradually convinced me that many of my attitudes towards myself and life were wrong.

I am embarking on a great adventure. I'm getting off the old steam train which is fuelled by negative self-destructive thoughts and am getting aboard the express train which travels quickly and smoothly along tracks of determination, destined for health, hope and happiness. Even though my thinking and attitudes are taking a new direction, I must be patient. Rome wasn't built in a day – neither will the new Ray be. Sure, some people change overnight, but life is an ongoing experience.

A full account of Ray's story may be found in his book: Ray Brown (1993). *The second son of god: the autobiography of an inventor with schizophrenia.* Fast Books. A portion of the profits from the sale of this book is donated to research and support of people with schizophrenia. The book may be purchased by writing to Ray Brown at PO Box 654, Glebe, NSW 2037, Australia.

MURIEL

Muriel is now in her middle age and continues to enjoy a full and busy life. She is an active advocate for people with short stature. Her account demonstrates that one of the greatest sources of handicap in her life has been the attitudes and behaviours of others. However, she has not let these interfere with her life.

I was raised in an 'ordinary' family where I was the odd one out. My Mum was 5'1", Dad was 5'10" and my two brothers were 6' and 5'11". Then there was me – 4 feet.

My family was great and I was treated the same as everyone else. I attended the local Catholic school where I was accepted as the same as all the other children. I progressed through school at the same rate as my friends and attained the Intermediate Certificate.

As a child at home I wasn't aware of being different as I was treated the same as everyone else. It wasn't until I started school that I realised that I was 'special'. My school friends were great; however, travelling to and from school sometimes caused me to be ridiculed by other children. My friends always stood by me, sometimes to the point of embarrassment, as they defended me. Having two older and protective brothers also helped relieve any nasty situations.

During adolescence, I found life sometimes hard. When I went out with my girlfriends to dances it was rare that I'd get asked to dance, but when I did, boy I'd enjoy myself.

I was always encouraged to try almost anything and this, I think, made me more confident.

I was employed as a typist for my first job, saved my money and headed off overseas at the age of 18 where I worked for three years in the United Kingdom. Upon my return I re-entered the workforce to work at Bankstown Police Station as a typist.

During this time I met my husband while on holidays in Port Macquarie. We married and we saw a genetics doctor to establish the probability of having children with short stature. We learned that we had a 50 per cent chance of having a little person, 25 per cent chance that the child would be of average stature and 25 per cent chance that the child would have a double dose of genes (causing respiratory difficulties). Unfortunately, we experienced this problem twice; however, we have two lovely children, both of whom are 'little people'.

Our older daughter is now 19 and engaged to another 'little person'. They are to be married next year. Our younger daughter is now 12 and has just started high school. Both girls are very capable and I hope I have imparted my confidence to them.

Both my husband and I enjoy indoor carpet bowls as well as lawn bowls. I have always encouraged my children to participate in as many activities as they feel able to do comfortably.

Whether small, tall or disabled in any way, your attitude towards yourself, as well as other people, makes you who you are. I trust the way I was raised and have brought up my children to accept what they are and to be aware of what they can contribute to others.

MARGARET

Margaret is the mother of two young children, one, Julian, has cerebral palsy. In this account she vividly explains her experiences dealing with professionals and then recounts her joy in coming to realise that her child is a gift and has much to give to the world.

We moved to a small country town in the Central West of NSW three years ago, full of enthusiasm. We were expecting our second child and felt a sense of freedom, buying our first home. The people seemed to be friendly, which was what we had expected from the 'real' Aussies, out on the land. Unfortunately, this has not always been the case.

After three months our son, Julian, was born in April 1994. There were no complications during pregnancy or labour; however, he was very sleepy and difficult to arouse for feeds. When he did feed, he had problems sucking because his cheek muscles were weak; consequently, he lost weight. At age seven weeks, the early childhood nurse pointed out that Julian was delayed in his milestones. The implications of the word 'delayed' meant nothing serious to me, I just thought 'oh well, he'll catch up'.

Julian contracted bronchiolitis when he was four months old and was rushed to Orange Base Hospital. I then had my first, but not my last, experience of being spoken to in an inappropriate and unprofessional way by health care staff. This was very upsetting, as I felt very vulnerable. During this time, I met another mother whose son had cerebral palsy, and some of his symptoms sounded the same as Julian's. It was the first time that a possible description came to light. I wasn't sure what cerebral palsy entailed and when I did find out I was horrified.

A child born with cerebral palsy is an enigma – no child is exactly alike in presentation. There are different types of cerebral palsy: shaky (ataxic), floppy (athetoid) and stiff (spastic), and varying types of paralysis (partial, paraplegia, quadriplegia). The future can also hold epilepsy, difficulties with hearing, speech and sight, and recurrent chest infections, just to name a few.

It is a common misconception that physical and intellectual disabilities coincide, however, with cerebral palsy, this is most often not the case. A fact I clung to!

Two months later, a leading paediatric neurologist informed us that Julian appeared to be severely brain damaged. I was in a kind of mental and emotional 'fog' for many months and could only cope one day at a time. The main problem was lack of sleep. Unfortunately, I was isolated from my family and was not told about available services straight away, otherwise most of this exhaustion could have been averted.

I experienced grief, helplessness, worry, fear, confusion, guilt, anger, and loneliness. All of which resulted in bodily stress – extreme fatigue, headaches, loss of hair, aches and pains, feelings of vulnerability, bursting into tears quite often, and the inability to be assertive just when I really needed to be.

You grieve for the loss of a dream and for your child who deserves the same chances in life as anyone else (but you know he probably won't get those same chances); you grieve for what your child may never experience. You feel uncertain, because in the early stages, professionals can't tell you exactly what is wrong or what the future may hold. You fear that you mightn't be able to cope, that your marriage won't survive, that you aren't spending enough time with your other children. You worry about your child's health, about finances, about finding the right services and doing enough therapy.

You worry about what will happen if you die, or will your child die? How will other people treat him and his siblings? Will he be able to speak, hear, walk or think? Will he have fits? Will he be able to go to school, have friends, get married, have children and be happy?

I initially spent 12 hours a day feeding Julian. He also had reflux so I was worried whether he was getting enough nutrition. It is only now, after two years that he is able to eat the same food as the rest of the family. A major achievement for both of us!

His hearing is very sensitive, which makes it difficult in noisy places such as shopping centres. He is tactile sensitive and, although this is improving in his hands, his feet are not improving. This inhibits his ability to stand and walk.

Without the help we needed earlier, Julian is afraid of being held by strangers. Now that I can get some help (paid), it is too late, as he is too distressed. For the first 18 months I monitored his breathing all night, getting up at least once to turn him over; however, this is improving.

Of course, there are also lots of good times! The love you share for each other, the joy when each child learns something new and with Julian each success is even sweeter. Our three year old daughter, Susannah, is a big help and adores Julian.

In December 1994, when Julian was eight months old, the fog began to clear, and we looked at alternative therapies, since doctors couldn't help. We visited a chiropractic clinic. I'd had many consultations in the past and felt confident with the expertise of professionals here, especially when manipulating such a delicate area as the neck. They are also skilled in laser acupuncture (no needles, no pain) combined with electro meridian imaging (a diagnostic computer used by many GPs in the United States).

They discovered that Julian's neck was badly out of alignment. My husband then recalled the obstetrician having to turn Julian during the birth, twisting his neck severely. Immediately after Julian's neck was realigned we could see him truly come alive. Rather than looking sleepy, hunched and not moving his arms and hands, Julian now straightened his back, and looked around him with interest. For the first time, he focused on me with recognition and love, and with the most beautiful smile! We couldn't believe the transformation – you could see the lights switch on in his eyes and mind. He brought his arms and hands forward, discovering them for the first time and for several months from that day he continuously played with and studied his fingers, catching up on lost time. The 28th December 1994, a fabulous day that we shall always remember, and no more migraines for Julian! With a combination of mainstream and alternative type therapies, I am sure Julian will catch up by the time he starts school.

It is August 1996 and Julian is able to sit unsupported, and can say three words. It is music to my ears! Each week he has progressed in some small but significant area – he is bright, alert and enjoying life. We are very grateful to all those therapists, alternative and mainstream, who are helping us enjoy life. For me, it has been a crash course in self-development and enrichment.

Julian is a special gift, like all children, and we shall do our best to allow him to enjoy the best life has to offer. early intervention is vital, as is getting information on resources and services. There is not enough information in doctors' surgeries nor community health centres on available services or treatments. Information is not circulated to all staff, nor is it displayed for all visitors/patients to see. There is so much that can be done to improve the lives of children like Julian and I pass on my good news to everyone in the hope that someone else may be helped by our story. One day Julian will be able to tell you his story *himself*!

BIBLIOGRAPHY

Aaseng, N. (1991). *Cerebral palsy.* USA: Venture.

Ablon, J. (1988). *Living with difference: families with dwarf children.* New York: Preager.

Ablon, J. (1990). Ambiguity and difference: families of dwarf children. *Social Science and Medicine,* 30, 870–87.

Aboriginal Medical Services Cooperative (1991). *NSW Aboriginal mental health report.* Sydney: AMSC.

Ackehurst, S. (1989). *Broken silence.* London: Collins.

Ainlay, S. (1989). *Day brought back my night: ageing and new vision loss.* London: Routledge.

Alsop, L. (1988). *Mothers with disabilities: their needs.* Canberra: Office on the Status of Women.

Altman, B. M. (1985). Disabled women in the social structure. In S. E. Browne, D. Connors & N. Stern (eds.). *With the power of each breath: a disabled women's anthology.* Pittsburg: Cleis.

American Academy of Orthopaedic Surgeons (1981). *Atlas of limb prosthetics. Surgical and prosthetic principles.* St. Louis: C. V. Mosby.

American Association on Mental Retardation (1990a). *Mental retardation: definition, classification and systems of supports* (9th edn). Washington, DC: AAMR.

American Association on Mental Retardation (1990b). Proposed definition. *AAMR News & Notes,* 3, Nov–Dec.

American Association on Mental Retardation (1992). *Mental retardation* (9th edn). Washington, DC: AAMR.

American Psychiatric Association (1994). *Diagnostic and statistical manual of mental disorders* (4th edn). Washington, DC: APA.

Ammer, C. (1991). *Getting help: a consumer's guide to therapy.* New York: Paragon House.

Anderson, K., Henderson, G. & Whittaker, C. (1995). No small task. *Diabetes Dialogue,* 42 (3), 6–13.

Arthritis Foundation of Australia (undated, a). *Osteoarthritis.* Sydney: AFA.

Arthritis Foundation of Australia (undated, b). *Rheumatoid arthritis.* Sydney: AFA.

Arthritis Foundation of NSW (1995). *The arthritis handbook* (2nd edn). Sydney: MacLennan & Petty.

Arthritis Foundation USA (1990). *Living and loving: information about sex.* Atlanta, GA: Arthritis Foundation.

Arthritis Foundation USA (1993). *Primer of rheumatic diseases* (10th edn). Atlanta, GA: Arthritis Foundation.

Arthritis Society of Canada (1991). *The arthritis treatment team.* Toronto, Ontario: ASC.

Arthritis Society of Canada (1994a). *Arthritis, diet and nutrition.* Toronto, Ontario: ASC.

Arthritis Society of Canada (1994b). *Corticosteroids.* Toronto, Ontario: ASC.

Asch, A. & Fine, M. (1988). Introduction: beyond pedestals. In M. Fine & A. Asch (eds). *Women with disabilities: essays in psychology, culture and politics.* Philadelphia, PA: Temple University Press.

Australian Bureau of Statistics (1981). *Handicapped persons in Australia, 1981.* Canberra: Australian Government Publishing Service. Cat. No. 4343.0

Australian Bureau of Statistics (1988a). *Disability and handicap.* Canberra: Australian Government Publishing Service. Cat. No. 4120.0

Australian Bureau of Statistics (1988b). *Disabled and aged persons.* Canberra: Australian Government Publishing Service. Cat. No. 4118.0

Australian Bureau of Statistics (1990). *National health survey: musculo-skeletal conditions.* Canberra: Australian Government Publishing Service.

Australian Bureau of Statistics (1993). *Disability, ageing and carers: summary of findings.* Canberra: Australian Government Publishing Service. Cat. No. 4430.0

Australian Federal Government (1993a). *Carer support: intellectual disability.* Canberra: Department of Health and Community Services.

Australian Federal Government (1993b). *Carer support: mental illness.* Canberra: Department of Health and Community Services.

Australian Federal Government (1993c). *Carer support: multiple sclerosis.* Canberra: Department of Health and Community Services.

Australian Federal Government (1993d). *Carer support: spinal cord injury.* Canberra: Department of Health and Community Services.

Australian Health Ministers Conference (1992). *National mental health policy.* Canberra: Australian Government Publishing Service.

Australian Quadriplegic Association (various dates). *Quad Wrangle.* Sydney.

Australian Quadriplegic Association (1988). Home Care Service of NSW. *Quad Wrangle,* Autumn, 3–4.

Australian Quadriplegic Association (1990). United stand on personal care. *Quad Wrangle,* Winter, 6.

Bailey, I. L. & Hall, A. (1990). *Visual impairment: an overview.* New York: American Foundation for the Blind.

Barnes, L. & Krasnoff, A. (1973). Medical and psychological factors pertinent to the rehabilitation of the epileptic. In A. B. Cobb (ed.). *Medical and psychological aspects of disability.* Springfield, Ill: Charles C. Thomas.

Barnes, C. & Oliver, M. (1995). Disability rights: rhetoric and reality in the UK. *Disability and Society,* 10, 111–16.

Barry, P. D. (1989). *Psychosocial nursing: assessment and intervention* (2nd edn). Philadelphia: Lippincott.

Batterham, G. (1986). *Everything you want to know about attendant care but were too afraid to ask.* Sydney: Department of Community Services and Stormbringer Film Productions.

Baume, T. & Kay, K. (1995). *Working solution.* Canberra: Australian Government Publishing Service.

Baumgart, D. (1990). *Augmentative and alternative communication systems for persons with moderate and severe disabilities.* Baltimore: Paul H. Brookes.

Beaumont, M. (1987). *Epilepsy in education, a manual for teachers.* Melbourne: National Epilepsy Association of Australia Inc.

Benz, C. (1994). *Coping with multiple sclerosis.* London: Optima.

Bergman, T. (1991). *Going places: children living with cerebral palsy.* Milwaukee: G. S. Childrens' Books.

Bergman, J. S. (1994). Protecting the mobility of the aging person with cerebral palsy or spina bifida. *Preventing secondary conditions associated with spina bifida or cerebral palsy: proceedings and recommendations of a symposium.* Washington: Spina Bifida Association of America.

Bidmeade, I. (1994). *Legislation and integration: an audit of legislation which impacts upon the integration of people with a disability in Australia.* Intellectual Disability Services Council.

Biggs, A. (1994). *Congenital limb deficiencies, a course in lower extremity prosthetics.* 5.17–5.22. Sydney: Centre for Continuing Medical Education, University of New South Wales.

Blair, E. & Stanley, F. C. (1988). Intrapartus asphyxia: a rare cause of cerebral palsy. *Journal of Paedicatrics,* 112, 515–19.

Bloom, B. A. & Seljeskig, E. L. (1988). *A parent's guide to spina bifida*. Minnesota: University of Minnestoa Press.

Bogod, N. (1995). A family affair. *Disability Today*, 4 (1), 26–40.

Booth, T. & Booth, W. (1994). *Parenting under pressure: mothers and fathers with learning difficulties*. Buckingham, UK: Open University Press.

Boschen, K. (1995). Variables affecting independent living for persons with physical disabilities. Paper read at the Colloquium on the environmental determinants to social participation. Quebec, Canada, September.

Bostock, L. (1991). Access and equity for people with a double disadvantage. *Australian Disability Review*, 2, 3–8.

Bowe, F. (1983). *Disabled women in America*. Washington, DC: President's Committee on Employment of the Handicapped.

Bowman, D. & Virtue, M. (1993). *Public policy. Private lives*. Canberra: Australian Institute on Intellectual Disability.

Boyd, R. D. & Otos, M. B. (1981). Hearing disorders. In J. E. Lindemann (ed.). *Psychological and behavioral aspects of physical disability*. New York: Plenum Press.

Boyd, R. D. & Young, N. B. (1981). Hearing disorders. In J. E. Lindemann (ed.). *Psychological and behavioral aspects of physical disability: a manual for health practitioners*. New York: Plenum Press.

Bozic, S., Hermann, H. & Schofield, H. (1993). *A profile of carers in Victoria: analysis of the ABS survey of disabled and aged persons 1988*. Melbourne: Victorian Health Foundation.

Brackenridge, B. P. & Dolinar, R. O. (1993). *Diabetes 101: a pure and simple guide for people who use insulin*. Minneapolis: Chronimed Publishing.

Brain Injury Women's Network (1995). *Perceptions of a mother after brain injury*. Sydney: Brain Injury Association of NSW.

Brentnall, B. & Dunlop, M. (1985). *Distance and disability: a survey of children with disabilities in isolated areas of Australia*. Sydney: Uniting Church National Mission Frontier Services.

Brewer, E. J. & Angel, K. C. (1993). *The arthritis sourcebook*. Los Angeles: Lowell House.

Brintnell, E. S., Madill, H. M., Montgomerie, T. C. & Stewin, L. L. (1992). Work and family issues after injury: do female and male client perspectives differ? *The Career Development Quarterly*, 41, December, 145–60.

Brintnell, E. S., Madill, H. M., Montgomerie, T. C. & Stewin, L. L. (1994). Disruption of life roles following injury: the impact on women's social networks. *WORK*, 4, 137–46.

Brooks, N., Campsie, L., Symington, C., Beattie, A. & McKinlay, W. (1986). The five year outcome of severe blunt head injury: a relative's view. *Journal of Neurology, Neurosurgery and Psychiatry*, 49, 764–70.

Brown, R. (1993). *Young people and epilepsy*. Melbourne: National Epilepsy Association of Australia Inc.

Brown, R. (1994). *The second son of God*. Sydney: Fast Books.

Buchanan, N. (1987). *Epilepsy and you*. Sydney: MacLennan & Petty.

Buchanan, N. (1989). *Epilepsy questions and answers*. Sydney: MacLennan & Petty.

Buchanan, N. (1994). *Understanding epilepsy*. Sydney: Simon and Schuster.

Burdekin, B. (1993). *Human rights and mental illness: report of the national inquiry into the human rights of people with mental illness*. Sydney: Human Rights and Equal Opportunity Commission.

Burgess, E. M. & Rappoport, A. *Physical fitness: a guide for individuals with lower limb loss*. Washington, DC: Department of Veterans Affairs.

Butler, S. R. (ed.) (1990). *The exceptional child*. Sydney: Harcourt Brace Jovanovich.

Campion, S. (1992). *A handbook on pregnancy for women with a physical disability*. New York: Routledge.

Campling, J. (1981). *Images of ourselves*. London: Routledge & Kegan Paul.

Canadian Diabetes Association (1994). *Your student with diabetes: a practical guide.* Toronto, Ontario: CDA.

Canadian Diabetes Association (1995a). *Diabetes and pregnancy.* Toronto, Ontario: CDA.

Canadian Diabetes Association (1995b). *Just like any other kid.* Toronto, Ontario: CDA.

Canadian Diabetes Association (1995c). *Planning meals for your guest with diabetes.* Toronto, Ontario: CDA.

Campling, J. (1981). *Images of ourselves.* London: Routledge & Kegan Paul.

Canadian Government (1982). *Canadian charter of rights, prohibitions and freedoms.* Ottawa, Canada.

Canadian National Institute for the Blind (1988). *Statistical information on the client population of the CNIB.* Toronto: CNIB.

Caras, S. (1994). Disabled, one more label. *Disability, Handicap and Society,* 9, 89–92.

Carroll, D. L. & Dorman, J. D. (1993). *Living well with MS: a guide for patient, caregiver and family.* New York: Harper Perennial.

Carter, G. & Jancar, J. (1985). Mortality in the mentally handicapped: a 50 year study of the State Park Group Hospitals (1930–1980). *Journal of Mental Deficiency Research,* 27, 143–56.

Cathels, B. A. & Reddihough, D. S. (1993). The health care of young adults with cerebral palsy. *Medical Journal of Australia,* 159, 444–6.

Chamberlain, M. A. (1984). Work for the disabled. *British Medical Journal,* 639–40.

Chedd, N. A. (1995). Getting started with augmentive communication. *Exceptional Parent,* May, 34–9.

Chubon, R. A. (1982). An analysis of research dealing with the attitudes of professionals toward disability. *Journal of Rehabilitation,* 48, 25–9.

Cobb, A. B. (1973). *Medical and psychological aspects of disability.* Springfield, Ill: Charles C. Thomas.

Cocks, E. (1989). *An introduction to intellectual disability in Australia.* Canberra: Australian Institute on Intellectual Disability.

Cocks, E. & Ng, C. P. (1983). Characteristics of those persons registered with the Mental Retardation Division. *Australian and New Zealand Journal of Developmental Disabilities,* 9, 117–21.

Cogher, L., Savage, E. & Smith, M. (eds.) (1992). *Cerebral palsy: management of disability series.* London: Chapman Hall.

Cohen, M. (1982). *Diabetes: a pocket book of management* (3rd edn). Sydney: Commonwealth Serum Laboratories.

Cohen, M. (1986). *Diabetes: a pocket book of management* (4th edn). Sydney: Commonwealth Serum Laboratories.

Colman, P. (1989). Type I diabetes: how to make prevention work. *Diabetes Conquest,* 21–7.

Commonwealth Department of Human Services and Health (1993). *Disability services standards handbook.* Canberra: Department of Human Services and Health.

Commonwealth of Australia (1986). *Disability Services Act.* Canberra: Australian Government Publishing Service.

Commonwealth of Australia (1992). *Disability Discrimination Act.* Canberra: Australian Government Publishing Service.

Commonwealth of Australia (1994). *Disability Services Standards.* Canberra: Australian Government Publishing Service.

Cooper, M. (1993). Discrimination against women with disabilities. *Australian Disability Review,* 4, 69–72.

Corbett, J. & Ralph, S. (1994). Empowering adults: the changing image of charity advertising. *Australian Disability Review,* 1–94, 5–14.

Corrick, J. A. (1992). *Muscular dystrophy.* Venture: New York.

Covington, G. (1995). Submission to the North American revision of the international classification of impairments, disabilities and handicaps. Quebec, September.

Crandall, R. (ed.) (1994). *Dwarfism: the family and professional guide*. Irvine, CA: Short Stature Foundation and Information Center Inc.

Crisp, R. A. (1984). Locus of control as a predictor of adjustment to spinal injury. *Australian Disability Review*, 1, 53–7.

Crisp, R. A. (1987). Helping relationships: key issues. *Australian Disability Review*, 1, 56–9.

Crisp, R. A. (1992). Return to work after traumatic brain injury. *Journal of Rehabilitation*, Oct/Nov/Dec, 27–33.

Cristall, B. (1992). *When a parent has multiple sclerosis*. New York: Rosen.

Cuff, C. (1987). *Brain injury program for New South Wales: GIO's commitment under Transcover*. Sydney: Cuff Consultants Pty Ltd.

Dahl, J. (1992). *Epilepsy*. Seattle: Hogrefe & Huber, Publishers.

Davis, F. (1963). *Passage through crisis: polio victims and their families*. Indianapolis: Bobbs-Merrill.

Dawson, D. (1994). Tricks for better recall: overcoming memory problems after a brain injury. *Abilities*, Summer, 23.

De Loach, C. & Greer, B. G. (1981). *Adjustment to severe physical disability*. New York: McGraw-Hill.

Dempsey, I. (1994). Parental empowerment: an achievable outcome of the national disability standards. *Australian Disability Review*, 1–94, 21–31.

De Souza, L. (1990). *Multiple sclerosis: approaches to management*. London: Chapman & Hall.

Devinsky, O. (1994). *A guide to understanding and living with epilepsy*. Philadelphia: F. A. Davis Co.

Diabetes Australia Association (1988). *Diabetes in Australia*. Canberra: DAA.

Dickson, H., Martens, D., Dever, L. & Tonkin, J. (1993). *Spinal injuries handbook*. Sydney: The Prince Henry Hospital.

Disability Services Coordination Unit (1989). *Statement of principles for people with disabilities and their families in NSW*. Sydney: NSW Government.

DisAbled Women's Network (DAWN) (1995). The risk of physical and sexual assault. *Abilities*, Spring, 32–3.

Disablement Income Group (1990). *Disablement doesn't bear thinking about*. London: Millmead Business Centre.

Dormans, J. P. & Pellegrino, L. (in press). *Caring for children with cerebral palsy: a team approach*. Baltimore: Paul H. Brookes.

Dorval, J. (1994). Achieving and maintaining body systems integrity and function: clinical issues. *Preventing secondary conditions associated with spina bifida or cerebral palsy: proceedings and recommendations of a symposium*. Washington, DC: Spina Bifida Association of America.

Doucette, H. (1986). *Violent acts against disabled women*. Toronto, Ontario: Disabled Women's Network.

Douglas, C. (1987). Queensland parents of the disabled. *Australian Disability Review*, 1, 2–3.

Drake, H. (1981). *It's only a leg!* Sydney: Sydney Better Communication.

Ducharme, S. H. & Gill, K. M. (1997). *Sexuality after spinal cord injury: answers to your questions*. Baltimore: Paul H. Brookes.

Duckworth, S. (1987). *The vacation activity centre and people with disabilities*. Sydney: NSW Department of Sport, Recreation and Racing.

Dumpleton, H. (1989). *Addups and takeaways*. Sydney: Kezza Enterprises.

Dunbar, R. E. (1991). *Mental retardation*. New York: Franklin Watts.

Durrance, J. (1992). The aging process and its effect on body systems. Paper presented at the Aging with a lifelong disability workshop, Ontario Federation for Cerebral Palsy, Toronto, May.

Eckerman, A., Dowd, T., Martin, M., Nixon, L., Gray, R. & Chong, E. (1992). *Binan Goonj: bridging cultures in Aboriginal health*. Armidale: University of New England.

Eicher, P. S. & Batshaw, M. L. (1993). Cerebral palsy. *Paediatrics Clinics of North America*, 40, 537–51.

Ellis, J. & Whaite, A. (1987). *From me . . . to you: advice to parents of children with special needs*. Sydney: Williams & Wilkins and Associates.

Elsass, L. & Kinsella, G. (1987). Social interaction following severe closed head injury. *Psychological Medicine*, 17, 57–78.

Emery, A. E. H. (1991). Population frequencies of inherited neuromuscular diseases: a world survey. *Neuromuscular Disorders*, 1, 19–29.

Emery, A. E. H. (1994). *Muscular dystrophy: the facts*. Oxford: Oxford University Press.

Epilepsy Canada. (1994). *Epilepsy: answers to your questions*. Toronto: Epilepsy Canada, Montreal, Quebec.

Evans, J. H. (1976). Changing attitudes towards disabled persons. *Rehabilitation Counseling Bulletin*, 19, 572–9.

Everson, J. M. (1995). *Supporting young adults who are deaf-blind*. Baltimore, MD: Paul. H. Brookes.

Fanning, P. (1993). Issues in the provision of mental health services in remote and rural areas. Paper presented at the Rural Health Forum, Bowral, November.

Fegan, L. & Rauch, A. (1993). *Sexuality and people with intellectual disability*. Sydney: MacLennan & Petty.

Ficke, R. C. (1991). *Digest of data on persons with disabilities*. Washington, DC: National Institute on Disability and Rehabilitation Research.

Fine, M. & Asch, A. (1988). *Women and disabilities*. Philadelphia, PA: Temple University Press.

Fink, A. (1994). *Carers news*. Sydney: Carers Association of NSW.

Fletcher, S. (1986). *The challenge of epilepsy*. Mill Valley, CA: Aura Publishing Co.

Foley, C. (1995). Interventions for women with disabilities. Paper read at Conversation on disability issues II: secondary conditions and ageing with a disability. Syracuse, New York, September.

Fougeyrollas, P. (1995). Explanatory models of the consequences of disease and trauma: an anthropolitical point of view on the handicap production cultural process. Contemporary historical evolution and international debates. Paper read at the Colloquium on the environmental determinants to social participation. Quebec, Canada, September.

Fragomeni, C. (1994). Kristopher's new world. *Disability Today*, 4 (1), 26–9.

Frank, M. (1995). Growing up. *Diabetes Dialogue*, 42 (3), 24–5.

Freeland, A. (1989). *Deafness: the facts*. Oxford: Oxford University Press.

Freeman, J., Vining, E. & Pillas, D. (1993). *Seizures and epilepsy in childhood*. Baltimore: The Johns Hopkins University Press.

Fries, J. F. (1990). *Arthritis: a comprehensive guide*. Reading, MA: Addison Wesley.

Frith, J. (1988). History of multiple sclerosis: an Australian perspective. *Clinical Experimental Neurology*, 25, 7–16.

Fritz, G. & Smith, N. (1985). *The hearing impaired employee: an untapped resource*. London: College-Hill Press.

Fullwood, D. (1993a). *Chances and choices: making integration work*. Sydney: MacLennan & Petty.

Fullwood, D. (1993b). *Here, there and everywhere: integration in our community*. Sydney: NSW Council for Intellectual Disability.

Fuhrer, M. (1995). The role of research. Paper read at Conversation on disability issues II: secondary conditions and ageing with a disability. Syracuse, New York, September.

Garner, A. M. (1981). Diabetes mellitus. In J. E. Lindemann (ed.). *Psychological and behavioural aspects of physical disability*. New York: Plenum Press.

Garner, A., Lipsky, D. & Turnbull, A. (1991). *Supporting families with a child with a disability*. Baltimore: Paul H. Brookes.

Geralis, E. (1991). *Children with cerebral palsy: a parents' guide*. Rockville, MD: Woodbine House.

Gerrits, C. (1994). Epilepsy care in a non-clinical setting: a medical–anthropological study among the Bassa and Kpelle in the rainforest of Liberia, West Africa. *Tropical and Geographical Medicine*, 46, Supplement, 13–17.

Geskie, M. A. & Salasek, J. L. (1988). Attitudes of health care personnel toward persons with disabilities. In H. E. Yuker (ed.). *Attitudes toward people with disabilities.* New York: Springer.

Gething, L. (1984). Cumberland's strategy of changing attitudes towards disabled people. *Australian Disability Review*, 1, 44–52.

Gething, L. (1988). The effects of physical disability on perceptions of health professionals. Paper read at the XXIVth International Congress of Psychology, Sydney, August.

Gething, L. (1990). *Working with older people.* Sydney: W. B. Saunders.

Gething, L. (1992a). Attitudes towards people with disabilities. *Medical Journal of Australia*, 157, 725–6.

Gething, L. (1992b). Judgements by health professionals of personality characteristics of people with visible disabilities. *Social Science and Medicine*, 34 (7), 809–15.

Gething, L. (1994a). Aboriginality and disability. *Aboriginal and Islander Health Worker Journal*, 18, 29–34.

Gething, L. (1994b). The interaction with disabled persons scale. *Journal of Personality and Social Behavior*, 9, 23–42.

Gething, L. (1995). A case study of Australian Aboriginal people with disabilities. *Australian Disability Review*, 95–4, 77–87.

Gething, L. & Fethney, J. (1995). Australian community and professional attitudes towards ageing. Paper presented at the Australian Association of Gerontology Rural Conference, Bathurst, September.

Gething, L., Leonard, R. & O'Loughlin, K. (1986). *Person to person: community awareness of disability.* Sydney: Williams & Wilkins, Adis Press.

Gething, L., Papalia, D. E. & Olds, S. W. (1995). *Lifespan development: second Australasian edition.* Sydney: McGraw Hill.

Gething, L., Poynter, T., Redmayne, G. & Reynolds, F. (1994). *Across the divide: distance, diversity and disability* (Volumes I and II). Sydney: The University of Sydney.

Gething, L. & Wheeler, B. (1992). The interaction with disabled persons scale: a new Australian instrument to measure attitudes toward people with disabilities. *Australian Journal of Psychology*, 44, 75–82.

Glauser, H. C. (undated). *Living with osteogenesis imperfecta: a guidebook for families.* Tampa, FL: OI Foundation Inc. Tampa, Florida.

Goffman. E. (1965). *Notes on the management of a spoiled identity.* Harmondsworth: Penguin.

Goldfarb, L. A., Brotherson, M. J., Summers, J. A. & Turnbull, A. P. (1986). *Meeting the challenge of disability or chronic illness: a family guide.* Baltimore: Paul H. Brookes.

Goodman, S. & Nunn, C. (eds.) (1992). *Coaching amputee athletes.* Canberra: Australian Sports Commission.

Goodwill, G. (1994). The social semiotics of disability. In M. H. Rioux & M. Bach (eds.) *Disability is not measles: new research paradigms in disability.* North York, ON: Roeher Institute.

Goss, S. (1989) *Ragged owlet.* Sydney: Houghton Mifflin.

Goss, S. (1995). *I can live with that.* Melbourne: Epilepsy Foundation of Victoria.

Government Insurance Office. (1988). *Support for self-determination and independence: GIO's commitment to people with spinal cord injury.* Sydney: GIO.

Gram, L. & Dam, M. (1995). *Epilepsy explained.* Copenhagen: Munksgaard.

Greenberg, J. S., Seltzer, M. M. & Greenley, J. R. (1993). Aging parents of adults with disabilities: the gratifications and frustrations of later-life caregiving. *The Gerontologist*, 33, 542–50.

Griffith, E. R. & Lemberg, S. (1993). *Sexuality and the person with a traumatic brain injury: a guide for families.* Philadelphia: Davis Co.

Gronwall, D., Wrightson, P. & Wadell, P. (1990). *Head injury, the facts: a guide for families and care-givers*. Oxford: Oxford University Press.

Gumnit, R. (1995). *The epilepsy handbook*. New York: Raven Press.

Halcrow, J. (1994). *The amputee in the community, a course in lower extremity prosthetics* – course manual. 5.29–5.36. Sydney: Centre for Continuing Medical Education, The University of New South Wales.

Halpern, A. S., Close, D. W. & Nelson, D. J. (1986). *On my own: the impact of semi-independent living programs for adults with mental retardation*. Baltimore: Paul H. Brookes.

Handler, B. S. & Patterson, J. B. (1995). Driving after brain injury. *Journal of Rehabilitation*, April/May/June, 43–9.

Hannaford, S. (1989). Women, disability and society. *Interface*, June, 10–12.

Harrison, J. (1993). Ageing in the international year of the world's indigenous people: what are the issues? Paper presented at the 28th Annual National Conference of the Australian Association of Gerontology, Adelaide, November.

Henderson, C. (1992). On the question of pregnancy. *Inside MS*, Spring, 11–13.

Hillson, F. (1996). Personal communication.

Hillson, R. (1987). *Diabetes: a beyond basics guide*. London: Macdonald & Co.

Hillson, R. (1992). *Diabetes: a new guide*. London: Optima.

Hiscock, V. (1991). Women's forum. *Australian Disability Review*, 3, 1–2.

Hollins, M. (1989). *Understanding blindness*. Hillsdale, NJ: Lawrence Erlbaum Associates.

Holmes, G. E. & Karst, R. H. (1990). The institutionalisation of disability myths: impact on vocational rehabilitation services. *Journal of Rehabilitation*, 56, 20–7.

Hope, M. & Mallos, T. (1995). *Duchenne muscular dystrophy: a guide for teachers*. Sydney: Muscle Diseases Clinic, Prince of Wales Children's Hospital.

Horsfall, J. (1987). Psychiatric non-institutionalisation. Whose needs are served? *Australian Journal of Social Issues*, 22, 530–41.

Human Rights Commission (1984). *Epilepsy and human rights*. Occasional Paper No. 7. Canberra: Australian Government Publishing Service.

Humphreys, J. Rolley, F. & Weinand, H. (1992). How healthy is life in the bush? Problems associated with the assessment of health status in rural Australia. *Australian Journal of Rural Health*, 1, 17–27.

Hunter, E. (1992). Aboriginal health awareness: an overview. Part 1. *Aboriginal and Islander Health Worker Journal*, 16, 14–17.

Hunter, E. (1993). Aboriginal mental health awareness: an overview. Part 2. *Aboriginal and Islander Health Worker Journal*, 17, 8–10.

Hyde, M. & Power, D. (1991). *The use of Australian Sign Language by Deaf people*. Brisbane: Griffith University.

Illinois Department of Rehabilitation Services (1994). Handicapping language: a guide for journalists and the public. *Remedial and Special Education*, 15, 60–2.

ILR Program on Employment and Disability (1994). *Workplace accommodations for persons with musculo-skeletal disorders*. Ithaca, NY: Cornell University.

Jacobs, L. (1988). *A Deaf adult speaks out*. Washington, DC: Gallaudet College Press.

Jacobson, A. (1989). Physical and sexual assault histories among psychiatric outpatients. *American Journal of Psychiatry*, 146, 755–8.

Jacobson, A. & Richardson, B. (1987). Assault experiences of 100 psychiatric inpatients: Evidence for the need for routine enquiry. *American Journal of Psychiatry*, 144, 908–13.

Jeavons, P. M. & Aspinall, A. (1985). *The epilepsy reference book*. London: Harper & Row.

Jennett, B., Teasdale, G., Braakman, R., Minderhound, J. & Knill-Jones, R. (1976). Predicting outcome in individual patients after severe head injury. *The Lancet*, 1031–4.

Joachim, R. (1985). A history of intellectual handicap: permanent acceptance or change? *Australian Disability Review*, 4, 48–54.

Jones, L. E. (1990). Lower limb amputation in three Australian states. *International Disability Studies*, 12, 37–40.

Johnston, C. (ed.) (1993). *Does this child need help: identification and early intervention*. Sydney: NSW Education and Training Foundation and the Australian Early Intervention Association (NSW Chapter) Inc.

Johnston, T. (1989). *Auslan dictionary*. (A dictionary of the sign language of the Australian Deaf community.) Melbourne: Deafness Resources Australia.

Jurisic, V. (1993). Sex and spinal cord injury. *Abilities*, Spring, 18–20.

Kalb, R. & Scheinberg, L. (1992). *Multiple sclerosis and the family*. New York: Demos Publications.

Kass, F. I., Oldham, J. M. & Pardes, H. (1992). *Complete home guide to mental health*. New York: H. Holt.

Kaufman, S. Z. (1988). *Retarded isn't stupid, Mom*. Baltimore: Paul Brookes Publishing Co.

Kemp, J. D. (1995). The impact of secondary conditions and other age-related problems on the lives of persons with disabilities. Keynote address at Conversation on Disability Issues II: secondary conditions and ageing with a disability. Syracuse, New York, September.

Kenihan, K. (1981). *How to be the parents of a handicapped child and survive*. Ringwood, Vic: Penguin.

Kerr, L. (1994). Care for the carers: bridging the gaps. Paper presented to the International Cerebral Palsy Society, Cambridge.

Knopfler, A. (1989). *Diabetes and pregnancy*. London: Macdonald & Co.

Kreutzer, J. S. & Wehman, P. (1990). *Community integration following traumatic brain injury*. Baltimore: Paul H. Brookes.

Krotoski, D. M., Nosek, M. A. & Turk, M. A. (1996). *Women with physical disabilities: achieving and maintaining health and well-being*. Baltimore: Paul H. Brookes.

Kübler-Ross, E. (1969). *On death and dying*. New York: Macmillan.

Landau, E. (1994a). *Deafness*. New York: Twenty First Century Books.

Landau, E. (1994b). *Epilepsy*. New York: Twenty First Century Books.

Lane, H. (1993). *The mask of benevolence: disabling the Deaf community*. New York: Vintage Books.

La Plante, E. (1993). *Seized*. New York: Harper Collins.

LaPlante, M. P. & Carlson, D. (1996). *Disability in the United States: prevalence and causes, 1992. Disability statistics report No. 6*. Washington, DC: National Institute on Disability and Rehabilitation Research.

Lawrence, A. (ed.) (1989). *I always wanted to be a tap dancer*. Sydney: Womens' Advisory Council.

Lee, I. (1988). *Double disability: a training kit*. Sydney: Multicultural Centre, Sydney College of Advanced Education.

Lee, R. (1992). *Deaf liberation*. Middlesex, UK: National Union of the Deaf.

Levine, K. & Wharton, R. (1995). Facilitated communication: what parents should know. *Exceptional Parent*, May, 40–53.

Lewin, T. (1990). As the retarded live longer, anxiety grips aging parents. *New York Times*, 28 Oct.

Lewis, N. (1987). Deaf culture. *CHIPS, 12*, September.

Lim, C. (1993a). Linda the trail blazer. *Link* (Special issue: focus on Aborigines and disability), September, 9.

Lim, C. (1993b). Needs of the young and old in Pitjanjatjara land. *Link*, November, 56.

Lindemann, J. E. (1981). *Psychological and behavioral aspects of physical disability: a manual for health practitioners*. New York: Plenum Press.

Lindemann, J. E. & Stanger, M. E. (1981). Progressive muscle disorders. In J. E. Lindemann (ed.) *Psychological and behavioral aspects of physical disability*. New York: Plenum Press.

Lippman, L. & Loberg, D. E. (1985). An overview of developmental disabilities. In M. P. Janicki & H. M. Wisniewiski (eds.). *Ageing and developmental disabilities: issues and approaches*. Baltimore: Paul H. Brookes.

Little, M. (1991). *Diabetes*. New York: Chelsea House Publishers.

Littlejohn, G. (1989). *Rheumatism: a consumer's guide*. Ivanhoe, Vic: Fraser Publications.

Little People's Association of Australia (1981). *Information guide on persons of short stature*. Sydney: Wentworth Press.

Livanos, C. & Karraz, T. (1992). Ethnicity and disability: the NSW experience. Meeting the challenge: proceedings of 1st national conference on the impact of disability within ethnic communities in Australia, Melbourne.

Livneh, H. (1988). A dimensional perspective on the origin of negative attitudes toward persons with disabilities. In H. E. Yuker (ed.). *Attitudes toward people with disabilities*. New York: Springer.

Lollar, D. J. (1994). Encouraging personal and interpersonal independence. *Preventing secondary conditions associated with spina bifida or cerebral palsy: proceedings and recommendations of a symposium*. Washington: Spina Bifida Association of America.

Lorig, K. & Fries, J. F. (1990). *The arthritis help book*. Reading, MA: Addison Wesley.

Lubin, R. A. & Keily, M. (1985). Epidemiology of ageing in developmental disabilities. In M. P. Janicki & H. M. Wisniewski (eds). *Ageing and developmental disabilities: issues and approaches*. Baltimore: Paul. H. Brookes.

Lundy, A. (1990). *Diagnosis and treatment of mental illness*. New York: Chelsea House.

Matthews, B. (1993). *MS: the facts* (3rd edn). Oxford: Oxford University Press.

McCall, R. (1991). *Hearing loss: a guide to self help*. London: Hale.

McCarthy, B. (1995). In profile with Duane Wagner. *Disability Today*, 4 (4), 43–9.

McCarthy, W. & Fegan, L. (1984). *Sex education and the intellectually handicapped*. Sydney: Adis Health Science Press.

McCleary, B. (1995) cited by D. Lipovenko. Alzheimer's risk for Down adults. *The Globe and Mail*, 19 July, pp. 1 and 5.

McCrindle, K. (1995). War on words: label versus euphemism. *Disability Today*, 4 (4), 18–22.

McDougall, V. (1993a). Koori leader presses for survey. *Link*, November, 57.

McDougall, V. (1993b). Kooris see people first. *Link*, November, 54.

MacElroy, I. (1987). No support for families. *Australian Disability Review*, 1, 11–12.

McGowen, T. (1989). *Epilepsy*. New York: Franklin Watts.

Maclean, A. (1990). *Deaf people in the workplace: a guide for employers*. Melbourne: Victorian School for Deaf Children.

Madden, R, Black, K. & Wen, K. (1995). *The definition and categorisation of disability in Australia*. Canberra: Australian Government Publishing Service.

Madill, H. M., Brintell, E. S. G., Macnab, D., Stewin, L. L. & Fitzsimmons, G. W. (1988). The delicate balance: working and family roles. *International Journal for the Advancement of Counselling*, 11, 219–30.

Mairs, N. (1986). *Plain text*. New York: Harper & Row.

Makas, E. (1981). *Perspectives*. Washington, DC: Regional Rehabilitation Research Institute, George Washington University.

Makas, E. (1988). Positive attitudes toward disabled people: disabled and nondisabled persons' perspectives. *Journal of Social Issues*, 44, 49–61.

Maksym, D. (1990). *Shared feelings*. North York, ON: G. Allan Roeher Institute.

Mancuso, L. L. (1993). *Case studies on reasonable accommodations for workers with psychiatric disabilities*. Washington, DC: Washington Business Group on Health. Washington, DC.

Marchi, S. & Migliorino, P. (1994). *People with disabilities from a non English-speaking background*. Sydney: NSW Council for People with Intellectual Disability and People with Disabilities Inc.

Marge, S. (1994). Toward a state of well-being: promoting healthy behaviors to prevent secondary conditions. *Preventing secondary conditions associated with spina bifida or cerebral palsy: proceedings and recommendations of a symposium*. Washington: Spina Bifida Association of America.

Marge, S. (1995). Preventing secondary conditions: costs and alternatives. Keynote address at Conversation on disability issues II: secondary conditions and ageing with a disability. Syracuse, New York, September.

Marsh, D. T. (1992). *Families and mental retardation: new directions in professional practice*. New York: Praeger Publishers.

Matson, J. L. & Barrett, R. P. (eds) (1993). *Psychopathology of the mentally retarded* (2nd edn). New York: Grune & Stratton.

Matthews, B. (1993). *Multiple sclerosis: the facts* (3rd edn). Oxford: Oxford University Press.

Matthews, R., Graham, S. & Doyle, J. (1988). The extra costs borne by families who have a child with a disability. *Australian Disability Review*, 1, 11–18.

Maxman, J. & Ward, N. (1995). *Essential psychopathology and its treatment*. New York: W. W. Norton.

Maynard, F. (1995). Treatment and care of secondary conditions: The role of the health care service provider. Paper read at Conversation on disability issues II: secondary conditions and ageing with a disability. Syracuse, New York, September.

Mental Health Consumer Outcomes Task Force (1991). *Mental health statement of rights and responsibilities*. Canberra: Australian Government Publishing Service.

Meyerson, L. (1988). The social psychology of physical disability: 1948–1988. *Journal of Social Issues*, 44, 173–88.

Miles, A. (1979). Some psycho-social consequences of multiple sclerosis: problems of social interaction and group identity. *British Journal of Medical Psychology*, 52, 321–31.

Miller, K. (1993). My body, my self. *Abilities*, Summer, 18–19.

Miller, N. B. (1994). *Nobody's perfect: living and growing with children who have special needs*. Baltimore: Paul H. Brookes.

Minnes, P. (1992). Coping with change: consumer and caregiver needs. Paper presented at the Aging with a lifelong disability workshop. Ontario Federation for Cerebral Palsy, Toronto, May.

Mira, M. P. & Tyler, J. S. (1991). Students with traumatic brain injury: making the transition from hospital to school. *Focus on exceptional children*, 23, 1–12.

Mitchell, R. (1986). Human rights and hearing impairment. *Australian Disability Review*, 3, 34–9.

Mittan, R. (1988). *Living well with epilepsy*. Wellington: New Zealand Epilepsy Association.

Molloy, S. (1995). *Handling it: you and your long-term illness*. Melbourne: Hill of Content.

Moore, M. S. & Levitan, L. (1993). *For hearing people only*. New York: Deaf Life Press.

Morgan, G. (1996). Personal communication.

Moss, I. (1993). Double disadvantage. *Australian Disability Review*, 23–7.

Mouat, W. (1990). Respite care. *Interaction*, (4) 32. National Council on Intellectual Disability.

MS Society Canada (1982). *Someone you know has multiple sclerosis: a book for families*. Canada: MSS Canada.

MS Society NSW (1993). *Work issues for people with multiple sclerosis. Fact sheet No. 6.4*. Sydney: MS Society NSW.

Munford, R. & Martin, S. (1994). *Disability studies: thinking critically about disability*. Palmerston, NZ: Massey University.

Munro, L. (1993). Aboriginal culture: mental health. Paper read at the National Aboriginal mental health conference, Sydney, November.

Muscular Dystrophy Associations of Australia (1990–91) *Fact sheets*. (A series of fact sheets about muscular dystrophies, myotonias and spinal muscular atrophy.)

Muscular Dystrophy Association of NSW (undated). *My friend has muscular dystrophy*. Sydney: MDA.

Muscular Dystrophy Association of South Australia (undated a). *Facts about Duchenne and Becker muscular dystrophy*. Adelaide: MDA.

Muscular Dystrophy Association of South Australia (undated b). *The myotonias*. Adelaide: MDA.

Muscular Dystrophy Association of South Australia (undated c). *Spinal muscular atrophy*. Adelaide: MDA.

Naeyaert, K. (1990). Living with sensory loss: vision. In *Writing in gerontology: living with sensory loss*. Ottawa, ON: National Advisory Council on Aging.

National Association of Multiple Sclerosis of Australia (1989). *Multiple Sclerosis: the mystery disease*. Melbourne, NAMSA.

National Association of Multiple Sclerosis of Australia (1990). Living with *Multiple sclerosis: a book for the newly diagnosed*. Melbourne, NAMSA.

National Epilepsy Association of Australia (1986). *A guide for parents*. Melbourne: NEAA.

National Health Strategy (1993). *Help where help is needed: continuity of care for people with chronic mental illness*. Canberra: Department of Health, Housing and Community Services. Issues Paper No. 5.

National Information Center for Children and Youth with Handicaps (1990). Having a daughter with a disability: is it different for girls?. *News Digest*, 14 (3).

Neisser, A. (1990). *The other side of silence: sign language and the deaf community in America*. Washington, DC: Gallaudet University Press.

Neurological Centre, The (1993). *Epilepsy: a booklet for the information of patients*. Sydney: Westmead Hospital.

Neurological Centre, The (undated). *Epilepsy*. Sydney: Westmead Hospital.

New South Wales Council on Intellectual Disability (1988). *A decent life: policy statement*. Sydney: NSWCID.

New South Wales Council on Intellectual Disability (undated). *Dealing with professionals*. Sydney: NSWCID.

New South Wales Department of Community Services, NSW Department of School Education, NSW Department of Health and Office on Disability (Social Policy Directorate) (1994). *Early intervention coordination project: proposed forward directions community consultation paper*. Sydney, June.

New South Wales Department of Health (1991). *Leading the way: a framework for NSW mental health services, 1991–2001*. Sydney: NSW Government.

New South Wales Government (1990). *NSW Mental Health Act*. Sydney.

New South Wales Government (1993). *Disability Services Act*. Sydney.

New South Wales Office of the Aged (1987). *Behind the statistics: some points about aged people in NSW*. Sydney: Premier's Department.

Nisbett, A. (1973). The path of light. In A. B. Cobb (ed.) *Medical and psychological aspects of disability*. Springfield, Ill: Charles C. Thomas.

Nosek, M. A., Rintala, D. & Young, M. E. (1995). *Findings on reproductive health and access to health care*. Houston, TX: Center for Research on Women with Disabilities, Baylor College of Medicine.

Oliver, M. (1991). *Social work: disabled people and disabling environments*. London: Kingsley.

Olivett, B. L. (1995). Conventional fitting of the adult amputee. In J. M. Hunter, E. J. Mackin, & A. D. Callahan (eds.). *Rehabilitation of the hand: surgery and therapy* (4th edn). St. Louis: Mosby.

Ontario Federation for Cerebral Palsy (1993). *Health, aging and cerebral palsy*. Toronto: Ontario Federation for Cerebral Palsy.

Ontario Federation for Cerebral Palsy (1994). *A guide to cerebral palsy.* Toronto, Ontario: Ontario Federation for Cerebral Palsy.

Ontario Federation for Cerebral Palsy (undated). *Ten plain facts about cerebral palsy.* Toronto, Ontario: Ontario Federation for Cerebral Palsy.

Ontario Provincial Government (1994). *Ontarians with Disabilities Act (ODA).* Toronto, Ontario.

Ontario Provincial Government (1995). *The Ontario Long Term Care Act.* Toronto, Ontario.

Orchison, R. & Simpson, G. (1995). Sexuality after head injury. In the *Head injury training kit.* Sydney: Lidcombe Head Injury Unit.

Orlans, H. (ed.) (1989). *Adjustment to adult hearing loss.* College Hill Press Inc.

Orr, K. (1984). Consulting women with disabilities. *Australian Disability Review*, 3, 14–18.

Overeyender, J., Turk, M., Dalton, A. & Janicki, M. P. (1992). *I'm worried about the future: the aging of adults with cerebral palsy.* Albany, NY: New York Developmental Disabilities Planning Council.

Oxley, J. & Smith, J. (1991). *The epilepsy reference book.* London: Faber & Faber.

Padden, C. and Humphries, T. (1988). *Deaf in America: voices from a culture.* Harvard University Press.

Paneth, N. & Stark, R. I. (1983). Cerebral palsy and mental retardation in relation to indicators of perinatal asphyxia. An epidemiologic overview. *American Journal of Obstetrics and Gynaecology*, 147, 960–6.

Paraplegic and Quadriplegic Association of NSW (undated). *Manual of welfare equipment.* Sydney: PQA (NSW).

Park, R. (1977). *Swords and crowns and rings.* Melbourne: Thomas Nelson.

Patrick, D. L., Richardson, M., Starks, H. E. & Rose, M. A. (1994). A framework for promoting the health of people with disabilities. In D. J. Lollar (ed.). *Preventing secondary conditions associated with spina bifida and cerebral palsy: proceedings of a symposium.* Washington, DC: Spina Bifida Association of America, 3–6.

Pearce, J. (1993). Returning to farming after spinal cord injury. *Paraquad*, 19–20.

Perlez, A., Furlong, M. & McLachlan, D. (1989). Family-centred rehabilitation: family therapy for the head injured and their relatives. In R. Harris, R. Burns & R. Rees (eds.). *Recovery from brain injury: expectations, needs and processes.* Adelaide: Institute for the Study of Learning Difficulties.

Pettit-Crossman, S. (1994). Diabetes and nutrition. *Abilities*, Fall issue, 28–31.

Pfeiffer, D. (1994). *Letter to Dr M. Thuriaux, Epidemiological Surveillance and Statistical Services, World Health Organization.* Distributed at Colloquium on the environmental determinants to social participation. Quebec, Canada, September.

Phifer, K. (1979). *Growing up small: a handbook for short people.* Middlebury, VT: Paul Eriksson, Human Growth Foundation.

Phillips, P., Ozer, M., Axelson, P. & Chizeck, H. (1987). *Spinal cord injury: a guide for patient and family.* New York: Raven.

Picard, A. (1990). No cure known for disease of boys. *Globe & Mail*, 28 June, Toronto.

Pillemar, K. & Moore, D. W. (1990). Highlights from a study of abuse of patients in nursing homes. *Journal of Elder Abuse and Neglect*, 2, 5–29.

Pillet, J. & Mackin, E. J. (1995). Aesthetic hand prosthesis: its psychologic and functional potential. In J. M. Hunter , E. J. Mackin, & A. D. Callahan (eds.). *Rehabilitation of the hand: surgery and therapy* (4th edn). St. Louis: Mosby.

Pillon, J. P. (1995). Hearing impairment and hearing aids. *Exceptional Parent*, May, 30–4.

Pimm, P. (1992). Physiological burnout and functional skill loss in cerebral palsy. *Interlink*, 4, 18–21.

Pitzele, S. K. (1985). *We are not alone: learning to live with chronic illness.* Minneapolis: Thompson & Co. Inc.

Ponsford, J. (1987). Practical issues in working with people with the head injured. Paper presented at the Headway Victoria Kaleidoscope Conference, Melbourne.

Ponsford, J., Sloan, S. & Snow, P. (1995). *Traumatic brain injury: rehabilitation of everyday adaptive living.* Hillsdale, Ill: Lawrence Erlbaum & Associates.

Poor, C. R. (1975). Vocational rehabilitation of persons with spinal cord injuries. In *Comprehensive vocational rehabilitation for severely disabled persons.* Washington, DC: Job Development Laboratory: The George Washington University Medical Center.

Powell, T. H. (1993). *Brothers and sisters: a special part of exceptional families* (2nd edn). Baltimore: Paul H. Brookes.

Powers, M. C. (1992). *Arthritis.* New York: Chelsea House Publishers.

Pueschel, S. M. (1990). *A parent's guide to Down syndrome.* Baltimore: Paul H. Brookes.

Quinn, P. (1994). America's disability policy: another double standard? *Affilia,* Spring, 45–57.

Racino, J., Walker, P., O'Connor, S. & Taylor, S. (eds) (1993). *Housing, support and community. Choices and strategies for adults with disabilities.* Baltimore: Paul H Brookes.

Ramsay, M. (1994). *Woe or go! A discussion paper on the disability discrimination standards.* Sydney: National Coalition for the Development of the DDA Standards.

Randall-Davis, E. (1989). *Strategies for working with culturally diverse communities and clients.* Washington, DC: Association for the Care of Children's Health.

Rappaport, J. (1981). In praise of paradox: a social policy of empowerment over prevention. *American Journal of Community Psychology,* 9, 1–25.

Ravot, K. (ed.) (various dates). *Amputee News.* (Newsletter available to members of The Amputee Association of NSW.)

Reiss, S. (1994). Issues in defining mental retardation. *American Journal on Mental Retardation,* 99, 1–7.

Resources for Rehabilitation (1993). *Living with low vision: a resource guide for people with sight loss.* Lexington, MASS.

Review team to consider hearing impairment among Maori people (1989). *Whakarongo mai: Report to the Minister of Maori Affairs.* New Zealand: Review team to consider hearing impairment among Maori people.

Rey, J. M. (1992). The epidemiologic catchment area (ECA) study: implications for Australia. *Medical Journal of Australia,* 156, 200–3.

Richard, A. & Reiter, J. (1990). *Epilepsy: a new approach.* New York: Prentice Hall.

Ringel, S. P. (1987). *Neuromuscular disorder: a guide for patient and family.* New York: Raven Press.

Rioux, M. H. (1995). Ethical and socio-political considerations associated on the use and revision of the ICIDH. Paper read at Colloquium on the environmental determinants to social participation. Quebec, Canada, September.

Rioux, M. H. & Bach, M. (1994). *Disability is not measles: new research paradigms in disability.* North York, Ontario: Roeher Institute.

Rix, P. (undated). *Living with a disability and dying for a break: a study of respite care.* Sydney: Disability Council of NSW.

Robinson, I. (1988). *Multiple sclerosis.* London: Routledge.

Roeher Institute (1989). *The power of positive thinking.* North York, ON: G. Allan Roeher Institute.

Roeher Institute (1992a). *No more victims: a manual to guide families and friends in addressing the sexual abuse of people with a mental handicap.* North York, ON: G. Allan Roeher Institute.

Roeher Institute (1992b). *No more victims: a manual to guide the police in addressing the sexual abuse of people with a mental handicap.* North York, ON: G. Allan Roeher Institute.

Roeher Institute (1993). *Answering the call: police response to family and caregiver violence against people with disabilities.* North York, ON: G. Allan Roeher Institute.

Roeher Institute (1995). *Harm's way: the many faces of violence and abuse against persons with disabilities.* North York, ON: G. Allan Roeher Institute.

Roessler, R. T., Shriner, K. F. & Price, P. (1992). Employment concerns of people with head injuries. *Journal of Rehabilitation*, Jan/Feb/March, 17–22.

Rosen, F. (1989). *Hearing loss: the invisible handicap.* Sydney: SHHH Australia Inc.

Rosner, L. J. & Ross, S. (1992). *MS: new coping and practical advice for people with MS and their families.* New York: Simon Schuster.

Ross, M. (1988). National attendant care program. *Quad Wrangle*, Autumn, 5.

Roush, S. E. (1976). Health professionals as contributors to attitudes toward persons with disabilities. A special communication. *Physical Therapy*, 66, 1551–4.

Royal Australian College of General Practitioners (1989). *A guide to the management of diabetes in general practice.* Canberra.

Sacks, O. (1989). *Seeing voices.* London: Picador.

Saunders, J. (1992). *Tinnitus: what is that noise in my ear?* Auckland: Sandalwood Enterprises.

Schaefer, B. (1985). *The isolation of country women.* Paper presented at the Australian Federation of University Women 26th Conference, Adelaide.

Scheinberg, L. (ed.) (1987). *Multiple sclerosis: a guide for patients and their families.* (2nd edn). New York: Raven Press.

Schembri, A. (1995). What is manual communication? Sydney: The University of Sydney, unpublished paper.

Schleien, S. J., Myer, L. H., Brandt, L. A. & Briel, B. (1995). *Lifelong leisure skills and lifestyles for people with developmental disabilities.* Baltimore, MD: Paul H. Brookes.

Schloss, P. & Miller, S. R. (1982). The effects of the label 'institutionalized' versus 'regular school student' on teacher expectations. *Exceptional Children*, 48, 361–2.

Schwier, K. M. (1994). *Couples with disabilities talk about living and loving.* Rockville, MA: Woodbine House.

SCI Care System (1994). *Spinal cord injury: facts and figures at a glance.* Birmingham, AL: University of Alabama-Birmingham.

Scott, L. (1993). Changing the story: CRS's first Aboriginal and Torres Strait Islander liaison officer relates her experience. *Link*, November, 55.

Seligman, M. (1975). *Helplessness.* San Francisco: W. H. Freeman.

Seligman, M. (1992). *Helplessness: on development, depression and death.* New York: W. H. Freeman.

Seltzer, M. M. Krauss, M. W. & Janicki, M. P. (1994). *Life course perspectives on adulthood and old age.* Washington, DC: American Association on Mental Retardation.

Setachi, Y. & Rosenfelder, R. (eds.) (1982). *The limb deficient child.* Springfield, Ill: Charles C. Thomas.

Shorvon, S. (1988). *Epilepsy: a general perspective.* Basel: CIBA GEIGY.

Sillence, D. O. & Barlow, K. K. (1991). *Osteogenesis imperfecta: a handbook for medical practitioners and health care professionals* (2nd edn). Sydney: IMS Publishing.

Slater, R. and Terry, M. (1990). *Tinnitus: a guide for sufferers and professionals.* London: Chapman & Hall.

Smith, D. W. (1993). *Schizophrenia.* New York: Franklin Watts.

Smith, J. D. (1994). The revised AAMR definition of mental retardation. *Education and Training in Mental Retardation and Developmental Disabilities*, 179–83.

Smith, W. L., Forbes, K. & Cooke, D. (1993). Head injury, family intervention and rehabilitation in a rural setting. Paper presented at the Second National Rehabilitation Conference, Commonwealth Rehabilitation Service, Sydney.

Sobsey, D. (1994). *Violence and abuse in the lives of people with disabilities: the end of silent acceptance.* Baltimore, MD: Paul H. Brookes.

Speigle, J. A. & Van den Pol, R. (1993). *Making changes: family voices on living with disabilities.* Cambridge, MA: Brookline Books.

Spender, L. (ed.) (1995). *Mental health rights manual.* Sydney: Mental Health Coordinating Council Inc, Redfern Legal Centre Publishing, Ltd.

Standards Association of Australia (1991). *AS1428-1 Access standards manual,* Sydney.

Stanley, F. J. & Watson, L. (1988). The cerebral palsies in Western Australia: trends: 1968–1981. *American Journal of Obstetrics and Gynaecology,* 158, 89–93.

Stanley, F. J., Watson, L. & Mauger, S. (1987). *Second report of the Western Australian cerebral palsy register.* Perth: National Health and Medical Research Council.

Stanton, M. (1992). *Cerebral palsy: a practical guide.* London: Optima Publishers.

Statistics Canada (1988). *1987 Health and activities limitations survey.* Ottawa: Statistics Canada.

Statistics Canada (1992). *1991 Health and activity limitations survey.* Ottawa: Statistics Canada.

Stewart, T. D. & Rossier, A. B. (1979). Psychological considerations in the adjustment to spinal cord injury. *Rehabilitation Literature,* 39, 75–80.

Stimson, L. & Best, M. (1991). *Courage above all: sexual assault against women with disabilities.* Toronto: DisAbled Women's Network (DAWN).

Stopford, V. (1988). *Understanding disability: Causes, characteristics and coping.* Caulfield, Vic: Edward Arnold.

Storrs, A. (1973). Rehabilitation: medical aspects of hearing disorders. In A. B. Cobb (ed.). *Medical and psychological aspects of disability.* Springfield, Ill: Charles C. Thomas.

Stuifbergen, A. (1995). Health promotion for persons with disabilities: preventing secondary conditions and maintaining one's health. Paper read at Conversation on disability issues II: secondary conditions and ageing with a disability. Syracuse, New York, September.

Sullivan, P. M., Vernon, M. & Scanlan, J. M. (1987). Sexual abuse of deaf youth. *American Annals of the Deaf,* 32, 256–62.

Sutton, E., Factor, A., Hawkings, B. A., Heller, T. & Seltzer, G. B. (1993). *Older adults with developmental disabilities.* Baltimore: Paul H. Brookes.

Taylor, D. (1987) Epilepsy and prejudice. *Archives of Diseases in Childhood Vol. 1.* 62, 209–11.

Taylor, F. & Bishop, J. (1990). *Being deaf: the experience of deafness.* London: The Open University.

Tetreault, S. (1994). Predictors of the extra load perceived by the mother living with a child having a motor disability. *Colloquium proceedings of Environmental determinants of social handicaps: in order to better act on handicap situations, ICIDH and environmental factors international network.* Quebec: Canadian Society of the ICIDH, 7–8, 58–63.

Thompsett, K. & Nickerson, E. (1992). *Missing words: the family handbook of adult hearing loss.* Washington, DC: Gallaudet University Press.

Ticoll, M. (1994). *Violence and people with disabilities: a review of the literature.* Ottawa, Ontario: Family Violence Prevention Division, Health Canada.

Tiessen, J. (1995). Bill 173: Red ribbon or red tape? *Disability Today,* 4 (3), 23–33.

Toleno, J. (1994). Finding sexual identity: the journey to becoming whole. *Abilities,* Summer, 19 and 78.

Traustadottir, R. (1990). *Obstacles to equality: the double discrimination against women with disabilities.* Syracuse, NY: Center on Human Policy, Syracuse University.

Traustadottir, R. (1991). Mothers who care: gender, disability and family life. *Journal of Family Issues,* 12, 211–28.

Trieschmann, R. B. (1979). The role of the psychologist in the treatment of spinal cord injury. *Paraplegia,* 16, 212–19.

Trocher, M. (1995). The road to wellness. *Diabetes Dialogue,* 43 (2), 23–6.

Turk, M. A. (1994). Attaining and retaining mobility: clinical issues. *Preventing secondary conditions associated with spina bifida or cerebral palsy: proceedings and recommendations or a symposium.* Washington: Spina Bifida Association of America.

Turnbull, A. P., Patterson, J. M., Behr, S. K., Murphy, D. L., Marquis, J. G. & Blue-Banning, M. J. (eds.) (1993). *Cognitive coping, families and disability.* Baltimore: Paul H. Brookes.

Turnbull, H. R., Turnbull, A. P., Bronicki, G. J., Summers, J. A. & Roeder-Gordon, C. (1989). *Disability and the family*. Baltimore: Paul H. Brookes.

Twigg, J. & Atkin, K. (1994). *Carers: perceived policy and practice in informal care*. Oxford: Oxford University Press.

Ulicny, G., White, G., Bradford, B. & Matthews, M. (1990). Consumer exploitation by attendants: how often does it happen and can anything be done about it. *Rehabilitation Counselling Bulletin*, 33, 240–6.

United States Department of Justice (1990). *The Americans with Disabilities Act (Public Law 101–336)*. Washington, DC: Civil Rights Division, US Department of Justice.

Van Etten, A. M. (1988). *Dwarfs don't live in doll houses*. Rochester, NY: Adaptive Living.

Vargo, J. (1985). A 'needs satisfaction' view of adjustment. *Rehabilitation Digest*, Winter, 15.

Vierck, E. (1991). *Keys to understanding arthritis*. New York: Barron's Educational Series.

Wagle, H. (1994). She wants to work hard for the money!: women with disabilities speak out on the issue of employment. *Abilities*, Summer, 40–5.

Walker, L. & Rickards, F. W. (1992). *Report to the Department of School Education, Victoria*. Melbourne: Deafness Studies Unit, The University of Melbourne.

Walmsley, J. (1993). Contradictions in caring: reciprocity and interdependence. *Disability, Handicap & Society*, 8, 56–8.

Walsh, J. (1989). *Actuarial research into physical disablement*. Sydney.

Washington Business Group on Health (undated). *Reasonable accommodations for workers with psychiatric disabilities*. Washington DC: Washington Business Group on Health.

Watts, R. (1995). Arthritis. *Disability Today*, 4 (4), 10–17.

Wehman, P., Inlow, D., Altman, A., Munday, A., West, M., Coplin, B., Kreuzer, J. & Zasler, N. (1991). Return to work for individuals recovering from stroke or traumatic brain injury: three case studies. *Canadian Journal of Rehabilitation*, 5, 45–50.

Weir, G. (1987). *How to live with a hearing loss*. Sydney: Deafness Resources Australia.

Weitz, D. (1992). 'Disabled': another look at labels. *Entourage*, 7, 7.

Weller, D. J. & Miller, P. M. (1977). Emotional reactions of patient, family and staff in acute-care period of spinal cord injury. *Social Work in Health Care*, 2, 369–77.

White, G. W., Gutierrez, R. Gardner, S. & Steward, J. (1994). *SCI and aging: a state of body and mind*. Kansas: The Research and Training Center on Independent Living, the University of Kansas.

Whiteneck, G. (1989). The management of high quadriplegia. *Comprehensive Neurological Rehabilitation, Vol. 1*. New York: Demos Publications.

Whiteneck, G., Charlifue, S., Gerhart, K., Lammertse, D., Manley, S., Menter, R. & Seedroff, K. (1993). *Aging with spinal cord injury*. New York: Demos Publications.

Williams, B. (1994). Increasing access to personal assistance: Americans with disabilities' insurance policy for staying healthy, well and productive. *Preventing secondary conditions associated with spina bifida or cerebral palsy: Proceedings and recommendations of a symposium*. Washington: Spina Bifida Association of America.

Williams, J. M. & Kay, T. (1991). *Head injury: a family matter*. Baltimore: Paul H. Brookes.

Wolfensberger, W. (1972). *The principle of normalisation in human service*. Toronto: National Institute on Mental Retardation.

World Health Organization (1980). *International classification of impairments, disabilities and handicaps*. Geneva.

Wright, B. A. (1975a). Social-psychological leads to enhance rehabilitation effectiveness. *Rehabilitation Counseling Bulletin*, 18, 214–23.

Wright, B. A. (1975b). Sensitizing others to the position of the insider. *Rehabilitation Psychology*, 22, 119–35.

Wright, B. A. (1980). Developing constructive views of life with a disability. *Rehabilitation Literature*, 41, 274–9.

Wright, B. A. (1983). *Physical disability: a social–psychological approach*. New York: Harper.

Wright-Felske, A. & Hughson, E. A. (1991). Enhancing inclusive communities. *Entourage*, Winter, 6–8.

Wynn Parry, C. B. (1981). *Rehabilitation of the hand* (4th edn). London: Butterworths.

Yanko, S. (1992). *Coming to terms with epilepsy*. Sydney: Allen & Unwin.

Youngson, R. M. (1991). *How to cope with tinnitus and hearing loss*. Oxford: Isis.

Yuker, H. E. (1988). The effects of contact on attitudes toward disabled persons: some empirical generalizations. In H. E. Yuker (ed.). *Attitudes toward people with disabilities*. New York: Springer.

Ziersch, T. (1990). The reintegration of Aboriginal children with significant physical disabilities into remote communities. *Australian Disability Review*, 3, 24–30.

Zola, I. K. (1982). Denial of emotional needs to people with handicaps. *Archives of Physical and Medical Rehabilitation*, 63, 63–7.

INDEX